The Pitcher

The Pitcher

JOHN THORN
AND
JOHN B. HOLWAY

PRENTICE HALL PRESS • New York

For our children—
The Holways: Jim, John, Diane, and Mona;
The Thorns: Jed and Isaac.

*   *   *

Published by Prentice Hall Press
A Division of Simon & Schuster, Inc.
Gulf + Western Building
One Gulf + Western Plaza
New York, NY 10023

PRENTICE HALL PRESS is a trademark of Simon & Schuster, Inc.

Library of Congress Cataloging-in-Publication Data

Thorn, John, 1947–
The pitcher.

Includes index.
1. Pitching (Baseball) I. Holway, John. II. Title.
GV871.T46 1987   796.357′22   86-43168
ISBN 0-13-157652-6

Designed by Irving Perkins Associates
Manufactured in the United States of America
10 9 8 7 6 5 4 3 2 1
First Edition

Contents

Pitcher

His art is eccentricity, his aim
How not to hit the mark he seems to aim at

His passion how to avoid the obvious,
His technique how to vary the avoidance.

The others throw to be comprehended. He
Throws to be a moment misunderstood.

Yet not too much. Not errant, arrant, wild,
But every seeming aberration willed.

Not to, yet still, still to communicate
Making the batter understand too late.

—Robert Francis

Introduction:
The Game within the Game

Hitting is timing. Pitching is upsetting timing.
—Warren Spahn

Viewed from the bleachers, baseball can seem child's play, simple, clear, and sweetly pure of intent. Throw and catch, hit and run—these are things we can do (or once could) and, we may flatter ourselves, not so much worse than those fellows down there. The pitcher slings the ball toward the catcher; the batter swings to intercept it; the fielders, coiled, await the outcome. Broad expanses of green and brown frame the players as they spring into motion at the crack of the bat. The brilliantly white ball soars or bounds where it will, the batter takes his base or is denied it—and inning after inning, game after game, year after year, the ceremony is reenacted. Harmony. Grace. Justice.

Baseball is not really so routine of course, or we would not care about it as intensely as we do. Is there a single action in all of sport more difficult than hitting a pitched ball, or one more intricate than pitching to a batter? What can appear more natural yet be more practiced than catching a fly ball? The beauty of baseball, its sustaining satisfaction, is that it is both simple and complex, slow and sudden, predictable and surprising—a tangle of paradoxes that, like art, like life, reveals itself only by degrees. The astute fan may weigh the merits of a sacrifice bunt or a steal of third base; after much study he may even solve an age-old enigma; yet the essential mystery of baseball—what goes on between pitcher and batter—remains forever hidden in plain sight.

* * *

We enter the national pastime's labyrinth of deception with the opening words of the official rules: "Baseball is a game between two teams of nine players. . . ." While basketball may be a game of five against five, and football, of eleven against eleven, *no* part of a baseball game pits nine men against nine. One might as well describe the sport as a free-for-all matching two rosters of twenty-four players each. In fact, baseball is a joint enterprise before the game's first pitch and after its last one, and at precious few points in between.

As a team game, baseball is an aggregate of individual games played for individual goals. It may be seen as the lonely struggle of one man, the batter, to overcome nine

1

opponents. Or, if we consider the seven men in the field to be of no concern if the batter cannot first hit the ball, the conflict narrows to one against two, hitter against the battery. But even in this game within the game, the catcher plays a passive role: His wisdom may direct the battery attack, but little that he does with the ball can set the larger game in motion. And so baseball's conflict telescopes further, to the primal combat of pitcher and batter, one against one.

Locked in concentration, the antagonists devise their strategies, ready their weapons, and face each other across the odd distance of 60 feet, 6 inches. The batter is armed with a tapered club, ideally of white ash, up to 42 inches long and of unlimited weight (although approximately 2 pounds is the current standard), with a diameter of 2¾ inches at its widest point. The pitcher grips a cowhide-covered sphere fashioned from layers of tightly wound woolen yarn, rubber, and at the center, composition cork; it weighs 5¼ ounces and is of a diameter slightly greater than that of the bat. He must apply speed, spin, and guile to the ball while directing it over (or tantalizingly close to) a plate 17 inches wide, within a vertical strike zone of 2 to 3½ feet depending upon the height and stance of the batter and the predilection of the umpire.

A good major-league fastball, traveling 90 miles per hour, will traverse the 55 to 56 feet between the pitcher's point of release and the heart of home plate in 0.42 seconds. Within the first 0.22 seconds after the ball leaves the hand, the batter must pick up the flight of the pitch, identify it by its rotation, predict its location, and decide whether to swing or not. He will need the remaining 0.20 seconds to stride, rotate his hips, and apply torque to the bat through the muscles

at the shoulder, elbow, and wrist. To drive the ball into fair territory, he must meet it within an arc of 15 degrees in front of or behind the point at which the bat is perpendicular to the path of the ball—a space of about 2 feet, through which the good major-league fastball will pass in 15 *thousandths* of a second.

Even if he connects squarely, however, he has little control over where his hit will go. Because both the ball and the bat are round at the point of impact, the batter cannot direct and manipulate the ball as golfers or tennis players, with their flat-surfaced clubs and racquets, can. Thus, there exists the phenomenon of the hard-hit out, which any batter will tell you is not compensated for by an equal number of scratch hits; and thus, we define the successful hitter as one who fails only seven times in ten. The major-league pitcher is a formidable foe, so formidable that only four batters in this century—Ted Williams, Mickey Mantle, Rogers Hornsby, and Babe Ruth—have ever been his equal, reaching base as often as they were retired, for even a single season.

Pitcher and batter are constantly looking for some key to obtaining momentary advantage. The batter will alter his stance, his location in the box, his grip; the pitcher will change his speeds, his selection of pitches, his delivery. Through this series of adjustments, the game within the game stays in traditional balance, with the average major-league hitter batting between .250 and .275 and the average major-league hurler yielding 3.50 to 4.00 runs per nine innings.*

But sometimes the combatants' adjustments are not enough to prevent the long struggle from tilting radically in favor of one or the other, as it did for the hitter in 1930

---

*These norms are a matter of practice, not a product of physical law. The earned run average for all play from 1876–1986 is 3.66, and the batting average is .268.

and for the pitcher in 1968. At such moments, just as the fight seems a mortal mismatch and the public outcry is at its greatest, strings are pulled from above the fray and a *deus ex machina*—in the form of a designated hitter, a redefined strike zone, a livened or deadened ball—restores equilibrium. The owners and rules makers know that the object of the year-in, year-out competition between pitcher and batter must be, not final victory, but eternal unresolved conflict if the fans are to maintain interest and profits are to be made. These handicappers will provide the balance between offense and defense that they imagine the public demands. If the customer clamors for a bushel of .350 hitters, he may have them. More home runs? As many as he would like.

Providing the hitter with an advantage requires tinkering with the game, which can be and has been done. But if you want more low-scoring classics, no problem: Just leave the rules and the ball alone for a generation and the .300 hitter will go the way of the dinosaur. Left unfettered, pitching is an irresistible force and will prevail. The progress of baseball from a boys' game of the 1830s to the national pastime and passion of today is the product of, on the one hand, a steady rise in pitching skill, fueled by advances in physiology, training, and technique; and, on the other hand, the repeated restraints placed upon that rise. These shackles permit hitters, dependent as they are on reaction time and electrical impulses to the brain, the chance to reestablish their former efficiency, thus maintaining the soothing illusion that, of all things, baseball, at least, remains the same.

But baseball has changed, and the steady onslaught of pitching has changed it most.

1

Pitching: Evolution and Revolution

THE EARLY DAYS: 1845–75

In the first codified rules of baseball, drafted by Alexander Cartwright for the Knickerbocker Base Ball Club in 1845, Article 9 (the only one pertaining to the pitcher) read:

The ball must be pitched, not thrown, for the bat.

Only ten words, but how much they reveal about the humble origins of baseball's prime player! First, we see that the pitcher came by his name from the underhand, stiff-armed, stiff-wristed pitch borrowed from cricket's early days—a delivery much like that seen today at the bowling alley. Second, we see the disdain of the "gentlemanly" Knickerbockers of New York for the uncouth throw, which characterized the rival version of baseball that flourished in New England until the Civil War. (Indeed, the term *pitcher* has been a misnomer in baseball ever since the mid-1860s, when the widespread—though not yet legal—wrist snap transformed the respectable pitch into the lowly throw.) And third, we see that the pitcher was not required to throw strikes rather than balls (the former did not exist until 1858, the latter until 1863), but instead to pitch *for the bat*: In other words, he and the batter were not adversaries but very nearly allies, each doing his utmost to put the ball in play for the valiant barehand fielders! Of all the positions in the game's original 1845 design, only right field was less demanding and less prestigious than pitcher.

That began to change in the game's second decade, as pitchers realized that, despite the restrictions on their motions, they could muster considerable speed and, with no "called ball" system in place, could whiz fastballs wide of the bat for as long as fifteen minutes until the impatient batter finally fished for one. The former alliance of batter and pitcher was breached and the breach was soon to widen.

Jim Creighton, a seventeen-year-old pitcher for the amateur Niagaras of Brooklyn (all teams were amateur then), created a stir in 1858 with a pitch that was not only faster than any seen before but also sailed or tailed or climbed or dipped; the result was "fairly unhittable," in the words of John "Death to Flying Things" Chapman, a contemporary star with the Brooklyn Atlantics. How did Creighton do it? By adding an imperceptible snap of the wrist to his swooping bowler's delivery. The first baseball pitcher to impart spin to the ball, he was soon wooed away from the Niagaras by the Star of Brooklyn club, with filthy lucre no doubt the bait. Now he was baseball's first professional, and by the following year, when the Excelsiors of Brooklyn offered him a still more lucrative deal, he had become baseball's first great pitcher and idol of the fans. Even twenty years after his last performance, observers of such worthies as Hoss Radbourn and Tim Keefe would say, "They're fine pitchers, to be sure, but they're no Creighton."

That last performance, alas, came against the Unions of Morrisania on October 7, 1862, when the twenty-one-year-old Creighton sustained a ruptured bladder, which a few days later proved fatal. He incurred the injury with heroic flair, while hitting out a home run.

The year after Creighton's death brought the system of "called balls" to speed up the game, but inasmuch as the lone umpire stood in foul ground along the first base line, balls and strikes could not be accurately judged. Moreover, the batter could demand a pitch high in the strike zone (waist to top of shoulder) or low (waist to a foot or so above the ground) and the pitcher had to comply. The pitcher was therefore working with a batter-imposed strike zone that was theoretically half that of today (but in practice much the same, since the strike zone of the last fifteen years has effectively shrunk to the "low strike" definition of the 1860s).

What advantages did a pitcher of the ear-liest days have? *First,* he worked behind a line, and after 1865 within a box, that was only 45 feet from home plate. An 80-mile-per-hour fastball thrown by George "Charmer" Zettlein would reach the plate in 0.38 seconds, precisely the time it takes Nolan Ryan to hurl 100-m.p.h. heat past a batter today. *Second,* with the pitcher's box—which until its abolition in 1893 varied in width from 12 feet to 4 and in length from 7 feet to 3—the hurler might move pretty much as he pleased, permitting him a wide-angle crossfire or even a running start, as in cricket bowling. *Third,* he could record outs on one-bounce catches until 1864, on one-bounce fouls until 1883, and on foul tips at any point in the count until 1888; uncaught fouls were not to register as strikes until the next century. *Fourth,* even though the batter's high-low option narrowed the strike zone and thus gave him an edge, a walk was awarded on nine called balls prior to 1876, and that number was not reduced to the current four until 1889.

And *fifth,* once Creighton snapped his wrist, it was only a matter of time before the other spinning pitches—notably the curve, but also the drop (sinker), the rise, the in-shoot (screwball), and spitter—were invented. The many claimants to creation of the curveball include Candy Cummings, Fred Goldsmith, Deacon White, Tommy Bond, Bobby Mathews, and college pitchers Charles Avery and J. M. Mann. The spitter is attributed to Bobby Mathews, but surely his version dropped less spectacularly than the reinvented wet one thrown by Jack Chesbro and Ed Walsh.

The prohibition against the wrist snap and the throw (or bent-elbow delivery) was only rarely observed by the late 1860s, so in 1872 Henry Chadwick proposed that the wrist snap be legalized, and it was. At the same time, the requirement that the pitcher's arm swing perpendicular to the ground was relaxed so as to permit, in effect, a below-the-hips throw not unlike that of Joe McGinnity or Dan Quisenberry. By 1875, Hartford's Tommy Bond was living at the edge of the rule by throwing low sidearm with tremendous speed, paving the way for the batting decline of the late 1870s and the frantic series of rule changes in the 1880s.

Before these pitching innovations came about, the baseball games of the 1860s typically featured 35 or more combined runs per game, with scores of 60–100 runs not unusual. Many of these were unearned because of general ineptitude in the field, greatly abetted by a rock-hard ball of incredible resiliency. One player of the period recalled in later years that the ball was so lively that, if dropped from the top of a two-story building, it would rebound nearly all the way back up. Low-scoring games were such a rarity that the annual guides would feature a list of "model games," defined as those in which the teams combined for fewer than ten runs.

In addition to the different pitching techniques, the late 1860s brought the famous dead ball and with it a sudden rush of low-scoring contests characterized by comparatively dazzling fielding. The fans and sportswriters were overjoyed with the new "artistic" game, at last a worthy rival to cricket. In a famous game of July 23, 1870, Rynie Wolters of the New York Mutuals shut out the "braggart" Chicago White Stockings; this whipping gave rise to the term *Chicagoed,* meaning shut out.* On May 10, 1875, Chicago fell victim to Joe Blong of St. Louis in baseball's first 1–0 game and to Boston's Joe Borden in history's first no-hitter on July 28 of the same year.

The opening season, 1871, of the National Association, baseball's first professional league, produced six shutouts. Only five years later, the National League's inaugural schedule of seventy games featured a whopping sixteen shutouts by St. Louis' Grin Bradley *alone.*

THE RISE OF THE MAJORS: 1876–1900

Baseballs were now being manufactured in mass, with deplorable quality control: The dead ball was, by midgame, often the mush ball. The fans no longer considered low scores so remarkable. National League batting averages declined every year from 1877 to 1880, falling from .271 to an alarming .245. The number of strikeouts nearly tripled as pitchers perfected the curves and slants introduced only a decade before. The league ERA was 2.37. The fledgling circuit, which in those years included franchises in such marginal sites as Troy, Syracuse, Worcester, and Providence, was losing money and in big trouble.

To the rescue came Harry Wright, the organizer of the Cincinnati Red Stockings and "Father of Professional Baseball." He perceived the threat as early as 1877 when, in the Boston Red Stockings' final exhibition contest, he had the pitcher's box moved back 5 feet. The following year, in a September exhibition contest against Indianapolis, he arranged for the game to be played with: a walk awarded on six balls rather than the nine that then prevailed; every pitch counting as either a strike or a ball, thus eliminating the "warning" call an umpire made when a batter watched a good pitch sail by; and complete elimination of restrictions on

---

*Prior to that game a few shutouts had been recorded—the first authenticated one, pitched by Creighton, on November 8, 1860—but never against so formidable a foe.

Harry Wright

a pitcher's delivery—he might throw any way he wished. In the winter prior to the 1880 season, Wright proposed a flat bat and a cork-centered lively ball. And in December 1882, by which time most of the above proposals had been tried and some instituted—the box at 50 feet, the abolition of warning pitches, the walk awarded on seven balls, soon to be six—he proposed denying the batter the right to call for a high or low pitch and, most dramatically, a pitcher's box of 56 feet—very much the pitching distance of today. (The pitching distance at that time was measured from home plate to the *front* of the box, or true point of delivery, while today's distance is measured from the plate to the rubber, from which the pitcher's front foot strides some 4 to 4½ feet forward.)

Hitting revived briskly in 1881, the first year of the new 50-foot pitching distance, but soon slid back again. The rule makers continued their tinkering with the ball/strike count (raising the strike count to four for 1887* and lowering the ball count to four by 1889), the length of the pitcher's box (from 7 feet to 6 feet to, in the final adjustment before replacement by the rubber, 5½ feet), the pitcher's windup (banning the running start and, for 1885, the raised-leg windup), and, most important, the delivery itself.

Once Tommy Bond began to raise his sidearm delivery slightly above the waist in the mid-1870s, it was only a matter of time before "anything goes" became the standard. Pitchers' motions were creeping up to a three-quarters, "from the shoulder" style

*In effect, raising it again, since the old warning pitch had prevailed until 1880 and was granted with two strikes until 1881.

in the early 1880s, and despite a few warnings and even a few forfeits, the practice was well in place before the rule that permitted it in 1883. In 1884 the National League removed all restrictions from pitchers, permitting a full overhand delivery that benefited primarily Charlie Sweeney of Providence, whose record of nineteen strikeouts in a game was not surpassed until Roger Clemens struck out twenty 102 years later. The American Association, the rival major league of the day, held to the from-the-shoulder rule until a June 7 meeting in 1885.

In 1887 the rule makers granted the most absurd capitulation to the hitters: not only were four strikes allowed against only five balls (although, to be fair, the division of the strike zone into high and low regions was eliminated), but walks were to be counted as *hits*. The resulting proliferation of .400 batting averages was broadly ridiculed, and in 1888 an out was again based on three strikes, walks resumed their previous nonhit status—and batting averages resumed their decline, dropping a whopping thirty points in the National League and thirty-five in the American Association as strikeouts increased dramatically.

The slide in batting performance was finally arrested in 1893 by adoption, one decade after its proposal by Harry Wright, of an effective pitching distance of 56 feet. The box was eliminated in favor of a slab placed 60 feet 6 inches from home (rejected was a proposal that the pitcher's position be midway between home and first, or about 63 feet 7 inches from home). Writers ever since have attributed the explosion of hitting in the mid-1890s to the ten-foot increase in the pitching distance, but in fact it was only a five-foot increase: The box of 1892 was 5½ feet long, and the distance to home plate of 50 feet was measured from the front of the

box; moreover, since 1887 the pitcher had to have his back foot in contact with the *back* line of the box. The old chestnut about the 60-foot 6-inch pitching distance being the result of a surveyor's error in reading a blueprint has no basis in fact: The rule makers simply moved the pitching distance back 5 feet, just as they had done in 1881.

The hitting explosion produced, at its zenith in 1894, a league ERA of 5.32, a team batting average of .349 (for the *fourth-place* Phillies), and nearly twice as many walks as strikeouts. That such a boost could have been anticipated was demonstrated by a little-known experiment in the Players League of 1890. In its attempt to win fan favor through increased scoring, the rival major league moved its pitching box back 1½ feet and, with the addition of a new lively ball, produced a batting average twenty points higher than those in the two established major leagues.

The 1890s were a hitter's heyday. Pitchers throwing breaking pitches at the new distance tired more quickly than their predecessors of the 1880s had; staffs now typically featured three and sometimes four starters where two had sufficed in the 1880s and one was enough in the 1870s. The pitcher's craft was advancing, but refinement created a new level of physical exertion. The curveball of the 1890s was no longer the roundhouse or schoolboy curve that featured only a lateral break, and the better pitchers had learned to throw a slow ball (change-up) with the same motion as the fast one, making it just as taxing on the arm. Hoss Radbourn threw for 679 innings in 1884, but he would not have been able to do it in 1894, when no pitcher exceeded 450 innings.

In 1895 the bat was widened to 2¾ inches in diameter, and the foul tip was for the first time ruled a strike. As the former change benefited the batter and the latter the pitcher, the balance between offense and defense was maintained. The other notable new wrinkle of the 1890s was pitcher Clark Griffith's introduction of the scuffed, or cut, ball; his practice was to bang the ball brazenly against his spikes. (In the 1920s, oddly, Griffith's voice was one of the loudest against the spitball.) Griffith's cut ball was significant primarily as a harbinger of the dead ball era to come, which might as aptly be termed the doctored ball era.

THE DEAD BALL ERA: 1901–19

Rule changes slowed in the 1890s—now was one of those anomalous times in major-league history when the battered pitchers needed a boost. And they drew considerable comfort from the ruling that the foul ball was a strike (NL, 1901; AL, 1903) and from the advent of such now illegal if not exactly defunct pitches as the spitball, shine ball,

mud ball, emery ball, and cut ball as well as the legal knuckleball and forkball. In 1900, the National League batting average was .279, and walks exceeded strikeouts by 12 percent. One year later, the mark was .267, and strikeouts exceeded walks by 58 percent. Parallel figures mark the experience of the American League in the years surrounding its adoption of the foul strike.

A hitting famine took hold for the rest of the decade, with the grimmest year being 1908. Shutouts were common and extra-base hits scarce. Base stealing and the bunt were potent offensive weapons, but the home run was a freakish occurrence—more often than not, the league home run leader would have fewer than ten, and in 1908 the entire Chicago White Sox team, who contended for the pennant into the final week, had only three. The popularity of the game itself was not in jeopardy—indeed, 1908 may have provided baseball with its greatest pennant

COURTESY OF JOHN THORN.

Christy Mathewson

races in each league. Such pitchers as Christy Mathewson, Ed Walsh, Cy Young, and Walter Johnson had become heroes with stature equal to Ty Cobb, Nap Lajoie, and Honus Wagner. The game was fast, strategic, and exciting, and fans were delighted with the rivalry between the American and National leagues after a decade of NL domination. But the owners had long memories, and they worried what might happen if hitting did not pick up soon: The press had been grumbling about baseball becoming a dull duel between pitchers rather than a contest between teams.

So in midseason of 1910, the National League introduced the new cork-centered ball (rejected in 1882). Both leagues agreed to its use in the World Series that year and during the regular 1911 season. The result was a mild boost in batting averages but a marked increase in extra-base hits—notably home runs—and run scoring. But was the cork-centered ball truly that much more lively than the rubber-centered ball of old? Did it have a higher coefficient of resiliency? In 1911, one oldtimer noted astutely that:

> *It isn't the cork center that makes the ball lively and causes so much hitting; it's the fact that the pitchers find the ball too hard to curve with their former skill. You see, the cork center is so large that twine has to be wound more tightly than formerly and when the cover is sewed on the ball is like the one used in cricket. It is like wood and the pitchers in gripping it between the thumb and fingers find that the surface does not give. You can make a soft ball curve almost at will. Anybody who knows will admit that. But the hard ball, such as the big leagues are using now, is far different. The pitchers can't get the old breaks and shoots, and as the ball necessarily cuts the plate*

> *straight and fast the good batsmen kill it. You'll find that all the best pitchers are having trouble this year and most of them will tell you that the old curves are impossible. The ball used two years ago was just soft enough near the surface to permit a tight grip, and that meant plenty of effectiveness.*

This observation applies equally well to later, still more lively versions of the baseball. The bane of pitchers is not the rabbit at the center of the ball, but the nature and tightness of the twine or wool that wraps around it, and the elevation of the stitching. The rest of the decade continued to be dominated by pitchers such as Russ Ford with his emery ball, Eddie Cicotte with his shine ball, and legions of pitchers with spitballs, Ed Walsh being paramount.

The cork-centered ball may have been more lively, but its *joie de vivre* was certainly diminished by the fifth inning or so, for in these days only two or three balls might carry the teams through an entire game.

By the mid-1920s—surely due in some measure to Ray Chapman's fatal beaning—stained or mutilated balls were taken out of play, a batter could request a fresh baseball, and the teams no longer insisted upon the return of foul balls (sample figures: the NL of 1919 used 22,095 baseballs; in 1924 it used 54,030). And those foreign-substance pitches were banned. And Babe Ruth, who had sounded the death knell of the dead ball era when he hit 29 homers for the Red Sox in 1919, came to New York. And the lively ball, whose existence at any point in history is still denied by everyone connected with Organized Baseball, hit the American League.*

---

*What made the heart of the 1920 ball race was the use of Australian wool, unavailable during World War I, and the tighter winding made possible by new machinery. An official of the Reach Company, manufacturer of AL baseballs, later admitted that the winding would be periodically tightened or loosened as requested.

THE RUTHIAN ERA: 1920–41

During the dead ball era, the National League batted over .270 only once and the American League only in its first two years as a major circuit, when pitching quality was marginal. Beginning in 1920, NL batters hit over .270 *every year* until 1933, and AL batters did so *every year* until 1941. From 1919 to 1921 alone, home runs doubled; by 1930, they had nearly doubled again. In 1919 the National League's leading slugger, Hi Myers, had a slugging average of .436; in 1930, *the entire league* slugged at a .448 clip. In 1919 the National League had no .350 hitters, the American League four; in 1930 they had twenty. Perhaps most incredible, the top-hitting team in the NL of 1919 was the second-place New York Giants, who batted .269; in 1930 the Phillies hit .315 and finished last as their shellshocked hurlers permitted 7.7 runs per game.

The Dark Age for pitching had set in: Pitchers found themselves short on ammunition and ideas, as they had in 1893—but now it would take them a long time, far longer than ever before or since, to resume their historic advantage.

Was the batting truly so awesome or the pitching so awful? Probably neither. This was an extraordinary period during which several forces combined to give the offense the sort of overwhelming superiority it had enjoyed in the mid-1890s. A whole generation of strongboys, their path illuminated by Ruth, was learning the joys of fencebusting. The push-and-poke attack, advancing runners one base at a time, went the way of the dodo almost overnight. And the pitchers, shorn of much of their arsenal, were caught unprepared for the new offensive—they simply fired those fastballs a bit faster and resignedly watched them rocket by their ears.

A fastball and a curve (the latter almost never thrown when behind in the count, except by the great ones) used to be enough to get by when the ball was dead and the outfielders could play shallow. Now the ball was, comparatively, a grenade, and every man in the lineup could hurt you—no more opportunities to pitch around strong batters and coast whenever you had a three-run lead. The plan of pacing oneself to go nine innings, à la Christy Mathewson, was becoming passé; relief pitchers were becoming respectable. Indeed, the advent of such relief specialists as Firpo Marberry, Mace Brown, and Johnny Murphy was the principal strategic innovation of the Ruthian era.

The great pitchers of the dead ball era were gone or, like Walter Johnson and Grover Alexander, in decline. Stars like Lefty Grove, Dizzy Dean, Dazzy Vance, and Bob Feller came along, but most of the pitchers of the twenties and thirties were pretty straightforward chuckers, daring the big boys to hit their best. Their stuff was probably no worse than that of the bulk of dead ball pitchers, but the consequence of their mistakes was far greater. New pitches? The slider, or nickel curve, may have been created in the mid-1920s by George Blaeholder of the Browns or Tommy Thomas of the White Sox, but its era of impact was yet to come. The knuckler of Dutch Leonard was not new, and its glory too was in the distance. The screwball of Carl Hubbell had of course been used by Mathewson and with less celebrated effect by a handful of nineteenth-century pitchers. Paul Richards, a great student of pitching and architect of the dazzling Orioles' staffs of the 1950s and 1960s, once said:

> *Pitchers are much better than they used to be. The oldtimers only remember the outstanding ones. They forget about the soft touches who couldn't hold a job today. Let's go back to the 1930s, and that means*

we're actually talking about the modern era. Most of the pitchers threw a fastball and a curve. That was it. There were some cute ones around, too, but they weren't the stars. Even some of the stars had a curve that was nothing special and today they couldn't make it with just the pitches they had.

When Richards spoke of cute ones, he may have had in mind Ted Lyons or Tommy Bridges. Some say Bridges had the best curve ever seen. And his curveless wonders might have included Red Ruffing, Dizzy Dean, and a bevy of other notables, including Hall of Famers.

But the pitchers' debacle of this period cannot be blamed entirely on their penchant for meeting power with power. The ball was livened and deadened, league by league, as the owners scrambled to attract the scarce dollars of Depression era fans. The NL ball was juiced in 1921, one year later than in the AL, when senior circuit officials saw how the fans liked the home-run heroics of Babe Ruth in the rival league. Certainly it was inflated further for the bruising 1930 season, then deflated the following year as homers declined mysteriously from 892 to 492. By 1933 the National League's ERA had come down by 33 percent; Carl Hubbell managed one of 1.66, a level not seen in either league since . . . 1919.

From 1931 to 1942, the American League was the hitter's circuit. Its ERA reached a high of 5.04 in 1936 (the only time a league ERA has ever exceeded five runs except for 1894) and stayed over 4.00 every year from 1921 to 1941, barring a 3.99 mark in 1923. Yankee fans may have loved the carnage their batters in particular wrought, but these were not classic years in baseball history.

Nor in truth were the next four, but they laid the groundwork for the period many observers feel was the game's greatest, the 1950s.

THE CLASSIC PERIOD: 1942–60

Baseball during World War II (1942–45) may have been inferior to that played immediately before and after, but the reason was not just the manpower shortage, which was not severe until 1944–45. The shortage of wartime materials forced baseball manufacturers to use an inferior grade of wool that produced a dramatically softer, deadened ball. Home runs in the American League, for example, plummeted from 883 in 1940 to 401 in 1946; league batting averages dipped below .250 for the first time since 1917, when another war for America had just commenced.

The marathon batting orgy of the twenties and thirties was over, and pitching seemed poised to reassert the dominance it had enjoyed in the early years of the century; even the return of stars like Williams, Musial, and DiMaggio from the service for the 1946 season failed to boost overall batting. But 1947 was a year of momentous change: Jackie Robinson broke the color line, television became a force. Of less obvious but more immediate impact, the ball was livened again. Home runs jumped by an incredible 62 percent, and, not surprisingly, complete games declined and saves increased (in the AL, by a whopping 45 percent). The fans loved it.

So the rule makers fanned the flame, lowering the strike zone in 1950 from the top of the shoulder to the armpit and raising it from the bottom of the knee to the top—the first mandated change in this area since 1887. As a result, home runs soared again, to a new high—but oddly, so did strikeouts. The die was cast for the rest of the decade: Batters would swing from the heels, forsaking batting average for power, and pitchers—many of them newly armed with the slider, or "nickel curve," as Cy Young disparagingly termed it—would keep them off balance. The strikeout-to-walk ratio, which had been roughly 1:1 since the introduction of the lively ball in 1920, was nearing the 2:1 (and higher) ratio of the 1960s. Despite the plentiful home run,* batting averages and bases on balls declined, testifying to the advancing skill of the pitchers and the managers who discovered the bull pen. The scoring level in 1960 was lower than that in 1950, and batting was already on its downhill slide to the vanishing point of 1968: the year of the pitcher.

THE EXPANSION ERA: 1961–

Only commissioner Ford Frick did not know it. He saw the prodigious slugging in the American League's expansion year of 1961: Colavito, Gentile, Killebrew, Cash, Mantle, and Maris plus a Yankees' team that hit 240 homers. He was particularly irked that a low-average hitter like Maris could break the cherished home run mark of Babe Ruth. After the National League's expansion and increased run production in the following year, he said: "I would even like the spitball to come back. Take a look at the batting, home run, and slugging record for recent seasons, and you become convinced that the pitchers need help urgently." He saw fit to rescue them by restoring the old strike zone that had been reduced in 1950.

Whoops! Strikeouts rose, walks declined; batting averages fell to the mid-.240s in both leagues, reaching the lowest combined level since 1908, and the woeful New York Mets batted .219, the lowest in NL annals since 1908. The batters were in disarray, and in the seasons that followed they would scurry into full retreat. Young strikeout artists—

Gibson, Marichal, Koufax, McDowell, Chance, McLain, and others—dominated. New stadiums favoring pitchers, such as Shea, Busch, and Dodger stadiums, replaced older parks that were hitters' havens—the Polo Grounds, Sportsman's Park, the Coliseum. The forkball and the knuckler, two pitches that had been around for generations, were revived with devastating effect; every kid pitcher seemed to hit the big time with a slider in addition to his curve and fastball, and such firemen as Larry Sherry, Roy Face, Ron Perranoski, Lindy McDaniel, and Dick Radatz had years when they seemed unhittable.

Baseball officials were becoming concerned that the grand old game appeared stodgy to fans of the sixties, that professional football was capturing the hearts and minds of America. The events of 1968 helped convince them. In the National League Bob Gibson had an ERA of 1.12, including thirteen shutouts. The American League had a batting champion who hit .301, surpassing his nearest rival by eleven points; five pitchers with ERAs under 2.00, one of them, Denny McLain, winning thirty-one games; a league batting average of .230, with the once proud Yankees hitting .214. Paul Richards recommended setting the pitching distance back another 5 feet, to 65 feet, 6 inches.

This was rejected, but the remedies of 1969 were almost as radical. The strike zone was reduced again, to the region of 1950–62. The mound was lowered to a maximum height of 10 inches from the 15 inches that had prevailed since 1903. In all likelihood, the ball was juiced again. Scoring was boosted by about 15 percent in each league, and homers (adjusted for the expansion to twelve-team circuits) jumped by about 30

*In 1954, National League teams averaged 158 homers, the game's highwater mark until 1986, when American League teams averaged 164 four-baggers.

percent. The lowered mound flattened out wicked curveballs and sliders and took the hop off all but the elite of fastballs. The strike zone change was of little significance in itself, but at about this time, without an explicit rule change, the top of the strike zone mysteriously came down not from the shoulders to the letters but to the midriff. By 1987 the high strike would become defined in practice as anything above the belt buckle.

These innovations resuscitated hitting for a while. Whereas in 1968 there had been only six .300 hitters, 1969 produced eighteen; where 1968 saw only three men with 100 RBIs, 1969 brought fourteen; the number of forty-plus home-run hitters rose from one to seven. But by 1972 the pitchers had adjusted, and batting in both leagues slid back to near-1968 levels. In the American League particularly, the situation was grim: Home runs (on a team-average basis) hit their lowest level since 1949 and batting averages dipped below .240 yet again.

The response this time was the designated hitter. It produced a tilt back toward the batters, inasmuch as pitchers now had to face nine true batters rather than eight. (How remarkable an achievement was Nolan Ryan's strikeout record of 383 that season. If he had faced pitchers in the nine-hole of the lineup, he might have added sixty more Ks.) Not only did the d.h. produce more scoring, it also produced more complete games, as managers no longer needed to pinch-hit for a starter who trailed in a low-scoring game. This tendency, however, was short-lived: AL pitchers completed 33.5 percent of their starts in 1974, but only 15.7 percent a decade later (although this was still higher than the 11.6 percent figure for NL).

Strangely, hitting perked up in the National League at about the same time, without benefit of the d.h. Could the new cowhide ball, manufactured in Haiti, have had something to do with it? Or was it the incredible shrinking strike zone? (Consider how sharp today's pitchers must be in comparison to their mates of, say, the 1920s, when the strike zone printed in the rule book corresponded to the strike zone during the game.) In any event, the pitcher/batter war seemed a standoff in the late seventies and early eighties, as batters fattened up on the new flock of breaking-ball cuties while older hard-stuff stars like Seaver, Palmer, Carlton, and Ryan continued to shine. Some of the newcomers—Soto, Guidry, Richard, Morris, Valenzuela—threw hard and made their marks, but the general opinion in baseball was that if the fastball was the pitch of the sixties and the slider the pitch of the seventies, the mixed bag of curve and change, cut fastball and split-finger fastball, would dominate the eighties. Then along came Dwight Gooden and Roger Clemens and Mark Langston, and we stopped hearing about the death of the fastball.

Nonetheless, the split-finger fastball was the sensation of the 1986 season. Popularized by relief pitcher Bruce Sutter in the early eighties, it had been invented back in 1908 by Bert Hall, who called it a forkball, and later was employed by Tiny Bonham, Roy Face, and Lindy McDaniel. For all of them it served as a dry spitter, an offspeed sinker that batters would beat into the ground or, in the case of Sutter, who threw it harder than the others, fan on. The gospel of the split-finger fastball was spread in the 1980s by Roger Craig when he was pitching coach of the Detroit Tigers, whose staff fell in love with the pitch.

It seems anyone whose fingers were long enough to throw the pitch added it to his repertoire. But one of Craig's disciples, Mike Scott of the Houston Astros, threw it harder than anyone and transformed it, in

1986, from a freakish change-up to the greatest menace batters have faced since the hard sliders of Lyle, Guidry, and Carlton a decade earlier. The pitch thrown by Sutter had a bit of a screwball tail to it, but its primary trait was its drop; Scott's split-finger pitch sails and swoops unpredictably at some 85 m.p.h.—and sinks, too.

In the second half of 1986, carrying over into the National League Championship Se-ries, Scott's pitch was as nearly unhittable as any ever seen on a diamond—as discouraging as Ryan's fastball, Carlton's slider, Koufax's curve, Wilhelm's knuckler, Walsh's spitter, Creighton's blue darter. Is this the end for the batter? Of course not; he will adjust, even if it takes a little help from the rule makers.

And then the pitcher will come up with something new.

2

Profile of a Pitcher

The pitcher runs the show. He holds the ball, and nothing happens until he lets go. He is in *control*.

Or at least that is the necessary illusion. In Jim Bouton's words, "You spend a good piece of your life gripping a baseball, and in the end it turns out that it was the other way around all the time." That little white sphere brings with it enormous demands for dexterity, strength, and concentration, "tremendous, sustained concentration," in the words of Mets' team physician James C. Parkes. "A batter makes an equally intense mental effort, but only four or five times per game. A pitcher must concentrate with every pitch."

Standing at the center of the goldfish bowl that is a major-league stadium, the pitcher must focus so fiercely on the task at hand that he blocks out not only the crowd but, when he has hit his rhythm, everyone else on the field, sometimes including the batter and catcher; the pitcher can raise himself above and outside the game to perform for himself, for art, for the pursuit of a perfect

pitch. Pitching may not be 70 percent of the game, as Connie Mack said long ago, or 80 percent, as Herman Franks said more recently, but the pitcher certainly bears a greater responsibility for victory or defeat than anyone else.

The pitcher is not simply an athlete; he is an artist in that while his talent shapes the game, he never knows beforehand whether his mysterious gift—his "stuff"—will be with him on a given day. He creates his work of art pitch by pitch, each pitch carrying a part of himself bearing his unique mark. The ball may be released but is still, magically, under his control and, if it is not hit, returns to him. The magic resides in his arm, that best friend and most dreaded enemy, which a pitcher may talk about as if it were detached from his body and going about on its own.

On the mound the pitcher attempts to create a rhythm (or connect with a cosmic one). For some, intense mental effort is the key: Skip Lockwood said, "I don't think you *can* think too hard. Baseball, when you really

Our nomination for the best lead on a story about pitching goes to the St. Louis writer of the 1920s who wrote:

"Alan Sutton Sothoron pitched his initials off today."

analyze it, is a game within a game within a game." For others, baseball's KISS rule applies: Keep It Simple, Stupid. Bill Lee wrote, "When cerebral processes enter into sports you start screwing up. It's like the Constitution, which says a separate church and state. You have to separate mind and body." Sparky Lyle echoed that sentiment, saying, "When you start thinkin' is when you get your ass beat."

Lockwood, Lee, and Lyle are all correct. A pitcher does have to think, and he has to think hard enough to go beyond thought and let his body talk.

What is the psychological profile of the pitcher? The tea leaves reveal that he is a perfectionist; independent; egotistical; sensitive and distrustful, his feelings easily bruised; brave; very, very tough; and often enough, totally off the wall. To wit, some case studies follow.

FLAKES AND FRUITCAKES

Baseball has always had flakes, and for every Casey Stengel, Babe Herman, Pepper Martin, and Germany Schaefer who played in the field, there were twice as many flaky pitchers. Branch Rickey called them men whose arms are twenty years ahead of their brains.

Don Stanhouse of the Orioles liked to hang upside down in the bullpen to get a new perspective on the game. He ended his career when he fell on his head. "He could have been a star," fellow flake Bill Lee said wistfully.

Randy Miller, another Orioles' pitcher, believed that curveballs were absolutely straight; the earth turning beneath them made them appear to curve.

Clyde King, a Brooklyn pitcher, was rushed into a game from the bullpen without a chance to warm up. To delay the game and give King time to loosen up, shortstop Peewee Reese feigned a foreign object in his eye. While Peewee gave an Oscar-winning performance rubbing the injured eye and a teammate elaborately tried to daub the speck out with a handkerchief, the pitcher stopped throwing, trotted over to his obviously pain-stricken teammate, and asked if there was anything he could do to help.

Sparky Lyle used to leap nude onto birthday cakes. Sparky also once put black shoe polish on a teammate's towel hanging outside the shower and waited for the victim to wipe the soap from his eyes. To see if his World Series diamond ring was real, he tried to scratch the glass on a coffee table with it. The coffee table, he concluded, was more valuable than the ring.

Kooky Rookies

Rookies are always the butts of jokes. Many a kid has trustingly rested his pitching arm overnight in the hammock intended for clothes that used to hang in Pullman upper berths. Back in 1890 nineteen-year-old Amos Rusie, taking the overnight boat from New York to Boston, spent the night sleeping in a life preserver on the advice of a helpful teammate.

Kansas City Monarchs' pitcher Bill Drake told John Holway of one rookie who was told to go out to left field and shag some flies. "Which way is left field?" he asked. "I've never been in this park before."

Then there was the rookie pitcher who, when asked why he did not use the rosin bag, replied, "I couldn't get it open."

18

18 The Pitcher

Sore Losers

Baseball has had many a famous sore loser. Wes Ferrell was one of the greatest at smashing up locker rooms. Lefty Grove was close behind. He would smash his fist into his locker, but always his right fist—Ted Williams noted: "Grove was a careful tantrum thrower." Mark Lemongello bit his shoulder until it bled; after one game he dived into a table laden with snacks and lay in the mustard and mayonnaise for an hour.

Rube Waddell

George "Rube" Waddell was the original baseball flake. In the early days of the century, he could be found diving into a Florida lake to wrestle alligators, heroically sitting on the ledge of a burning building with a hose, leading a parade and hurling his baton high in the air, or turning cartwheels off the mound after beating Cy Young in twenty innings.

Rube was an alcoholic, and he sold the ball used in that Cy Young game for drinks. About twenty bartenders around the league displayed the historic ball above their bars.

The man-child had a child's heart of gold. He once dashed into a burning house, picked up an oil stove that had turned over, and threw it into a snowbank. While duck hunting, he leaped into the water and rescued two men who had fallen from their boat. Another time, responding to a cry for help, he bravely dived off a ferry— heroically saving a log.

Waddell tried the patience of his manager, Connie Mack. He also exasperated his catcher and roommate, Ossie Schreckengost, primarily by eating crackers in bed. (In those days ball players slept two to a bed.) Schreck finally had a clause inserted in Rube's contract prohibiting him from eating crackers in bed.

Schreck was a little weird himself. One night when both were in their cups, Rube announced that he could fly and leaped out the window to prove it. When he came to in the hospital the next day, he asked his roomie why Schreck did not stop him. "Heck," said Schreck, "I bet you could do it."

Bugs Raymond

Arthur "Bugs" Raymond, also an alcoholic, pitched for the New York Giants about the same time Waddell was pitching for the Philadelphia A's. Waddell cartwheeled off the mound; Raymond walked off on his hands.

In the minor leagues, at Charleston, South Carolina, Raymond won the first game of a July 4 doubleheader, took a lunch break at the local bar, returned to the park, and pitched a perfect game in the night-cap. On another day he stuck his hand into the blades of a fan in a bar, then pitched an eleven-inning four-hitter.

Bugs Raymond

18 NATIONAL BASEBALL LIBRARY, COOPERSTOWN, N.Y.

A spitball thrower, as a major-league pitcher Bugs tied the great Honus Wagner into knots with his spitter. When his drinking pals asked him to demonstrate, he hurled a glass through the tavern window and said proudly, "Notice the break."

At games he tossed baseballs over the bullpen wall in return for drinks. When John McGraw posted guards on the gates, Raymond lowered a bucket of baseballs from the clubhouse window and hauled the beer back up. McGraw tried withholding his paycheck and sending it directly to Raymond's wife. "If she gets the money," Bugs said, "let her pitch."

Eventually McGraw had to let him go. Two years later Raymond got into a playground fight and was kicked in the head. He died of a fractured skull at the age of 30.

Nick Altrock and Al Schacht

The two funniest comedians in baseball were, naturally, pitchers—Nick Altrock and Al Schacht.

For two years, 1905–6, Altrock had been a twenty-game winner with the Chicago White Sox and beat the great Mordecai Brown 2–1 in the 1906 World Series. He was a fine fielder, setting several records in the regular season and the Series. He also had a great move to first. He would dare the runners to step off and once picked off seven out of eight. It was said that he walked batters on purpose as the best way to get them out. Nick said he once picked the same man off base five times, each time hitting him in the chest before the runner realized the ball was coming.

Long after he was relegated to the coaching lines, Nick nevertheless went to bat once each season, the last time in 1933 at the age of fifty-nine, the oldest man ever to play a big league game until Satchel Paige.

Craig Carter of *The Sporting News* reports

Nick Altrock

that Altrock discovered his comic talent in the coach's box in Milwaukee in 1912, when he started shadow-boxing with himself between innings. The crowd roared as he slugged himself and sprawled rubbery-legged to the ground, staggered up, and slugged himself again. He pulled the routine later while with the Washington Senators, and the opposition pitcher, Vean Gregg, laughed so hard he could not pitch. Washington won the game 4–2, and Gregg's owners complained to the league president, Ban Johnson, who asked for a demonstration and could not keep a straight face himself. He told Nick to keep the act—but not during the game.

When Al Schacht flunked out of the Senators' pitching rotation, he joined Altrock on the coaching lines. Schacht coached third base—he was good at waving in runners, he said, since he had watched so many of them score while he was pitching. Nick and Al did their comedy routine together—Al was the straight man who revived the prostrate fighter with a bucket of warm water, although pranksters were known to substitute ice-cold water whenever they could. Al's trademark outfit was a top hat, long tails, and a pillowy catcher's mitt.

Another crowd-pleaser involved running to the dugout when a shower began, reappearing in galoshes. If the ump still did not call the game, Altrock would open an umbrella. If that failed too, he would sit on a plank of wood and "row" furiously for dear life.

For some reason, Nick and Al had a falling out, and though they continued to perform together, they took separate cabs to their gigs and did not talk to each other for the last six years of their partnership. No one ever knew why, and neither one ever told anyone. But it did not affect their comedy. "Luckily," Schacht explained, "it was pantomime."

Dazzy Vance

One of the game's best pitchers in the 1920s, Dazzy Vance contributed more than anyone, except perhaps Babe Herman, to the Dodgers' reputation as the Daffiness Boys. They were both in the middle of the famous incident in which Herman tripled into a double play. The bases were loaded, with Vance on second, when Herman smashed a hit deep to the outfield. One man scored and Vance rounded third, then, fearing he would be thrown out, slid back into the base as the man on first slid in from the other direction and Herman charged around second with his head down. Both Dazzy and Babe were called out, giving rise to the vaudeville joke, "The Dodgers have three men on base." "Oh yeah? Which base?"

Vance was leader of the "0-for-4 Club" of free spirits who liked to party after curfew. One night they got back to find one of the team's coaches waiting for them in the lobby, so they piled back into the cab and visited another bar. Each time they returned, the coach was still there, so what could they do but return to their drinking? At last, by 3 A.M. the coach gave up and went to bed, and the boys finally were able to reach their rooms undetected.

On a train trip, Vance, pitcher Burleigh Grimes, and a couple of other Dodgers made Ku Klux Klan hoods out of pillow cases and invaded the car where the Boston Braves were sleeping. They dragged their victims out of their berths, bedclothes and all, and choked terrified catcher Mickey O'Neil until he gave them all his signs.

Satchel Paige

Because he pitched in the Negro leagues for most of his career, few whites had the chance to see Satchel Paige pitch. But all can enjoy his humor secondhand. His remark "never look back, someone may be gaining on you" is today as much a part of American speech as Leo Durocher's "nice guys finish last."

Paige was a skinny kid ("If I turned sideways you couldn't see me"), who self-consciously wore two pairs of socks to flesh out his legs, but still his baseball knickers hung loose around his calves. The vicissitudes of life in the Negro leagues shaped Satch's humor. He regaled audiences with his stories of traveling, crammed with his knees up to his chin, in a roadster full of ball players, trying to catch some sleep between games. In the latter half of his career, when he was with the Kansas City Monarchs, he was advertised to pitch almost every game to draw a crowd. Of course he pitched only two or three innings, but he once said he pitched 165 ball games one year. "I began to learn to pitch by the hour.'' If he did not pitch, he said at his induction into the Hall of Fame, ''they didn't want us—in town, let alone in the ball park.''

The black teams took their baseball seriously and, contrary to popular opinion, did not clown as, for instance, the Harlem Globetrotters do. But a few teams did have players with a comic talent who both played ball and entertained the fans. The Ethiopian Clowns, for example, were a minor-league black club that wore clown makeup and clown suits or grass skirts over their uniforms and put on comic routines before the game.

Paige was not a formal clown like these. But he had a droll humor that was all the funnier for being genuine.

Monarchs' catcher Othello Renfroe calls Satchel ''the most comical man you ever saw in your life. When we were warming up, he'd take infield practice at third. Just *throw* it over that diamond, man, flip it to second.'' Fans came out early just to see the infield practice.

Satchel was actually a serious man, in addition to being a witty one. Monarchs' first baseman (and later Cub coach) John ''Buck'' O'Neil recalls standing silently with Satch at the old slave market in Charleston, South Carolina, before Satch broke the silence by saying, ''I feel like I've been here before.'' ''Me too, roomie,'' O'Neil agreed.

On a fishing trip in the Everglades, Satch would not let O'Neil shoot the deadly water moccasins around their boat. The swamp was their domain, Satch said, and the men were the intruders in it.

Satch had nicknames for everyone. O'Neil was ''Nancy.'' He was given the name on a trip through the prairies, when Satch had an Indian girl in one hotel room and another girl in a second room. Stealing out of

the second, he tapped on the first door, calling softly, ''Nancy? Nancy?'' Suddenly the second door flew open, and an angry girlfriend demanded to know who Nancy was. At that moment, O'Neil opened his door, sized the situation up, and said, ''Yeah, Satch, what is it?''

''I'm not married,'' Paige once said, ''but I'm in great demand.''

Satchel liked fast women and fast cars and was habitually dallying, then speeding to the stadium, arriving just as the restive fans were demanding their money back and the owners were on the verge of suicide. One night Washington's Griffith Stadium was packed, and Satch was late. He had been stopped by a cop for speeding, and finally arrived with a police escort, sirens wailing.

Monarchs' owner J. L. Wilkinson finally assigned pitcher Chet Brewer to get Paige to the games on time. Brewer, who later scouted Dock Ellis, Reggie Smith, Enos Cabell, and others, recalls:

One time in Three Rivers, Michigan, 200 miles to go, game starts at three o'clock; it's one now. Satchel in the middle of the floor shooting dice with some woman for pennies. They had won his pennies. I said, ''Come on, Satchel, we're going to be late.'' He's still there. I said, ''Come on, let's go.'' ''Oh, Dooflackem, you worry too much,'' he said.

Satchel was driving this big Airflow Chrysler. We get in his car. He said, ''If the red lights are going to make us late, I won't stop at any more.'' He's blowing his horn, going right through the red lights. Satchel was going so fast, we went about a block past the ball park—had to turn around. We walk in in the fifth inning, people going home, demanding their money back.

One time in Philadelphia, he had this white Lincoln Continental car then. We were late again. Down this street he went. ''You can't go down that street! It's a one-way street!'' Traffic coming at us, Satchel ducking in and out. Big motorcycle cop, siren: "Pull over there." Satchel pulled over. "Doggone, don't you see that's a one-way street?"

Satchel looked up at him so innocently: "I'm only going one way."

They took him to jail, fined him $50. "You're going to have to make court tomorrow at nine."

Satchel said, "Sir, we're going to leave at eight."

The judge said, "Another $50, you can go." Satchel paid. Just speeding again. We got to the ball park in the third inning. Late again!

Out here in California he broke every traffic law in Los Angeles, making U-turns, going through the safety zone with people standing in it. Out in Bakersfield on his way to 'Frisco to play, the cops were after Satchel, didn't catch him until he was in Oakland. He just said, "I wanted to see how fast I could go before you caught me."

They said, "Man, you can't drive out here." They took his California driver's license from him.

I told J. L., "Now, instead of one pitcher being late, you got two late. I don't want to ride with Satchel any more. He's going to get both of us killed!"

Satch was the first to describe Cool Papa Bell as so fast he could turn out the light and jump in bed before the room got dark. Bell himself tells of the time he and Satch were roommates, and while Paige was out galavanting one night, Bell stayed in the room and discovered that the light switch malfunctioned; there was a few seconds' delay before the lights went out. He tested it carefully, put on his pajamas, and waited for Satch to return.

"Sit down," Bell said, "I want to show you something." He flicked the switch, strolled over to bed, got in, and pulled the covers up. Bing, the light went off. "See, Satch?" he grinned. "You been tellin' people that story 'bout me for years, and even *you* didn't know it was true!"

In 1981, suffering from emphysema and breathing through a tube attached to an oxygen pack, Paige was torn between accepting an invitation to lunch at the White House or to a reunion of Negro league veterans. "That meeting is for old black ball players, isn't it?" his wife, Lahoma, asked.

Satch admitted that it was.

"Well," she said, "that's you. Have you looked in the glass lately?"

Satch went to the reunion.

"Age," Satchel said, "is a question of mind over matter. If you don't mind, age doesn't matter."

Lefty Gomez

One of the great humorists of the game, Lefty Gomez was eighteen when he told a writer that Einstein was "an inventor—like me." Lefty's contribution to science? The revolving goldfish bowl for tired goldfish. He was called "Goofy" from that day on.

In his rookie year, Lefty was facing Al Simmons when the umpire walked out to the mound. "Simmons says you're throwing a spitball," the arbiter said sternly.

"Tell him," Lefty replied, "to hit it on the dry side."

Lefty denied throwing spitters, though he conceded that "I sweat easily."

Lefty had once worn glasses. Once, when they were smudged, he wiped them off and then looked at home plate. There was Jimmy Foxx, muscles bulging, standing up to bat. Foxx had muscles in his hair—Lefty once winced, "He wasn't born, he was trapped." Gomez was so unnerved that he never wore glasses again. Jimmy once slugged a home run off Lefty far into the third deck of Yankee Stadium. Next time Foxx came up, Gomez simply stood on the mound, holding the ball. Catcher Bill Dickey came out to see what was wrong. "Let's just wait a minute," Lefty said. "Maybe he'll get a long-distance phone call."

Manager Joe McCarthy bawled Lefty out one day for gawking at a plane while standing on the mound. "He could have hit a homer off you because you weren't paying attention," McCarthy said. "Joe," Lefty replied, "the day someone hits a homer off me while I have the ball in my hand, I'm finished."

When Gomez loaded the bases one day, shortstop Frank Crosetti came over to the mound. "There are three men on," he informed the pitcher. "Oh?" said Lefty, "I thought they gave me an extra infield."

Once a double-play ball was hit back to the mound, and while Crosetti moved over to take the throw at second, Gomez tossed it instead to second baseman Tony Lazzeri, who was 40 feet from the bag. "What did you do that for?" the startled Lazzeri asked. "I've been reading about how you're the smartest player on this club," Gomez replied. "I just wanted to see what you'd do with that one."

In Phil Rizzuto's rookie year, Gomez called the nervous youngster over to the mound. "Is your mother in the stands, kid?" he asked. "Yessir, Mr. Gomez," Phil replied. "Well, stand here and talk to me a minute," Lefty said. "She'll think you're giving advice to the great Lefty Gomez." The beaming Rizzuto hit his first big-league home run that day.

As it must for all pitchers, the end finally came for Lefty. He knew it was time to quit when he went to the mound, let fly a fastball, and "thought someone had dug up the mound and moved it back 15 yards." He was asked if he was throwing as hard as ever. "I'm throwing just as hard," he said, "but the ball isn't getting up there as fast."

Dizzy Dean

"Anybody who's ever had the privilege of seein' me play ball knows that I am the greatest pitcher in the world," Dizzy Dean once declared. For a couple of years in the 1930s he was right.

The son of a poor sharecropper from Arkansas, Diz dropped out of school after the third grade "so's not to pass my old man." He flunked out of second grade, Dean said. "And I wasn't so good in the first grade either."

As a Cardinals' rookie, Dizzy was sent down to their St. Joseph farm club. "Listen, Branch," he told general manager Branch Rickey, "don't waste no time sendin' me to St. Joe. If I can strike 'em out in one league, I can strike 'em out in the other. I can win the pennant for you, Branch."

"Judas priest!" Rickey said in retrospect. "I think he would have."

But the Mahatma, not knowing any better, sent Dean down anyway. Diz bombarded him with letters, keeping him posted on his exploits—seventeen wins with a last-place team. Each letter was signed "The Great Dean."

Once, tiptoeing in after curfew, Dean

Dizzy Dean

bumped into the president of the Texas League. "Good morning, Mr. President," Diz winked—and promised not to tell on him.

Diz was nineteen when Rickey finally brought him back up. In an exhibition against the A's, Dean kept pestering manager Gabby Street: "I jest wish I was a-throwin'." Finally, to shut him up, Street put him in against Al Simmons (.322), Jimmy Foxx (.364), and Mickey Cochrane (.293). Diz struck all three out.

Burgess Whitehead, a lifetime .266 hitter, had roomed with Dean in the minors, so Diz used to throw him easy pitches in the majors. Once Whitehead hit one back to the box, striking Dean on the forehead. "Little bitty buddy," Diz scolded, "you got to start pullin' that ball."

Dizzy's brother Paul, nicknamed Daffy, joined the Cards in 1934. On the team train one day Paul took a swig from a bottle just as the train entered a tunnel. "Diz," he asked in the dark, "have you tried any of this stuff?"

"No," Dizzy confessed.

"Well, don't. I did, and I've gone plumb blind."

Giant player-manager Bill Terry was Dean's special foil. After bursting into the New York clubhouse during the 1934 stretch drive, Diz was ordered out by a startled Terry. "We're going over the Cardinal hitters," Bill sputtered. "That's okay," Diz replied cheerfully, "I already know all their weaknesses anyway."

Dean promised some lame children in a hospital that he would strike Terry out with the bases loaded. In the game, he walked Hughie Critz deliberately to put three men on when Terry stepped in. "I kinda' hate to do this, Bill," he said, "but I done promised a bunch of kids I'd fan you with the bases full." Then he did.

Once, however, Bill drilled three line drives back to the box, almost killing Diz. Third baseman Pepper Martin strolled over. "Diz," he said worriedly, "I don't think you're playing him deep enough."

Dean's willing partner in much of his mischief was Pepper Martin. One day in a hotel, they put on some paint-spattered overalls, got some ladders, brushes, saws, and hammers, and carried them all into the banquet room, where a speaker was regaling the diners. Like a Laurel and Hardy movie, the two proceeded to knock things off tables, noisily setting their ladders up, calling questions to each other, banging with the hammers, and of course completely disrupting the speech. When some guests finally recognized them, they were invited onto the dais and given a loud round of applause.

Dean and Martin once rigged smoke bombs in several limousines parked outside a hotel. When the owners in fur coats and tuxes turned the keys and the smoke poured out, the startled guests ran back into the lobby, to be greeted by Dean and Martin, reassuringly wearing firemen's outfits.

In the 1934 World Series, Dean hit on a unique way to break up a double play. As he charged into second on a force out, he suddenly leaped and took the shortstop's throw right between the eyes. He was knocked cold and carried off the field. Worried Cardinals' fans were reassured by the next morning's headline:

X-RAY OF DEAN'S HEAD REVEALS NOTHING

In a booklet he wrote, *The Dizzy Dean Dictionary and What's What in Baseball*, Diz explained that his book filled a long-standing need, since "there ain't no good expert source where you kin look up some of the words. . . . I mean the real tecknical words that's used by the players and has growed right out of baseball." Though people sneered at his syntax ("Sin tax? What will them fellers in Washington think up next?'') and orthography, Dean observed correctly that ''a lot of people who don't say ain't ain't eatin'.''

In addition to the dictionary, the booklet carried some chapters in the back. The table of contents read:

Chapter 1. Who's the Greatest Pitcher in the World?

Chapter 2. Who's Got the Greatest Throwin' Arm in the World?

Chapter 3. Who's the Greatest Hitter in the World?

Chapter 4. Who's the Greatest Runner in the World (not countin' days I was tired)?

Dean once bet a friend that he could strike out Vince DiMaggio, Joe's older brother, four times. He got the first three, then Vince lifted a foul back toward the screen, which catcher Johnny Ogrowdowski went after. ''Drop it, damn it, drop it!'' Dean commanded. He then fanned DiMaggio for the fourth time.

Dean's pitching career came to a sudden end when Earl Averill drilled a pitch back into his foot during the 1937 All Star game. A doctor examined the foot and announced gravely that the toe was fractured. ''Fractured, hell,'' Diz exploded, ''the damn thing's broke!''

After retiring, Dean became an announcer, and his contributions to American speech then rank with his contributions to pitching science. ''He slud into third'' is a classic. Less famous are: ''The runners returned to their respectable bases,'' and ''The batter is standing confidentially at the plate.''

He once described a famous ball-park visitor, Queen Wilhelmina of the Netherlands, as ''some fat lady,'' and urged listeners, ''Don't fail to miss tomorrow's game.''

Dean's malaprops as an announcer are legend, but they could not obscure an unerring analytical approach to the game. After a 1-0 game, he informed his listeners that ''the game was closer than the score indicated.'' On another occasion, he confided that ''this series is already won, but I don't know by which team.''

Bobo Newsom

Norman Louis Newsom was sometimes called Buck but was usually called Bobo because that was what he called everyone else. A good ol' boy from South Carolina, Bobo was the Dizzy Dean of the American League.

He got his shot at the majors by winning thirty-three games in the Pacific Coast League in 1933. The record book says thirty, but as Bobo asks, ''Who ya' gonna believe, the record book or the guy what did it?'' Thirty or thirty-three, the record earned him a trip to the St. Louis Browns. The Browns finished sixth that year. Bobo lost twenty games, but he won sixteen, including a no-hitter; he lost the no-hitter and the game with two out in the tenth. He was once asked how many no-hitters he had pitched. ''Just the one,'' he said, ''They don't grow in bunches like bananas, son.''

Newsom was given the honor of opening the 1936 season in Washington before President Franklin Roosevelt and a capacity crowd. In the third inning, third baseman Ossie Bluege fielded a bunt and fired to first. Bobo forgot to duck, and the ball caught him on the side of his face. He clutched his face and staggered in agony; manager Bucky Harris told him to sit out for the rest of the game. ''Naw,'' Newsom said, 'Ol' FDR came out to see Bobo, and he's gonna see him all the way.'' He won the game 1-0. Afterward, they found out his jaw was broken in two places. It had to be wired shut,

Bobo Newsom with Bobby Shantz

cutting down on his loquaciousness for a short time anyway.

In another game, after the plate umpire repeatedly called his best pitches balls, Newsom finally got a strike call. Walking to home plate, he swept his cap off and bowed low from the waist. "Thank you very kindly, my dear fellow," he said. He was promptly thumbed out of the game.

Back with St. Louis in 1938, owner Don Barnes promised him a suit of clothes if he would win the opener. Newsom did, and Barnes pressed some money into his hand.

"Keep the sugar, Bobo," Newsom replied. "Bobo bought the suit before the game. The bill is on your desk." That year he won twenty of the fifty-five games the Browns won.

Newsom won twenty again in 1939, although he was traded in mid-season to Detroit, and that was also the year he had a fight with writer Robert Ruark. At least, Ruark was fighting; Bobo was drinking a soda and holding Ruark at arm's length with the other hand. In one game he publicly announced that he would beat his old club, the Senators. The park was packed with Washington fans who had come to boo him. Newsom pitched a two-hitter and thumbed his nose as he walked off the field.

He won twenty-one games in 1940, plus two in the World Series. When Bob Feller received a record salary of $30,000, Bobo topped him with $35,000. He walked into President Walter O. Briggs' office to sign the record-breaking contract, telling Briggs' son, "Step aside, little Bo; Big Bobo wants to see me."

With his new wealth, Newsom bought a car with neon lights that spelled "Bobo" and a horn that played "Tiger Rag," and he dined nightly on quail and champagne at his specially reserved table in the hotel restaurant. He lost twenty games, and general manager Jack Zeller cut his salary to $12,500. Zeller, who was bald, had just had ninety farm players cut because of a ruling by commissioner Mountain Landis. "Hell, Curly," Newsom said, "you lost ninety players, and I don't see you takin' no cut."

Zeller peddled him to the Brooklyn Dodgers, and Newsom wired his new manager, Leo Durocher: "Wish to congratulate you on buying pennant insurance." Instead of a pennant, Leo got trouble. He accused Newsom of causing a passed ball by throwing a spitter, which precipitated a mutiny among the players, who rallied to Newsom's defense.

The Dodgers sent him back to the Browns, the Browns sent him to his old pinochle partner, Clark Griffith, at Washington. In all, Newsom served five terms in Washington and boasted that he beat Franklin Roosevelt's record by one.

Van Mungo

In the 1930s Van Lingle Mungo of the Giants had a great fastball, a great weakness for the bottle, and a great eye for the ladies.

In the minors Van pitched for Montreal of the International League. "Montreal had a good drinking ball club," infielder Roy Hughes says. Mungo and fellow pitcher Jake Flowers were found drunk on the bench one day, and the other guys hustled them down to the bull pen to keep them out of sight of manager Clyde Sukeforth. They were too late. The following day, Sukey called a clubhouse meeting, and, while slowly walking around the training table, he informed the team gravely, "We're going to play a baseball game today. I want nine sober volunteers."

Leo Durocher reported that in Cuba one winter Van was caught in bed with somebody's wife and was pursued by the angry husband wielding a machete. His teammates smuggled him to the waterfront, where a Pan Am seaplane was waiting with motors running. With the police hot on his heels, Van sprinted down the wharf, grabbed a rope from the plane door, and was lifted to safety as the big plane gunned its engines and took off.

Joe Page

In *Dynasty* Peter Golenbock says Joe Page, the great Yankee reliever of the forties, once gave teammate Snuffy Stirnweiss the fright of his life by propping a bear's carcass on an outhouse toilet seat. When Snuffy opened the door, the bear fell forward on him, and only muffled cries of terror could be heard from Stirnweiss.

Page's roommate was Joe DiMaggio, who, on marrying Marilyn Monroe, observed that "it's got to be better than rooming with Joe."

Whitey Ford

Whitey Ford's nocturnal escapades with Mickey Mantle and oft times Billy Martin are legendary. Mantle always said that if he had not met Whitey, he would have added five years to his career—but he would not have had nearly as much fun. The two once led the Yankees' private detective in a merry chase through a church, around a block, and back to their hotel entrance. (The gumshoe could have just followed the trail of olives, writer John Lardner once suggested.)

Billy Loes

Brooklyn Dodger Billy Loes was a tough-talking Brooklyn kid who pitched in the fifties. He did not want to win twenty games, he said, because then everyone would expect him to do it every year. So he stopped at fourteen.

On train rides from Brooklyn to Philadelphia, he locked himself in the men's room to avoid a New Jersey process server in a paternity suit.

Before the 1952 Dodger/Yankee World Series, Loes was roundly criticized for predicting that the Yankees would win in six games. He hotly denied it—he had said seven games, he insisted.

In that Series he committed a balk when the ball squirted out of his hand. "Too much spit on it," he explained. Vic Raschi followed with a ground ball, which Loes booted. He said he lost it in the sun.

Dean Chance and Bo Belinsky

Or how about those two playboys of the western world, Dean Chance and Bo Belinsky of the California Angels? Dean, the "aw shucks" country boy from Appleton, Wisconsin, and Bo, the skirt chaser from the big city, quickly discovered they were soulmates. Curfews meant nothing to Dean and Bo. Chance came in at 4:30 one morning, then pitched in the All Star game, holding the NL to two hits. Bo usually went to sleep around 6 A.M. The first time was in 1962, before his first major-league start.

Bo once met a blonde, struck up a conversation, stayed out with her until 4 A.M., and then threw a no-hitter the next day. His big regret was that he never found her again. "She was my good luck charm. When I lost her, I lost all my pitching luck." Bo complained that he did not make money off his no-hitter; in fact, it cost him money: "I had to buy drinks for everyone. It was like a hole-in-one."

His only other regret was that he could not "sit in the stands and see [myself] pitch."

"Happiness," Bo said, "is a first-class pad, good wheels, an understanding manager, and a little action." He also said, "Sex always helped me relax. No one ever died of it."

The Angels' management must have wished Chance and Belinsky were more like Dodger pitcher Burt Hooton. Hooton was so square, said announcer Vin Scully, that "he went out and painted the town beige."

Once, while in the minors in the Baltimore organization, Bo and pitcher Steve Dalkowski chanced to room next door to the reigning Miss Universe. Dalkowski diligently drilled twenty holes in the wall. When Miss Universe discovered them, she raised a storm, and manager Paul Richards demanded an explanation for the holes.

"Holes?" Bo asked. "What holes?"

"The holes in your wall," Richards replied.

"Oh," said Bo, "those holes."

Luckily (or unluckily) for Bo, he ended up in Los Angeles with the Angels, not Baltimore. After his no-hitter, he quickly became a hot item in the Hollywood gossip columns. With columnist Walter Winchell helping with the introductions, Bo dated royal queens—ex-Queen Soraya of Iran—and movie queens—Tina Louise, Ann-Margret, Connie Stevens, and Mamie Van

Doren. Bo maintained the highest standards and insisted, "I didn't take out a broad without checking her references." He did make one exception. One night he said he found a beautiful woman hanging from his hotel windowsill. "What could I do?" he asked. "I had to invite her in to save her life."

One girl moved in to stay. But when she took him for $350 in a poker game, he kicked her out. "He sent her home in a cab," said his buddy Chance. "Bo had class."

Pitching for the major-league minimum wage of $6,000, the left-hander won ten and lost eleven on the field. He and Chance (who was 14–10) helped lift the Angels from seventh to third. Bo's off-field antics were equally valuable in doubling the Angels' attendance to 1.1 million. "Let's face it," he said without false modesty, "I put that team on the map."

The next year he reported late to spring training and explained that he had been delayed by a snowstorm in Texas. Another time he said he was held up by a pool tournament—Bo was actually a good player and was even offered a world tour shooting pool.

Bo was a victim of the sophomore jinx, and his record fell to 2–9. He was farmed out to Hawaii, where he spent the summer observing bikinis on Waikiki. "When the Angels called me back," he confessed, "I was depressed."

But Belinsky soon got back into the Hollywood swing. Arriving back from a road trip at dawn one morning, Bo dashed off the plane to the arms of three waiting women as his sleepy teammates cheered.

He and Chance threw champagne parties for teammates, drawing the name of the lucky guest of honor from a hat. Bo also fixed one lucky teammate up with a date, who turned out to be a drag queen.

Still another eager teammate, a fellow southpaw, was given a hot phone number, which turned out to be manager Bill Rigney's hotel suite. "Who the hell is this?" Rig bawled, and the lefty was soon on his way to the minors. Bo knew how to handle a rival.

But sometimes the joke was on Bo. He drove up to the hotel in his candy-apple convertible at 5 A.M. one morning to find the whole team, including Rigney, on the sidewalk because of a fire inside. It cost Bo a $500 fine.

The Angels finally gave up and traded him to Philadelphia. He quickly developed a distaste for the town. Fans there "would even boo a funeral," Bo said.

He ended his big-league career with a 26–51 record. "I've gotten more publicity for doing less than any player who ever lived," he grinned. Even his love life may have been exaggerated, Bo admitted to Bob Uecker: "If I did everything they said I did, I'd be in a jar at the Harvard Medical School."

Moe Drabowsky and Other O's

Moe Drabowsky could throw a tantrum when he lost—he once demolished a hotel room to the tune of $6,000. But he was also a happy spirit who kept a club loose. He liked giving hotfoots in the bull pen. A former Oriole, he hired a plane to fly over the Baltimore stadium at World Series time trailing a banner wishing the Birds good luck.

Moe used to make long-distance phone calls to Hong Kong on the bull pen telephone, ordering fried rice to go. In one game an O's pitcher was coasting to a lopsided win when Moe, knowing the Baltimore extensions, dialed the bull pen. "Get Hughes heated up," he barked. A surprised bull-pen coach sprang to his feet, grabbed a glove, and Hughes began throwing furiously, while Drabo doubled up laughing.

Moe once brought a life-size Chinese Buddha back to the hotel, put it in front of Charlie Lau's door, and rang the bell. When Charlie opened the door, Moe banged a huge Chinese gong, and Lau jumped so high he banged his head on the door jamb.

On another occasion, Drabowsky put a 5-foot boa constrictor in Paul Blair's locker and drove Blair, screaming and half-naked, out onto the field.

Moe's Baltimore bull-pen mate Dick Hall once ate a seventeen-year locust. "It was long and black and horrible looking," he said, but he bit it in half on a dare and swallowed it. The only ill effect he reported was blurry vision. "They won't come back again until 1987," he said, "so I haven't eaten one since."

Another Orioles' pitcher, Ross Grimsley, was known as "the Animal." He would not wash, use deodorant, or comb his hair, and mooned passing motorists from the team bus.

Baltimore pitcher Mike Flanagan's sense of humor was much more refined. In his first game in New York, he said, "I got into the bull-pen car, and they told me to lock the doors."

Tug McGraw

Some of Mets' reliever Tug McGraw's one-liners are destined for anthologies. He was the guy who said he didn't know whether he preferred grass or Astroturf—he had never smoked Astroturf. He also originated the line, since attributed to many others, that he was going to spend half his bonus on wine, women, and song, "and I'll probably just waste the other half."

McGraw reported to the Mets' training camp with a handlebar mustache and hair to his shoulders. Ironically, he was a graduate of barber school. He grew tomatoes in the bullpen and once put on Willie Mays' uniform, blacked his face, and signed Mays' name on baseballs.

"McGraw," smiled his teammate Tom Seaver, "has only about forty-eight cards in his deck."

Denny McLain

Perhaps modern baseball's most tragic figure, Denny McLain ended up in prison, but he had his fun before the end closed in on him, and he did not take himself seriously. He had as much fun "as a whore in a lumber camp," he wrote in his autobiography, *Nobody's Perfect*. Denny could turn a phrase with Dizzy Dean at his best. The Tigers, Denny once said, "were slower than the fog off manure."

He once told Joe Foy, in an 0-for-46 slump, what each pitch would be, but still Foy could not hit. "I was beginning to think I'd have to tee it up for him," Denny said.

Denny McLain

At last Foy got hold of one and blasted it nine miles. As McLain explained to him later, he was afraid Foy might be sent to the minors. "I can stand you on your head any time I want to," he said, "and I need all the Joe Foys I can get."

McLain modestly insisted that he was not the flakiest pitcher in the league: Teammate Bill Faul was. For starters, Faul never took showers, even after a game. In Puerto Rico one winter McLain and fellow pitcher Joe Sparma were playing gin rummy in the locker room when Faul stomped in, cussing for being lifted by the manager. That was no problem, they said. "Just put on someone else's uniform and go out there and start pitching again." Faul did, and almost got away with it. When manager Bob Swift found out, he let Faul off free but slapped $100 fines on McLain and Sparma instead.

Spaceman Bill Lee

Southpaw Bill Lee did not consider himself a flake; rather, it was the northpaw world that was odd. The very word *flake* was a "right-handed, egotistic, consumeristic, exploitative, nonrecycling, carnivorous" word that no left-hander would have coined.

Lee earned his flakehood when he publicly admitted using marijuana (he did not smoke it but sprinkled it on his pancakes). How did he like Montreal? It's okay, he said, "once I get past customs."

Perhaps the grass helped Bill fantasize about talking to a guru in the Himalayas while 30,000 fans thought he was pitching to Reggie Jackson. Fantasies reduced the pressure on him and greatly contributed to his success. Hitters did not know what he was going to throw, because he did not either—"It was hell on catchers though." Lee described his mental state as almost Zen-like: "You are the ball, and the ball is you." The arm and mind are in sync, the brain relaxed. And time slows down, so that a line drive back to the box actually floats back in slow motion.

Actually, aside from wearing an anti-Nixon T-shirt that proclaimed "Lick Dick," Lee was not that odd. True, he did read books by Gurdjieff, Ouspensky, and Paramahansa Yogananda, and he spoke his mind and adopted causes that were not always popular, such as public control of utilities, zero population growth, the Equal Rights Amendment, and school busing. He went to China. He called Boston a racist city and received an angry, misspelled missive from city councillor Albert O'Neil. Lee coolly wrote back to warn O'Neil that "some moron" was using his stationery.

Like Jim Bouton perhaps, Lee was just too intelligent to be an average jock. "In baseball," he said, "you're supposed to sit on your ass, spit tobacco, and nod at stupid things." He was not very good at it.

Jerry Reuss

Dodgers' manager Tom Lasorda's personal cross to bear was Jerry Reuss and his partner in mischief, outfielder Jay Johnstone. Tom once looked up between innings to see them both dressed in overalls dragging the infield with the ground crew. He fined them $250. When word got out, fans sent in donations to cover the fine. In fact, the two made a small profit, so Lasorda, insisting that he had been responsible, made them take him out to dinner.

They once removed all Lasorda's precious celebrity pictures of Frank Sinatra, Ronald Reagan, Don Rickles, and others from his office wall and replaced them with their own and a note: "How many games did these other guys win for you?"

During one spring training, the two disconnected Tom's phone and tied his motel door to a tree so he could not open it, trapping him inside for hours until a passerby heard his muffled cries for help.

And, Lasorda reports in his autobiography, *Artful Dodger,* Reuss once took his wife on a road trip when he was with Pittsburgh. This was against club rules, and Reuss became the first man in big league history to be fined for sleeping with his wife.

Dan Quisenberry

One of the best relievers of the eighties, Dan Quisenberry had a dry sense of humor. "I have seen the future," he once deadpanned. "It is much like the present, only longer."

Dan made fun of his own lack of strikeouts. He said he had more saves than strikeouts, "though recently I had a couple of 0–2 counts." Dan said he belonged to the 30-30-30 club: 30 saves, 30 strikeouts, and 30 great plays.

Terry Forster

In the mid-1980s, Atlanta's reliever Terry Forster was considered the fattest man in the game, and one of the fastest wits. He could even outduel comic David Letterman, who taunted him about his weight. "I haven't always been this big," Forster told him, "It just snacked up on me." Anyway, Forster insisted, "a waist is a terrible thing to mind."

The Count of Montefusco

John Montefusco had always craved the spotlight. In high school he played shortstop until he discovered that the pitcher always got his name in the paper, so he switched to pitching. But success came slowly.

At twenty-two in 1972, he was still outside organized baseball, too old for the scouts to consider seriously; even the lowly expansion-team San Diego Padres turned him down. But the San Francisco Giants finally took a chance, and late in 1974, a breathless

Montefusco arrived in Los Angeles just before the game and was rushed in in relief in the first inning against the pennant-winning Dodgers. Ignoring the golf cart waiting to transport him from the bull pen, John sprinted to the mound, got one out on a ground ball, the next two on strikeouts, and marched off with both hands raised in victory. Then he hit a home run in his first at bat.

Next the "Count of Montefusco" announced that he would knock the second-place Reds out of the pennant race, would pitch all nine innings, would handle Johnny Bench (.280) with ease, and would hit another home run. He did. He shut them out, struck Bench out three times, and hit another homer. Again he strode triumphantly off the mound, both fists in the air.

The next year, 1975, the Count told the Atlanta Braves he was going to shut them out. He did. "I pitch best under pressure," he said, "so I say things that help the pressure build."

He ended with a 15–9 mark, struck out 215, and helped lift the Giants to third place. The strikeout figure irked him, because he missed Grover Alexander's rookie mark of 227. "I should have done better; I want to be the best pitcher in baseball," he said.

His goal: to rent a Rolls Royce and have a chauffeur drive him to the park in top hat, cape, and white gloves. "I will take them off, hand them to my attendant, and proceed to the mound."

"I am the best pitcher around," Montefusco insisted. "I'm not boasting or bragging. I'm just telling the truth." Baseball is show business, and he was good for the game. "I'm not cocky. I'm just confident."

He was an urban Dizzy Dean, and baseball needed him, but he too never fulfilled his early promise. A bad back ultimately proved the end of his career in 1986.

Houston Astros' reliever Dave Smith says he was once sprinkled with pee from a fan in the Shea Stadium stands above the visitors' bull pen. "That's the first time I've ever been used for long relief," he said.

Other Flakes

Dutch-born Bert Blyleven explains that he is able to throw the best curve in the American League because of his extremely long fingers, developed "from sticking my fingers into dikes."

Knuckleballer Joe Niekro was said to be so slow that it took him an hour and a half to watch "60 Minutes."

Boston's Dennis "Oil Can" Boyd got his nickname back home in Mississippi, where "oil" was the slang word for beer. In Boston, the high-strung Boyd carries on a constant monologue, struts around the mound after strikeouts, waves to the crowd, gives infielders high-fives for great plays, gives opposing batters clenched-fist out calls, and utters such Dizzy Dean-isms as "My family babified me."

And, of course, who can forget that sui generis rookie Mark "Big Bird" Fidrych of the Detroit Tigers, who created a sensation in 1976 by talking to the ball, patting the mound, and winning nineteen games. His success prompted Lefty Gomez to confide that he had often talked to the ball himself.

"What did you say?" he was asked.

"I said, 'go foul, you @#$%&, go foul!' "

3

Control

I'm working on a new pitch. It's called a strike.
—Jim Kern

All the great pitchers and coaches agree: Control is the key to pitching.

"Control," Cy Young said, "is what kept me in the big leagues for twenty-two years."

"When I've got my control and my good stuff," Bob Gibson said, "I can beat any team I pitch against."

Control means less walks, of course. If a pitcher gives up a hit an inning, every walk puts a second man on base that inning. Then the hurler is in real trouble.

Control also means getting ahead in the count so the pitcher can work the batter to make him swing at the pitcher's chosen pitch, rather than the fat fastball that might bring a strikeout or a home run. But control involves more than just getting the ball over the plate. It means putting the ball where it is hard to hit—in Casey Stengel's words, "as close to the plate and as far from the bat as possible."

"The plate is 17 inches wide," Warren Spahn said. "But I'm only concerned with 5 inches—2½ on the one side and 2½ on the other. I never use the rest." The middle foot belongs to the hitter—if he can find anything there.

Steve Carlton's catcher, Tim McCarver, calls these "the fertile lanes." That's what the pitcher has to concentrate on. Carlton visualized the strike zone before every game, McCarver says. He sat in the training room with his eyes closed and concentrated on those two narrow lanes, each one exactly the width of the ball and no more.

Sinkerball pitchers such as Kent Tekulve and Doug Corbett rotate the plate in their minds so that the fertile lane is running across the plate at the batter's knees.

Jim Merritt had a fair fastball and curve, but most of all, said his catcher, Johnny Bench, Merritt could "graze the edges of the plate. When he's at his best, he can put only the seams over." "Nipping the frosting off a cake," Satchel Paige called it.

Pitching coach George Bamberger preached that an 87-m.p.h. fastball on the

34

corner will win more games than a 90-m.p.h. strike down the middle.

Tom Seaver says he can throw a ball within a quarter-inch of any spot nine times out of ten. And Paige's control was so fine, they could catch him in a rocking chair, and often did in exhibition games. (You had to be rocking forward when you caught it, catcher Pepper Bassett said; if you were rocking backward, the pitch would knock you back to the grandstand.)

When Denny McLain won thirty-one games in 1968, he threw 95 percent of his pitches for strikes, umpire Bill Kincannon told Larry Gerlach. "He threw more different pitches for strikes than anybody I ever saw," Kincannon said admiringly.

That can be a misleading statistic, Sandy Koufax said; it may simply mean the pitcher is not hitting the corners. "The wildest pitch is not necessarily the one that goes back to the screen. It can also be the one that goes right down the middle." This leads to what pitchers call being "wild in the strike zone"—they get the ball over the plate but not in the spot where they want it. When a pitcher is wild in the strike zone, he does not give up many walks, but he probably gives up a lot of hits.

Wildness can drive batters out of their wits, pitchers out of the league, and managers out of their minds. When old-time Braves manager George Stallings suffered a heart attack, his doctor asked to what he ascribed his hypertension. "Bases on balls, you son of a bitch, bases on balls!" Stallings growled.

Christy Mathewson said the 1910 Cubs, who won a record 116 games, lost the World Series because their pitchers lost their control. A's manager Connie Mack, realizing this, ordered his hitters to wait everything out. With the Cubs' pitchers constantly in the hole, the A's hitters were in a position to guess which pitch was coming and frequently guessed right. The hurlers complained that catcher Johnny Kling was tipping his signs, and Kling was traded to Boston that winter. But the A's hadn't stolen any signs, Matty said, they were simply taking advantage of the pitchers' wildness.

THROWING BALLS FOR STRIKES

Many good pitchers deliberately throw outside the strike zone. Most hitters don't "know" the strike zone, they say, and often the best out pitch is not over the plate at all. With two strikes against him, a hitter has to protect the plate, and Jim Palmer said half of all third strikes are out of the strike zone.

Steve Carlton's slider and Fernando Valenzuela's screwball are rarely strikes, ex-catcher Tim McCarver wrote in *Sport* magazine. Ninety percent of their strikeouts come on balls.

Willie Mays chased high fastballs out of the strike zone. Bob Gibson confided, "You can get him out with a bad pitch."

Yogi Berra was famous for swinging at bad pitches. Once, when he struck out on one way outside, he came back to the dugout fuming, "How can a pitcher that wild stay in the league?"

In 1948 Gene Bearden bedeviled American League hitters with a knuckler that broke sharply down. He won twenty games, including the playoff against the Red Sox, then won one Series game and saved another. The next year his old minor-league manager, Casey Stengel, took over the Yankees. Casey told Yankee hitters that Bearden's ball broke so much that it was not in the strike zone when it crossed the plate. He told his hitters to lay off it; with three balls, Bearden then had to come in with a fastball, which they murdered. Word quickly spread throughout the league, and Bearden's victories shrank to eight, four, and finally three. Until Casey spread the word, Gene had been winning games by throwing balls.

Of course, hitters do not see the same strike zone the pitcher and the umpire see. The hitter is looking at it sideways. Still, if batters knew the strike zone as well as pitchers and umpires (and Ted Williams), men like Joe DiMaggio, Dave Parker, and Willie Stargell would have walked a lot more than forty or fifty times a year. "The best-kept secret in all of baseball is Steve Garvey's poor pitch selection," McCarver wrote. One year, in 625 at bats, Garvey walked just twenty times, and ten of them were intentional.

Control, then, is more than throwing strikes or not issuing walks. Control depends on the game situation, Warren Spahn pointed out. Do you want the hitter to hit it on the ground? To the left side of the infield? Can a pitcher throw high in a bunt situation and low in a double-play situation?

PITCHING HIGH: SACRIFICE BUNTS

Nobody has ever figured a pitcher's sacrifice hit average: SHs divided by SHs foiled, that is, when the on-base runner is thrown out, the bunt is popped up, or the sacrifice sign has to be taken off. Nor has anyone determined which pitcher gave up the fewest SHs. But Seymour Siwoff's *Book of Baseball Records* says Stanley Coveleski and Ed Rommel gave up the most in one year, fifty-four, though that may have included some sacrifice flies.

In more recent times, Fernando Valenzuela led the majors by giving up twenty-seven SHs in 1983, though he cut that down to nine the following year. Steve Carlton also tended to give up a lot.

PITCHING LOW: SACRIFICE FLIES

In 1983 Larry Gura pitched 200 innings and gave up 17 sacrifice flies, most in the majors. Ferguson Jenkins also threw a lot of pitches that resulted in long flies while men were on third.

In contrast, in 1968 Luis Tiant went 258 innings without allowing any sacrifice flies. The next year Phil Niekro went 284 innings (more than 1,850 batters) and did not permit any.

The all-time leader was Billy Pierce, who pitched almost 1,900 innings in the 1950s and 1960s and permitted only 21 SFs. Bill Hands of the Giants and Cubs was next— only twenty-seven in 1,570 innings. Don Drysdale, Bob Gibson, and Claude Osteen were also good at preventing sacrifice flies.

PITCHING LOW FOR DOUBLE PLAYS

White Sox' manager Eddie Stanky used to reward his pitchers with suits of clothes for throwing twenty ground balls or more a game. In one game in 1931 the Red Sox infielders made a total of twenty-five putouts.

The eternally curious statistician and author Bill James has made a study of double plays turned behind pitchers. His findings are inexact, as he realizes, because it is impossible yet to apportion DPs among starter and relievers. He therefore uses DPs per game started to give him a rough guide.

Big-league clubs average about one double play per game. In 1985 the best team, the California Angels, turned 1.2 per game, and the worst, the Pittsburgh Pirates, 0.8.

There is a school of thought that poor-pitching teams turn more DPs because they put more men on base to be doubled up.

The 1948 Browns set a DP record with a team ERA of 5.01. The next year the A's broke it with an ERA of 4.23, worst in the league. They almost broke their own DP record the next year with a team ERA of 5.49.

James found, however, that, while this rule may apply to whole teams, individual pitchers varied widely. In 1985 Tommy John of the California Angels had 1.5 per start, while Mike Krukow of the San Francisco Giants had only 0.4. Bill plotted the ten pitchers in each league with the best DP support and the ten with the worst. As might be expected, all ten NL leaders pitched for the league's best DP clubs, while all the ten worst pitched on the league's worst DP clubs.

However, in the American League, the plotting produced more mixed results. The Texas Rangers ranked twelfth in DPs, but Ranger Rick Honeycutt was second in DP support. The Detroit Tigers were last in team DPs overall, but they were the fourth-best DP team in the league when Dan Petry was on the mound, whereas Tiger Jack Morris had one of the poorest DP records in the league.

HIT BATSMEN

Many batters are hit by pitchers every year—more than 690 in 1985. American League pitchers hit more than 400 batters; National League pitchers, about 280. That is one man hit in every four games in the NL and one every three in the AL. The difference is obviously accounted for by the presence of the designated hitter in the American League: AL pitchers do not have to bat and thus are safe from retaliation. (For the same reason the dirtiest sliders, such as Ty Cobb, were always outfielders, not infielders.)

The all-time leader in hitting batsmen was Cannonball Gus Weyhing, who drilled 286

batters in the nineteenth century—many of them at the old 55-foot distance. Chick Fraser, whose career spanned both centuries, hit 217 men, or one every 15.1 innings.

In this century, Walter Johnson holds the record, 208. Yet the gentle Johnson lived in fear of hitting someone and killing him, a fact that hitters like Ty Cobb knew and took outrageous advantage of. Joe McGinnity hit the most men per inning. And he hit 41 men in 341 innings in 1900.

MOST FREQUENT HB

Pitcher	HB	IP	IP/HB
McGinnity	184	3,459	18.8
Drysdale	154	3,432	22.2
Bunning	160	3,760	23.5
Plank	188	4,505	24.0
Johnson	208	5,924	28.5

LEAST FREQUENT HB

Pitcher	HB	IP	IP/HB
Koufax	18	2,324	129
Spahn	41	5,244	128
Ford	28	3,170	113

Howard Ehmke, the old submarine-baller, led the American League in hitting batters six times between 1920 and 1927. Dodger Don Drysdale and the Yankees' Tommy Byrne each led five times. With Don it was probably intentional; with Byrne, just wildness—he usually led in walks too.

Tommy John and Moe Drabowsky hit four in one game, Dock Ellis and Wilbur Wood, three in one inning. Early 1900s pitcher Deacon Phillippe also shot down three in one inning, which raises suspicions since he was normally a fine control pitcher.

By contrast, Montreal's Jay Tibbs pitched 456 innings in his career before he hit his first batter. Alvin Crowder went 327 innings in 1932 without hitting a man.

The Hitters' Responsibility

Of course, the hitters bear some responsibility for their own undoing. Otherwise, why was Ron Hunt of the Mets hit once every 21 at bats, but Vern Stephens of the Browns and Red Sox plunked only once every 1,083? Don Baylor is the all-time champion clay pigeon, getting 262 purple hearts in 12 years.

Hitter	HB	AB	AB/HB
Don Baylor*	262	7,746	29.6
Ron Hunt	243	5,235	21.5
Frank Robinson	198	10,006	50.5
Minnie Minoso	187	6,569	34.7

*Still active.

Minoso led the league ten times, Frank Crosetti of the old Yanks led eight, Hunt and Robinson seven each.

The record for one season is fifty, by Hunt in 1971, or once every ten times up. That same year Sandy Alomar went to bat 689 times without getting hit.

Some batters get hit because they crowd the plate. Frank Robinson took what Earl Weaver called "a death-defying stance," actually curling his upper body and head over the plate.

Getting hit is often a deliberate offensive tactic. Some pitchers swore Hunt used to dive at the ball. Ty Cobb was good at it, said Ted Lyons. So was Fred Snodgrass of the old Giants.

Baylor admits that if he has an 0–2 count against him "and I'm two-third struck out, anything close and I'll risk it." He even took to wearing a bull's-eye on his T-shirt.

Batters sometimes get hit because they are expecting a curve that does not break. Or they get a false sign that the curve is coming when it is not. "Eagle Eye" Jake Beckley, the old first baseman, once stepped into what he thought would be a Christy Mathewson curve that turned out to be a fastball, and it knocked him unconscious for two days. "Were you tipped off by Joe Kelley?" Matty asked when Beckley came to. "Then it was Joe's fault, not mine." "I felt no qualms about hitting him," Matty wrote.

Joe Adcock of the Braves once got beaned twice in one at bat. Ruben Gomez hit him, and when Adcock charged the mound, Gomez, who had gotten another ball from the ump, beaned him again.

Jake Stephens could not hit much, so he wore a loose-fitting shirt and let the ball graze the flannel, then shouted to the umpire: "Look! Look! He hit me!" Ty Cobb was good at that too, said Ted Lyons. So was Fred Snodgrass of the old Giants.

Headhunting

The most controversial pitch in the pitcher's arsenal is the beanball or brushback. One hitter, Ray Chapman, was killed by a pitched ball. Another, Tony Conigliaro, nearly lost an eye. And every hitter lives in fear that the next pitch may be the one to end his career. The ball speeds toward the hitter's ear at more than 90 m.p.h. "You lean back, and then you dive forward," said little Jake Stephens of the old Homestead Grays. "I mean, you leave your hat in the air."

When is a pitch a brushback? And when is it a knockdown, thrown with malicious intent?

"When the ball is thrown at the head," says Bob Gibson. "You know that's no mistake, because there's no way you can miss the plate that far."

The simple brushback is more common. It sends a signal to the hitter to back away from the plate. "A brushback is not to scare a hitter or to hit him," Gibson writes. "It is to make him think.'' When the hitter does give ground, the next pitch is usually on the outside corner, where he can no longer reach it. That is a basic part of baseball strategy. Hitters do not get hit with brushback pitches.

Early Wynn was once accused of being mean enough to throw at his own grandmother. He denied it. ''Only if she was digging in,'' he said.

Johnny Allen of the Yanks denied a similar charge, though he admitted he might ''brush her back a little.''

There are three purposes for the knockdown—to intimidate the hitter, to pay him back for hitting a homer (or because the previous batter hit a homer), and to retaliate when the other team throws at your club. There are two schools of thought about it.

One, led by Walter Johnson, Robin Roberts, and Sandy Koufax, says there is no excuse for endangering a man's life to win a ball game. Koufax went through a season of 366 innings in 1966 without hitting a batter, pretty good for a man with a reputation for being wild. Lefty Grove—''he's never wild inside''—also belonged to that school. He might throw close to Ruth's chin once in a while, but generally, he did not want to wake anyone up. Bob Gibson refused to throw at a man ''just because he hits me hard,'' he wrote in *From Ghetto to Glory*. ''If he hits a home run off me, it's because I made a mistake. It's my fault, not his.''

Headhunting is an unfair, one-way battle, wrote Jim Bouton in *Ball Four*. ''How the hell can you throw at the guy?'' he demanded of a teammate. ''He's just doing his job. He has no comeback at you if you get him out, so why should he have to risk getting injured just because he's successful?''

Actually, some hitters can retaliate. Some bunt the ball to first, then spike the pitcher, who is covering the bag. Little Chino Smith, a spitfire of the Negro leagues, knocked down by Cincinnati's Adolfo Luque, blasted the next pitch straight back at Luque's head, and the two were soon rolling on the grass between mound and home.

The beanball is potentially lethal. Besides Chapman and Conigliaro, others have been seriously injured. Don Mincher was hit in the face by Sam McDowell, who was fast and wild and was not necessarily aiming at him. Jim Ray Hart was hit by Bob Gibson in his rookie year and missed the rest of the season. Dickie Thon of Houston was never the same player after his beaning by Mike Torrez in 1984.

Paul Blair was almost killed by a pitch from Ken Tatum, an overpowering fastballer. Blair crowded the plate, and Ron Luciano, who was umpiring, says he does not think Tatum tried to hit him. But the last split second of that pitch is ''frozen in my memory,'' Luciano wrote in *The Umpire Strikes Back*. It hit just below Blair's helmet with a ''splat,'' like slapping Jello, Luciano said. ''It was the worst sound I ever heard. He went down hard. Blood started trickling out of his nose and mouth and ears into the dirt. I thought he was dead.''

Luciano got sick on the field. Blair was rushed to a hospital and required two years of hypnosis before he could hit again. ''Tatum was never the same pitcher after that,'' Luciano wrote. ''Blair was never the same hitter. And I was never the same umpire—after seeing Blair lying unconscious in the dirt I couldn't tolerate pitchers trying to hit a batter in the head.'' When Billy Martin of the Rangers ordered his pitchers to throw at Brewer Robin Yount, Luciano refused to umpire any more Rangers' games in protest.

Morality aside, Bouton reasoned that "my most precious possession is the three balls I'm allowed to throw before I walk somebody. If I give up one of them simply to frighten the hitter, I'm giving up half my attack."

"Personally," Vic Raschi added in an interview with Donald Honig (*Baseball Between the Lines*), "I never thought it very good strategy to throw at Joe (DiMaggio) or Ted Williams. They could beat you when they were happy; get them mad and they'd kill you."

Satchel Paige agreed: "I don't call that no baseball if I got to cave your ribs out to get you."

Paige did make one exception—Jimmy Piersall, who, he says, called him "a black so-and-so." Next time "when he came up, he went down. He chased his hat and belt for half a block."

Though this was unique for Paige, the knockdown was a normal tactic used in both the white and black majors. Bill Drake says he would run the hitters across the plate with the first three balls, "then I'd pitch." In 1926 one of his victims, Willie Wells, got a miner's helmet, took the gas spigot off, and wore it to the plate, thus inventing the batting helmet.

Leo Durocher said the first helmets in the white major leagues were worn by the Brooklyn Dodgers of 1941 to combat "Beanball, Inc.," the alleged plot to get the pennant-bound Dodgers that year. Owner Larry MacPhail distributed the headgear after the Dodgers' Joe Medwick was felled by a pitch from Pittsburgh's Joe Bowman. Medwick "dropped like the trunk of a tree," Leo wrote in *Nice Guys Finish Last,* and was carried off unconscious on a stretcher as fistfights erupted all over the field.

The Dodgers were not blameless themselves, however. Durocher tells of old Freddie Fitzsimmons, who called Johnny Mize "picklehead" and promised Leo, "He ain't gonna hit me, I'm gonna knock his cap off." With an awful grunt—"like a rhinoceros in heat," Durocher laughed, Fitz uncorked one 6 inches behind Mize's ear, while Leo prayed that a wild pitch would not send in the go-ahead run. Fitz followed with a knuckler for a strike. Then, "Get ready, picklehead," he snarled, "you're going down again." Mize did, bat and hat flying in different directions. Then another knuckler, strike two. Fitz walked halfway to home. "Right at that pickleheaded skull of yours," he roared. Oh no, Durocher moaned, he's not going to go to 3–2. But he did. Then with another mighty roar, Fitz unleashed the slowest curve Mize had ever seen. "He started to swing eleven times," Leo laughed, and he struck out.

Mize told Donald Honig that "any guy that threw at me knew I could hit him." John was hit in the head twice, once by Harry Gumbert and once by Harry Brecheen. Deliberate? "One was a sinkerball pitcher, and the other one was a control pitcher. And on each occasion I'd hit a home run the time before. Take it from there."

Joe DiMaggio called the Dodgers' Whitlow Wyatt "the meanest guy I ever saw." Pete Reiser told Honig that when Joe tried to dig in in the 1941 Series, Wyatt knocked him down twice, then yelled, "Joe, you do that against me again, you'll be in a squat position the rest of your life." Later, as Phillies' pitching coach, Wyatt tried to get Robin Roberts to throw at hitters. "They ought to hate you on the field," he said. But Roberts never would.

"Baseball was a form of warfare," Durocher wrote. Pat Malone of the Cubs used to get insulted if a banjo-hitter like Durocher took a good swing. He'd walk in and snarl, "I think I'd just better knock your cap off."

Lefty O'Doul told Lawrence Ritter in *The Glory of Their Times* that when he was a pitcher for San Francisco in 1921, "I hit nineteen men. On purpose. No telling how many I missed."

Burleigh Grimes of the same era was another mean pitcher. According to writer Tom Meany, he'd throw behind them, or at their feet, making them skip rope. "He only gets three shots at me," Frankie Frisch growled, "then he has to pitch." Grimes crossed him up by throwing a fourth one at his head. Frank dived for the dirt, his hat floating down after him. "It was one of the few times in baseball I was really scared," he admitted, "and Burleigh just stood out there and laughed at me."

Charley Root of the Cubs was another one. Did Babe Ruth really point to center field and hit a home run off him? Root's teammate, Charlie Grimm, sneered at the idea. "Root would have put the next pitch right in Ruth's ear if Babe had tried that on him." Ruth would have ended up with his feet in the air, agrees another teammate, Billy Herman. Grimm managed in the same school. He once told pitcher Gene Conley, "They've been digging in on you. Set a couple guys down on their butts."

Even the ebullient Dizzy Dean got mad when a hitter dug a hole with his back foot. "You all done? You comfortable?" he would ask. "Well, get a shovel, because that's where they're gonna bury you." "I saw him hit seven straight Giants" in one spring training game, Durocher said. "I don't think the Giants beat him a game that year."

In the 1967 World Series, Carl Yastrzemski hit two home runs in the second game, and Boston pitcher Jim Lonborg was quoted as saying he was going to brush Lou Brock back next time they met. Instead, Cardinals' pitcher Nelson Briles started off by hitting Yaz in the leg. "Nellie reads the newspapers," Bob Gibson nodded.

Mickey Mantle never seemed to worry when pitchers threw at his head. But he had weak legs throughout his career, and he could not tolerate it when they threw close to his ankles.

Sal Maglie of the Giants and Dodgers threw close to the hitters, hence his nickname, Barber. As a pitching coach, he preached the same philosophy: "If you go 3–0 on a guy, go ahead and flatten his ass. If you're going to walk him anyway, do it real good."

Stan Williams of the Dodgers kept a book on hitters. When a hitter got four stars, he was in danger. Hank Aaron got five stars. Williams hit Aaron in the helmet and later apologized: "Sorry I hit you on the helmet, Hank. I meant to hit you on the neck."

When Daryl Spencer was traded to the

Sal Maglie

Dodgers from the Giants, Williams debated whether to take him out of his book. ''No,'' he decided, ''I think I'll keep you in there. You'll probably get traded again.''

Back in the 1930s, Wes Ferrell told Donald Honig, when a guy hit a homer, the next two hitters expected to go down. After one home run, Fat Bob Fothergill stepped in. Ferrell put one over his head. The next hitter strode to the plate and laid down in the dirt. ''Heh, Wes,'' he said, ''you don't have to throw at me, I'm already down.''

Russ Meyer of the Cubs was one of the few pitchers who confessed to throwing at hitters. ''Why beat around the bush?'' he shrugged. ''I played under nine managers, and only one, Eddie Sawyer, didn't tell me to knock somebody down.''

Alvin Dark kept a little book on pitchers who had thrown at his team, Gaylord Perry said. He would not order his pitchers to retaliate right away, as that would be too obvious. ''It might take a year or even two,'' Perry said, ''but that man would get his.''

Luciano had many famous battles with Orioles' manager Earl Weaver. But ''one of the many things I've always respected about Weaver is that he will not allow his pitchers to throw at a batter. Umpires never have to warn Orioles' pitchers about beanballs.'' The long list of Baltimore twenty-game winners and Cy Young winners is proof, Luciano wrote, that pitchers can win without the beanball.

WILD PITCHES

The all-time leaders in wild pitches are Walter Johnson and Red Ames, each with 156. Johnson did it in almost 6,000 innings, Ames in about 3,200. Ames threw thirty of them in 1905, the modern record.

The all-time record was set in 1886 by Bill Stemmyer, who uncorked 64 of them in 349

innings, or about one every 5.5 innings. In 1986 rookie Bobby Witt of Texas came close to that; he threw 22 in 158 innings, or one every 7.2 innings

Year	Pitcher	WP	IP	IP/WP
1886	Bill Stemmyer	64	349	5.5
1905	Red Ames	30	263	8.7
1986	Bobby Witt	22	158	7.2
1963	Earl Wilson	21	211	10.0
1977	Nolan Ryan	21	299	14.2
1910	Walter Johnson	21	374	17.7

Another Ryan, John, heaved ten in one game in 1876. It was, not surprisingly, the only game he pitched in the majors. The modern record is six by Bill Gullickson in 1982. Walter Johnson and Phil Niekro each uncorked four in one inning. Larry Cheney of the Cubs and Dodgers led the league six times.

On the other hand, Dick Hall, the Baltimore reliever, pitched more than 1,200 innings from 1955 to 1971 and threw only one wild pitch. Joe McGinnity in 1906 pitched 340 innings without throwing one.

Those Bases on Balls

There are thus many ways to judge control. But bases on balls have always been the traditional index. ''Walks kill teams,'' said George Bamberger. In 1977, the year before he took over the Brewers, Milwaukee pitchers had walked 565 men, or 3.5 per game. Bamberger cut that to 398, or 2.5, and he estimated the extra 167 walks had cost the Brewers 20 to 25 games the previous year.

In 1983 LaMarr Hoyt walked only 1.1 men per nine-inning game. That was the lowest average in the American League since Tiny Bonham back in 1941.

Just as it is getting easier to record strikeouts, however, it has become more and more difficult to hold down walks. Most of the all-time stingiest hurlers worked back in the nineteenth century or the early years of this century. The lifetime list:

Pitcher	BB/9 Inn.
Pud Galvin	1.1
Dan Quisenberry	1.3
Deacon Phillippe	1.3
Babe Adams	1.3
Addie Joss	1.4
Cy Young	1.5
Christy Mathewson	1.6
Jesse Tannehill	1.6
Red Lucas	1.6
Nick Altrock	1.6
Noodles Hahn	1.7
Grover Alexander	1.7
Tiny Bonham	1.7
Fritz Peterson	1.7
Carl Hubbell	1.8
Lew Burdette	1.8
Juan Marichal	1.8
Ed Walsh	1.9
Paul Derringer	1.9
Ken Raffensberger	1.9

There are two unusual things about this list. First, it contains only one active player, Dan Quisenberry. Since Quiz is a reliever, often called on to give intentional walks, Bill James estimates that his unintentional walk average is about 0.7. Second, the list contains only one left-hander, Hubbell.

Since 1901 the stingiest pitchers in a single year were Christy Mathewson in 1913 and Babe Adams in 1920. Each issued only 0.62 bases on balls per nine-inning game. That's control! The all-time leaders in this century:

Year	Pitcher	BB/9 Inn.
1913	Mathewson	0.62
1920	Adams	0.62
1914	Mathewson	0.66
1904	Young	0.69

Year	Pitcher	BB/9 Inn.
1933	Lucas	0.74
1906	Young	0.78
1919	Sallee	0.79
1919	Adams	0.79
1922	Adams	0.79
1918	Sallee	0.82
1908	Joss	0.83
1905	Young	0.84
1902	Phillippe	0.86
1923	Alexander	0.88
1901	Young	0.90
1903	Phillippe	0.90
1902	Tannehill	0.97
1903	Young	0.97
1908	Mathewson	0.97
1915	Mathewson	0.97
1908	Burns	0.98
1912	Mathewson	0.99

Fritz Peterson of the Yankees led the league five straight years in least walks per game. That ties him with Young in the American League and puts him just behind Matty and Alex of the National League.

Before 1901

Perhaps the most remarkable control pitcher of all time was Cy Young. For thirteen years, from 1893 to 1906, Cy led his league in least walks per nine innings eleven times. He finished second the other two years. Grasshopper Jim Whitney was another great control pitcher, recording the least walks per nine innings five years in a row, from 1883 to 1887.

Least Walks, Most Strikeouts

Five men have led their leagues in least walks per nine innings and most total strikeouts, both in the same year: Christy Mathewson, Walter Johnson, Grover Alexander, Urban Shocker, and Robin Roberts. Their records were as follows:

	Year	IP	W	SO
Mathewson	1908	391	42	259
Johnson	1913	346	76	296
Johnson	1915	337	56	203
Alexander	1917	388	58	201
Shocker	1922	348	59	149
Roberts	1953	347	61	198
Roberts	1954	337	56	185

However, none of them led the league in strikeouts per game in those years. Only two men have led in both most strikeouts per game and least walks per game in the same year. Jim Whitney, in 1883, with 6.0 strikeouts per game and 0.6 walks per game; and Walter Johnson, in 1920, with 4.9 strikeouts per game and 1.7 walks per game. Oddly, 1920 was probably the worst season of Johnson's career; he won only eight and lost ten as the Senators finished sixth. But 1883 was the best year of Whitney's career, with thirty-seven wins for the champion Bostons.

In 1904 Cy Young struck out 200 and walked only 29. In 1971 Ferguson Jenkins struck out 263 and walked 37. Neither, however, led his league in Ks. Jenkins set an impressive career record—the only man ever to strike out more than 3,000 and walk less than 1,000. He just made it, with 997 walks.

Innings without a Walk

Leaders in consecutive innings without a walk are:

	Year	Innings
Bill Fischer	1962	83
Christy Mathewson	1913	68
Randy Jones	1976	68
Doc White	1907	65

Fischer, then of the Kansas City Athletics, says he did not know he was approaching a record until the scoreboard announced that he had passed fifty innings. He broke Mathewson's record against the seventh-place Orioles. "I was scheduled to pitch Friday night, but it was a rain-out," he told John Holway. "I got myself all psyched up, then had to back off." He started the second game of a doubleheader Saturday and, just two outs away from the record, went 2–1 on pitcher Robin Roberts. "I'm going to walk the pitcher!" he thought. But Roberts took strike two, then missed strike three. Jerry Adair, who rarely walked, also struck out, enabling Fischer to tie Mathewson. Then Brooks Robinson hit a ground ball back to Fischer, and he broke the record. In the streak, Bill had only fifteen 3–2 counts and gave up just five home runs. He wound up with only 0.56 walks per nine innings, but his won/loss record was only 4–12 for the A's, who came in next to last.

Fischer later coached the 1986 Red Sox' pitching staff and brought it from tops in walks in 1985 to least in 1986. His star pupil, Roger Clemens, struck out a record twenty men in one game without issuing a single walk. The Sox as a whole had the best ERA in the league for the first time since 1914.

Babe Adams set the record for number of innings without walks in an individual game, pitching such a twenty-one inning game in 1920. Cy Young went twenty innings in 1905. Carl Hubbell pitched an eighteen-inning shutout in 1933 without giving up a walk. Stan Coveleski once pitched seven innings without throwing a single ball.

FEWEST PITCHES PER GAME

Cy Young, Eddie Plank, Sam Jones, and Bob Gibson are among those who felt they had only so many pitches in their arms, so that the more pitches they threw, the less they had left. Young took a minimum number of warm-up throws, and Plank and Jones would not even make pickoff throws to first base. (Jones did once, and the first baseman was so surprised that he dropped it.)

Red Barrett, who won nine and lost sixteen for the 1944 Boston Braves, pitched one game that year using only fifty-eight pitches, the all-time record, report Ted DiTullio and Ron Liebman of the Society for American Baseball Research (SABR). That's about six pitches per inning, or two pitches per out. That beat the old record of sixty-one, shared by Ben Sanders (1891) and Red Faber (1915).

BEST CONTROL TEAMS

According to SABR's Evelyn Begley, the 1904 Boston Pilgrims (later Red Sox) gave up fewer walks than any club in this century, with 233, or 1.5 per game. Cy Young issued only 29, and Jesse Tannehill was right behind, with 33. The 1902 Pirates were also tightfisted, yielding only 1.8 walks per game. Tannehill, then with the Pirates, gave up a mere 25, Deacon Phillippe, only 26, and Sam Leever, 31. Both the Pilgrims and the Pirates won the pennant in those years.

WILDEST TEAMS

The wildest team in history, Begley reports, was the last-place Philadelphia A's of 1915, who gave up 827 free passes, 5.4 per game. John Wyckoff issued 165 to lead the league; Rube Bressler gave up another 118, and Bruno Haas gave up 16 in *one* game. Poor Connie Mack. He used to like to wave his outfielders into position with his scorecard when he had had Rube Waddell, Chief Bender, Herb Pennock, and Eddie Plank pitching: "They had control, and I knew where the ball was coming in, and therefore what the batter would do with it." But with the 1915 club, Connie had to put the scorecard down and suffer.

Wildness does not attack last-place clubs exclusively, however. The second wildest team in history was the world champion New York Yankees of 1949, with 5.3 walks per game. Tommy Byrne gave up 179 (in only 196 innings); Vic Raschi, 138; and Allie Reynolds, 123. Still, the Yanks finished second in ERA and, most important, first in wins, beating Boston on the final day.

THE WILD MEN

Washington's Sam "Dolly" Gray holds the record for bases on balls in one inning—eight—in 1909; seven came in a row. (Where was the bull pen in those days?)

Henry Mathewson, Christy's kid brother, walked fourteen men in one nine-inning game in 1906.

Nine years later lefty Bruno Haas of the A's walked sixteen men in his first big league game, still the record.

If Satchel Paige used to warm up by pitching over matchbooks, lefty Tommy Byrne warmed up by throwing over card tables—and missing. But, like Nolan Ryan, he was saved because he was so darned hard to hit, yielding 1,138 hits compared to 1,037 walks. In 1949 he gave up 179 walks but only 125 hits. He won fifteen and lost seven.

Dick Weik rarely pitched a nine-inning game. But Pete Palmer said he once walked thirteen men in a six-inning game.

According to John Grabowski's *Baseball Trivia Newsletter*, when San Francisco's Mike Krukow was pitching for Cal Poly, he once walked seventeen men—and pitched a no-hitter!

Rex Barney, the Dodgers' right-hander, would have been a great pitcher, columnist Dick Young once wrote, "if home plate were high and outside."

Rex's predecessor as wild man of Flatbush was Luke "Hot Potato" Hamlin, of

CONTROL LEADERS

Year	Pitcher (AL)	BB/G	Pitcher (NL)	BB/G
1901	Young	0.90	Orth	1.02
1902	Orth	1.11	Phillippe	0.86
1903	Young	0.97	Phillippe	0.90
1904	Young	0.69	Hahn	1.06
1905	Young	0.84	Phillippe	1.55
1906	Young	0.78	Phillippe	1.07
1907	White	1.17	Phillippe	1.51
1908	Joss	0.83	Mathewson	0.97
1909	Joss	1.15	Mathewson	1.18
1910	Walsh	1.48	Suggs	1.62
1911	White	1.47	Mathewson	1.11
1912	Bender	1.74	Mathewson	0.99
1913	Johnson	0.99	Mathewson	0.62
1914	McHall	1.55	Mathewson	0.66
1915	Johnson	1.50	Mathewson	0.97
1916	R. Russell	1.43	Rudolph	1.10
1917	R. Russell	1.52	Alexander	1.35
1918	Cicotte	1.35	Sallee	0.82
1919	Cicotte	1.44	Adams	0.79
1920	Johnson	1.69	Adams	0.62
1921	Mays	2.03	Adams	1.01
1922	Shocker	1.53	Adams	0.79
1923	Shocker	1.59	Alexander	0.88
1924	S. Smith	1.53	Alexander	1.33
1925	S. Smith	1.82	Alexander	1.11
1926	Pennock	1.45	Donohue	1.23
1927	Quinn	1.61	Alexander	1.28
1928	Quinn	1.45	Alexander	1.37
1929	R. Russell	1.59	Vance	1.83
1930	Pennock	1.15	Lucas	1.88
1931	Pennock	1.43	S. Johnson	1.40
1932	C. Brown	1.71	Swift	1.09
1933	C. Brown	1.65	Lucas	0.74
1934	Ferrell	2.44	Hubbell	1.06
1935	Harder	1.66	W. Clark	1.22
1936	Lyons	2.22	Lucas	1.33
1937	Stratton	2.02	J. Dean	1.50
1938	Leonard	2.14	Derringer	1.44
1939	Lyons	1.35	Derringer	1.05
1940	Lyons	1.79	Derringer	1.46
1941	Lyons	1.78	C. Davis	1.57
1942	Bonham	0.96	Warneke	1.79
1943	Leonard	1.88	Rowe	1.31

Year	Pitcher (AL)	BB/G	Pitcher (NL)	BB/G
1944	C. Harris	1.34	Raffensberger	1.57
1945	Bonham	1.10	C. Davis	1.26
1946	Hughson	1.65	Cooper	1.76
1947	Galehouse	2.48	Jansen	2.07
1948	Hutch	1.95	Jansen	1.75
1949	Hoatkman	2.61	Koslo	1.82
1950	Hutch	1.86	Raffensberger	1.51
1951	Hutch	1.29	Raffensberger	1.37
1952	Shantz	2.03	Roberts	1.23
1953	Lopat	1.61	Roberts	1.58
1954	Lopat	1.75	Roberts	1.50
1955	Gromek	1.84	Newcombe	1.46
1956	Stobbs	2.02	Roberts	1.21
1957	Sullivan	1.79	Newcombe	1.49
1958	Donovan	1.92	Burdette	1.63
1959	H. Brown	1.76	Newcombe	1.09
1960	H. Brown	1.24	Burdette	1.14
1961	Mossi	1.76	Burdette	1.09
1962	Donovan	1.69	B. Shaw	1.76
1963	Donovan	1.22	Friend	1.47
1964	Monbouquette	1.54	Bunning	1.46
1965	Terry	1.25	Marichal	1.40
1966	Kaat	1.62	Marichal	1.05
1967	Merritt	1.19	Pappas	1.57
1968	F. Peterson	1.23	B. Hands	1.25
1969	F. Peterson	1.42	Marichal	1.62
1970	F. Peterson	1.38	Jenkins	1.73
1971	F. Peterson	1.38	D. Wilson	1.02
1972	F. Peterson	1.58	Pappas	1.34
1973	Kaat	1.73	Marichal	1.59
1974	Jenkins	1.23	Capra	1.75
1975	Jenkins	1.87	Nolan	1.24
1976	Bird	1.41	Nolan	1.02
1977	Rozcema	1.40	Candelaria	1.95
1978	Jenkins	1.48	Christenson	1.86
1979	McGregor	1.18	K. Forsch	1.77
1980	Matlack	1.24	B. Forsch	1.38
1981	Honeycutt	1.20	G. Perry	1.43
1982	John	1.58	Bird	1.41
1983	Hoyt	1.07	Hammaker	1.67
1984	Hoyt	1.64	Gullickson	1.47
1985	Saberhagen	1.45	Hoyt	0.86
1986	Guidry	1.78	Eckersley	1.93

whom another columnist, Tom Meany, wrote, "If he fell off the Brooklyn Bridge, he couldn't hit the water."

Monte Kennedy of the 1951 Giants could throw a ball through a wall—if he could hit the wall, laughed his teammate Monte Irvin. When Leo Durocher ordered Kennedy to "stick it in (the batter's) ear," the pitcher replied earnestly, "I'll try, but I'm not sure I can."

Another pitcher, Tom Walker of the 1985 Cleveland Indians, also tried to throw a knockdown pitch but got a called strike instead. "That's the kind of control I had," he said sheepishly.

Steve Dalkowski, a Baltimore farm hand in the 1950s, once threw a pitch through a 2-inch-thick board that represented the strike zone. Unfortunately, it took him forty minutes to hit the board. In nine years in the minors, Dalkowski averaged 12.3 walks per nine innings. His high was 18.7 in 1957. In 1960 he walked 262 hitters, approaching Amos Rusie's big-league record of 289.

"He never made it to the majors," Baltimore coach Jim Russo said. "But it wasn't for lack of trying. The kid must have thrown millions—literally millions—of balls on the sidelines, trying to work on his control. The sad part about the story is that just about the time Dalkowski finally got a semblance of control, he came up with a sore arm, and that finished him." After spending years in the low minors, Dalkowski ended his career as an alcoholic.

Billy Werber of the Red Sox dug two holes with his cleats at home plate and got set for the first pitch from the farmyard phenom Bobby Feller, the new kid in the league. Bob twisted, kicked, and fired a blazer behind Werber's head. Bill dived for the dirt and came back up "a white and shaken man," according to Red Sox' coach Al Schacht.

Feller would turn his back, raise his leg,

twist back toward home, and fire. "Man, he'd blind you," said Atlanta sportscaster Othello Renfroe, who faced him as a Negro leaguer. "Can you imagine him having that delivery when he was wild?"

On one overcast afternoon in New York, Lefty Gomez walked timidly to the plate against Feller, holding up a lighted match. "What's the matter? Can't you see him?" the umpire growled.

"Yeah, I can see him," Lefty said. "I just want to be sure he sees me."

For 16 years the wild man from Iowa would walk 1,764 batters (4.1 per 9 innings). If not for the war, that was another record he would have had without any competition. As it was, teammate Early Wynn edged him out then, with eleven more walks in seven more years. That is, until Nolan Ryan came along and swept both their records away. Through 1986, Ryan had 2,268 walks in 4,116 innings, or 5.0 per nine-inning game. He led the league in walks nine times and would have led seven years in a row, 1972 to 1978, if Mike Torrezhad not beaten him out in 1975. Amos Rusie and Sam McDowell are next with five league-leading years.

Yet Ryan, Feller, and Wynn were terrific

Nolan Ryan

pitchers. Their wildness may even have been an asset, as hitters shivered and quaked looking up at that hill just 60 feet away and the loose cannon standing there about to go off.

"It helps," Ryan says, "if the hitter thinks you're a little crazy."

Feller and Ryan were and are what Uncle Wilbert Robinson of the old Dodgers used to call "pleasingly wild." They kept the hitters loose.

Yankees' reliever Ryne Duren had a fastball like a rifle bullet and glasses like a pair of Coke bottle ends, the players laughed. The Yankees would steer him in the general direction of the sound, and he would squint toward the plate for a sign, then uncork a pitch into the screen behind the plate. That usually gave the hitters something to think about.

Ed Reulbach of the old Cubs, who also suffered from poor eyesight, had his catcher wear a white-painted glove, another ploy not calculated to reassure the batter.

Negro leaguer Bill Drake, nicknamed "Plunk" for obvious reasons, also liked to throw the first warm-up into the screen and yell, "Look out!" as though frightened by the imminent tragedy he foresaw. Lew Burdette of the Milwaukee Braves—a fine control pitcher—was another master at this. He would wind up, fire, and yell, "Look out!" As the batter fell back, one of Lew's "dinky little sliders" would snake over the outside corner.

When the White Sox' Joe Cowley pitched a no-hitter against the California Angels in 1986, half his pitches were outside the strike zone. "His wildness was what made him so good," complained California's Wally Joyner, one of his victims. "He either walked you, or you were swinging at bad pitches."

The wildest men in history are listed in the following tables.

MOST LIFETIME WALKS

Pitchers	Walks
Nolan Ryan*	2,268
Early Wynn	1,775
Bob Feller	1,764
Steve Carlton*	1,742
Phil Niekro*	1,743
Bobo Newsom	1,732
Amos Rusie	1,716
Gus Weyhing	1,566
Red Ruffing	1,541
Bump Hadley	1,442

*Still active; figures through 1986.

However, if you arrange them in order of most walks per nine innings, you get quite a different picture:

MOST WALKS PER NINE INNINGS

Pitcher	BB	IP	BB/9 Inn.
Tommy Byrne*	1,037	1,362	6.9
Rex Barney	410	597	6.2
Ryne Duren	392	589	6.0
Jim Kern	444	793	5.0
Nolan Ryan†	2,268	4,116	5.0
Sam McDowell*	686	1,305	4.7
Bump Hadley	1,442	2,944	4.4
Bob Feller	1,764	3,827	4.1
Bobo Newsom	1,732	3,759	4.1
Amos Rusie	1,704	3,769	4.1

*Left-handed.
†Still active; figures compiled through 1986.

For decades left-handers have been ridiculed as wild men. In 1933 writer Heywood Broun watched Carl Hubbell pitch a ten-inning shutout without walking a man or even getting behind on a batter. "Such control in a left-hander is incredible," Broun marveled. "There must be a skeleton in Hubbell's closet somewhere, such as a right-handed maternal grandmother."

It makes a good joke, but it is a bum rap. The first eight men on the lifetime total-walks list are all right-handers. In fact, Warren Spahn, ranked ninth, is the only lefty in the top twenty. Sam McDowell ranks twenty-one, and Hal Newhouser, twenty-three. The notorious Lefty Grove does not even make the top twenty-five.

If you look at walks per season, you will find that Amos Rusie gave up 218 walks in 1893, the first year of the present, longer pitching distance. No one since has exceeded that, although Bob Feller and Nolan Ryan have given it good tries. In 1938 the nineteen-year-old Feller walked as many as 208 in only 277 innings, or 6.7 per game. Ryan could not quite catch either Rusie or Feller. In 1974 he reached 202 (5.5 per game) and in 1977 walked 204 (6.1 per game).

Strangely, Rusie had more control problems at the old, fifty-foot distance. He had walked 267 men the year before that, and 289, over 548 innings, in 1890, the second year in which the four-balls rule was in effect. That last figure comes out to 4.6 walks per nine innings.

The leaders, since 1893:

Year	Pitcher	BB	BB/9 Inn.
1893	Amos Rusie	218	4.1
1898	Cy Seymour	213	5.4
1938	Bob Feller	208	6.7
1977	Nolan Ryan	204	6.1
1974	Nolan Ryan	202	5.5
1894	Amos Rusie	200	4.1
1941	Bob Feller	194	5.1
1938	Bobo Newsom	192	5.2
1894	Ted Breitenstein	191	3.8
1893	Tony Mullanc	189	4.7

A number of pitchers have led their leagues in both walks and strikeouts for a season. Nolan Ryan did it six times; Amos Rusie and Bob Feller, four times; Toothpick Sam Jones and Sam McDowell, three times;

Mark Baldwin, Cy Seymour, and Wild Bill Hallahan, twice; and Larry Corcoran, John Clarkson, Jack Stivetts, Lefty Grove, Van Mungo, Clay Bryant, Kirby Higbe, Johnny Vander Meer, Warren Spahn, Bob Turley, Al Downing, Bob Veale, Steve Carlton, Phil Niekro, and J. R. Richard, once.

Eight other men led their leagues in most walks and most strikeouts, though not in the same year: Hoss Radbourn, Cy Falkenberg, Bobo Newsom, lefty Hal Newhouser, Allie Reynolds, Early Wynn, Bob Gibson, and Mel Stottlemyre.

The Walking Hitters

Why do some hitters walk a lot and others don't? Ted Williams demanded a strike; others will swing at anything close. Some, such as Eddie Yost, who could not hit, work the pitcher for a walk as a major offensive weapon.

Some clubs walk a lot—the Expos of the early 1980s, for example. By contrast, the Pirates of that time did not walk often. One theory is that poor-hitting clubs wait out the pitcher more, while good-hitting teams jump on the first good pitch, figuring that it may be the only good one they will see. Yet the hard-hitting Cincinnati Reds of the 1970s led the league in drawing walks as often as they led it in winning games.

Intentional Walks

Walks make sense in many cases. As Allie Reynolds cheerfully said about pitching to Ted Williams, "I'm overmatched. If there's a run in scoring position, I've got to walk him."

Bill Nicholson set a record with four home runs in a doubleheader in the Polo Grounds in 1944. When he came up a fifth time with the bases loaded, the New York pitcher walked him intentionally. He figured one run was better than four.

Intentional walks (IBB) were first compiled as a separate statistic in 1955. Since then, Carl Yastrzemski has drawn more than anyone, 190. Jim Palmer gave up the least IBBs per total batters faced, about one per 400. Al Downing was next, with one per 300.

John Schwartz of SABR says National Leaguers give up far more IBBs, presumably because there is no designated hitter: Many IBBs are to get to the pitcher. Relievers yield more than starters, because they generally come into the game with men on base, when IBBs are more apt to be called for.

In their book *The Hidden Game*, however, Pete Palmer and John Thorn found that the IBB is a losing strategy most of the time. If the pitcher does not make the final out as hoped, the leadoff hitter comes up in the next inning with no outs. They recommend the strategy only in the eighth or ninth inning. Baltimore's manager Paul Richards took the concept a step further. With two outs, he gave the pitcher an intentional walk to prevent the leadoff man from batting first in the next inning.

Satchel Paige was famous for arriving late at the park, and hitters soon learned that the best time to hit him was early in the game, before he had warmed up. Buck Leonard remembers Satch loading the bases in the first inning, waving away his teammates' protests, and intentionally walking in a run. "I know what I'm doing," he insisted.

"Now," he announced, "that's all you're gonna get today." And, says Buck, "that's the only run we did get. He beat us 8–1."

LEARNING CONTROL

How do you learn control? Satchel Paige started out as a wild colt in 1927 until two Birmingham veterans, Harry Salmon and Sam Streeter, took him in tow. Streeter, now eighty-six, told Satch he was taking his eye off the plate before he released the ball. They made him throw over matchbooks and Coke bottle caps until Paige could name his fastball his "be" ball, "cause it be where I want it to be."

Jerry Reuss is one man who learned control. In 1973 he led the National League in walks, averaging 3.8 per nine innings. By 1982 he was down to only 1.6 per game, second best in the league.

Nolan Ryan has also gradually brought his walks down, though he will never lose his wildness entirely—and does not want to. On the other hand, Ryan complains, perhaps with justice, control pitchers like Catfish Hunter, Ferguson Jenkins, and Randy Jones have such a good reputation for control that the umpires give them all the close calls on the edges, much as Ted Williams used to get close pitches called in his favor. Said Ryan: "Because I have a reputation for wildness, I don't get the close calls."

There are two reasons why a pitcher is wild, Bill Fischer says. First, poor mechanics, and second, fear of getting the ball over and having the batter hit it. After a home run, Fischer observes, a pitcher often is shy about throwing over the plate. "If you can throw strikes in the bull pen," Fischer says, "you should be able to throw strikes in the game."

Working Too Fine

Fischer might have added a third reason—working too fine, aiming exclusively for those fertile lanes McCarver mentioned. Walks are not always a symptom of bad control. Early Wynn, for example, consistently ran the count to 3–2, not because he could not throw strikes but because he did not want to give the hitter a good pitch to hit. He worked the batter thoroughly, and if he lost a few of them, well, he won 300 games. Jim Palmer points out that more walks are usually given up in close games because the pitchers are trying to pitch fine.

Rick Sutcliffe, when he was rookie of the year in 1979, was another who tried to pitch too fine. "The people who really hurt me the most were the contact hitters," said Rick. Against such men as Pete Rose or Keith Hernandez, "you try to make your curveball break a little better, and consequently you're behind them, and then they're that much better hitters."

Bullet Joe Rogan of the Kansas City Monarchs was also always on the corners. Catcher Frank Duncan, who caught both Rogan and Satchel Paige in their primes, much preferred Satch. "Satchel threw in a quart cup," he says. But Rogan was all over the plate—high, low, inside, outside. "He'd walk five or six men, but he didn't give up many runs." Rogan was just keeping the hitters off balance. He could "thread a needle with that fastball or curve" when he wanted to, said Bill Foster, his rival from Chicago.

Concentration, Lack of Work

Mostly control is concentration. Bob Gibson talked to himself before pitching, as Mark Fidrych did. "Inside, outside," Gibson would repeat, fixing the concept in his mind. "The more I think about them [the corners], the more I'll hit them." If he had to miss, he preferred to miss outside. "If you make a mistake away," he told Tim McCarver, "it's a single; if you make a mistake inside, it's a home run."

Another reason for lack of control is lack of work. Gibson chafed on the bench as a youngster. The longer he sat, the rustier and the wilder he became. The layoff actually made him too strong, "and the ball would go every which way."

Most good control pitchers in the era of the lively ball give up a lot of home runs. Tom Seaver and Bert Blyleven do.

Robin Roberts did. Batters crowded the plate, confident Robin would not throw at them, and Roberts himself said he "put Christianity into practice. To prove I was not prejudiced, I served up home-run balls to Negroes, Italians, Jews, Catholics alike. Race, creed, nationality made no difference to me." But Roberts figured that even Willie Mays hit only 50 homers in 500 at-bats, or one in every 10. Those are good odds—it did not make sense to walk him. But, insisted Roberts' pitching mate Steve Ridzik, most of the home runs came when Robin was leading 5–1 or 5–0. He rarely gave up homers in close games.

In *The Bronx Zoo*, Sparky Lyle wrote of ribbing Catfish Hunter about throwing so many gopher balls. "That's right, and I'll probably give up 240 more before I retire," Hunter shot back. " 'Cause I'll throw the damn ball in there every time. I'm going to make them hit it. They gotta hit it out, and I don't care if they do. I'll keep throwing it in there, and I'll keep getting most of them out."

Hunter was the greatest control pitcher umpire Ron Luciano ever saw. Cat could wave his fielders into position and then make the hitter hit to that exact spot—or over it into the stands. He gave up some "majestic" shots, Luciano wrote—"Launchings." Cat actually admired them himself. "You think that was a good one?" he would laugh disdainfully. "You ought to see the shot Rice hit off me in Boston. Brought rain."

THE GOPHER KINGS

When Pedro Ramos pitched, the old joke went, the ground crew dragged the warning track. The sluggers could not wait to take their swings against him. The big Cuban pitched for fifteen years, 1955–70, and altogether yielded 315 home runs, or one every 7.5 innings. In 1957, when he threw forty-three gopher balls, then an AL record, Ramos allowed one home run every 5.5 innings. And Pete pitched in Griffith Stadium, the biggest park in the majors. Imagine how he would have fared in Ebbetts Field! Or the Metrodome, where Bert Blyleven gave up a record 50 home runs in 1986. Blyleven averaged one homer every 5.4 innings.

But Ramos was far from the biggest gopher-ball pitcher ever. Robin Roberts was way ahead of him, with 502 for a career and 46 in one year, 1956—both big-league records—until Blyleven smashed the second one. In 1956 he was tossing them up on an average of one every 6.5 innings and led the league in losses. The home runs weren't necessarily to blame however: The year before he served up forty-one homers and led the league in wins.

Raymond Gonzalez of SABR, building on data first compiled by the late John Tattersall, has made a magisterial study of gopher pitchers. Everett Cope has brought it up to date. Gonzalez divided the history of the game into four home-run periods: Nineteenth Century, Dead Ball Days, Ruth's Transition Era, and the present Homer Happy Days.

Nineteenth Century

To right-hander Bill "Cherokee" Fisher belongs the honor of throwing the first home-run ball in the modern major leagues, in 1876. Fisher, who had been pitching in the National Association for several years, served it up to Ross Barnes of Al Spalding's Chicagos. It was the only home run Barnes hit all year—in fact, he hit only one other in his life, although he led the league in batting, with .429, and led the Chicagos to the pennant. As for Fisher, he won only four games and lost twenty for the last-place Cincinnati and was soon out of the game for good.

Aside from Fisher's exploit, little else is known about nineteenth-century home-run pitchers. Gonzalez says Frank Dwyer gave up twenty-six in one season, the hit-crazy year of 1894, when hits were cheaper than ever before or since. The league average was .309 (it was only .303 in the infamous 1930 NL season). Four men hit over .400, topped by Hugh Duffy's .438. Duffy also led the league in homers, with eighteen. Like Fisher, Dwyer pitched for the Cincinnatis, who were then led by Charlie Comiskey. Frank won 19 and lost 22 that year, but bounced back with 24 wins two years later and retired with 176 victories and 152 defeats.

Dead Ball Days, 1901–19

By 1901 the dead ball curtain had descended over baseball, and teams scratched for runs. A walk, a sacrifice, and an infield error constituted a batting rally. Those were the halcyon days for pitchers, when there was plenty of room for outfielders to run down the longest drive.

Ed Killian of Detroit, almost unknown today, went almost four years, from 1903 to 1907, without giving up a home run. At 1,001 innings, that was more than 100 nine-inning games.

In 1916 Babe Ruth pitched 324 innings without permitting a home run (while hitting three himself). And he was not even the best in the league—Walter Johnson went

371 homerless innings that same year (Johnson also hit more than he yielded—one).

In all, seven men during the era pitched 300 innings without yielding a home run:

Year	Pitcher	IP	ERA	W–L	Team Standing
1916	Walter Johnson	371	1.89	25–10	7
1910	Jack Coombs	353	1.30	31–9	1
1904	Ed Killian	332	2.44	14–20	7
1916	Babe Ruth	324	1.75	23–12	1
1906	Vic Willis	322	1.73	22–13	3
1905	Ed Killian	313	2.27	22–15	3
1908	Rube Vickers	300	2.34	18–19	6

In his career, Killian pitched almost 1,600 innings and gave up only 9 homers, or one every 178 innings, only one for about every 20 games—the stingiest record in history. The seven stingiest pitchers of the two decades, and thus of all time, were:

Pitcher	HR	IP/HR	ERA	W–L
Ed Killian	9	178.0	2.38	101–79
Joe Wood	7	159.0	2.03	116–57
Ed Walsh	24	123.5	1.82	195–126
Addie Joss	19	123.0	1.88	160–97
Babe Ruth	10	122.0	2.28	94–46
Eddie Plank	42	107.5	2.34	327–192
Ed Cicotte	32	101.0	2.37	210–148

Interestingly, as a pitcher Babe Ruth allowed one homer every thirteen games, but as a batter he slugged one every three games.

The Ruthian Era, 1920–41

From 1920, when the lively ball was born, to World War II, home-run totals rose almost yearly. The dead ball was dead, and left fielders and first basemen swung from the end of the bat, but every shortstop on the bench had not started trying to emulate them yet.

In 1921 Eppa Rixey was still able to hurl 301 innings while yielding only a single homer; that's the best single-season record in the last 65 years. In 1926 Stan Coveleski could hold hitters to one in 245 innings. But each year it got tougher and tougher.

On a lifetime basis, Rixey was also tops for his era with one home run for every five-plus games. The leaders:

Pitcher	HR	IP/HR	ERA	W–L
Eppa Rixey	94	48	3.14	266–251
Stan Coveleski	67	46	2.88	214–141
Carl Mays	70	43	2.92	208–126

Coveleski pitched in Cleveland's chummy League Park, a pitcher's nightmare, with a right-field fence only 290 feet away. He also pitched in spacious Griffith Stadium, a pitcher's delight, with the left-field foul pole 405 feet away. Apparently it did not make any difference: He kept the ball in the park wherever he pitched.

The home-run totals in the Ruthian era were not quite as horrifying as they are today. The gopher king of that period, Red Ruffing, served up only 254—half as many as Robin Roberts. Close behind Ruffing was Carl Hubbell with 246.

Altogether, seven Hall of Famers are on the list of the eleven most generous pitchers. Surprisingly, Grover Cleveland Alexander, a finesse pitcher who played part of his career during the dead ball days, gave up more home runs than Lefty Grove, a fastballer who played entirely during the lively ball era. (Grove's wildness probably helped keep his total down; hitters could not dig in against him as they could against Alexander.)

Homer-Happy Days, 1946–Present

Beginning in about the mid-1940s, the best home-run hitters were not improving—but the worst ones were. Today everyone swings from the heels, and the league totals show it. So, unhappily, do the pitchers' totals.

While Pete Ramos and Robin Roberts may epitomize the era, they are not alone. Right behind Roberts, with 502 home runs yielded, comes Ferguson Jenkins with 484, and Warren Spahn with 434. Others who would surely be up there with them if they had pitched longer are Sandy Koufax, Juan Marichal, and Catfish Hunter. Obviously, there is no longer a stigma attached to a pitcher giving up home runs, as there is no longer a stigma attached to a hitter striking out.

Denny McLain was another one who could throw home runs and win games with equal ease. Over his career he tossed 242, or one every 8 innings; in 1966 he threw 42, more than anyone except Roberts and Ramos, yet he still won 20 games. Two years later Denny served up a league-leading 31 homers—one for every game he won. If he had changed his style to throw fewer homers, would he have won as many games? Probably not. When a pitcher begins nibbling the corners of the plate, he begins throwing more balls and gets behind the hitters, and that means he has to come in with the hitter's pitch even more often.

Imagine how many homers Roberts, Jenkins, and Spahn would have given up if they had faced the designated hitter! Of the leading gopher throwers, only Hunter suffered that punishment. How much difference does the d.h. make? In 1984 eleven of the top fifteen home-run hurlers were in the American League, led by Mike Smithson of the Minnesota Twins with thirty-five. Bill Gullickson of Montreal led the National League with twenty-seven.

Gonzalez's data show that most of the top home-run pitchers have been junk pitchers with good control. In contrast, the toughest men to hit home runs off of have been fireballers who were too wild to dig in on—J.R. Richard, Bob Veale, and Nolan Ryan. Richard yielded less than one home run per two-and-a-half games—twenty-two innings. Veale was close behind, with one per twenty-one innings pitched. Ryan, who credits his sinkerball as much as his speed and wildness, held the hitters to one home run every other nine-inning game.

Grand Slams

Four pitchers have given up nine grand-slam home runs in their careers—Ned Garver, Lindy McDaniel, Milt Pappas, and Jerry

Reuss. Two men—Ray Narleski in 1959 and Tug McGraw in 1979—gave up four grand slams in one year; both were relievers who were brought in to stop rallies, not to groove grand slams.

On the other hand, Jim Palmer pitched almost 4,000 innings and never gave up a grand slam. With the bases full, he said, he would not throw anything good to hit; he would rather have walked the batter, figuring one run is a lot better than four.

Home Runs per Game

Everett Cope reports that five pitchers have given up six or more home runs in one game, all of them between 1930 and 1940: Larry Benton, 1930; Sloppy Thurston, 1932; Al Thomas, 1936; Bill Kerksieck, 1939; and George Caster, 1940.

Kerksieck and Caster gave up four in a single inning. Eight other pitchers have also done that. Paul Foytack gave up his four in 1963 to consecutive hitters; ironically, one of those hitters was Pedro Ramos.

4

Strikeouts: The Power and the Glory

The power pitcher—the man who can rear back and fog it by the hitter—is the brightest star in the pitching firmament. When he takes the mound, it is *showtime*.

The strikeout is pitching's grand slam, its slam dunk, its slap shot. The strikeout does not just quietly retire the hitter, a fate he expects to befall him two times out of three; it humiliates him.

Yet, unlike the power hitter or the power forward in basketball, the power pitcher is shackled by his sport, made to overcome obstacles not presented to other players. Consider:

The fastball comes in, and the hitter tees off. The ball climbs high and far into center field. The fielder races to catch up with it, crashes against the fence 430 feet away, and snares the ball. The hitter, cursing and muttering, jogs back to the dugout and slams his helmet against the water cooler. And who can blame him?

The next hitter steps in. He also swings from the heels—and misses the ball by 3 inches. He has just failed as thoroughly as a

hitter can fail. The pitcher has succeeded as completely as a pitcher can. But is this batter sent back to the dugout? No. He is given two more swings. The poor hurler is required to beard the lion again and see if he can get away with it two more times. And at one time, as mentioned earlier, the hitter was actually given five strikes before he was called out (1887, when the batter was allotted four strikes and the first called strike, the so-called warning pitch, did not count).

Wouldn't the rules be more just, and the action more compelling, if baseball were played "one swing and you're out"? We might give the hitter more than three called strikes to compensate him, but the first swinging strike would be the only one. (We have not decided how to treat foul balls yet. They are also failures, compared to the 430-foot fly, but who said life, or baseball, could ever be completely fair?)

How would this affect the game? We once did a study of what happened to hitters after they missed with their first swing. It revealed that with one swinging strike against him, the average hitter's batting average dropped to about .100. In fact, the odds were good that he would swing and miss again, and even again. (Of course this study was done before the designated hitter, and many weak-hitting pitchers were included in the data. But even eliminating pitcher at-bats, the average would probably be under .200.)

A one-strike-you're-out rule would speed up the game. It would save the power pitcher's arm. It would restore science and inside baseball to the game. And frankly we are not convinced that this change would be unpopular with the fans.

The rule would probably throw the Reggie Jacksons and Dave Kingmans right out of the major leagues. But it might not affect sluggers like Joe DiMaggio or Ted Williams very much; both these men sometimes had more home runs than strikeouts. Yogi Berra, Frank McCormick, Tommy Holmes, and Arky Vaughan were among many others who could hit with authority without flailing the air. Williams once said he thought he was a better hitter with two strikes on him, because he choked up, protected the plate, and just met the ball. He later modified that a bit, but he was still a fine two-strike hitter.

Under the present three-strike rule, the power pitcher is forced to throw many more pitches than the defensive pitcher, who wants to make the hitter hit the pitch and hit it to a certain place. This makes the power pitcher throw a lot more pitches per game, with consequent wear and tear on his arm. It also, as Bill James points out, gives base runners many more opportunities to steal.

Catcher Thurman Munson thought the strikeout pitch was overrated. Sam McDowell, for instance, "always seemed more interested in embarrassing a hitter than in just retiring him." Munson himself said that

when he called a game, he never tried for a strikeout unless it was really needed. Munson's thought was, "How can we get this guy to hit off stride, away from his strength?"

Bob Gibson also did not pitch for strikeouts for the same reason. They are the most inefficient way to get an out. He would much prefer to get three outs on three pitches than on nine—or twelve, or fifteen—as a strikeout pitcher must. (Of course, with a man on third and none out, a strikeout is the only safe outcome and so is desired.)

Not only is baseball prejudiced against its power pitchers, it does not even know how to use them. James asked the sensible question: Wouldn't power pitchers be more effective at night? He found that they are indeed more effective under the lights. Some power pitchers, James found, cut their ERAs by as much as two runs under the lights.

But James also found that managers had never thought of this and were not giving their strikeout pitchers any more starts after dark than the finesse pitchers were getting. Baseball is such a conservative game that, fifty years after the first night game, managers have yet to notice that change presents opportunity.

WHAT IS SPEED?

Nolan Ryan's pitches were timed and found to be faster than Bob Feller's, but under different test conditions. Walter Johnson was timed with an even more primitive device. How would a Cy Young or Amos Rusie do in a test with today's radar devices? It may not matter, for there are three components of every pitch, according to Tom Seaver— speed, location, and movement—and the least important of these is speed. More important questions are: Does the fastball have a hop on it? Does it tail away? Does it sink? Or is it straight as an arrow?

And does it *seem* fast? That may be more important than being measured fast by the JUGS gun. Speed is a relative thing, Albert Einstein noted. A Stu Miller fastball, traveling barely 80 m.p.h., can seem a blue dart to a hitter after facing a diet of 60–65-m.p.h. junk. Moreover, a smooth, deceptive motion can make a hitter think the pitch is slower than it really is. Ted Williams said that the first time he faced Satchel Paige, he marveled at the fluid, easy style. Before he woke up from the reverie, three strikes were over the plate. Walter Johnson had that kind of effortless delivery too.

The most important question, though, is how does the pitcher set up his fastball? The classic pattern is the slow curve down and away, then the fastball under the whiskers. Coming right after the curve, the fastball seems even faster.

Some oldtimers did not have a curve at all. Johnson and Grove did not, not until so late in their careers that it hardly mattered. Feller, Koufax, and Ryan had great ones. Today the curve is often used as the "out" pitch, even for the flamethrowers. Ryan, for one, goes to his curve more and more after the fourth inning. He used primarily his bender in his fifth no-hitter because his fastball was not overpowering that night. "You can't win with one pitch," he said. "It doesn't matter how fast you can throw."

Pitchers formerly used the curve to set up the fastball. Now it is often the other way around, just as football teams now routinely commit the one-time heresy of using the pass to set up the run.

Several fastball pitchers use the slider, rather than the curve, as their second pitch; Mets' reliever Jesse Orosco is one. Generally the slider has less of a dropoff in speed; while relievers can get away without a change of pace, or even a second pitch, few starters can.

Strikeout totals have exploded since World War II. One reason is Ralph Kiner's crack about home-run hitters driving Cadillacs. Hitters feel four or five strikeouts are a cheap price for a home run. Hitters used to be proud of making contact; even Babe Ruth, with his prodigious sweeping swing, infrequently had even half as many strikeouts as Juan Samuel did in 1985. Now the fashion is to just whale away, and if you fan, well, "a strikeout is better than a double play" (Darryl Strawberry).

Then, too, there is more pressure on today's pitchers to gather strikeouts, as the Astroturf single makes a mockery of many perfect pitches.

The rise of the bull pen, especially since 1959, is also a factor promoting higher strikeouts. If the starter has a Dave Righetti, Todd Worrell, or Jeff Reardon to come to his aid when he tires, he can pitch as tough to the eighth-place batter as he does to the clean-up man.

LIFETIME STRIKEOUT LEADERS

Masaichi Kaneda*	4,490
Nolan Ryan†	4,277
Steve Carlton†	4,040
Tom Seaver†	3,640
Gaylord Perry	3,534
Walter Johnson	3,508
Don Sutton†	3,431
Phil Niekro†	3,278
Ferguson Jenkins	3,192
Bob Gibson	3,117
Bert Blyleven†	3,090
Jim Bunning	2,855
Mickey Lolich	2,832
Cy Young	2,799
Warren Spahn	2,583
Bob Feller	2,581

*Japanese major leagues.
†Still active; figures compiled through 1986.

SPECIAL K'S

Who is the greatest strikeout pitcher in history? We cannot say, but any of the following pitchers might be considered the greatest.

Nolan Ryan

Nolan Ryan is awesome. His fastball has been clocked at more than 100 m.p.h., and not a single hitter doubts it. He has struck out 383 men in one year (1973), 19 in one game twice (1974).

Ryan achieved both marks in spite of the American League designated hitter rule, the only great strikeout pitcher besides Roger Clemens so handicapped. If he had hurled against the patsy-hitting pitchers of other leagues and other years, he might well have whiffed 400 per year on four occasions. Surely he would have passed twenty in a game. And how many more no-hitters could he have tossed?

Ryan has his critics, who say that he is wild, that he cannot win twenty games consistently, and the line. But no pitcher in history has so dominated batters as has this taciturn Texan, whose biggest problem may be that he just has no color.

Ryan's fastball was and is so fast that the ball literally seems to explode. Umpire Ron Luciano said that it left the pitcher's mound as big as a golf ball, and then when it reached the top of the plate, it burst into a million blinding specks of white. An optometrist explained it logically: The ball arrived so fast that the human eye could not adjust quickly enough. When the eye finally did adjust, the ball suddenly reached normal size with what seemed like an explosion.

Complained one hitter: "Why doesn't he throw a spitball like everyone else?"

Bob Feller

Bob Feller ended his career with only 2,581 lifetime strikeouts, but in our book, he should be second on the all-time-great strikeout pitcher list. He estimated that World War II cost him 1,200 strikeouts, and his estimate is not immodest, considering the four prime years he gave up.

When he enlisted in the navy at the age of 23, right after the Japanese attack on Pearl Harbor, he had struck out 1,235 batters, more than any man his age in history. At the same age Walter Johnson had 707; Sandy Koufax, 313; Steve Carlton, 233; Nolan Ryan, 231; and Gaylord Perry, 70.

As a seventeen-year-old, Bob had struck out sixteen men in one game, tying the modern big-league record. A week later he blew the record away by striking out seventeen. Then two years later, as a twenty-one-year-old in 1938, he shot his fastball past eighteen Tigers in one game.

He whiffed 260 in his last peace-time year, 1941. He struck out 348 more in his first full year back. That's 300 a year average, or 1,200 for four years. And his service years were arguably the four best years of his athletic life, ages twenty-three to twenty-six. Johnny Vander Meer pitched his double no-hitters at twenty-three, Don Larsen his perfect Series game at twenty-six.

Feller does not regret entering the navy. His father was dying of cancer, and he could have gotten a deferment. "But I didn't think it was the right thing to do. Not that I'm a hero. But I don't regret it. We did what we thought was best. I wouldn't do it differently. I'd do a lot of things differently; that's not one of them."

Back in baseball in 1946, Feller struck out 348. "I didn't start trying to strike everybody out until the middle of July," he told us. Wheaties had offered him $5,000 to break Rube Waddell's record, so he wrote to the league office to ask what the record was. He was told it was 343. Bob topped that with 348. "Later they came back and said Waddell had 349. I just wish they'd told me that before the season was over. You can bet your last buck I'd have pitched a few more innings and gotten it."

At the end of his career, he might have hung on, like Steve Carlton and Pete Rose, to go for 4,000. And he probably could have made it.

Like Ted Williams, Feller missed the mountaintop years in the middle of his career. Comparing others to him is to compare them at their peak to Bob before and after his peak. What did the war cost him? "We'll never know, will we?" he shrugs.

In our book, we put Bob right up there with Ryan.

Tom Seaver

Steve Carlton

Steve Carlton and Tom Seaver

Steve Carlton and Tom Seaver are two strikeout stars who are at once both great and lucky. Do not get us wrong: They deserve their greatness. But they had no war to rob them of their peak seasons, no sore arms or illnesses, no designated hitters to face until very late in their careers. They pitched most of their games under the friendly lights in the most strikeout-prone era the game has ever known. They would have been stars in any era, under any conditions, but they realized their potential more fully than the other strikeout artists.

Both men beat Ryan to striking out nineteen hitters in a game. Carlton did it against the Mets in 1969, thus setting a modern record (though losing the game, 4–3 on two two-run homers by Ron Swoboda). Seaver matched it a year later against the San Diego Padres. Ryan joined them in 1974, and Roger Clemens topped them in 1986 by fanning twenty.

Seaver incidentally ended his nineteen-strikeout game with record-breaking fireworks. He fanned the last ten men he faced, more consecutive batters than any pitcher had ever struck out. To the last man, Al Ferrara, Seaver threw a slider for a strike, another for a ball, then went to a fastball, which Ferrara swung at and missed. Though Seaver had a two-hitter going, he was leading by only one run. "I was worried about him hitting it out," he said later. "I had to challenge him. I just let a fastball rip." The ball came in at Ferrara's knees. Ferrara swung and missed, and Seaver had his share of the record.

The closest anyone has ever come to Seaver's ten straight is nine by Mickey Welch, back in 1884. In this century, only Max Surkont, Jim Maloney, and Johnny Podres had struck out eight in a row before Seaver, and only Nolan Ryan, Roger Clemens, and Jim Deshaies have done it since.

Lefty Grove

While the debate used to rage over who was faster, Johnson or Feller, there were some who insisted that the fastest man they ever saw was neither. In their book Lefty Grove was the speed king. Grove threw a straight ball, with no hop or sail like most fastball pitchers have. Still, even without the hop, the hitters could not touch it.

The ace of the champion A's, from 1929 to 1931, Grove led the league in strikeouts seven straight times, though his highest season total was only 209 in 1930. He finally retired with 2,266 in his big-league career. Neither number is terribly impressive by today's standards, but two factors held Lefty's totals down.

First, he played in the transition era, as did Feller, between the punch-and-judy hitters of the dead ball days and the roundhouse swingers of the expansion era. If he played today, he would probably have more.

Second, Grove, like Feller, may have missed some of the best years of his career, not in the military but in the minor leagues. He did not even get to the majors until he was twenty-five, although he was obviously ready three years before that.

Grove, from the western Maryland mountains, signed with the Baltimore Orioles of the International League in 1920 at the age of twenty. He won twelve and lost three that year, and then in 1921 he really took off. He won twenty-five, eighteen, twenty-seven, and twenty-seven for them over the next four seasons, as the Orioles swept to pennant after pennant with a club that many regarded as better than a lot of the big-league teams. Lefty was also striking out 254, 205, 330, and 231 hitters over the same stretch. Why, then, didn't he get the call?

In those days there was no major-league-controlled farm system as there is today. Some minor-league clubs might have had working agreements with big-league teams, but most were free to sell their best players to the highest bidder or to retain them if the players were of more value at the turnstiles. Today the minor leagues act as a feeder system for the majors (excepting a few independent clubs like those in Miami and Utica), and a big-league club can keep a boy down on the farm only so long until he is fair game to be drafted by any other team. Back in the 1920s Orioles' owner Jack Dunn had put together a great team and paid his stars as much as they could get in the majors. Legally, he did not have to sell Grove, and Lefty did not want to leave his home state anyway. He was rich and happy with the Orioles. Connie Mack finally did pry Grove loose, along with several other Orioles' players who went on to play on the A's championship clubs. The price for Grove: $100,600, the most ever paid for a ball player up to that time. The old record was the $100,000 that the Yanks reportedly gave the Red Sox for Babe Ruth (in fact it was much, much more and included New York's assumption of the mortgage on Fenway Park!).

So Grove finally made the majors at the age of twenty-five and promptly led all American League hurlers in strikeouts with 116. Lefty was terrific after he reached the majors. But he may have been even better in the three years before that. How many strikeouts did he lose? Perhaps 100 to 150 a year for three years, or about 400 in all, enough to move up several notches in the all-time list.

In 1928 Grove twice struck out the side on nine pitches. This feat has been performed by only fourteen other pitchers, beginning with Rube Waddell in 1902 and ending with Ron Guidry in 1984. Only two other men—Sandy Koufax and Nolan Ryan—have done it twice, but only Grove did it twice in the same year. One of the two was against the Yanks' "Murderers' Row"—Babe Ruth, Lou Gehrig, and Bob Meusel. The only pitch any of them touched was a foul by Meusel.

Lefty almost did it four times. Once in Philadelphia he entered in relief with the bases full and Ruth, Gehrig, and Tony Lazzeri coming up. This time it took ten pitches, all of them strikes. "Lazzeri hit a couple of fouls," Lefty said.

Dazzy Vance

Another pitcher who achieved the ultimate strikeout efficiency was Dazzy Vance, who, like Grove, did not reach the big leagues until late in life. In Vance's case, he was thirty-one before he made it to stay, with the Dodgers of 1922. His problem was that he could not win with only three days' rest; he needed four. He would come up from the

minors, get a cup of coffee, look bad, and go back down to St. Joe or Toledo or Memphis. Finally, in New Orleans, his manager gave him four days' rest, and Dazzy took off for the big leagues to stay.

Like Grove, Vance immediately led the league in K's and continued to lead for seven straight years. His high was 262 in 1924, when he went 28–6 and won the National League MVP award over Rogers Hornsby, who only hit .424 that year. He had 17 strikeouts in a 10-inning game in 1925 and finally ended up with 2,045 for a career, all but 18 after the age of 31. If he had come up today, he would have been right at home with the modern five-day rotation.

Amos Rusie

As Babe Ruth revolutionized baseball in the 1920s, transforming the "inside" game of the dead ball era into the power game of the next fifty years, so did Amos Rusie revolutionize it in the 1890s. The Hoosier Thunderbolt, with his terrifying fastball and scarcely less speedy curve hurtling in from a distance of 50 feet, made batters fear for their lives. He was the prime mover, in 1893, of the pitching distance to its current 60 feet 6 inches.

Even at the increased distance, he was awesome. In 1894 he won thirty-six games and posted an ERA *2.5 runs* below the league average!

Walter Johnson

For more than half a century Walter Johnson, the Big Train, stood alone atop the all-time strikeout list, outlasting Babe Ruth's home-run marks. Batters would suddenly become "violently ill" when Johnson was due to pitch, Ring Lardner reported. His records fell to Nolan Ryan, Steve Carlton, and Gaylord Perry, principally because they pitched in an era when batters struck out 60 to 70 percent more often. Even so, Johnson led the league in strikeouts in twelve different years, and no one else is even close to that. Johnson pitched against punch-hitters whose aim was just to make contact. Even a Joe Jackson or a Home Run Baker, with their full swings, seldom fanned. There were no Mickey Mantles or Willie Stargells swinging for "all or nothing at all." If Johnson had pitched against today's home-run-happy hitters, his ERA might be a lot higher, but his strikeout total might still be unassailable.

Then, too, Johnson was not going after records. He bore down when he had to and coasted when he could. He liked to fool around with his curve, which was not much, when he was ahead, instead of applying the *coup de grace* with the fast one.

In one game his teammates had bet a lot of money on themselves, and Johnson put a couple of men on in the ninth. A teammate ran to the mound in alarm to remind him of the stakes. Johnson fanned the next three men—Tris Speaker, Dick Hoblitzell, and Duffy Lewis—on nine pitches.

One wonders how much more formidable Johnson would have been under the lights. One dark day catcher Eddie Ainsmith went to the mound and told Walter to fake the pitch. Johnson delivered an imaginary ball, Ainsmith smacked his glove, and the ump called it strike three. It is no coincidence that batting averages have gone down and strikeouts up since night ball was introduced.

On the other hand, Johnson pitched in what some consider an inferior league. The American League in the first two decades of this century may not have had the deep talent that the older National League had. It had Ty Cobb, of course, and Nap Lajoie and Joe Jackson and some other big names, but the talent quotient for the league as a whole, top to bottom, was not as high as that in the National League.

Of course, ability was far less than in the majors of today, when population has exploded much faster than major-league expansion can keep pace, so that now pitchers must face great hitters three times as often as Johnson's generation did.

And without a decent curve, it is a fair question whether Johnson could survive today. If Nolan Ryan and Dwight Gooden know they cannot be effective in the big leagues today with only one pitch, it is doubtful if Johnson could.

Rube Waddell

Rube Waddell had all Johnson's handicaps and advantages, plus one big handicap that Sir Walter never had—alcoholism. It cut short his years of stardom and led to his early death at the age of thirty-eight.

But when Rube was right, he could not be touched. He led the league in strikeouts seven times, six of them in a row. Waddell's 349 strikeouts in 1904 remained inviolate—although disputed, some sources crediting him with 346, others with 343—until Sandy Koufax finally surpassed it in 1965. Johnson did not even come close.

In 1902 Waddell began the season with Los Angeles of the Pacific Coast League, at that time—when the majors went no farther west than St. Louis—a super-strong circuit, perhaps the equal of the fledgling American League. After winning twelve of his nineteen starts, Rube joined the Philadelphia Athletics on June 26—and won twenty-four more!

In 1908, after even patient Connie Mack had given up on him and shipped him into exile with the St. Louis Browns, Rube had enough left to strike out sixteen of his old teammates in one game, an amazing total with the choke-hitting batters of that day.

And yes, Rube really did call in his out-field and infield and strike out the side, though never in a big-league game. Once when he did that, the local batters just plunked the ball over the empty infield. His mates laughingly refused to budge while Rube huffed and puffed running the little pop singles down. But he finally did strike the last man out.

Sandy Koufax

Anyone who saw Sandy Koufax pitch will never forget the sight. Many feel that, just as Ted Williams was the perfect image of the hitter, Koufax was the picture-perfect pitcher of the last half-century.

The Brooklyn Dodgers had sent a scout to look over the young Koufax. His report is a model of some sort: "First," the scout wrote, "he's from Brooklyn. Second, he's Jewish."

Uprooted from his home and trans-planted 3,000 miles away in Los Angeles, he would win immortality. As a kid, he walked as many men as he struck out. In Los Angeles, all that began to change, and by 1965, when he broke Rube Waddell's forty-one-year-old season's strikeout mark, he was whiffing more than five men for every one he walked.

Koufax first shook up the baseball world in 1959 by striking out eighteen men in one game, tying the existing record for this cen-tury set by Bob Feller in 1936. Koufax had struck out thirteen the game before, for a two-game total of thirty-one, a record even Feller had not achieved. He followed it with ten more the game after, making forty-one in three games, another record. He struck out eighteen again in 1962. (Neither 1959 nor 1962 was a big victory year for him be-cause of injuries.)

Not until 1963 did Koo, as the New York tabloids tagged him, become a star, but by October 1966 his career was over, ended prematurely by a bad arm. Because of his late start and his early retirement, Koufax's lifetime totals do not compare to others who pitched longer. But for those few years at his peak, he showed the game perhaps the most dominating pitcher of all time.

He led the league in ERA for five straight years, a record. He won more games, twenty-seven, and pitched more shutouts in one year, eleven, than any National League left-hander in this century. He pitched a no-hitter a year for four straight years, the last one a perfect game. He compiled a World Series ERA of 0.95 in four Series. He won three Cy Young Awards, at a time when the award was given to only the best pitcher in *both* major leagues.

Sudden Sam McDowell

In 1965, at the age of twenty-two, Sam McDowell was the greatest strikeout pitcher the game had ever seen. He whiffed 325 men in only 273 innings, making him not only the youngest pitcher ever to reach 300 strikeouts, but giving him 10.71 per nine-inning game, a figure that even Nolan Ryan, with a best of 10.57 per game in 1973, has not been able to match although Dwight Gooden passed them both with 11.37 per game in 1984.

McDowell won seventeen games for the sixth-place Cleveland Indians that year, posted a 2.18 ERA, and pitched one-hitters back to back. He had the world at his feet.

"McDowell has done things that Koufax couldn't do at that age," Indians' manager Alvin Dark would say in 1969. "He can go on and be better than Koufax ever was. Sam has a change-up, which Sandy didn't have. When Sam fully realizes just how good he is, there's no limit to what he can do."

The next year, 1970, Sam posted 304 strikeouts and 20 wins, but that was the crest of the wave. His victories fell to thirteen, ten, six, one, and finally two. The whispers that circulated around the league were that Sam McDowell was a lush.

"I was the biggest, most hopeless, and most violent drunk in baseball," McDowell now agrees. As he told Shirley Povich of the *Washington Post,* he demolished barrooms, battled cops, lied to managers. In 1975, having drunk himself off the Indians, Giants, and Yankees, Sam came to the end of the line as a reliever for the Pirates.

McDowell took to selling insurance and finally—ironically—to counseling kids in trouble, at a salary of $7,000 a year. It was then that he sought help for himself too and turned his life around. By the spring of 1985, he was back in baseball, on the payroll of the Texas Rangers, with eight other teams calling and asking for his help. His job: counseling alcoholic and drug-addicted ball players.

Smokey Joe Williams

While Lefty Grove and Dazzy Vance were laboring in the minors, a black–Indian pitcher was also toiling in obscurity, unable to show his talents before major-league crowds and writers who could have made him an American legend. His name was Smokey Joe Williams.

Joe was a lanky, hawk-nosed Texan who, from 1912 to 1933, faced the greatest pitchers in the country, black and white. Against white big leaguers, he won twenty-three, lost seven, and tied one. Two of his losses came at the age of forty-five; two others were by scores of 1–0. Among his victims were five men now enshrined in the Hall of Fame: Walter Johnson, Grover Alexander, Chief Bender, Waite Hoyt, and Satchel Paige.

In 1952, when the Pittsburgh *Courier* asked a panel of black veterans and sportswriters to name the best black pitcher of all time,

Smokey Joe Williams was the winner, 20–19, over Paige. Satchel, who split two games against Joe in the early 1930s, rated Joe the fastest he saw. One game that Williams reputedly pitched in 1917 was a ten-inning no-hit masterpiece with twenty strikeouts against the National League champion New York Giants. No confirmation has yet been found of this feat, but the game remains a centerpiece of black baseball's oral tradition.

One of Williams' greatest games came in 1930 at the age of forty-four. He faced the Kansas City Monarchs under the Monarchs' new traveling lights. The bulbs may have been a bit dim, for in twelve innings he and Kansas City's Chet Brewer dueled scorelessly. Williams liked to spit tobacco juice on the ball, which did not help matters any. For twelve innings the outfielders on both teams stood with their arms folded. By the time Williams finally won it 1–0, Brewer had struck out nineteen, Williams, twenty-seven.

Bullet Joe Rogan

"Rogan was one of the world's greatest pitchers," said Satchel Paige, who followed Bullet Joe as ace of the Kansas City Monarchs. "He was a chunky little guy"—Rogan stood only 5 feet 6 inches—"but he could throw hard. He could throw hard as Smokey Joe Williams. Yeah."

Rogan spent his best years in the army in Honolulu and Arizona before Casey Stengel discovered him playing for a black infantry team on the Mexican border in 1918 and recommended him to the owner of the new Monarchs. Joe was already thirty years old.

Chet Brewer, later a scout for the Pirates, saw Walter Johnson, Grover Alexander, Bob Feller, and Sandy Koufax pitch. "Rogan was the best pitcher I ever saw in my life," he says flatly. "Smokey Joe Williams was next in my book. Both were better pitchers than Satchel, but Satchel got all the publicity. Rogan could throw a curveball faster than most pitchers could throw a fastball. And he was the inventor of the palmball. He'd just walk it up there. Hitters were well off stride. I saw him one winter just make Al Simmons crawl trying to hit that ball.''

Satchel Paige

Of course the most famous black pitcher was Satchel Paige, and those too young to have seen Smokey Joe Williams or Bullet Joe Rogan consider him the best. He is the black pitcher they wish had reached the major

Satchel Paige

NATIONAL BASEBALL LIBRARY, COOPERSTOWN, N.Y.

leagues two decades before he finally did, with the Cleveland Indians in 1948 at the age of forty-two.

Satch called his fastball his ''thoughtful stuff.'' It did give hitters plenty to think about.

''He just changed the size of the ball,'' said oldtime sportswriter Ric Roberts. Hitters said it looked like a fifty-cent piece. It actually had a buzz or hum to it. Complained one hitter after being called out on strikes: ''That last one sounded a little low, didn't it, ump?''

Late in his career, Satch pitched three innings a day to draw a crowd, but earlier, when he was with Birmingham, he took his full turn in the rotation as everyone else did. In 1929, according to Dick Clark, chairman of SABR's Negro league committee, Satch turned in three high strikeout games. On May 29 he whiffed seventeen Cuban Stars and beat them 6–2 on a two-hitter; he walked only one man. Six days later he struck out eighteen Nashville hitters in a fourteen-inning nonleague game. Then on July 14 he fanned seventeen Detroit Stars, beating them 5–1 on another two-hitter. Again he walked only one.

In California in the winter of 1933, reportedly stung by a racial remark while pitching against some white big-league stars, Satch actually did call in his outfield and strike out the side—Babe Herman, Frank Demaree, and Wally Berger.

In 1934 Paige hooked up in one of his many games against Dizzy Dean of the world champion St. Louis Cardinals. Satch won it 4–1, pitching six innings with thirteen strikeouts and no hits. Dean trotted by the Crawfords' dugout between innings, mopped his brow, and grinned, ''Satch, if you and Josh [Gibson] played with me 'n Paul on the Cards, we'd win the pennant by July 4 and go fishin' the rest of the year.''

In Los Angeles in the fall of 1946, he faced another white all-star team, and a young right-hander pounded a homer off him. Paige's mouth dropped as he watched the hitter round the bases. "Who he?" he asked incredulously.

"That's Ralph Kiner," first baseman Buck O'Neil replied.

"Who he?" Paige repeated, uncomprehending.

"He just led the National League in home runs."

"*Did* he? Well, tell me when he comes up again," Satch said.

Two innings later O'Neil called, "Here's Kiner." The catcher stooped to waggle his fingers for a sign. "Don't put those fingers down," Satch commanded. "I'm gonna throw him nothing but fastballs outside." Kiner swung at three and missed them all.

"Nobody hits Satch's fastballs," Satch said, strolling off the mound.

Masaichi Kaneda

The jewel of Japan's pitchers was a lanky Japanese-born Korean lefty by the name of Masaichi Kaneda (*ka-nay-da*), the "Golden Arm"—*kane* means gold in Japanese. Kaneda struck out Mickey Mantle three straight times in 1955, and his 4,490 strikeouts far surpassed Walter Johnson's record long before Nolan Ryan or Steve Carlton did. It will be a great race to see if Ryan can catch "The Emperor," as he is also called because of his temperamental, independent ways. Ryan needed 213 more at the start of the 1987 season.

We saw Kaneda pitch for the last-place Kokutetsu (National Railway) Swallows from 1952 to 1955 and fell in love with his stylish, economical motion. From 1951 through 1974 Kaneda won between twenty and thirty-one games every year for a team

that averaged about fifty-five wins. Like most Japanese, Kaneda relieved about as often as he started. His best ERA was 1.30 in 1958.

Kaneda led the league in strikeouts eleven times. His high was 350 in 400 innings in 1955.

Eiji Sawamura

The first great Japanese hurler was Eiji Sawamura, an eighteen-year-old schoolboy who struck out Babe Ruth two times in one game in 1934. He whiffed Charlie Gehringer (.356), Ruth (.288), Jimmy Foxx (.334), and Lou Gehrig (.363) in a row. He went into the ninth inning tied 0–0 against Earl Whitehill, before Gehrig beat him 1–0 on a home run.

Largely as a result of Ruth's tour, the first Japanese pro league was born, and Sawamura was its first star. He pitched three no-hitters before going into the army; he was killed in the South Pacific. Today he is a legend of Japanese baseball. The Japanese Cy Young Award is named the Sawamura Award.

Yutaka Enatsu

"The purpose of my life is strikeouts," lefty Yutaka Enatsu once said. In 1968, his second year in the league, he needed one more to tie the single-season Japanese record. He struck out the legendary Sadaharu Oh to tie it, then waited dramatically for Oh to come up again so he could whiff him once more to break the record.

One would suppose that managers would stand in line to get someone like Enatsu on their team. Instead, he was bounced around. As a cocky rookie in 1967, Enatsu elbowed past the veteran stars to take his bath first instead of waiting submissively as a good rookie should. As punishment, his manager ordered him to kneel at attention. Enatsu showed his contempt by holding the position all night.

In 1985, at the age of thirty-six, Enatsu reported to the Milwaukee Brewers' camp to try out for the U.S. major leagues, hoping to be the first Japanese to make it since Masanori Murakami in 1965. His big dream of striking out Reggie Jackson ended quickly when Jackson hit a single to center against him. The Brewers let him go in one of the final spring cuts.

STRIKEOUT RECORDS

Matt Kilroy: 513

In 1886 Matt Kilroy pitched for the old Baltimore Orioles in the American Association, which was then one of the two major leagues. Kilroy struck out more batters that year, 513, than anyone else ever has.

Of course, Kilroy had some advantages that today's Nolan Ryan or Dwight Gooden

SINGLE-SEASON STRIKEOUT LEADERS
The 300 Club

	AL				NL	
1971	Mickey Lolich	308		1978	J.R. Richard	303
1910	Walter Johnson	313		1986	Mike Scott	306
1965	Sam McDowell	325		1972	Steve Carlton	310
1976	Nolan Ryan	327		1979	J.R. Richard	313
1972	Nolan Ryan	329		1966	Sandy Koufax	317
1977	Nolan Ryan	341		1965	Sandy Koufax	382
1946	Bob Feller	348				
1904	Rube Waddell	349				
1974	Nolan Ryan	367				
1973	Nolan Ryan	383				

The 400 Club

1968	Yutaka Enatsu	401	(Japan)
1884	Charlie Buffinton	417	(587 IP)
1938	Virgil Trucks	418	(Alabama-Florida league)
1884	Hoss Radbourn	441	(679 IP)
1946	Bill Kennedy	456	(280 IP, Coastal Plain league)
1884	Hugh Daily	483	(501 IP)
1886	Toad Ramsey	499	(589 IP)

The 500 Club

1886	Matt Kilroy	513	(583 IP)

do not. First, he pitched at a distance of only 50 feet. Second, he pitched 583 innings.

A handsome, strapping man, Kilroy was the idol of little Henry (H.L.) Mencken, the future newspaper pundit. Mencken's father, a prosperous cigar manufacturer, named one of his cigars the Kilroy in Matt's honor.

That year was a strikeout year. Thomas "Toad" Ramsey fanned 499 men and finished second.

In 1884 Hugh Daily, the one-armed wonder, whiffed 483. That's the year he got 20 in one game. A revolutionary change in the rules had just been mandated—pitchers were allowed to throw overhand, and before the batters could adjust, no less than 11 pitchers that season scored 300 strikeouts or more, including Hoss Radbourn with 441, and Charlie Buffinton, 417.

Dwight Gooden: Most Ks per Game

It remained for a nineteen-year-old, Dwight Gooden, to dim all the old stars by striking out more men per game than any other pitcher. In his rookie year, 1984, Gooden fanned 276 men in only 218 innings, 11.4 per game. (As an eighteen-year-old minor leaguer at Lynchburg, he had averaged an astounding 14.1 whiffs per game.)

His 11.4 demolished the old major-league record of 10.7 by Sudden Sam McDowell. Even Nolan Ryan could fan only 10.6 per nine innings in his best year. The top ten:

Year	Pitcher	SO	SO/9 Inn.
1984	Dwight Gooden	276	11.4
1965	Sam McDowell	325	10.7
1973	Nolan Ryan	383	10.6
1962	Sandy Koufax	216	10.6
1972	Nolan Ryan	329	10.4
1966	Sam McDowell	225	10.4
1976	Nolan Ryan	327	10.4
1965	Sandy Koufax	382	10.2
1960	Sandy Koufax	197	10.1
1986	Mike Scott	306	10.0

Gooden had four days' rest between starts. Less rest and more starts may have increased his total strikeouts but cut down on his per game average.

Strikeouts per game sheds a new light on strikeout stats. Christy Mathewson led the NL five times in strikeouts, but only once in strikeouts per game. His overshadowed teammate, the unlucky Red Ames, never led in strikeouts, because he did not pitch enough innings. He led in whiffs per game four times. The all-time season leaders in strikeouts per game:

AL Pitcher	Seasons	NL Pitcher	Seasons
Walter Johnson	8	Dazzy Vance	8
Nolan Ryan	7	Sandy Koufax	6
Rube Waddell	7	Tom Seaver	6
Sam McDowell	6	Red Ames	4
Lefty Grove	5	Grover Alexander	4
Bob Feller	5		

The lifetime leaders are:

AL Pitcher	SO/9 Inn.	NL Pitcher	SO/9 Inn.
Nolan Ryan*	9.32	Sandy Koufax	9.28
Sam McDowell	8.86	J. R. Richard	8.37
Rube Waddell	7.04	Bob Veale	7.96
Bert Blyleven*	6.96	Jim Maloney	7.81
		Sam Jones	7.54
		Bob Gibson	7.22
		Steve Carlton*	7.19

*Still active; figures compiled through 1986.

Steve Dalkowski: Strikeout King

The all-time strikeout pitcher was Steve Dalkowski, who according to legend, threw the fastest ball ever. In 1957, at the age of eighteen, with the Orioles' farm team in the Appalachian league, Steve struck out an average of 17.6 hitters every nine innings he pitched, or just about two men per inning. The only trouble was he walked as many men as he whiffed. He never pitched an inning in the majors.

Twenty Ks: Roger Clemens and One-Armed Daily

When Roger Clemens struck out 20 men in one game in 1986, the papers raved that not in the history of major-league baseball—111 years and 150,000 games—had anyone done what Clemens did. That is not quite true.

Back in 1884 One-Armed Hugh Daily struck out twenty in the old Union Association. The record books say nineteen, but he lost one strikeout under the rules then in effect because his catcher dropped a third strike. Under today's rules we would count that as a whiff. Of course it was an expansion year with three leagues and 33 teams, and the strike zone and ball-strike rules were different. Still, Clemens actually shares the record with Daily.

Twenty-one for Sweeney?

SABR's Frederick Ivor-Campbell says Clemens and Daily may actually be in second place, behind Charlie Sweeney of the 1884 Providence Grays. Sweeney is the man whose rivalry with Hoss Radbourn that year spurred Hoss on to win sixty games. On June 7 he struck out at least nineteen of the second-place Bostons and, under today's rules, possibly twenty-one. Foul tips were counted as outs then, no matter how many strikes were on the batter. If a foul tip occurred when the third strike would have, it was not scored as a strikeout. Ivor-Campbell says Sweeney got two such outs in the game. It is not known from the game accounts if they came on third strikes, which would qualify as strikeouts today. If they came earlier in the count, they would be strikes today, not outs, and might have become strikeouts if Sweeney had been allowed to finish pitching to each man.

Ron Necciai: Twenty-seven in Nine Innings

The all-time professional strikeout mark is twenty-seven, by nineteen-year-old Ron Necciai of Bristol in the Class-D Appalachian league on May 13, 1952. It was also a no-hitter, of course. But it was not a perfect game.

MOST STRIKEOUTS, NINE-INNING GAME

Year	Pitcher	SO	Opponent
1986	Roger Clemens	20	Seattle Mariners (.253, finished last)
1884	Hugh Daily	20	Boston, UA (.236)
1884	Charles Sweeney	19	Boston, NL (.254)
1969	Steve Carlton	19	New York Mets (.242, pennant winner)
1970	Tom Seaver	19	San Diego Padres (.246, finished last)
1974	Nolan Ryan	19	Boston Red Sox (.264)
1975	Frank Tanana	19	Texas Rangers (.256)
1884	Dupee Shaw	18	St. Louis, UA (.292)
1884	Henry Porter	18	Boston, UA (.236)
1938	Bob Feller	18	Detroit Tigers (.272)
1940	Leon Day	18	Baltimore Elites (Negro League)
1959	Sandy Koufax	18	San Francisco Giants (.261)
1962	Sandy Koufax	18	Chicago Cubs (.253)
1968	Don Wilson	18	Cincinnati Reds (.273, led majors)
1976	Nolan Ryan	18	Chicago White Sox (.255)
1978	Ron Guidry	18	California Angels (.259)
1980	Bill Gullickson	18	New York Mets (.257)

Ron, a gangling 6-foot, 5-inch right-hander, now a partner in a sporting goods firm outside Pittsburgh, says he actually faced thirty-one batters. His catcher dropped one third strike, his shortstop made an error, and he walked one man and hit another. The twenty-eighth out was a grounder. He says he struck out the first thirteen men in a row, setting a record that still stands.

In his next start, Ron pitched a 24-strike-out two-hitter. In 43 innings with Bristol, he struck out 109 men.

Promoted to Burlington, North Carolina, he struck out eleven straight men to break former Congressman Vinegar Bend Mizell's league record. That led to a shot with the Pittsburgh Pirates, where he won only one game and lost six for the last-place Bucs, with an ERA of 7.08. Necciai says he struck out 312 men in three leagues that year.

The next summer he had arm trouble, which forced him out for two years. He tried a comeback in 1955 but finally gave up.

Will anyone ever tie his record? Walter Johnson reputedly struck out all twenty-seven hitters in a high school game.

"I keep thinking some day some kid's going to do it," Necciai says. "But as time goes on, it gets tougher and tougher. Kids [batters] get bigger, stronger, better athletes. It's been thirty-four years now." And Ron Necciai gives a philosophical shrug.

Extra-inning Games

The most whiffs in an extra-inning major-league game are twenty-one by the Washington Senators' Tom Cheney in 1962 in a sixteen-inning game. (Number 21 was Dick Williams, a .247 hitter who soon after that decided to take up managing instead.) Cheney incidentally went through eight straight hitless innings, from the eighth to the sixteenth. Yet for the year he struck out only 147 men and ended with a 7–9 won–lost record for tenth-place Washington. His big-league won-lost record was 19–29.

MOST CONSECUTIVE STRIKEOUTS

Year	Pitcher	SO	SO/Season	W–L	ERA
1970	Tom Seaver	10	283	18–12	2.81
1884	Mickey Welch	9	345	39–21	2.50
1884	Charles Buffinton	8	417	47–16	2.15
1885	Ed Cushman (UA)*	8	47	4–0	1.00
1953	Max Surkont	8	168	11–5	4.18
1963	Jim Maloney	8	265	23–7	2.77
1963	Johnny Podres	8	196	14–12	3.54
1972	Nolan Ryan	8	284	19–16	2.28
1973	Nolan Ryan	8	326	21–16	2.87
1986	Roger Clemens	8	238	24–4	2.48
1986	Jim Deshaies	8	128	12–5	3.25

*Cushman never had a winning record for a full season; he lost twenty games in 1885, 1886, and 1890.

WORLD SERIES STRIKEOUT RECORDS

Year	Pitcher	SO	Opponent
1906	Ed Walsh	12	Chicago Cubs (.262, led league)
1929	Howard Ehmke	13	Chicago Cubs (.303)
1953	Carl Erskine	15	New York Yankees (.273, led league)
1963	Sandy Koufax	15	New York Yankees (.252)
1968	Bob Gibson	17	Detroit Tigers (.235)

MOST STRIKEOUTS, EXTRA-INNING GAMES

Year	Pitcher	SO	Innings	Opponent
1930	Joe Williams	27	12	Kansas City Monarchs (Negro league)
1962	Tom Cheney	21	16	Baltimore Orioles (.248)
1917	Joe Williams	20	10	New York Giants (.261; no-hitter)
1968	Luis Tiant	19	10	Minnesota Twins (.237)
1974	Nolan Ryan	19	12	Boston Red Sox (.264)
1974	Nolan Ryan	19	11	Detroit Tigers (.247)
1977	Nolan Ryan	19	10	Toronto Blue Jays (.252)

Smokey Joe Williams, in the Negro leagues, holds the all-time record, striking out twenty-seven Kansas City Monarchs over twelve innings in 1930.

All Star Game Strikeouts

Carl Hubbell struck out six of the greatest hitters in history in succession in the All Star game of 1935: Babe Ruth, Lou Gehrig,

Carl Hubbell

Jimmy Foxx, Al Simmons, Joe Cronin, and Bill Dickey.

The two starting lineups for the game contained seventeen future Hall of Famers (only Wally Berger of the National League did not make it). The AL lineup included:

Player	Average	HR
Charlie Gehringer	.339	26
Heinie Manush	.349	11
Babe Ruth	.282	22
Lou Gehrig	.363*	49*
Jimmy Foxx	.334	44
Al Simmons	.344	18
Joe Cronin	.284	7
Bill Dickey	.322	12
Lefty Gomez	.131	0

*Best in major leagues that year.

"We didn't discuss weaknesses (before the game)," Hubbell recalled. "They didn't have any, except Gomez."

Catcher Gabby Hartnett told him to waste everything except the screwball and keep the fastball and curve outside. In the Polo Grounds, with the short foul lines, "we can't let 'em hit it in the air."

Was the All Star game just an exhibition? "They talk about those All Star games being exhibition affairs, and maybe they are," Hub would tell John P. Carmichael in *My Greatest Day in Baseball*. "But I've seen very few players in my life who didn't want to win, no matter whom they were playing. If I'm playing cards for pennies, I want to win. Besides, there were 50,000 fans there, and they wanted to see the best you've got."

Hubbell started the game. Hartnett came to the mound at the beginning of the inning and told him, "Forget about being careful. Just throw your screwball over. Hell, I can't hit it, and neither will they."

Against Gehringer, Hartnett called for a waste pitch, but it was a little too close, and Charlie singled. Down from the stands came a yell, "Take him out!"

Manush was next. Hubbell got two strikes on him, then lost him, with Ruth up next. Infielders Bill Terry, Frank Frisch, and Travis Jackson—all Giants' teammates—converged on the mound and wanted to know if Hub was all right. He assured them that he was, while more fans began calling to take him out before it was too late.

Striking Ruth out was "the last thought in my mind," Carl said; the screwball would not be effective, breaking in as it would toward the left-handed Ruth. Hubbell hoped to make Babe hit it on the ground for a double play. Babe never took the bat off his shoulder. Hub wasted a fastball, then threw three straight screwballs, and Ruth just stood there. "The Babe must have been waiting for me to get the ball up a little, so he could get his bat under it. He always was trying for that one big shot at the stands, and anything around his knees, especially a twisting ball, didn't let him get any leverage.'' Still waiting for a pitch to belt, Babe heard the umpire call strike three. ''You could have knocked me over with a feather,'' Hubbell said. As for Babe, ''it was funny, how he looked. . . . He wasn't mad, he just didn't believe it.''

Gehrig, another lefty, was next, and Hubbell was still thinking DP. ''By golly, he fanned,'' Hub exclaimed—on four pitches, the last one swinging at the screwball. ''You should have heard that crowd.''

As Gehrig passed Foxx in the on-deck circle, he whispered, ''You might as well cut, it won't get any higher.''

Gehringer and Manush pulled a double steal. Now Hubbell was going for the strikeout, and Hartnett did not call for any more waste pitches. Foxx was right-handed, and the left-handed screwball was invented for just this situation. Foxx hit a foul then, said Hubbell, ''I threw three more screwballs, and he went down swinging. We had set down the side on twelve pitches.''

Simmons, another right-hander, led off the second. Earl Averill had told Al to walk up on the pitch. ''Yeah, I walked up on it,'' Simmons muttered. ''I wound up swinging toward right field and looking the catcher in the eye.''

The right-handed Cronin was next, and he too struck out.

Then Dickey, a lefty, stepped to the plate. ''He outsmarted me,'' Hubbell would recall. ''All the other fellows were committing themselves too soon. But he didn't do that.'' Dickey took two strikes and a ball. On the next pitch, ''he just stood flat-footed. He didn't stride at all. Just slapped it to left field.'' That broke the string.

Gomez then whiffed, the sixth strikeout in two innings. (Lefty always complained that he gets left out when the list of illustrious victims is mentioned.)

In the third, Hubbell faced Gehringer, Manush, Ruth, and Gehrig again; he gave up another walk but no hits, then retired. To show that Hubbell had not been taking advantage of patsy batters, the American Leaguers then roused themselves and pounded the next four pitchers—Lon Warneke, Van Mungo, Dizzy Dean, and Fred Frankhouse—for thirteen hits and nine runs. Simmons smacked two doubles and Cronin one.

In 1986 Fernando Valenzuela finally tied the King's record. His victims were: Don Mattingly, hitting .339 at game time; Cal Ripken, Jr., .299; Jesse Barfield, .305; Lou Whitaker, .263; and Teddy Higuera, .000.

Mattingly had just been voted the greatest player in the game by 400 of his peers. It would be lefty against lefty. Val threw a sensational breaking ball that hit the dirt, as

Fernando Valenzuela

Mattingly, completely fooled, lunged at it and missed. With the count at 2–2, Val fed Mattingly a low screwball. Mattingly missed it completely.

Val also started right-hander Cal Ripken, Jr., off with a strike, then two balls and another strike to even the count. The fifth pitch was off the plate to make it a full count. Val went with the screwball as his out pitch again. It was on the inside corner, and Ripken just looked at it.

Barfield was leading the majors at the time in home runs. Undaunted, Val put the first pitch in there again, then, on the 1–2 pitch, threw one low and inside, near the same spot where Ripken had been fooled. Barfield also watched this one break, for strikeout number three.

Whitaker led off the next inning. He had cracked a home run off Dwight Gooden in his previous at-bat. Val followed the same pattern he had with Barfield. He got the first pitch over again, missed with two balls, evened the count with strike two, then threw a third strike over for strikeout number four.

Finally, his fellow countryman, pitcher Teddy Higuera, stepped in. Higuera, the AL pitcher, had not swung a bat since 1981. He did not swing it this time either: Val disdainfully threw three straight strikes and walked off the mound, carrying with him a piece of Carl Hubbell's record.

Hubbell's and Valenzuela's records pale in comparison to the records of Japanese pitchers in their All Star games, however. In the 1971 Japanese All Star game, Yutaka Enatsu pitched three innings, faced nine men, and struck out all nine. In the 1984 game, Suguru Egawa of the Tokyo Giants struck out the first eight men he faced.

5

Endurance

The greatest workhorses of all time were Cy Young and Pud Galvin. Young pitched more innings, 7,377, and more complete games, 756, in 22 years than any other man.

Galvin was second to him with 5,959 innings and 639 CG, in only 14 years. The best of the modern players in CG is Warren Spahn with 382.

MOST INNINGS PITCHED		MOST COMPLETE GAMES	
Pitcher	*IP*	*Pitcher*	*CG*
Cy Young	7,377	Cy Young	756
Pud Galvin	5,959	Pud Galvin	639
Walter Johnson	5,923	Tim Keefe	557
Gaylord Perry	5,352	Kid Nichols	533
Phil Niekro*	5,265	Walter Johnson	532
Warren Spahn	5,246	Hoss Radbourn	489
Grover Alexander	5,188	John Clarkson	485
Kid Nichols	5,067	Tony Mullane	462
Steve Carlton*	5,055	Jim McCormick	466
Tim Keefe	5,043	Gus Weyhing	448

*Still active; figures through 1986.

The biggest single-season workhorses were Will White and Hoss Radbourn.

Year	*Pitcher*	*IP*	*G*	*GS*	*CG*	*W–L*
1879	Will White	680	76	76	76	43–31
1884	Hoss Radbourn	679	75	73	73	60–12

And the most innings pitched in a single season, broken down by old-time and modern pitchers, were by Ed Walsh for the Chicago White Sox in 1908 and Wilbur Wood, also for the White Sox, in 1972.

1901–19

Year	Pitcher	IP
1908	Ed Walsh	464
1904	Jack Chesbro	455
1903	Joe McGinnity	434
1907	Ed Walsh	422
1902	Vic Willis	410
1904	Joe McGinnity	408

1920–PRESENT

Year	Pitcher	IP
1972	Wilbur Wood	377
1971	Mickey Lolich	376
1946	Bob Feller	371
1920	Grover Alexander	363
1973	Wilbur Wood	359
1923	George Uhle	358
1922	Red Faber	353
1944	Dizzy Trout	352

OLDTIMERS

Amos Rusie

The record for innings pitched since 1893, when the pitchers' mound was moved back to its present distance, was set by the man who was responsible for moving it back, Amos Rusie. He went 482 innings the first year of the new mound.

A 200-pounder, Rusie pitched 444 innings the following year and added three more seasons with 300 or more before his arm finally gave out.

"The pitchers were under too hard a strain in my day to last many years," Rusie said. "In New York especially the practice

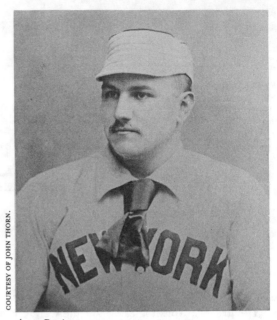

Amos Rusie

prevailed of working a winning pitcher as much as he would stand. The crowd demanded it. I was young. I didn't think my arm would ever wear out, and I even asked to be allowed to work sometimes when not called upon. Later I paid the price."

Rusie, the Nolan Ryan of his day, was washed up at the age of twenty-seven.

Ironman McGinnity

Joe McGinnity was indeed an iron man. He pitched both ends of a doubleheader five times. In his big year, 1903, he started 48 games, completed 44 of them, relieved in 7 others, and pitched a total of 434 innings. He won thirty-two games. It was the fifth season in a row he had gone over 300 innings; the next year he pitched 408 innings and won 35 games, as his club, the Giants, won the pennant.

Joe pitched more than 300 innings for three more years. Even after the Giants let him go at the age of thirty-seven there was

Jack Chesbro

Ed Walsh

still plenty of iron left in his arm. He pitched 400 innings for two years with Newark, winning 29 and 30 games; he pitched 436 innings, the most in his life, with Tacoma at the age of 43, and was still winning at Dubuque in 1925, at the age of 54.

Happy Jack Chesbro

In 1904, Happy Jack Chesbro started fifty-one games for the old New York Highlanders, or about one of every three the team played. He completed forty-eight of them, a modern record, and won forty-one, another record.

Big Ed Walsh

Like Chesbro, Walsh was a spitballer. Big Ed always maintained that the spitter was easy on the arm. Gaylord Perry, the happy spitter of recent years, seemed to bear that out. Picus Jack Quinn, another spitballer, pitched to the age of forty-nine.

In 1908 Walsh pitched like a superman in the White Sox' stretch drive. He hurled every third day for the last month, and in one ten-day stretch was pitching every other day—complete games. In all, he hurled 464 innings and won 40 games. Nobody since then has pitched more.

The following year, Walsh pitched only half as many innings and won only fifteen games, though his ERA was still an excellent 1.41. But he bounced back with three more workhorse years of well over 300 innings, so the hard work in 1908 did not seem to affect him adversely.

In 1912 Ed won twenty-seven and saved ten others. He pitched a league-leading 393 innings.

That October, manager Jim Callahan called on Walsh for some superhuman pitching in the Chicago city series against the Cubs. Ed was twenty-seven years old, in the prime of his powers. He had already pitched 393 innings in the regular season, but the city series was a grudge match, and who else did the White Sox have? Joe Benz was 12–18, Frank Lange 10–10, rookie Eddie Cicotte 9–7, and Doc White 8–9.

On October 9 Walsh opened the series, pitched a one-hit shutout for nine innings, but had to settle for a 0–0 tie. White Sox catcher Ray Schalk called it one of the greatest games he ever saw.

The next day Walsh pitched the final three innings of a twelve-inning tie. That made twelve innings in two days.

The Cubs won the third game over White.

Walsh pitched the fourth game and lost to Ed Reulbach 4–2. He had now pitched 21 innings in four days.

The Cubs won the fifth game over Cicotte, to put them ahead three games to nothing.

Both clubs packed their bags before the sixth game. Walsh would go again—"he was all we had left," Schalk told Lloyd Lewis in *My Greatest Day in Baseball*. Big Ed went eleven innings to win. That was thirty-two innings in six days.

The Sox won the seventh game 7–5.

They still packed their bags for game eight, but the White Sox won it 8–5, Ed Walsh pitching the final inning to make thirty-three innings in eight days.

Now it was the ninth and final game. Of course it would be Ed Walsh again. "I'll always see him," Schalk said, "a great, handsome figure of a man, with shoulders like a schoolhouse, dark face, sharp eyes, smashing that spitter in there, snapping his arm to make it sink past the bat, pitching harder and harder as we got near the end of the long game in what had been the longest drawn-out postseason series."

The Sox scored early and often, but still Walsh would not let them take him out.

"No, indeed. He not only stayed out there, but he kept pouring it through harder and harder the further he went. He was out to get even with the Cubs. He was out to humiliate them, rub their noses to the dust. He wanted a shutout."

He got it, 16–0 on five hits, none after the fifth inning. Walsh had pitched forty-two innings in nine days, giving up twenty-four hits and eight runs. When the last batter rolled out, the fans mobbed him.

But that was all for Big Ed. The next year his arm went bad. "It wasn't sore or anything," he said. "Just tired." He asked owner Charlie Comiskey for a year off to rest, but Comiskey would not hear of it. That season Walsh pitched only ninety-seven innings and won eight games. By 1914 he was down to forty-two innings and two wins.

(Walter Johnson thought the real explanation for Walsh's ruined career lay in his many relief appearances: seventeen in 1908, nineteen in 1911, a league-leading twenty-one in 1912.)

The new Federal League offered Walsh $75,000 to jump to them, but Comiskey had ruined his arm, and Big Ed had to turn the offer down. He won only three more games the rest of his life.

(Two other durable oldsters: Lefty George, who ended his big-league career in 1918 at the age of thirty-two, was still pitching minor-league ball in 1943 at the age of fifty-seven. Nick Altrock pitched in the majors until age forty-seven and pinch-hit for the Senators at the age of fifty-six—he got a triple.)

MODERN PITCHERS

The game has changed radically since Iron Man, Happy Jack, and Big Ed were young. Pitchers cannot coast now; every pitch is

CONSECUTIVE COMPLETE GAMES SINCE 1920					
Pitcher	*CG*	*Years*	*Pitcher*	*CG*	*Years*
Lyons	28	1941–46	L. Benton	17	1928
Roberts	28	1952–53	Alexander	16	1921
Lucas	27	1931–32	Marichal	16	1968
Langford	20	1980	Tanana	14	1977

potential disaster in the rabbit-ball era. And now there is the bull pen: Pitchers work every fifth day and throw as hard as they can for five innings, followed by two relievers who throw as hard as they can for the last four. Any manager who tried to use one workhorse the way the White Sox used Walsh would not stay up very long.

The lighter workload is a result of many factors. Night ball; coast-to-coast jet lag; new breaking-ball pitches, which are harder on the arm; fewer days off in the schedule— all these things make it hard to be an iron man today. Then too, a 1908 inning was an easier inning than a 1980 inning. Walsh, McGinnity, and the others could let the eighth and ninth men hit the ball, confident it would stay in play. Now even Bucky Dent can end your whole season with one swing. The old-time managers used a five-man pitching staff. Now managers have ten men they can bring in when needed. And a lot of the oldtimers' complete games were actually losses. Today's managers will not— and do not have to—stick with a starter when the other team is starting to hit him. Today's pitchers could throw fifty-eight complete games, just as today's Olympic athletes can do anything their grandfathers could. But it is a losing tactic to leave the starter in too long. Now the strategy is to get an early lead and call in the bull-pen aces to save it.

Since 1917 only two men have pitched more than 375 innings—Mickey Lolich, with 376 in 1971, and Wilbur Wood, with 377 in 1972. Significantly, Wood was a knuckleballer. Hoyt Wilhelm and Phil Niekro were two other knuckleballers who just kept rolling along.

Warren Spahn topped the moderns with twelve seasons of twenty complete games or more. (Cy Young is the all-time leader, with sixteen.) In twenty-four years Spahn had only one sore arm.

Ted Lyons completed more than 73 percent of his starts; in 1942, at the age of forty-one, he completed all twenty games he started, although he pitched only once a week. Lyons was followed by Wes Ferrell, who finished 70 percent of what he began.

PACING

Some great pitchers learned to pace themselves. Outfielder Paul Hines, who played with Hoss Radbourn in 1884, when Hoss had his sixty-victory year, said, "Rad had plenty of speed, but he never let it loose until it was absolutely necessary. That's why his arm lasted for so many years."

Cy Young was another one who could pace himself. He gave up an average of almost a hit an inning throughout his career. But he won 510 games by bearing down when it counted.

Christy Mathewson preached holding something in reserve for when it was needed most. Sportswriter Fred Lieb once saw him pitch a fourteen-hit shutout. Matty got the first two men in each of the first seven innings, gave up a hit or two, then got the last out. He had plenty left in the eighth and ninth and retired the last six men in order. John McGraw once blew up at him for losing a big lead late in the game. "Don't worry," Matty laughed, and struck out the side.

Walter Johnson agreed with Matty. "I never go at top speed except when it comes to the pinch," he said.

Red Ruffing used to pace himself, Bob Feller said. He would win by scores of 7–5, 2–1, whatever it took. Modern pitchers like Nolan Ryan should do the same, Feller said. But, Bob admitted, "in the old days the ball was softer, you didn't have to pitch so fine. You could throw 70 to 90 pitches, you didn't have to throw 125 to 140. You could stay well under 100, pitch more often, with less wear and tear."

On the other hand, the young Tom Seaver pitched all-out. Like Nolan Ryan, he was accused of trying for perfection every time out, and his teammates complained that he didn't have much left in September. When the Mets won the 1973 pennant with a 29–14 stretch drive, Seaver's contribution was only four won and four lost in that period.

After moving to the Cincinnati Reds, Seaver, at the age of thirty-six, learned to pace himself. The secret, he said, was to "pitch within yourself." He is still winning games at the age of forty-one.

REST

How much rest should a pitcher have? Three days used to be standard. Dazzy Vance could not pitch in the majors until he found a manager, Wilbert Robinson, who would give him four. Now four is standard.

A few can pitch with two days' rest, at least for short periods, like the last week of a pennant race or the World Series. A very few, like Wilbur Wood of the White Sox, could do it regularly. In 1971 he won twenty-two games; fourteen came with only two days' rest. But then Wood threw the knuckleball, which, like the spitter, is a godsend to pitchers' arms.

Too much rest, on the other hand, is bad. Gaylord Perry, a spitballer, hated the five-day rotation. So did Warren Spahn. Many pitchers have chafed on the bench or in the bull pen, pleading for more work. Sparky Lyle said that when his arm got too strong, his slider did not break sharply. Control is no longer razor sharp. Fastballs tend to come in too high. When the arm gets tired, the pitches behave correctly again.

Mets' pitching coach Mel Stottlemyre says finesse pitchers Ron Darling and Bob Ojeda can get by on three days' rest but insists that his power pitchers, Dwight Gooden and Sid Fernandez, need four. As a result, everyone has to have four days too.

But the power pitchers of the past disagree with him. Walter Johnson, for example, thought the four-day rotation was just right.

"I don't think the rest had anything to do with it," Bob Feller told us. "Three days' rest is enough. Two is okay." Like Johnson, Bob sometimes relieved in the middle day between starts.

"When you get too much rest," wrote Sandy Koufax, "your arm seems strong at the beginning, but your control tends to be haphazard, and the bottom falls out on you in the middle of the game."

Nolan Ryan, who pitched in both four-day and five-day rotations, prefers four; at the age of thirty-eight, he conceded an occasional extra day's rest might be okay.

Weather can be a factor in rests. Ted Lyons of the old White Sox pitched a twenty-one-inning game once but said it did not take as much out of him as some nine-inning games at 100 degrees in St. Louis. Gene Conley agreed: "You lose from twelve to fifteen pounds, and for the next two days you feel sick." (With night baseball, of course, the average summer temperature at game time is probably 10 to 20 degrees less than in the old days.)

CONDITIONING

How much conditioning does a pitcher need? The question has been a subject of heated debate for a century. Conley, who went from baseball to pro basketball, says basketball players are in much better shape than baseball players, and have to be, constantly running up and down the court. (When outfielder Tom Brown went from the Washington Senators to the Green Bay Packers, he was the object of derision for the bad shape he was in.)

Pitchers, and pitching coaches, are sharply divided over how much work a pitcher needs. Johnny Sain, Art Fowler, and Satchel Paige never believed in running. As Sain and Satch said, you do not run the ball over the plate; if you did, Jesse Owens would win twenty games. Paige's advice for exercising properly was "rising gently up and down on the bench."

"The reason I don't like running," Fowler explained, "is that it tires me out." Denny McLain agreed. "The only thing running and exercise do is make you healthy," he said.

But the traditional wisdom is to run pitchers back and forth across the outfield. Seaver subscribes to it. The legs are the key to pitching, he says; they are the biggest muscles in the body, "and legs are solely the product of blood, sweat, and conditioning."

Lyons agreed. "It's not the arm, it's the legs. When they start to get weak, you don't get the ball over." Eighty years old in 1985, Lyons was still doing a lot of hunting.

Don Sutton is fanatical about caring for his legs, massaging them regularly. At the age of forty-plus, he is still winning as many games as he had at twenty-five.

A pitcher's legs get tired from lifting them to throw 100 to 120 times a game, says George Bamberger. "You can lose coordination, and that leads to loss of control and sore arms." Within reason, Bamberger claims, "there's no way you can overdo the running and throwing that pitchers do in spring training. The more work you do, the more endurance you will build."

Ray Miller, Bamberger's successor as pitching coach for the Orioles, explains: "For a pitcher to throw a baseball hard, he must drive with his legs. If he doesn't condition his legs by running, then late in a game when his legs start to weaken, he will start throwing high and put stress on his arm."

Mike Marshall, the reliever who also holds a Ph.D. in physiology, jogged four miles a day. When he relieved in his 101st game in 1974, a record, he insisted he was not tired at all.

WEIGHT

Some pitchers, such as Seaver and Koufax, were equally obsessive about their weight in the off-season. But Mickey Lolich and LaMarr Hoyt, two hurlers with straining buttons on their uniforms, are testimony to the fact that you do not have to be in good shape to be a good pitcher. Lolich used to boast that "all the fat guys watch me and say to their wives, 'See? There's a fat guy doing okay. Bring me another beer.'"

Fattest pitcher of all time was Walter "Jumbo" Brown, who was built like a sumo wrestler, at 6 feet, 4 inches and (officially) 295 pounds. However, in twelve years, from 1932 to 1941, Brown won only thirty-three games with the Yankees and Giants.

Jumbo's Yankee teammate, Lefty Gomez, a slender 170 pounds, won twenty-one and twenty-four games in his first two years with the Yankees. They urged him to put on thirty pounds over the winter and promised he would make them forget Lefty Grove. He did and won sixteen games the next year. Another season like that, he said, "and I'll make them forget Lefty Gomez."

PAIN

A big problem pitchers face is just plain pain, that is, sore arms.

Sandy Koufax's arm would puff up the day after a game. "I could see it blow up." When he tried to move it, "it sounded as if I were squeezing a soggy sponge." Just combing his hair was "a very gritty" experience.

Steve Barber of the Orioles compared pain to colors. On bad days his arm felt bright red; less bad was hot pink. In *Ball Four* Jim Bouton compared his own sore arm to a toothache in the biceps.

Randy Jones recalled the day his arm snapped after he had won twenty-two games and seemed on the way to thirty. A nerve was severed, and "my arm began to shrink. It just withered. There was no muscle, no bicep."

"Your arm is your best friend," said Tom Seaver, "but you've got to treat it like it was your worst enemy. It'll get you if it can." Seaver would change his plane seat if his right arm was under the air-conditioning. He could not sleep on his right side, waking instinctively if he did roll over onto it.

The human arm was not meant to throw

baseballs. Ancient cavemen took a stick and clubbed their prey to death, Bob Gibson once told John Holway; they did not throw rocks at it. If anything, doctors say, throwing underhand is more natural than overhand. The arm is designed to hang down.

The lower arm turns inward at the elbow; screwballers must bend it outward. Carl Hubbell had a permanently bent arm after a while, but even fastballers like Seaver usually cannot straighten their arms.

"Pitching is an unnatural and harmful act," said Dr. Anthony Saraniti of the Sports Medicine Institute in New York. Pitching creates tremendous unnatural strains in muscles, joints, bones. Photos of pitchers at the top of their delivery show grotesquely bent arms, as if the elbow had been forced back by some jujitsu hold. Imagine doing that 110 times a game, 5,000 times a year, 80,000 or more times a career!

Throwing 100 fastballs a day ruptures countless minute blood vessels. Curve balls pull tendons and erode the bone in the elbow. Sheer muscle mass impairs circulation. George Medich, who was both a pitcher and a medical student, called it "volume overload." Many pitchers end up, like Whitey Ford, buying tailored shirts with one sleeve longer than the other.

Many pitchers suffer circulation problems. Ford did not have a pulse in his wrist for a year, as blood stopped flowing from the shoulder because of a blocked artery. "My left hand went numb; it just went dead." He finally required surgery.

Koufax rubbed Capsolin, an irritant, on his arm; it whipped up the circulation but almost blistered him in the process.

Milt Wilcox of the Tigers used DMSO, ordinarily used on race horses. It smelled awful and gave him bad breath, but he was 8–6 before DMSO, 7–1 after it.

Adhesions also form on the muscles over

the winter. Koufax compared them to mucilage spread on a rubber band. When the band is stretched in spring training, the adhesions, which do not stretch, crack and tear away—usually painfully.

Sometimes simple stretching will help. Bobby Shantz hung from the dugout roof between innings. George Uhle won 200 games with mediocre teams in the twenties and thirties by simply stretching his arm behind his head. The Yankees' orthopedist Dr. Maurice Cowens put Catfish Hunter under anesthesia, Sparky Lyle says in *The Bronx Zoo*, and stretched his pitching arm to break the adhesions. The treatment worked for a while, and Cat threw some good games in 1978.

BIOMECHANICS

Not only the amount of throwing needs to be studied, but also the technique. Oddly, a major-league owner, who has paid upward of $40 million for his franchise, will not protect his most valuable assets, his players, by applying the growing science of biomechanics to his business. The U.S. Olympic team has a sophisticated biomechanics department in Colorado Springs, applying the principles of engineering to everything from a shot-putter's heave to a marathon runner's stride. Slow-motion films and the most sophisticated modern equipment are focused on the athletes. A small flaw in a marathon runner's pattern of placing his foot can, after twenty-six miles, lead to a permanent, career-ending injury. The USOC has professors all over the country doing research for it. Yet baseball has not tapped into this knowledge. Ted Williams and Charlie Lau could debate long and loudly whether to hit off the front foot or the back foot, but no one has ever tried to focus scientific light on the debate.

This is slowly changing. "By looking at films and studying videotape, we can now predict where or when an injury will occur to a pitcher's arm," Dr. Saraniti said. The Orioles film every pitcher and every pitch from two angles in every game.

SPORTS MEDICINE

One of the tragedies of pitching history is that modern medicine was not ready to help Sandy Koufax when he needed it. He was thirty years old in April 1966, at the height of his powers, when the team doctor told him it would be his last season or he risked permanent injury to his arm. He had bone spurs in his elbow and took cortisone shots continuously just to endure the pain and get through the year. Today doctors could have performed arthroscopic surgery, a common procedure, over the winter and had him back in action in the spring.

A tougher problem is the rotator cuff, four muscles that can be torn away from the bone of the upper arm. Many pitchers had their careers ended with it: Don Drysdale, Ron Perranoski, Wayne Garland, Steve Busby, Don Gullett, and Jim Bibby. Drysdale had masked the pain with medication instead of getting treatment early. He was so doped up, sometimes he could not even read the scoreboard. Not until Roberto Clemente almost killed him with a batted ball did Don decide to get help. By then it was too late.

Tommy John had a 13–3 record in July 1974 and seemed headed for twenty victories and the Cy Young award, when the pain in his arm from a torn ligament drove him to consult Dr. Frank Jobe, who had operated successfully on basketball stars Wilt Chamberlain, Jerry West, and Elgin Baylor. Jobe removed a ligament from John's right arm and reconstructed it around his left (pitching) elbow. There followed a year of rehabilitation—ice packs alternating with almost scalding hot water, ultrasound, and massages.

After a year out of the game, John came back to win ten and lose ten in 1976. The next year he was 20–7. In all, John pitched (through 1986) eleven years after coming off the operating table and won 140 games—more than he had won in the twelve years before the operation. In fact, he was a better pitcher with his new arm, going 124–106 before the surgery and 141–104 afterward.

John laughed that his body was almost forty, but his arm was only five. He also laughed that he had told Jobe to "put in a Koufax fastball. He did, but it was Mrs. Koufax's."

Baltimore's reliever Don Aase submitted to the same operation, the first power pitcher to come back from such an injury.

Helpful though it may be, one has to question the ethics of surgery—and the ethics of pitching to the point of needing surgery. Any activity that requires a human being deliberately to abuse a valuable part of his body is essentially immoral. What is the difference between surgery to regain a competitive edge and the use of steroids to give an Olympic weight lifter an edge? Both give the user an unfair advantage. Both are unnatural and harmful to the body.

Jobe and other specialists now discourage surgery and stress prevention in the form of exercise. Perranoski, now the Dodger's pitching coach, has all his pitchers doing exercise.

But the problem is to get the pitcher to ask for help. Not one of the 1981 workhorse Oakland Athletics' hurlers—all later afflicted by sore arms—blames manager Billy Martin or coach Art Fowler for his subsequent miseries. Each admits he had been pitching in pain and blames himself for not heeding the danger signals earlier.

"There's only one cure for what's wrong with all of us pitchers," Jim Palmer said, "and that's to take a year off. Then, after you've gone a year without throwing, quit altogether."

That day comes sooner or later to every pitcher.

Even Cy Young's rubber arm finally gave out, at the age of forty-five. He had slowed down to a 4–5 record the year before, then in the spring of 1912 admitted to catcher Johnny Kling, "It's no use, John; the arm feels like a pump handle."

It was time at last to pay for those 510 victories.

THE SURVIVORS

Satchel Paige

In spite of all the hazards, some pitchers do survive into ripe middle age.

Satchel Paige pitched three innings of shutout baseball for the Kansas City A's in 1965 at the age of fifty-nine, the oldest man ever to play, let alone pitch, in a big-league game. (Nick Altrock once came to bat at the age of fifty-seven as an end-of-season stunt.) Satch pitched the three innings so he could draw a pension, but they were big-league innings. He gave the ninth-place Red Sox only one hit, walked none, and struck out one.

The question of Satchel's exact age was more a shrewd publicity gag than a legitimate question. We have no trouble accepting the 1906 date usually given for his birth. He broke into the Negro minor leagues with Chattanooga in 1925, when he would have been nineteen, and made the black majors with Birmingham the next year.

Thus Paige was forty-two when Bill Veeck gave him a job on the Indians. "Everybody kept telling me he was through," Veeck said. "That was understandable. They thought he was human.'' Satch rewarded Bill with six victories against one defeat as the Indians won the pennant in a playoff. Later, when Veeck took over the St. Louis Browns, he found a job for Satch there too, giving him his own easy chair in the bull pen. Satch was forty-seven then.

Actually, Paige said cheerfully, he never could have pitched that long in the Negro leagues, because they would have bunted on him. Inexplicably, the white hitters did not think of that.

If Satch's twenty-one years in the black major leagues are added to his six in the white majors, he is by far the all-time champ in years pitched, with twenty-seven. It is a mark that may endure as long as the legend of Satchel will. (To be a purist about it, the black leagues folded for several years during the Depression, and Paige had to pitch semi-pro ball in North Dakota and Latin America. But it was not his fault that there was no league to pitch in.)

Picus Jack Quinn

Of all the men who have grown old gracefully while pitching, perhaps none are more remarkable than Phil Niekro and Hoyt Wilhelm—two knuckleballers—and Picus Jack Quinn, the old spitballer. These men demonstrated that the knuckler and the spitter are indeed the survivors.

Who today has heard of Quinn, the Pennsylvania coalminer who won 247 big-league games, the last three at the age of forty-eight? When the ballots for Cooperstown are counted, Quinn always gets overlooked, but he enjoyed a remarkable career and pitched twenty-three years in all, from 1909 to 1933.

As a youngster, Picus Jack was trapped in a coal-mine fire and staggered through smoke to escape. He used to sharpen his control by trap shooting. In 1930, at the age

of forty-seven, he became the oldest man ever to pitch in a World Series and six years later was still throwing them over the plate in the minor leagues.

Eleven Tough Old Birds

Jim Kaat is next to Paige in longevity, with twenty-five years of big-league pitching. Quinn had twenty-three. Phil Niekro also had twenty-three at the end of the 1986 season. Early Wynn would have had twenty-three too if he had not spent 1945 in the service. Starting as a nineteen-year-old with Washington in 1939, he was still pitching in 1963, when he finally won his 300th game. The eleven toughest old birds in the game in terms of total years pitching were:

Pitcher	Years	Ages
Satchel Paige	27*	21–65
Jim Kaat	25	20–44
Early Wynn	25†	19–43
Warren Spahn	24‡	21–44
Herb Pennock	23†	18–40
Jack Quinn	23*	25–49
Phil Niekro	23	25–46
Cy Young	22	23–44
Gaylord Perry	22	23–44
Sam Jones	22†	21–42
Eppa Rixey	22	21–42
Grover Alexander	20†	22–43
Bobo Newsom	20*	21–45

*Not continuous.
†Includes one year of military service.
‡Includes three years of military service.

Again, the knuckleballers and spitballers predominate.

Smokey Joe Williams

One should really add fastballer Smokey Joe Williams to the list. Joe's career spanned twenty-four years, from 1909 to 1933. He had pitched with local teams around Texas before that.

He said he was trying to beat Ironman McGinnity's record of pitching until fifty-four in the minors. To keep in shape, he said he ate little meat and lots of vegetables, especially spinach.

There was a dispute over Williams' true age—in fact, that was where Paige got the idea of making a mystery out of his own age. Joe said he was born in 1876, which would have made him thirty-three when he got to the big time and fifty-seven when he finally retired. This is the age the Grays publicized, but it is hard to credit. Our own research indicates Joe was probably born in 1885, according to a baptismal record, or 1886, the date on his marriage license, making him a mere child of forty-six when he quit.

Oldies and Goodies

These men all grew old gracefully. Quinn pitched in the World Series at the age of forty-seven, Jim Kaat at the age of almost forty-four. Gaylord Perry won the Cy Young award at forty. Spahn and Sal Maglie pitched no-hitters at thirty-eight. At the same age, Steve Carlton worked 283 innings. At thirty-eight Fat Freddy Fitzsimmons set the National League won–lost record (since broken by Roy Face) of 16–2.

Through 1986, Phil Niekro had won 114 games after passing his fortieth birthday. Quinn is next, with eighty-nine after forty. Niekro has more innings pitched, strikeouts, and walks than any graybeard after blowing forty candles out on his cake.

Some other robust oldsters after forty: Cy Young, 119 complete games and fifteen shutouts, and Hoyt Wilhelm, 459 games, 115 saves, and a 2.11 ERA.

Gaylord Perry for one thinks Spahn should have gone on for several more years. They were teammates on the San Francisco Giants in Warren's last year. "He was forty-four and still a good pitcher," Perry said, but "no one gave him a chance to pitch again."

Luis Tiant was still pitching when well over the age of forty, according to his official age—his real age may have been even greater. His secret was having the trainer rub a mixture of linaments, honey, and marijuana onto his arm before each game. It may or may not have been good for the arm, but the trainer spent the rest of the day sitting around with a happy smile on his face.

PITCHERS BY AGES

At the young end of the scale, eighteen-year-old John Montgomery Ward won twenty-two games in 1878 and forty-seven the year after that. In 1985, twenty-year-old Dwight Gooden became the youngest pitcher ever to win the Cy Young award, beating record-holder Fernando Valenzuela by fifteen days. That same year Bret Saberhagen, twenty-one, became the youngest to win in the American League, edging out Vida Blue, who also was twenty-one when he received the award, by about nine months.

What is the optimum age for baseball greatness? We have checked the records of the twentieth-century pitchers and compiled the five best men at each age in victories and strikeouts.

(A word of caution: Many players probably fib about their ages. Jim Bouton tells of one "nineteen-year-old phenom," Rollie Sheldon, who upon investigation turned out to be a three-year air force veteran with three years of college. He was actually twenty-six. But if he had told the scouts his real age, "he never would have had a chance." After Jackie Robinson's signing, many a Negro league veteran told the scouts he was three or four years younger than he really was.)

Following are the greatest pitchers of all time by age. (On birthdays, we follow an arbitrary rule. For all men born before July 4, we use the age at the end of the season. For all born July 5 and after, we use the age at the beginning of the season. This works reasonably well in most cases. But three problems are Jack Quinn, Hoyt Wilhelm, and Frank Tanana. Jack was born July 5, Hoyt, July 23, and Frank, July 3. The reader is at liberty to adjust the charts accordingly if desired.)

WINS BY AGE, 1900–86

Age	Pitcher	Wins
16	McKee	1
17	Feller	5
	Miller	1
	Skeels	1
18	Feller	9
	V. McDaniel	7
	Dierker	7
	R. Wise	5
	Brillheart	4
	Clyde	4
19	Bunker	19
	Bender	17
	Feller	17
	Gooden	17
	Palmer	15
20	Feller	24
	Gooden	24
	Mathewson	20
	P. Dean	19
	Ruth	18
	Lush	18
21	Feller	27
	Marquard	24
	Hendrix	24
	Blue	24
	Ruth	23

Age	Pitcher	Wins
22	Wood	34
	Mathewson	30
	Marquard	26
	James	26
	Johnson	25
	Feller	25
	Ferrell	25
23	Mathewson	33
	J. Dean	29
	Newhouser	29
	Willis	27
	Gomez	26
24	Johnson	32
	Mathewson	31
	McLain	31
	J. Dean	28
	Alexander	28
	Uhle	26
25	Johnson	36
	Hendrix	29
	Roberts	28
	Walsh	25
26	Johnson	28
	Rudolph	27
	Willis	27
	Mays	27
	Cheney	26
27	Walsh	40
	Mathewson	37
	Coombs	31
	Alexander	27
	Johnson	27
	Uhle	27
28	Alexander	31
	Mullin	29
	Chesbro	28
	Coombs	28
	Shocker	27
	White	27
29	Alexander	33
	McGinnity	29
	Walsh	27
	Mathewson	27
	Mays	27

Age	Pitcher	Wins	Age	Pitcher	Wins
	Walters	27	38	Spahn	21
	Trout	27		Chandler	20
30	Chesbro	41		Young	18
	Bagby	31		Adams	17
	Alexander	30		Leonard	17
	Grove	28	39	Wynn	22
	Walsh	27		Plank	21
	Brown	27		Spahn	21
	Newcombe	27		G. Perry	21
	Koufax	27		P. Niekro	19
31	Grove	31	40	Young	22
	Brown	29		Alexander	21
	Vance	28		Spahn	21
	Walsh	27		P. Niekro	21
	Six with 26			Plank	16
32	McGinnity	31		Seaver	16
	Bagby	31	41	Young	21
	Brown	27		Spahn	18
	Luque	27		Alexander	15
	Five with 25			P. Niekro	15
33	McGinnity	35		Lyons	14
	Cicotte	28	42	Spahn	23
	Vance	28		Young	19
	Alexander	27		Quinn	10
	Hubbell	26		Faber	10
	Crowder	26		Dickson	10
34	Young	33	43	P. Niekro	17
	Grimes	25		Quinn	15
	Crowder	24		Wilhelm	10
	Six with 23			G. Perry	10
35	Young	32		Spahn	8
	Cicotte	29	44	Quinn	18
	McGinnity	27		P. Niekro	11
	Crowder	24		Wilhelm	8
	Carlton	24		Spahn	7
36	Young	28		Kaat	5
	Plank	26	45	P. Niekro	16
	Johnson	23		Paige	12
	Alexander	22		Quinn	11
	Roe	22		Wilhelm	7
37	Young	27		Newsom	2
	McConnell	25	46	P. Niekro	16
	Carlton	23		Quinn	9
	Vance	22		Wilhelm	6
	Spahn	22			

Age	Pitcher	Wins
	Paige	3
47	P. Niekro	11
	Quinn	5
48	Quinn	3

Before 1900 pitchers came up to the big leagues sooner and often matured sooner. Fred Chapman pitched a complete game for the 1887 Phillies at the age of fourteen; Willie McGill won eleven games at the age of sixteen (and twenty at the age of seventeen); at age nineteen Amos Rusie was a twenty-nine-game winner and John Montgomery Ward had an astounding 47–17 at that age.

STRIKEOUTS BY AGE

Age	Pitcher	Number of Strikeouts
16	Murphy	16
	Derrington	3
17	Murphy	42
	Feller	17
	Derrington	14
	Miller	9
	Dierker	5
18	Feller	150
	Dierker	109
	Clyde	74
	Gumbert	52
	M. McCormick	50
19	Gooden	76
	Feller	240
	Nolan	206
	Blyleven	135
	Bender	172
20	Gooden	268
	Feller	246
	Blyleven	224
	Mathewson	215
	Holzman	171
21	Blue	301
	Feller	261
	Valenzuela	240
	Marquard	237
	Wood	231
22	McDowell	325

Age	Pitcher	Number of Strikeouts
	Johnson	313
	Blyleven	269
	Mathewson	267
	Feller	260
23	Maloney	265
	Score	263
	Tanana	261
	Blyleven	249
	Drysdale	246
24	Johnson	303
	McLain	279
	Jenkins	260
	Lonborg	246
	McDowell	236
25	Ryan	329
	McDowell	283
	Seaver	283
	Newhouser	275
	Soto	274
26	Ryan	383
	Waddell	301
	Seaver	289
	McDowell	279
	Jenkins	274
27	Ryan	367
	Waddell	349
	Feller	348
	Carlton	310
	Koufax	306
28	Richard	303
	Waddell	286
	Lolich	271
	Tiant	264
	Seaver	251
29	Koufax	381
	Ryan	327
	Richard	313
	Veale	276
	Gibson	270
30	Ryan	341
	Koufax	317
	Lolich	308
	Walsh	255
	Chesbro	239

Age	Pitcher	Number of Strikeouts	Age	Pitcher	Number of Strikeouts
31	M. Scott	303		Carlton	163
	Ryan	260	40	P. Niekro	208
	Walsh	254		Wynn	157
	Lolich	250		Vance	150
	Seaver	235		Young	148
32	Gibson	268		Seaver	134
	Jones	225	41	P. Niekro	176
	Waddell	224		Young	150
	Ryan	223		G. Perry	135
	Bunning	219		Carlton	120
33	Gibson	269		Spahn	118
	Bunning	268	42	Young	109
	Vance	262		Wilhelm	106
	Falkenberg	245		Spahn	102
	G. Perry	234		Wynn	91
34	Gibson	274		Vance	67
	Bunning	252	43	P. Niekro	144
	Ryan	245		Perry	116
	G. Perry	238		Spahn	78
	Seaver	226		Wilhelm	76
35	Carlton	286		Jones	60
	Bunning	253	44	P. Niekro	128
	Ryan	245		Spahn	90
	G. Perry	216		G. Perry	82
	Gibson	185		Wilhelm	72
36	G. Perry	232		Young	55
	Gibson	208	45	P. Niekro	136
	Vance	184		Paige	91
	Young	183		Wilhelm	67
	Ryan	183		Quinn	28
37	Carlton	286		Newsom	16
	Young	203	46	P. Niekro	149
	Vance	200		Wilhelm	68
	Ryan	197		Paige	51
	Wynn	184		Quinn	28
38	Carlton	275		Lyons	10
	Ryan	209	47	P. Niekro	149
	Young	208		Quinn	25
	Wynn	179		Wilhelm	16
	G. Perry	177	48	Wilhelm	8
39	P. Niekro	248		Quinn	3
	Ryan	194	59	Paige	1
	Wynn	179			
	Vance	173			

George Bamberger of the Orioles, Brewers, and Mets said he liked his pitchers to go for complete games. "It gives the staff pride and makes those pitchers stronger as the season wears on. It gives them more stamina, so they get tougher in the late innings when they have to go the route. I use the bull pen only when I have to. If the pitcher on the mound is any good, I keep him there for as long as I can. After all, you know what he has, but you don't know what the reliever has on a particular day."

Lefty Gomez knew the end was near when someone asked him, "Are you throwing as hard as ever?" "Yeah," he replied, "I'm throwing just as hard, but the ball isn't getting there as fast." It was Gomez who once said the Yankees' bull pen was so old they ought to keep a priest out there.

THE DANGERS OF OVERWORK

Do today's owners and managers ruin their pitchers by demanding too much?

Catfish Hunter won twenty games for five seasons in a row, joining Walter Johnson and Lefty Grove, the only other two men to do it. He was one of the youngest men ever to win 100 games. In his first year with the Yankees, he pitched 30 complete games and 323 innings, the most by any Yankee in half a century.

And then his arm gave out.

In 1976 Cat fell victim to injuries and had his worst year since 1969.

Writing in the *Sporting News* in 1977, Leonard Koppett wondered if Hunter was not destroyed by overwork by greedy owners in Oakland and New York.

Koppett observed that Cat had enjoyed magnificent years in Oakland with a strong bull pen to relieve him after seven hard innings. But, in the tough pennant drive of 1974, Oakland worked him harder than ever. The Yankees obtained him in 1975 at a then record salary, and George Steinbrenner wanted his money's worth. Hunter could bring in the customers, and he could bring the Yanks a pennant.

Too much work for two years straight is risking a letdown the third year or possibly even a curtailed career, Koppett wrote. Complete games are significant, because the strain and therefore the danger is much greater in the last couple of innings than in the first seven. Ray Miller, Baltimore's pitching coach, agrees that most injuries come late in the game.

Miller's predecessor on the Orioles, George Bamberger, had the opposite philosophy. He believed complete games gave a pitcher pride and stamina. It's true that the Orioles racked up a record number of Cy Young awards with strong starters who completed their games. But there is a difference between working a pitcher hard and working him too hard. Under manager Earl Weaver, Bamberger's pitchers worked hard. When Bamberger became his own manager with the Mets and Brewers, he may have worked his hurlers too hard. None of his teams were winners.

Some other case histories:

Bob Feller reached 300 innings three times. A strikeout pitcher, he must have thrown about 3,000 pitches each year. He was finished as a big winner at the age of thirty-two. It might have been sooner if he had not had a forced four-year rest during World War II.

Brooklyn was notorious for sore arms.

Branch Rickey pushed pitchers hard in Florida. One of his managers, Charlie Dressen, objected. It is too easy to develop sore arms in the spring, he said. Many an arm has been left in Florida in April.

Cy Young agreed. He called spring training "the most exquisite agony."

Roger Craig got his big-league start because of all the sore arms on the Dodgers' staff. "Back then," he said, "Brooklyn had sixteen farm clubs (today most teams have five), so if some pitcher's arm fell off, they had someone else to take his place."

Joe Page, the Yankee relief ace of the late 1940s, always believed that Casey Stengel had cut Joe's career short by overworking him.

Pitcher Gene Conley with the Braves in the fifties tells of the day he tried a comeback only to get knocked out of the box by a club of minor leaguers. He wandered into a church and sat in the back pew, crying, when he felt an arm on his shoulder.

"What's the matter, son? Did you lose your mother?"

"No sir," Conley said, tears streaming down his cheeks, "I lost my fastball."

Robin Roberts pitched more than 300 innings five times. He had twenty complete games seven times. But Roberts began losing it at the age of twenty-nine. "I can pinpoint the week it happened," in August 1955, he said. It was his sixth straight twenty-victory year. But he never won twenty again. "I never again had the ability with a man on third base to rear back and overpower a hitter. It was just a pitcher's arm. It quits on you after a while."

Chuck Estrada, who later coached the San Diego Padres, said that as a kid with the Orioles under Paul Richards, "I would go out and throw 200 pitches. No one cared. It was not until we started losing our good arms at a very young age that the Orioles started thinking there weren't very many

great arms left. So we don't let that stuff happen any more." Estrada's victories dwindled steadily, from eighteen to fifteen to nine, three, and finally one. He was washed up at twenty-nine.

In 1965 and 1966 Sandy Koufax worked more than 300 innings and completed 25 or more games each year. That was it. He never pitched again, finished at the age of thirty-one.

Juan Marichal had similar stats—more than twenty wins, more than 300 innings—in 1968 and 1969, then fell to a 12–10 record and never was the real Marichal again. He was thirty-two.

In 1968 Denny McLain had that great season when he won thirty-one games, twenty-eight of them complete, and followed it in 1969 with twenty-four wins and twenty-three complete games. The next year his arm was dead. He was twenty-six years old.

Ferguson Jenkins pitched 289 innings or more for five years running, 1967 to 1972, then fell to 14–16 in 1973. He was traded to Texas, which began working him hard again, and pitched .500 ball thereafter.

In 1972 Steve Carlton had his super season with the last-place Phils—346 innings, 30 CGs, a 27–10 mark, and a 1.98 ERA. The next year his complete games were down to eighteen, his wins were cut in half, and his losses and ERA doubled.

David Clyde, a hard-throwing lefty, pitched his first game for the Texas Rangers at the age of seventeen in 1973. One year later he was in the minors with a shoulder impingement. Doctors say he was forced to pitch too hard too soon.

Mickey Lolich pitched 376 innings in 1971 and 1972. He was down to a 16–15 record in 1973.

Rawly Eastwick saved twenty-two games and won two World Series games for the Reds in 1975 at the age of twenty-five. He saved twenty-six more the next year. And that was it. He hung on with five clubs over five years before realizing it was over.

Randy Jones was a workhorse in 1976 and a has-been in 1978.

The Japanese leagues are notorious for destroying pitchers. A hot pitcher is worked every other day in the stretch and the Japan series. Kazuhisa Inao worked more than 300 innings six out of seven years (more than 400 twice), won forty-two, thirty-five, thirty-three, thirty, twenty-eight, twenty-five, twenty-one, and twenty games until he just could not do it any more.

Even youngsters are very vulnerable. Mark Fidrych (19–9, league-leading 2.34 ERA at the age of twenty-one) developed tendonitis and never starred again. He did not know how to pace himself, umpire Ron Luciano believes. "He'd be fabulous for seven innings, then lose it. First his fastball was gone, then his curveball was gone, then he was gone."

Steve Busby pitched two no-hitters in his first season in the majors. He had two more good years before a torn rotator cuff ended his career.

Don Gullett was 16–2 at the age of twenty and enjoyed seven good years with Cincinnati. Disabled with a torn rotator in 1979, he never came back.

Perhaps Fernando Valenzuela was lucky that the players' strike came in his rookie year and prevented overwork. Even so, Fernando is overweight, pitches many complete games, and pitches a screwball, which is notoriously hard on arms. One has to wonder about him having a long career.

Many authorities, such as ex-pitcher Joey Jay of the Reds, blame sore arms on Little League. Boys begin throwing a curve at age eleven. By the time they are out of high school, they have been throwing it for nine or ten years. Several authorities would outlaw curves in Little League and permit the spitter instead. Dr. Peter LaMotte, the former Mets' physician, urged that boys not be allowed to pitch more than two innings until they are over sixteen.

Others blame the big-league teams.

"The future is of no concern to the manager or general manager," John Denny said. "Do you think they were concerned with me burning myself out? I don't think so. There was somebody else to take my place, and there'll be somebody to take his."

Shades of Amos Rusie.

Billy Ball at Oakland

The A's had lost 108 games in 1979. Rick Langford had a 12–16 record, Mike Norris was 5–8, and poor Matt Keough lost his first fourteen games and ended up with a 2–17 mark. Langford led them all with 14 CG and a 4.27 ERA. Norris was so discouraged that he went to work selling used cars for Reggie Jackson in the off-season (he sold one).

Enter Billy Martin and his pitching coach, Art Fowler. With the Yanks they had had Sparky Lyle and then Goose Gossage and Ron Davis in the bull pen. But when they took a look at the A's bull pen, they decided they had better go all the way with their starters. They set up a five-man rotation, gave each man plenty of rest, and told him the game was his to finish, win or lose.

Pitcher Mike Norris described the look on Martin's face when Billy arrived at the mound. "He'd want to say something like, 'Hey, guy, I want you to come out,' but the look said, 'Please don't.' " Martin made the pitcher feel like a sissy if he wanted to quit. He would give Norris a pep talk: "You're my ace, big guy," and, said Mike, "I'd feel ten feet tall."

The pitchers seemed to thrive on it. The A's had the best team ERA in the league and leaped all the way to second place in their division. In all, the club finished ninety-four of its games. Langford (19–12) had twenty-eight complete games, including twenty-two in a row, which may be the most by any man since Bill Dinneen's thirty-seven in 1904. Norris (22–9) had twenty-four, in spite of throwing seventy-five screwballs a game, and Keough (16–13) had twenty.

Overworked? Martin and Fowler scoffed. Langford never threw more than 122 pitches in any of his games (except one fourteen-inning one, of course). Most of the time he was under 100. "Now how's he going to get tired throwing that much?" Fowler demanded.

And they all had plenty of rest between starts. Langford led the league in innings pitched, with 290. "I never got tired," he insisted.

The A's had several factors going for them. First, they probably could not have done it without the d.h. rule, which meant pitchers were not lifted for pinch-hitters in close games (the leading National League club in complete games that year was St. Louis, with 34). Second was the cool climate in Oakland (could they have done it in Texas or Atlanta or Kansas City?). Third, all three were accused of (and Norris admitted) throwing spitters, which are considered easy on the arm.

How did it affect them the following year, the strike-shortened 1981?

Langford again led in CG, with eighteen in the strike-shortened season. He won twelve and lost ten. Steve McCatty, the fourth starter the year before, was right behind him with sixteen and also won the ERA crown. Norris (12–9) had twelve CG. Keough (10–6) had ten. This time the A's finished first in their division.

Maybe Martin and Fowler were onto something.

In 1982 came the collapse. Here's how the A's ironmen did:

	W–L	ERA	CG	IP
Langford	11–16	4.21	15	237 (3rd in league in CG)
Keough	11–18	5.71	10	209 (led league in ER)
Norris	7–11	4.76	7	166
McCatty	6–3	3.99	2	129

The A's finished thirteenth in ERA out of fourteen teams. They completed forty-two games but lost ninety-four and came in fifth in the seven-team division.

By 1983 Martin and Fowler were gone, and Langford could not turn a door knob. His won–lost record was 0–4, he had surgery on his right elbow, and before the end of the year he was in the minors. Keough pitched in pain and ended with 5–7. Norris was 4–5, and McCatty 6–9. McCatty was high man in CG with three.

The next year only McCatty was left; his record was 8–14. The A's completed twenty-two games, twelfth in the league.

Martin and Fowler appeared to be onto something, all right. Whatever it was, they may have ruined the careers of three promising young pitchers.

Baltimore manager Earl Weaver admitted that "relief pitchers today are asked to make more appearances than ever before. So what if he burns his arm out? There are others to take his place."

Actually, Earl was not that cynical in practice, out of self-interest, if nothing else. He carefully charted how often his relievers threw, even if they did not get into the game. He had a rule against letting a reliever warm up more than three days in a row.

> Satchel Paige's prescription for staying young, in addition to "never look back," was:
>
> "Avoid fried meats; they angry the stomach."
>
> "If your stomach disputes you, lie down and pacify it with cool thoughts."
>
> "Keep the juices flowing by jangling around gently as you move."
>
> "Go very light on the vices, such as carrying on in society; the social ramble ain't restful."
>
> "Avoid running at all times."

Most teams also use charts to control how many pitches their hurlers throw. When a man reaches 120, he is usually pulled, no matter what the inning.

In 1985 John Holway asked Mets' general manager Frank Cashen (Weaver's former boss at Baltimore) if he would be tempted to use Dwight Gooden every fourth, or even third, day if the September pennant race got hot. Cashen insisted that he would not. He kept his promise, and it may have cost him the pennant, as the Mets lost the pennant during the stretch to St. Louis by three games.

THE MARATHON BATTLES

Oeschger and Cadore

Joe Oeschger and Leon Cadore battled each other for twenty-six innings one day in 1920—equal to almost three full games—and settled for a 1–1 tie. Oeschger gave up nine hits, Cadore, fifteen. Joe walked only four, Leon just five.

Actually this was Oeschger's second marathon battle in two years. Exactly one year and one day earlier, when he was with the Phils, Oeschger had struggled twenty innings against Burleigh Grimes of the Dodgers and had to settle for an inelegant if courageous tie, 9–9. Thereafter, the Phils let him go to the Giants, who also cut him loose, to the Braves. He ended the 1919 season with a 4–4 record for the three teams combined.

Leon Cadore, like Oeschger, was twenty-seven and had been kicking around for several years, compiling so-so records.

The two—Oeschger with a good fastball and Cadore, the curveballer—started 1920 by hooking up in an eleven-inning duel in April, Cadore winning 1–0.

Then, on a rainy Sunday morning the first of May, Braves manager George Stallings gave Oeschger the ball. Joe was a faithful churchgoer; and Stallings, one of the most superstitious men (as well as one of the cussingest) in baseball annals, wanted every edge he could get.

The Braves scored in the fourth on a walk, an infield out by Cadore, and a two-strike single. The Dodgers came back the next inning with a run on a triple and a single. Then both teams, tired of their offensive exertions, settled down to serious baseball.

In the seventh, Oeschger retired the side on three pitched balls.

In the ninth Cadore filled the bases with one out, but got Charley Pick (.274) on a double play to send the game into the history books.

In the seventeenth, the Dodgers almost ended it. They filled the bases against Oeschger with one out, but Zach Wheat was cut down at the plate on an infield grounder, and Ed Konetchy was also out trying to score on a play at first.

Oeschger admits he was tiring a bit in the eighteenth, but the Dodgers were tiring even more. Stubbornly they battled on as darkness crept across the field. Finally umpire Barry McCormick, as exhausted as the players, called it after three hours and fifty minutes.

Leon Cadore pitches twenty-six-inning game

Did the twenty-six-inning ordeal leave Oeschger and Cadore on stretchers? Hardly.

Oeschger was ready to pitch again four days later until he pulled a leg muscle while running. "But my arm was okay," he insisted. Nevertheless, Stallings ordered him to sit out a turn, although Joe was back on the mound for his next start. He ended up with a 15–13 record for a seventh-place club and went on to win twenty the year after that.

Cadore won fifteen and lost fourteen for the pennant-winning Dodgers of 1920, the best record of his life.

The game was the beginning of strange things for the Robins, as the Dodgers were called then. They had finished fifth in 1919. The day after the twenty-six-inning battle, they went thirteen innings against the Phils, with Burleigh Grimes going all the way. On May 3, back in Boston, they wrestled the Braves another nineteen innings before losing. Sherry Smith pitched the whole game without relief. (In 1916 he had pitched the longest World Series game, fourteen innings, and lost to Babe Ruth.)

MOST INNINGS PITCHED GAMES

Year	Pitcher	IP	Score	H	BB	Opponent	(Pos)
1920	Leon Cadore	26	1–1	15	5	Boston Braves	(7)
	Joe Oeschger	26	1–1	9	4	Brooklyn Dodgers	(1)
1906	Jack Coombs	24	4–1	15	6	Boston Red Sox	(8)
	Joe Harris	24	1–4	16	2	Philadelphia A's	(4)
1927	Bob Smith	22	3–4	20	9	Chicago Cubs	(4)
1914	Rube Marquard	21	3–1	15	2	Pittsburgh Pirates	(7)
	Babe Adams	21	1–3	12	0	New York Giants	(2)
1918	Lefty Tyler	21	2–1	13	1	Philadelphia Phillies	(6)
	Art Nehf	21	1–2	12	5	Pittsburgh Pirates	(4)
1905	Ed Reulbach	20	2–1	13	4	Philadelphia Phillies	(4)
	Tully Sparks	20	1–2	19	1	Chicago Cubs	(3)
	Rube Waddell	20	4–2	15	4	Boston Red Sox	(4)
	Cy Young	20	2–4	13	0	Philadelphia A's	(1)
1918	Mule Watson	20	1–2	19	4	Chicago Cubs	(1)
1919	Joe Oeschger	20	9–9	22	5	Brooklyn Robins	(5)
	Burleigh Grimes	20	9–9	15	7	Philadelphia Phillies	(5)
1945	Les Mueller	20	1–1	13	5	Philadelphia A's	(8)

1945: Les Mueller's Twenty-Inning Tie

In 1945 Les Mueller came out of the army to help the Tigers in their pennant drive and toiled to a twenty-inning 1–1 tie against the last-place Athletics. It was a crucial tie, as the Tigers won by only 1½ games over Washington, but Mueller was not invited back in 1946, when the other veterans returned from the service.

Only six other men have pitched eighteen innings or more during the lively ball era that began in 1920:

Year	Pitcher	W–L	IP	Opponent	(Rank)	Score
1920	Dana Fillingim	12–21	19	Brooklyn Dodgers	(1)	2–1
1921	Dixie Davis	16–16	19	Washington Senators	(4)	8–5
1927	Bob Smith	10–18	18	Chicago Cubs	(4)	3–1
1933	Carl Hubbell	21–12	18	St. Louis Cards	(5)	1–0
1955	Vern Law	10–10	18	Milwaukee Braves	(2)	4–3

Marathon Shutouts

Four men have pitched eighteen-inning shutouts: John Montgomery Ward in 1882, Ed Summers in 1908, Walter Johnson in 1918, and Carl Hubbell in 1933.

Minor-League Marathons: Burns, Clarke, Henley

In 1909 two minor leaguers preceded the Oeschger-Cadore feat of going twenty-six innings in the same game. According to the SABR publication *Minor League Baseball Stars,* Burns and Ed Clarke of the Three-I League struggled through a drizzle, as Burns gave up one run in the first, then pitched shutout ball for the next twenty-five innings. In the bottom of the twenty-sixth, Clarke hit a batter, who scored on an apparent triple. The batter was called out for not touching second, but the run was allowed to count, making Burns the winner, 2–1.

The longest shutout in history was recorded that same year by Cack Henley of San Francisco, who beat Jimmy Wiggs of Oakland 1–0 in twenty-four innings. Henley gave up nine hits and only one walk. The game lasted three hours and thirty-five minutes.

PITCHING DOUBLEHEADERS

There has not been a doubleheader victor in almost fifty years, since Dutch Levsen of Cleveland did it in 1926, and we will probably never see one again. The lively ball and the bull pen have combined to change the game too much to necessitate such heroics now.

Ironman Joe McGinnity

The most famous ironman was Joe Mc-Ginnity, who won his nickname perhaps from working in an iron foundry in Pennsylvania or from winning seven games in six days with Springfield in 1896. In the majors, he holds the record for doubleheaders pitched—five, three of them in one month in 1903.

On August 1 of that year, Joe whipped the Braves 4–1 and 5–2. One week later, August 8, he did it to the Dodgers 6–1 and 4–3. In the second contest, Joe scored the winning run himself on a single, sacrifice, and an error; while the Dodgers stood around arguing about the call, he dashed home. And on August 31 he administered two beatings to the Phillies, 4–1 and 4–3.

In the six games, he pitched fifty-four innings and yielded only ten runs and thirty-six hits. The six complete games were among forty-four he hurled that year, and the six victories put him over thirty wins for the year (his final record: 32–18). Needless

NATIONAL BASEBALL LIBRARY, COOPERSTOWN, N.Y.

Ironman Joe McGinnity

to say, McGinnity led the league in innings pitched, with 434.

Pitching doubleheaders was nothing new to McGinnity. Two years earlier, with the old Baltimore Orioles, who were then in the American League, he had pitched two twin bills in September. He split the first, on September 3, 10–0 and 1–6. Nine days later he split another pair, 4–3 and 4–5.

Mule Watson Pitches
Three Doubleheaders

John "Mule" Watson, a twenty-one-year-old rookie, pitched two doubleheaders for the Phils in 1918, but the best he could get was one victory, two losses, and a tie. (Watson's teammate Joe Oeschger must have watched with interest.) That same year the Mule pitched a twenty-inning game against the Cubs—and lost it 2–1. He ended the year with a 6–10 record.

In 1921 Watson and Oeschger both moved to the Braves, and the stubborn Mule tried pitching a doubleheader again, this time against his old club, and with better success. He won both games, taking the first 4–3 and, getting stronger as the shadows lengthened, shutting out the Phils 8–0 in the second.

DOUBLEHEADER WINNERS

1903	Joe McGinnity (3)
1905	Frank Owen
	Ed Walsh
	Doc Scanlon
1906	George Mullin
1908	Ed Summers
	Ed Reulbach
	Ed Walsh
1914	Ray Collins
1916	Dave Davenport
	Pol Perritt
	Al Demaree
	Grover Alexander
1917	Fred Toney
	Grover Alexander
	Bill Doak
1918	Carl Mays
	Mule Watson (2)
1921	Mule Watson
1923	John Stuart
1924	Hi Bell
	Urban Shocker
1926	Dutch Levsen

Ed Reulbach's Doubleheader Shutouts

In 1905 Ed Reulbach was a twenty-two-year-old rookie with the Chicago Cubs, just out of Notre Dame. On June 24 he hurled eighteen innings and scored a 2–1 victory, scattering fourteen hits. Two months later, August 24, Reulbach was locked in another pitchers' duel. This time he had to battle twenty innings before winning 2–1 over Tully Sparks of the fourth-place Phils.

In 1908 Reulbach was called on to perform more heroics: pitching a doubleheader in the midst of one of the hottest of all pennant races. The day was September 26, the race the famous Cubs–Giants–Pirates scrap, which featured the Fred Merkle incident and culminated in a one-game playoff for the flag. In fact, Reulbach's feat came right after the Merkle game, when Mordecai Brown, Jack Pfiester, and the other Cub hurlers were exhausted from the three-game Giants' series.

For some reason, Reulbach had not pitched in a week, when he had gone ten innings to a 0–0 tie against Philadelphia, so he volunteered to pitch both ends of a doubleheader against the seventh-place Dodgers. Ed threw eighteen innings without allowing a run, winning 5–0 and 3–0. He held the Dodgers to only eight hits all afternoon, to become the only man in the white major leagues to pitch two shutouts in one day.

Five days later, Ed pitched his fourth straight shutout, beating Cincinnati on only two hits.

Foster, Rogan Hurl
Black Playoff Doubleheader

The white majors have never seen two men hook up against each other in both ends of a doubleheader, but two of the greatest pitchers in Negro league history—Big Bill Foster and little Bullet Joe Rogan—did it in

"TETSU WAN" INAO

In 1958 Kazunisa Inao of the Japanese Lions wrote the most amazing World Series record ever—in any country, in any era.

A right-handed slider artist, Inao (pronounced e-noẃ) was an unheralded high school boy in 1956, not given much chance to make the Fukuoka Lions. Relegated to batting practice pitcher, he threw 500 pitches a day and acquired the control that later made him famous. Given a chance to pitch, he surprised everyone by winning twenty-one games, with a 1.06 ERA, and helped pitch the Lions to the world championship. Of 130 games played by the Lions, Inao pitched in sixty-one. That October he won three and lost none in the Japan Series.

The next year Inao went 35–6, plus two more in the Japan Series.

In 1959 he appeared in seventy-two games, winning thirty-three and losing ten. As the Lions just nipped the Osaka Hawks by one game, Inao hurled in the deciding contest. His next challenge was the Japan Series, a grudge match against the famous Tokyo Giants. Here, as reported by SABR's Yoichi Nagata, is what happened:

Right after the final regular season game, Inao caught a bad cold, running a high fever. To keep the newsmen from finding out, he struggled to the park to work out with the team, then slipped away in a taxi, driving through the city to throw any pursuing *papparazzi* off the track, then returned to a secluded inn to sleep.

Inao started the first game and was knocked out in the fourth inning, losing 9–3.

The Lions lost the second game 7–3. "The series is ours," Giants' manager Mizuhara exulted.

After an eighteen-hour train ride from Tokyo, Inao started game three with two days' rest. He gave up only three hits but lost 1–0. The Lions were now down three games to nothing.

The next day the Lions, as home team, canceled the game for "wet grounds," giving Inao an added day of rest. The Giants protested unsuccessfully.

Inao pitched game four and won it 6–4 to keep the Lions' hopes alive.

He relieved in game five in the fourth inning and pitched seven innings of shutout ball, giving up only one hit. In the bottom of the tenth he lashed a "sayonara" home run to win his own game, 4–3.

After another travel day, the Series resumed in Tokyo. Inao started game six and pitched a three-hit shutout, winning 2–0. The Series was now all tied up.

Naturally, Inao would pitch the finale the next day—who else? He pitched eight more innings of shutout ball, making a total of twenty-five straight scoreless innings, before the Giants got a home run in the ninth. But it was too late. Inao beat them the fourth game in a row and the Lions were champs.

The Lions had lost the first three games, then swept the last four, a feat never accomplished in either the United States or Japan Series. And "Tetsu Wan" Inao had pitched six games in eleven days, winning the last four in a row.

1926, and they did it in the final showdown in the pennant playoff.

Foster, younger brother of the great Rube Foster, was a twenty-two-year-old sophomore for the Chicago American Giants. Many authorities consider him the finest left-hander in Negro league history, though there is a lot of competition for that honor.

Rogan's Kansas City Monarchs had jumped out to a 4–3 lead over the American Giants in the nine-game playoff. Rogan had won three of the games and Foster had lost twice.

The season came down to one last doubleheader in Chicago, and each club went with its best—Foster against Rogan. Bill shut the Monarchs out 1–0 to even the series, and both teams retired to the clubhouse before the second contest.

"Well," Chicago manager Dave Malarcher asked the team, "it's all your ball game; who shall I pitch for the deciding game?"

"I feel all right," Foster replied, and the team nodded unanimously to send him back to the mound again.

As Rogan sauntered out onto the field and saw Foster warming up, he stopped in his tracks. "You gonna pitch?" he demanded.

"Yeah," Foster said, "I'm gonna pitch."

"Well, I'm coming back too then," Rogan declared, grabbing the ball out of Monarch rookie Chet Brewer's hand.

Rogan must have cooled off a little too much. He gave up five runs in the first inning, then shut the door. But it was too late. Foster beat him 5–0, and the American Giants were champs. Foster had pitched them into the World Series with a double shutout.

Other Black Doubleheader Pitchers

Two black pitchers, Ed Rile and Al "Steel Arm" Davis, pitched two doubleheaders in the 1920s. Some other Negro league iron-man performances, compiled by SABR's Negro league chairman, Dick Clark:

Year	Pitcher	Opponent
1920	Ed Rile	Chicago
1921	George Britt	Baltimore
1926	Bill McCall	Detroit
	Eddie Miller	Kansas City
	Slap Hensley	Indianapolis
1927	Ed Rile	Kansas City
1928	Steel Arm Davis	New York Cubans
1930	Steel Arm Davis	Birmingham

Johnny Taylor: Three Wins in One Day

Schoolboy Johnny Taylor of the Negro leagues is the only man we know of to win three games in one day. Pitching with the New York Cubans in 1937, he beat the Philadelphia Stars in the first game of a doubleheader in New York, 5–1. In the second game, he came in in the fourth inning to relieve Luis Tiant, Sr., and won that game too.

That night the Cubans drove to Long Island for a game against the Pittsburgh Crawfords. Once more Taylor had to come in in the fourth inning and scored his third victory of the day.

6

The Staff

COMPETITION

As pitching keys the game within the game—the one-on-one confrontation of batter and hurler—so are the pitchers a team within the team. They are a breed apart, united by common understanding of the pressures unique to their position. Mike Marshall described the pitching mound as an island, an apt metaphor for the pitcher's sense of isolation from his teammates. The weight of individual responsibility for victory or defeat creates something of a bunker mentality, with pitchers looking only to each other—and their coach—for support. But the fierce loyalties that may develop within a pitching staff are compromised by cutthroat competition.

Every man has to fight every other man to win his job on the staff—and to hold it. The struggle is especially keen among the thirty or more men in spring training who are battling for the last two spots.

Jim Bouton admitted that after he had been shelled from the box one night, "I didn't cry when the other guys got clobbered too."

The balance of competitiveness and camaraderie is difficult to attain and easily disturbed: as with love, you do not know precisely what created it, but you know when it is there and when it is not. Many think the ebullient Dizzy Dean, despite his twenty-nine wins and jovial ways, actually upset the chemistry of the St. Louis pitching staff in 1934. Wild Bill Hallahan, the ace of the pennant-winning 1931 club, lost his touch in 1934, possibly because of resentment for all the publicity Dean was getting.

Robin Roberts told of joining the Phils when the veteran Schoolboy Rowe was winding up his career. They teamed together for two years, and when Rowe finally got his release, he took Roberts aside to tell him he was a great pitcher, "but you give your curveball away. I thought I'd tell you that before I leave." Robin thanked him but thought to himself: "Wasn't that curious? As long as I was on the staff with him, in a sense competing with him, he wouldn't tell me I was tipping my curve."

The staff has its own pecking order, well recognized by everyone from management down. Gaylord Perry said Larry Dierker and Danny Coombs of Houston came in drunk together one night. Both got fined. But the club deducted Coombs' fine from his paycheck; Dierker's paycheck was not altered. Could it be, Perry wondered, because Dierker was a twenty-game winner and Coombs a marginal relief man?

COOPERATION

There is an ambivalence among pitchers. On the one hand, they want to stick pins in their rivals. On the other, they want to win and collect a World Series check. When Bouton was with Seattle at the end of his career, he watched teammate Diego Segui pitch a good game, while he warmed up in the bull pen, hoping for a call to go in and save it. "I was torn between wanting him to get bombed and wanting him to do well, because we could use a win and because he's a good fellow."

"We were a twenty-five man unit," former Yankee Eddie Lopat told Peter Golenbock in *Dynasty*. "I didn't give a damn who won, as long as New York won." Lopat shared his experience with Allie Reynolds, his roommate, and taught him to slow his pitches down to tease the overanxious hitter.

Bill Lee said Boston's pitching coach Darrell Johnson did not give him much advice. "What advice I did get came from my peers," Lee Stange, Ray Culp, Sparky Lyle, and Ron Kline. Kline was particularly helpful in showing him how to hold certain pitches, and, most important of all, how to hold a shot glass.

After Lyle went to the Yanks and he and Rawly Eastwick were in the New York bull pen together, Rawly went in in long relief and pitched hitless ball to finish the game. Lyle said he was "jumping up and down, waving my hands in the air and cheering

COURTESY OF THE NEW YORK YANKEES.

Sparky Lyle

him on. He saw us, and the next inning when he got to the mound, he tipped his cap to the bull pen."

That same year the two best relievers in baseball, Lyle and Goose Gossage, shared a bull-pen bench, and the situation was ripe for an explosive clash, especially since Lyle, the reigning Cy Young winner, was forced to watch Gossage get all the good assignments. Lyle complained all year, but to manager Billy Martin and owner George Steinbrenner, not to Gossage. He and the Goose got along well.

Later, after Lyle left, Ron Davis would play second violin. Goose helped the rookie.

Rich Gossage

Don Drysdale

"When I first came up I used to throw the ball as hard as I could when I was warming up," Davis said. But Gossage told him, "Just throw hard enough to get your arm loose; after that you can be ready in eight pitches."

In 1972 Fritz Peterson and his pitching mate, Mike Kekich, carried fraternal feelings to the extreme. They had double-dated so often that they decided to switch wives. ("There goes family day," general manager Lee MacPhail moaned.)

Sandy Koufax and Don Drysdale were the best one-two pitching punch of the 1960s. They twice struck out 500 men between them in one year and held that record until Nolan Ryan and Bill Singer of the Angels broke it. There could easily have been a lot of jealousy between them as to which would start a World Series or open the season.

"Don and I have been together too long for that," Sandy wrote. "We learned about pitching together. We lived together for six months in the army. He'd stay at my house on weekends while we were at Fort Dix. I'd spend Thanksgiving and other holidays with him and his folks after I moved to Los Angeles." They even held out as a team and negotiated better contracts jointly; as rivals, they would have been played off against each other by management.

Rookie Don Sutton got help from both of them. "Drysdale was more gregarious and outgoing. He would go over the hitters with me. He even told me what I should wear and how much to tip the waitresses." On his first road trip, "Invariably the waitress would say, 'The tall gentleman took care of your check.'"

Sutton would repay the kindness later by passing some of it on to young Bob Welch of the Dodgers. Overhearing Dodgers' scout Al Campanis tell Welch to abandon his slider and work on an overhand curve instead,

Sandy Koufax

Sutton told the kid he looked good throwing the slider. "I don't care what anybody says, you know what got you here. You've got to be your own pitcher." Welch called that "probably the best advice I've ever gotten."

Tom Seaver and Jon Matlack of the Mets were close friends off the field and in the dugout. Ron Guidry's best friend on the Yankees was fellow pitcher Dick Tidrow, who taught Ron to keep his pitches low. Another Yankees' hurler, Sparky Lyle, taught him the hard slider. Guidry might not have stuck with the Yankees without the tips he got from those two.

On the Orioles, Scott McGregor taught his fellow starter and Cy Young rival Mike Flanagan to throw a change-up with the same motion as the fastball. When Steve Stone joined the staff in 1979, the Orioles were in the pennant race and McGregor was taken out of a game when he was leading. The O's went on to win, but McGregor didn't get credit for the victory. "Tough luck," Stone told him.

"That's okay," Scotty replied cheerfully. "We won the game."

"I realized then," Stone said, "That the whole team had a collective pride, and I was impressed."

THE RELIEF REVOLUTION

Not since Babe Ruth cracked his twenty-nine home runs in 1919, ushering in the home-run revolution, has baseball witnessed a change as profound as the one we are in the midst of: The Relief Revolution. It has altered the strategy, and the record-keeping, of the game as irrevocably as Babe did.

Actually, it is a tide that has been flowing silently, inexorably, and almost unnoticed, for 80 years—ever since 1904, when the Boston Pilgrims' pitchers completed 148 of the 154 games they started. Only six times that year did relief pitchers come in to finish up. In 1977 the San Diego Padres completed only 6 of the 162 games they played.

It was an ex-pitcher, wily Clark Griffith, who first had a vision, albeit a dim one, of the future course of the game. In 1905, a year after the Pilgrims' ironman season, Griff's New York Highlanders became the first team in history to go a full season with less than 100 complete games. The Highlanders completed only eighty-eight, or just

about half, their games. Jack Chesbro, exhausted from winning forty-one games the year before, won only nineteen, and the Highlanders finished sixth.

In 1912 ex-catcher Roger Bresnahan brought the record down to sixty-two with the last-place Cards. Four years later Miller Hugins of the Cards took it down another peg, and in 1919 Branch Rickey, also of the Cards, took it to fifty-five, as the Cards finished seventh. Burt Shotton, Lou Boudreau, Bill Rigney, Ed Lopat, and Ted Williams whittled it down to eleven with Ted's 1972 tail-end Texas Rangers. Then John McNamara and Al Dark reached the present low of six in 1977, with the Padres, who finished next to last.

That was a decade ago. Is the game poised for another assault, perhaps to the ultimate level, zero?

Sadly, each time the CG record was lowered, it was usually a tail-end team that did it. Although a high total of CGs is usually a sign of a strong pitching staff—the 1904 Pilgrims were, after all, the AL champs—a low total of CGs usually points to trouble in the starting rotation. So in one sense the relief revolution has been an orphan of desperation.

Paradoxically, however, saves are the children of success. As CGs went down, saves slowly climbed, but the clubs that rocketed the saves' record upward were, by and large, the champions. There is a big difference between bringing in a reliever to mop up the battle damage left by the shell-shocked starter and bringing him in as a deliberate act of policy to save a game that the starter is winning.

John McGraw was the first genius who suspected the value of the save, although again, even he only dimly grasped the importance of his discovery. Some stops on the way in the progression of saves' records:

Year	SV	Team	(Rank)	Manager
1904	14	New York Giants	(1)	John McGraw
1913	22	Philadelphia A's	(1)	Connie Mack
1924	25	Washington Senators	(1)	Bucky Harris
1947	34	Brooklyn Dodgers	(1)	Leo Durocher
1953	39	New York Yankees	(1)	Casey Stengel
1965	53	Chicago White Sox	(2)	Al Lopez
1970	60	Cincinnati Reds	(1)	Sparky Anderson

It is clear that saves make sense. One can only wonder why the greatest brains of the dugout have taken eighty years to understand that two or three strong, fresh arms are better than one tired one.

For most of this century, the relievers were the second-stringers, not good enough to break into the starting four. The early firemen were starters who relieved between starts—Bender, Brown, Walsh, and the like. Only a few relief specialists emerged—Doc Crandall of McGraw's 1911 Giants, Firpo Marberry of Harris' Senators, Joe Page of Stengel's Yankees. Usually hitters hoped to knock the starter out so they could fatten up on the bull pen.

Now of course it is just the opposite. Rich Gossage and Jesse Orosco are specialists proud of their assignment, who can come in late in the game and blast the hitters out of the box. Now the strategy is to play for an early lead, then bring in the heat to save the game. It is a rare team nowadays that can come from behind in the late innings, and the complete game is almost extinct in the World Series.

Along with the revolution in strategy has come a revolution in record keeping. The old records are no longer relevant, and new ones have not yet emerged to measure the new phenomenon.

Some of the old ones:

Complete Games. Virtually irrelevant now. A starter who has any gas left at the end of the seventh is like the marathoner who still has a kick left after he breaks the tape: It implies that he was not pushing hard enough in the race.

Wins. Less and less significant. Today's hurlers find it more difficult to win twenty games. One reason is the five-day rotation, which eliminates about seven starts a year. The other reason is the bull pen, which is now determining the fate of the starters far more than it did in grandpa's day.

There were some symbiotic starter/reliever teams in the past. Satchel Paige usually started every game and went two or three innings to draw a crowd. Then the almost invisible Hilton Smith came in to finish the game. "My gosh, you couldn't tell the difference!" Roy Campanella whistled. Yet Smith had none of Satchel's color and received none of his publicity. Sighed Smith: "Next day I'd read in the papers, 'SATCHEL AND MONARCHS WIN AGAIN.' "

Another famous duo was Lefty Gomez and Johnny Murphy of the Yankees of the 1930s. Murphy, later general manager of the Mets, was known as "Fireman Johnny." Gomez was relieved by Murphy so often that he said he could go on pitching as long as Johnny's arm held out. Gomez won seven World Series games. When? "1932 and '36, '38, '39, and '41—no, Murphy was tired and I didn't pitch in '41."

Now it is commonplace for the starter to trudge into the dressing room, leaving the game tied or perhaps with a one-run lead, while a fresh young Hercules arrives in the bull-pen cart either to save the game or give up the hit that ties it or loses it. The starter is standing helplessly under the shower with the radio on listening to his fate being decided by someone else.

Consider the seventh game of the 1946 World Series, the one that Enos Slaughter won by dashing home from first on a double in the eighth.

Boston's starter Boo Ferris pitched the first four innings and left with St. Louis leading 3–1. Burrhead Joe Dobson came in to hold it for three innings.

Meanwhile Cardinals' starter Murray Dickson tired after seven innings and gave way to Harry Brecheen in the eighth. Brecheen promptly gave up the tying runs on Dom DiMaggio's double.

In the ninth Bob Klinger came in to give up a hit by Slaughter and Harry Walker's double that sent Enos home with the run that made a loser out of Klinger and a winner out of Brecheen.

Dickson got nothing for his seven innings of one-run ball.

Dobson got nothing for his three shutout innings of middle relief.

Brecheen, who almost lost the game, received the winner's laurel crown, thanks to Slaughter and Walker.

Wins for relievers. At best, meaningless, at worst fraudulent, as Brecheen illustrates. "I'm always suspicious of a lot of wins for relievers," said Bob Brown, publicist of the Orioles; they usually imply, as does Brecheen's, that the fireman failed to hold a lead.

In 1959 Pittsburgh reliever Elroy Face won eighteen games and lost one. In 1966 the Dodgers' Phil Regan won thirteen in a row in relief. How many of their wins were save opportunities that they failed to hold?

ERA. Increasingly misleading as well. The starter's ERA, as well as his win or loss, is often in the hands of the reliever. If the starting pitcher leaves two men on base, and the reliever lets them both score, they are charged to the starter. If his twin brother leaves two men on but his relief throws a double-play ball to end the inning, the starter gets away with neither runner charged against him.

ERA for relievers. In 1952 rookie Hoyt Wilhelm of the Giants became the only reliever ever to lead the league in ERA (he won fifteen and lost three). But, like the relief win, the reliever's ERA is a highly suspect statistic. In the 1985 All Star game, relief ace Willie Hernandez came in with two NL runners on and promptly gave up the hit to Darryl Strawberry that scored them both. You will not find either run in Hernandez's ERA, though he is paid—rather handsomely—to slam the door without letting inherited runners cross the plate.

Save. This is the first statistical attempt to come to grips with the relief revolution. It recognizes a reliever's role, although the *Sporting News' Baseball Register* still does not recognize it as a statistic. And the save does have problems. It is the most easily manipulated stat, as managers reward favorite firemen with easy save situations. The relievers call this the "Glory Time."

When the Yanks had both Cy Young winner Sparky Lyle and millionaire Goose Gossage in their bull pen, Billy Martin had orders to give Gossage the save opportunities when the team was ahead and give Lyle the thankless mop-up assignments when the team was behind.

Another example was game five of the 1985 World Series. Detroit's Aurelio Lopez was pitching strongly in relief and winning, 5–3. For no apparent reason, manager Sparky Anderson pulled Lopez out in the eighth and put in soon-to-be Cy Young winner Willie Hernandez to cash in on the save.

Hernandez gave up a run and almost lost the game, which would have served Anderson right.

Then, too, saves are getting more and more numerous while getting cheaper and cheaper. Sometimes a reliever can pick up a save by pitching to only one man with two out in the ninth. It is now possible to pick up three or four such saves a week.

Still, recording saves and relief points (wins plus saves) is an improvement over the old won–lost records.

The all-time relief leaders in saves and relief points:

Wins		Saves		Relief Points	
Hoyt Wilhelm	123	Rollie Fingers	341	Rollie Fingers	455
Lindy McDaniel	119	Bruce Sutter	286	Rich Gossage	379
Rollie Fingers	114	Rich Gossage	278	Bruce Sutter	353
Rich Gossage	101	Sparky Lyle	238	Hoyt Wilhelm	350
Sparky Lyle	99	Dan Quisenberry	229	Sparky Lyle	337

Team Won–Lost. Perhaps every player who contributes to a win should get a win—and that includes nonpitchers too. We started compiling such stats in 1946, and now others are taking up the task, at least for catchers and pitchers.

If the team won, then everyone should share the credit, both the starter who started and the relievers who finished. This would reward those starters who now get no decisions while the bull pens get the wins. It would also reward the middle reliever who gets nothing, while others get the win and the save.

On the other hand, if the team wins the game after the starter leaves, this implies that he left the field either tied or behind. But if it loses after he leaves, he deserves even more credit, since it implies that he left the game leading or at least tied. So team won–lost records can be more confusing than helpful.

Half-Runs and Half-Losses. When a starter leaves a runner on base and his reliever lets the run score, who is more responsible? Now we give the complete blame to the starter and none at all to the reliever. Yet obviously each was about equally responsible.

We say charge them each half a run. And if the run leads to a loss, charge them each with half a loss.

Scoring Ratio. Vince Nauss, on the public relations staff of the Phils has invented the scoring ratio. This measures the inherited runners the reliever allows to score.

In partial data for 1985, Nauss reports the following scoring ratios:

Pitcher	Runners	Runs	Ratio
Kent Tekulve	13	2	.154
Don Carman	33	9	.212
Larry Andersen	24	9	.375

In 1986 Andersen had moved to the Astros, whose bull-pen numbers looked like this:

Pitcher	Runners	Runs	Ratio
Aurelio Lopez	18	5	.278
Dave Smith	32	9	.281
Larry Andersen	33	10	.300
Charlie Kerfeld	33	17	.505

Davis Jackson, in his seminal study *The Last Word,* rated all 1984 pitchers, starters, and relievers on the basis of potential bases allowed compared to actual bases allowed (a home run is four bases, scoring from first is three, and so on). Relievers are penalized for bases by inherited runners as well as for runners they put on themselves. But they can earn points for stranding runners; thus a runner stranded on first is three bases to the good for the reliever.

Using this logic, Jackson deduced that Luis Aponte of Cleveland and Warren Brusstar of the Cubs were the most effective stoppers in 1984, though their conventional stats do not show it (Aponte 1-0, 4.11; Brusstar 1-1, 3.11). Other top stoppers that year were Ernie Camacho, Jeff Reardon, Goose Gossage, and Jesse Orosco.

The worst stoppers were Juan Agosto of the White Sox and Gary Lucas of Montreal. Surprisingly, Dave Righetti, Gary Lavelle, Tom Niedenfuer, and Doug Sisk also ranked low.

Jackson also calculated pitching averages with men in scoring position. Best men in the clutch, he says, were Roy Thomas of Seattle, .113, and Jeff Reardon of Montreal, .130.

Apparently relief support, like batting support, is distributed unevenly, even to pitchers on the same team. Yankee Phil Niekro (16-8) was luckiest of all, while teammate Ron Guidry (10-11) got very little help. Detroit's Juan Berenguer (11-10) and Dan Petry (18-8) saw most of their runners stranded by the bull pen; Jack Morris (19-11) saw most of his move up.

Jackson also pointed out that almost all of MVP Willie Hernandez's appearances that year were at the start of an inning with the bases empty, not quite the stereotype we have of the courageous fireman rushing into the crisis with the bases loaded, putting out the blaze. Only seven times did Hernandez come in in the middle of an inning that year.

Of those seven games, Jackson said, Hernandez let the runners score in four of them. Fortunately, Jackson said, Hernandez was very good at keeping the leadoff man off base, which seems to have been the key to his effectiveness.

Dan Quisenberry was another who usually came in at the beginning of an inning, rather than in the middle.

The real firemen, who were rushed in in emergencies, were Ron Davis, Jesse Orosco, and Bill Caudill.

Hold. The biggest heroes for the San Diego Padres in the 1984 World Series were not Tony Gwynn and their other hitters, or Eric Show and their other starters (who got bombed pretty hard). The stars were the Padres' middle relievers—Andy Hawkins, Dave Dravecky, and Craig Lefferts. Usually these middle relievers get nothing for their heroics.

The Orioles and the Phillies have devised a stat for them, called the hold. If the hold had existed in 1946, Boston's Dobson would have earned one in the climactic Series game against the Cardinals.

Squander. And, using the same system, Brecheen would have been given a squander, because he came in with a lead and lost it. (It is possible to get both a squander and a win in the same game, as Brecheen did.)

SABR member Peter Berkowsky calls this a fail and has been urging baseball's rules committee for years to recognize it as an official stat. The committee, which hemmed and hawed before approving the save, has hemmed and is still hawing over the fail.

Meanwhile, the Phils and Orioles go ahead and compile both holds and squanders, the brainchildren of Nauss and Baltimore's Bob Brown.

In 1984 Philadelphia's Al Holland won or saved thirty-four games. But he also lost or squandered thirty-one. His unsung bull-pen mates, Larry Andersen and Bill Campbell, got only five saves between them, but each had twenty-six holds. The line on the Phils' bull pen that year:

Pitcher	W	+	SV	+	H	–	SQ	–	L	=	Points
Andersen	3		4		26		19		7		7
Campbell	6		1		26		16		5		12
Holland	5		29		14		21		10		17

Nauss and Brown weight wins, saves, and losses as two points each, but we give them all equal weight.

The Up

In the final game of the 1960 World Series, the Pirates were knocking one Yankees' pitcher after another out of the box. Bob Turley and Bill Stafford each lasted one inning. Bobby Shantz pitched well for five innings before a double-play ball hit shortstop Tony Kubek in the throat. Jim Coates got two outs, then gave up a three-run homer to Hal Smith. And each time the Yankees got in trouble, Casey Stengel was on the phone to the bull pen to get Ralph Terry warmed up. Terry, who had gone six innings four days earlier, was up and down in the bull pen all day. By the time he got the call to rescue Coates, he had pitched almost an entire game in the bull pen.

Terry got the final out in the eighth.

In the ninth the tired Terry grooved one of the most famous home runs of all time to .273-hitting Bill Mazeroski, and the Yanks had lost the Series.

The Orioles have a statistic for this. It's called the *up*. Earl Weaver's rule was never to let a reliever have more than three ups in three days. If you do not count your ups, you can lose a world championship, as Stengel demonstrated.

Sparky Lyle said Cleveland manager Jeff Torborg had his bull pen up even before the Star Spangled Banner. He adds that Billy Martin kept the bull-pen phone ringing the whole game in New York.

"Bill Rigney wore out pitchers in the bull pen," said reliever Steve Ridzik. "Some managers, they warm you up five innings, sit you down, and get another guy in the game."

Gil Hodges of the Senators, and later the Mets, was a good manager, Ridzik said. "The second time you warm up, you're in the game. Hodges didn't get enough credit. He was probably the best handler of pitchers I've ever seen."

Dave Righetti liked Yogi Berra, the manager who made him a reliever. "He took care of me," Dave told Murray Chass of the *New York Times* in 1986. "I was strong the whole year. My arm didn't get tired until the last day of the season."

But Billy Martin was just the opposite. "Billy just basically didn't know how to use me," Dave said. Martin had him warming up without using him or put him into the game as early as the sixth inning. "I didn't know if I should pace myself or blow them away in one inning." If he pitched hard and stayed in for three innings, "the next day I'd be hanging a little bit."

Lou Piniella resumed the Berra technique, and Righetti reasoned, "If they used me for only three outs, I could pitch ninety games."

Some notable relief feats:

In 1952 rookie Hoyt Wilhelm of the Giants became the first reliever to lead the league in ERA. He ended with a 15–3 record and eleven saves.

In 1957, according to John Grabowski of *Baseball Trivia Newsletter,* Leo Kiely won twenty games in relief for San Francisco, then in the Pacific Coast league. It is probably the record for organized ball.

Two years later Pittsburgh's Elroy Face won eighteen and lost one in the National League. (Grabowski points out that Face's only loss was to the Dodgers' Chuck Churn, who won only two other games in his career.) Face's eighteen victories are misleading, since they imply that he failed to save a lot of games, then won them when the Pirates' hitters bailed him out. However, Face did save ten games that year. In the pennant-winning year of 1961, he lost twelve games in relief, a record, though again he saved seventeen.

In 1966 Phil Regan of the Dodgers won thirteen games in a row in relief. He ended the season with fourteen wins, one loss, and a league-leading twenty-one saves.

And in 1979 Atlanta's Gene Garber broke Face's record by losing sixteen games in relief.

QUALITY STARTS

The quality start is defined as a game in which the starting pitcher goes at least six innings and gives up three earned runs or less. The theory is that if a starter can do that, he has kept his club in the ball game,

and even if he does not get a win, he has done his job.

John Lowe of the *Philadelphia Inquirer* reports that Dave Stieb of Toronto racked up the most quality starts for the three years 1983–85. Stieb won only forty-seven games, about sixteen a year, but he tossed seventy-eight quality starts, or an average of twenty-nine per year.

Behind him was Jack Morris of Detroit, with fifty-five wins and seventy-six quality starts.

The leaders, according to Lowe:

QUALITY STARTS
1983–85

Pitcher	QS	W
Dave Stieb	78*	47
Jack Morris	76*	55
F. Valenzuela	70	44
Mario Soto	67	47
Joe Niekro	67	42
Rick Rhoden	67	37
Charlie Hough	63	45
Don Sutton	62	37
Nolan Ryan	62	36
John Tudor	61†	46
John Denny	60	37
LaMarr Hoyt	59†	53
Tom Seaver	59†	40
Bud Black	58*	37
Mike Smithson	58*	40
Dan Petry	56*	52
Phil Niekro	55†	43
Dave LaPoint	55	31
Frank Tanana	55*	40
Bill Gullickson	54	43
Ron Guidry	54*	53
Steve Carlton	53	29
Bert Blyleven	52*	43

*American League.
†American League and National League.

Stieb and Morris deserve extra credit, because they pitch in the American League, where the d.h. makes it more difficult to hold opponents to three runs in six innings.

It is interesting to see Nolan Ryan tied for eighth on the list. Ryan is much maligned because he rarely wins twenty games, but he insists quietly that he keeps his club in the game and says it is not his fault if they cannot win. The quality start data seem to bear him out.

Ron Guidry is the most efficient pitcher in converting quality starts into wins—fifty-four quality starts produced fifty-three victories. Steve Carlton was the least successful; he gave the Phils fifty-three quality starts, but they gave him only twenty-nine victories in the period.

The quality start is an interesting concept—certainly it has some advantages over the traditional but increasingly obsolete win. We are watching it with an open mind but offer a few comments that proponents may want to consider in making refinements before submitting it to the troglodytic rules committee as a possible new stat.

First, the threshold is too high. In 1986 the National League ERA was 3.72 for nine innings, or 0.40 per inning. That would work out to 2.46 for six innings. (The American League figures were 4.18, 0.46, and 2.76.) Thus, giving up three runs in six innings, far from being a "quality" performance, is actually a below-average performance. We would suggest two earned runs for six innings would better satisfy the title of "quality" start.

Second, under the present criteria, a pitcher who goes the full nine innings and gives up a fourth run loses his quality start. But one extra run in three extra innings would seem to be even more valuable to his team. A sliding scale would be fairer. Again, using 1986 data, average performances would be:

IP	NL ERA	AL ERA
6	2.46	2.76
7	2.87	3.17
8	3.28	3.63
9	3.69	4.09

Thus a quality start might be two earned runs or less for six or seven innings, three or less for eight or nine innings. The definition could be adjusted in future years to follow the league ERA up or down.

But the concept is sound. With proper refinements, we can recommend the quality start as a new tool to measure today's new starters.

Oh . . . and in game seven of the 1946 World Series, Murry Dickson would have received one.

CAPTAIN HOOK

The most important job a manager has is handling his pitchers. And the most important part of that job is knowing when to change pitchers—and when not to.

The trip to the mound is one of the great arts of managing or merely a transparent device for giving your reliever another few pitches to heat up—it depends on who you talk to.

In the 1957 World Series, Warren Spahn of Milwaukee had the Yankees down 4–1 going into the ninth inning of the fourth game. Although he had shown a few signs of tiring, he went out and got the first two batters, Hank Bauer (.259) on a fly and Mickey Mantle (.365) on a grounder. But Yogi Berra (.251) and Gil McDougald (.289) singled, and Milwaukee's manager, Fred Haney bounced out of the dugout and trotted to the mound, as the fans booed and implored him to let Spahn stay in. Had Haney made up his mind to make a change? What did he and Spahn say on the mound?

After a few words, Haney turned and jogged back to the bench, and Spahn peered in for the sign to pitch to Elston Howard (.253). Howard whacked a home run over the wall to tie the game up.

No pitcher wants to be taken out, and most will say anything to stay in. Said Whitey Ford of Casey Stengel: "He'd ask if I was tired and I'd say no, and a lot of times I'd be lying. And it hurt us, because we lost a couple of games that way."

Walter Johnson once said the reason he failed as a manager was that, as an ex-pitcher himself, he did not have the heart to take a man out.* "Just one more" can be as dangerous to pitchers as to alcoholics.

Honesty from relievers is just as vital. Earl Weaver wanted his relievers to tell him frankly before the game, "I don't have it tonight, Earl," or, "I can only get you one out today." Tippy Martinez was good at that. Occasionally, Weaver admits, he left a tired reliever in to take a pounding. The rest of the bull pen was overworked, and Earl sacrificed the game—and the pitcher's ERA—to save the rest of the staff for the next night. Once, in a celebrated strategic retreat, Weaver brought in outfielder Larry Harlow and bull-pen coach Elrod Hendricks to pitch, for the same reason.

Another ex-pitcher, Freddie Hutchinson, made up his mind whether to pull the starter before he crossed the foul line. "After I cross the foul line, no amount of pleading is going to make me change."

A trip to the mound may do nothing except upset the pitcher's rhythm and concentration. Catcher Thurman Munson did not like to do it; neither did Tim McCarver. When a manager comes out, says McCarver, often all he does is plant doubt in the pitcher's mind.

Then there are the absent-minded managers like Johnny Lipon, who met his reliever at the mound, handed him the lineup card, and took the ball back to the dugout with him.

Gaylord Perry tells of one experiment to do away with the trip to the mound. San Francisco's Vancouver farm team installed a radio receiver in pitcher Art Bamberger's cap, and the conversation went like this:

"Hello, Art?"
Bamberger nods.
"Art, this is Haller at bat."
Nod.
"Don't give him anything too good to hit. But don't walk him."
Nod.
Haller doubles.
"Okay, get him next time. Now here's Chuck Hiller. Throw him a curve."
Nod.
Base hit.
"Hello, Art? Runners on first and third and no outs. It's Dusty Rhodes. If he hits it to you, double play, second to first. You're not following through enough. Come up over the top more. Don't forget to take your stretch. Now waste a fastball away on him."
Six nods.
Rhodes clears the bases with a fastball thrown down the middle.
End of experiment.

Rogers Hornsby did not bother going to the mound. He just stood on the dugout steps and peremptorily waved the pitcher out.

Joe McCarthy sent a coach so there was no chance of being talked out of it by the pitcher. "What could I say to him?" Joe asked. "That it's very warm for this time of year?"

Jimmy Dykes once arrived on the mound to hear the pitcher say, "Gee, Skip, I've

*Not true. Actually, Johnson's teams had high save totals for their day.

only been missing by this much,'' holding his thumb and finger a half-inch apart. ''Yes,'' said Jimmy, ''but you've missed by that much sixteen straight times.''

Jim Kern once protested that he was not tired. ''No,'' the manager replied, ''but the outfielders are.''

Some trips to the mound are not to take the pitcher out, but to be seen on television, the pitchers charge. Or to give and get information. Other times the pitcher is left wondering what the purpose was. The skipper pats his rump and says, ''Don't give him anything good, but don't walk him.'' (''If I could do that,'' the pitcher sneers to himself, ''I wouldn't need a manager.'')

One decision American League managers do not have, but National Leaguers do is when to pinch-hit for the pitcher. If the pinch-hitter comes through, you are a genius; if he pops up and the reliever who enters blows the game, you are a chump. In 1982 the Dodgers were one game behind the Braves on the final day of the season. Fernando Valenzuela was pitching a strong game against the Giants. With the score knotted at two in the seventh inning, the Dodgers loaded the bases when Fernando was due up with two out. To pinch-hit or not? Lasorda thought his hurler was tiring and sent Jorge Orta up to hit. Orta made out, and the Giants' Joe Morgan went to slug a homer off the reliever to knock the Dodgers out of the running. ''The hard part of managing,'' said Lasorda, ''is that you get only one guess.''

Modern statistics can help a manager make a decision he used to make by the seat of his pants. If the starter is going well but Reggie Jackson is up, the printouts can tell that Jackson hits this starter at a .333 clip, but he is only hitting .214 against the man warming up in the bull pen. Said Weaver: ''The decision is made for you.'' (Not ex-

actly—a human element always eludes the powers of the computer, and successful managing lies in evaluation of this element.)

It is vital to know when to bring in a reliever. It is just as vital to know which reliever to bring in. Weaver for one rejected the righty-lefty rule. He did not care which way the next opponent batted; he brought in his hottest arm. Earl stayed with the hot man until he cooled off.

Each manager has a different way of telling if his pitcher is tired. Tom Lasorda told us he watches to see if his pitcher is dropping his shoulder or if his pitches are edging up into the ''red zone,'' the danger zone above the belt.

Charlie Dressen used to say, ''If your pitcher starts out high in the first inning, he'll adjust. But if he's high after the fifth inning, get him out.'' Another Dressen rule: ''A pitcher can get out of one jam or two, but not three. The third jam, get him out.''

Weaver's version of that rule was, do not let the starter lose the game. If the score is close and he is throwing well, leave him in. But if he has a lead and suddenly puts some men on and the winning run comes to the plate, yank him. Some pitchers, like Dennis Martinez, run out of gas fast, so do not wait.

But what of the pitcher who really can survive a rocky inning and bounce back? Mike Cuellar could not pitch until he broke a sweat. It was hard sometimes, but Weaver waited out a lot of rocky first innings with him, especially on cold days in October. Robin Roberts was also notorious for recovering from a bad inning, and it used to drive his managers crazy. If Roberts is good, they figured, he is much better than anyone in the bull pen. But if he is not. . . .

Fastest Hooks in the West

Some famous fast hooks:

Zack Taylor of the 1949 Browns used nine

pitchers in one nine-inning game. The Browns still finished seventh.

Luke Appling of the 1967 Kansas City A's used seven pitchers in one shutout. The A's still finished tenth.

Walt Alston of the 1965 Dodgers used six pitchers in one shutout. The Dodgers finished first.

Preston Gomez lifted two pitchers with no-hitters going after eight innings—Clay Kirby of the 1970 Padres and Don Wilson of the 1974 Astros. Both times the relievers gave up hits to spoil the bids. Kirby never got another chance; Wilson had already pitched two.

Lee Elia, manager of the 1983 Cubs, had more shutouts (ten) than complete games (nine). The Cubs finished fifth in their division. Frank Robinson of the 1981 Giants was even faster, with nine shutouts and eight complete games.

Three skippers—John McGraw, Sparky Anderson, and Dick Howser—frequently led the league in saves while coming in last in complete games. Were they fast on the draw? Or were they just lucky to have Doc Crandall, Willie Hernandez, and Dan Quisenberry in their bull pens?

Slowest Hooks in the West

George Stallings led the 1914 miracle Braves to the pennant with an ironman staff of Bill James (37 CG), Dick Rudolph (36), and Lefty Tyler (34). The Braves had only five saves. It was Stallings who left Joe Oeschger in for twenty innings against Leon Cadore in 1920.

As a coach with Baltimore, George Bamberger produced a record number of Cy Young winners. Later, as manager for the Mets and Brewers, he said he liked his pitchers to go for complete games. "It gives the staff pride and makes those pitchers stronger as the season wears on. It gives

them more stamina, so they get tougher in the late innings when they have to go the route. I use the bull pen only when I have to. If the pitcher on the mound is any good, I keep him there for as long as I can. After all, you know what he has, but you don't know what the reliever has on a particular day." Bamberger's teams were not notably successful.

When Dave Johnson took over the Mets in 1984, they went from twelve complete games to forty, to the complaints of relief ace Jesse Orosco.

Earl Weaver's teams led the league in complete games more than any other man—he did not produce all those Cy Young awards by yanking his pitchers too early.

Which Is the Best Policy?

Clearly, the best policy is to be neither too fast nor too slow, but right on time. If the starters are strong and the bull pen weak, the only wise policy is to leave the starters in. With weak starters and strong relievers, one must get the hook out fast. Billy Martin went to the bull pen often when he had Sparky Lyle and Goose Gossage out there. But in Oakland, where he had no bull pen, he worked his starters to death.

The manager who balances his starters and his relievers best is the one who will go to the most World Series. Four men—Bill McKechnie, Joe McCarthy, Al Lopez, and Walter Alston—are among the yearly leaders in both complete games and saves. In 1928 McKechnie's Cardinals led in both categories the same year; they were also tops in NERA—earned run average normalized for home park bias, as calculated by Pete Palmer—as the Cards won the pennant. (It's not surprising that the Astros, Cards, and Padres frequently have low ERAs and the Red Sox, Cubs, and Braves seldom do— where a pitcher pitches is crucial to his record, just as home park inflates or deflates batting records.) Ditto McCarthy's 1939 Yankees. The conclusion seems to be that they knew how to get the most from both their starting staffs and their bull pens. (McKechnie had the toughest job—while McCarthy had Fireman Johnny Murphy in the bull pen, McKechnie had no single relief ace to rely on.)

Connie Mack appears on both the most CG and the least CG lists, a commentary on the vicissitudes of fifty-three years of managing both pennant winners and tail-enders.

In 1986 the leaders were:

Most saves: Lou Piniella's New York Yankees, fifty-eight. Dave Righetti had a record forty-six of them.

Fewest saves: Billy Gardner's Minnesota Twins, twenty-four.

Most complete games: Gardner's Twins, thirty-nine.

Fewest complete games: Jim Frey's Chicago Cubs, eleven.

Ron Lewis' *Pitcher Performance Handbook* is an excellent tool to evaluate today's managers. For instance, the all-time leading bull pens are:

Year	Team	(Rank)	Manager	W	Pct.*	Bullpen
1984	Kansas City Royals	(1)	Dick Howser	84	92%	(Quisenberry)
1983	San Francisco Giants	(5)	Frank Robinson, Danny Ozark	79	90%	(Minton, Lavelle)
1986	New York Yankees	(2)	Lou Piniella	90	86%	(Righetti)

*Percent of team's wins either won or saved by bull pen.

In 1984, after Ron Guidry left the game, the Yankees' relievers were 5–2; after Phil Niekro was lifted, they did even better, 6–1. Manager Yogi Berra apparently knew what he was doing when he rescued both men—and when he made a reliever out of Dave Righetti.

Jim Frey of the Cubs also showed good judgment in pulling Dick Ruthven and Scott Sanderson. Lee Smith and the rest of the bull pen were 5–1 after Ruthven left, 7–4 after Sanderson.

But Tom Lasorda of the Dodgers had mixed results. After he yanked Jerry Reuss, the bull pen posted a 4–1 record. But after Alejandro Peña departed, the bull pen was 2–8. For Bob Welch the figures were 0–4. This suggests that Tom was right to pull Reuss but should have left Peña and Welch in longer.

Note the 1984 Pittsburgh Pirates. How could a team lead the league in ERA, as the Pirates did, and finish last in their division? Their bull pen let them down, that was how. Fireman Kent Tekulve had a fine ERA as usual, but he won only three and lost nine. Don Robinson was about as bad, 7–15.

Many managers may have sympathized with Gene Mauch, who, when asked why he had not yanked his pitcher sooner, muttered, "I was afraid I'd strangle him if I got him in the dugout."

7

Relationships

THE PITCHING COACH

"Of all the people who really help a pitcher the most, the pitching coach is the man," Eddie Lopat once said. He had worked with the best of the old line—Dolf Luque, Frank Shellenback, Mel Harder, Joe Becker, Jim Turner—and finally became one himself; his protegé, Whitey Ford, regarded him like a brother.

There are good coaches and bad. An example of the former, Jim Bouton said, was Jim Owens, an undistinguished pitcher but a perceptive coach. Owens had a great overhand curve when he first came up, "but they told me I had to throw a slider. So I worked on the slider until I lost my overhand curve. That taught me never to take a young pitcher and force him to come up with a new pitch. I give them their own head."

For pitchers, that sensitive, misunderstood caste of egomaniacs, their special coach serves as analyst, surrogate parent, and conduit to the boss. A good pitching coach can be controversial, sticking up for his staff against management doctrine, or he

can be laid back, dispelling the pressure that builds up around the staff from the outside. A good pitching coach may mean a pennant (though the manager will get the credit); a bad one may mean promising careers thrown away.

Who is the pitching coach on your favorite team? Chances are you do not know. Yet many an unsung pitching coach has changed baseball history.

Robinson and Marquard

They were calling Rube Marquard "the $11,000 lemon." Sold by Indianapolis to the New York Giants for a then record price, Rube spent two frustrating years on the Giants' bench, 1909–10, winning nine and losing eighteen. Then Uncle Wilbert Robinson took charge of him. Rube was the victim of his own overwhelming publicity: Failure was unthinkable; even today, expectations grow as a player's salary grows. Robinson, a former catcher with the Baltimore Orioles, was an avuncular cherub who was serving as a coach for his old teammate John McGraw. In the spring of 1911 he devoted himself almost entirely to changing the $11,000 lemon into an $11,000 beauty.

As Christy Mathewson told the story, Uncle Wilbert began working on Marquard's self-image, which was not too high after the newspapers had begun tagging him a lemon. "Rube, you've got a lot of stuff today," Robbie would say. "But don't try to get it all on the ball. Mix it with a little control, and it will make a great blend." He taught Rube the weakness of every hitter in the league. Marquard had been getting two strikes on a hitter, then letting him get away. Robbie began each day telling his protegé, "Now, Rube, you've got to start on the first ball to the batter. Always have something on him, and never let him have something on you." Wrote Matty in *Pitching in a Pinch:* "Out there in the hot Texas sun, with much advice and lots of patience, Wilbert Robinson was manufacturing a great pitcher out of the raw material."

Suddenly Marquard became a star. He was the ace of the staff with twenty-four victories and led the Giants to the 1911 pennant. Toward the end of the year, Rube began "to wabble a little bit" when the club was on its last western swing. He lost to the Cubs, and "Robinson hurried out to Chicago and worked with him for two days." Said Matty: "Rube turned around after Robinson joined us and beat them to death in the last contest."

Ahead lay two more twenty-game seasons, a record nineteen wins in a row, and the Hall of Fame. And none of it might have happened if it had not been for a pitching coach with the patience of Wilbert Robinson. What he did for Marquard seems simple enough—praise, praise, and then more praise before the first word of criticism—but how many tenderhearted, high-strung phenomenons have washed out for the lack of such handling?

Cy Perkins and Robin Roberts

Cy Perkins was a nineteen-year-old catcher with Connie Mack's A's in 1915. He was still catching for them in 1929, when he taught Lefty Grove self-control by making him slap the ball into his mitt three times between every pitch as a way to compose himself before firing. He also taught Lefty to pace himself in the early innings so he would finish with something in reserve. Perkins was Joe McCarthy's coach when the Yanks won the pennant in 1932 and was with the Tigers on their pennant-winning 1934–35 teams. By 1950 he was back in his old town, Philadelphia, coaching another phenom, Robin Roberts.

"He was a wise and compassionate man" who knew how to boost a kid's morale, Roberts said in *Baseball Between the Lines*. "Kid," Cy told Roberts, "I've been in baseball for thirty-five years, and the five best pitchers I've ever seen are Walter Johnson, Lefty Grove, Herb Pennock, Grover Cleveland Alexander, and you."

Perkins never told Roberts how to pitch: "Do it your way," he said. He never congratulated Robin on a victory, "but when I lost he'd always be there and never let me get morose or despondent about it." When Roberts once was knocked out in the first inning, Perkins told him that happens sometimes and recalled the day Lefty Grove got belted for seven runs in the first inning. Then he walked away and let Roberts draw his own conclusions.

When Roberts was released by the Phils in 1962, Perkins called immediately. "Don't let them drive you out of the game," he told the crestfallen Roberts. "You'll be pitching shutouts when you're forty." So Roberts joined the Orioles and began a second career as an American Leaguer, adding fifty-two more victories to his total.

"He was a very quiet man," Robin said. "He did the same for all the guys that he did for me, but always very quietly. The players always had tremendous respect and affection for him." When the Phillies let Cy Perkins go, Roberts begged them to let him pay Cy's salary. "I don't think you appreciate how much help he gives us," Robin said.

Joe Becker and Sandy Koufax

Young Sandy Koufax was wasting his great stuff about a foot over the batter's head. Manager Walter Alston credited another ex-catcher, Joe Becker, with teaching Koufax control and sending him on to the Hall of Fame. Becker (his entire big-league career consisted of forty games with the Indians twenty years earlier), worked by the hour with Koufax. "Joe would have Koufax pitching with a windup and without a windup, trying to discover some method that would put rhythm into his delivery." They tried a tighter windup. "Then suddenly," Alston told Si Burick, "just like that, they found it one day—all at once—just a little rocking motion on the pitching mound. Suddenly, he was a pitcher, not a thrower."

Johnny Sain, the Pied Piper of Pitchers

Johnny Sain did for pitching in the sixties what Babe Ruth and the lively ball did for hitting in the twenties said Jim Brosnan. Another famous pitcher-author, Jim Bouton, enthusiastically called Sain "the greatest pitching coach who ever lived."

For fifteen years, from 1961 to 1974, one could plot Sain's travels through the league by following the twenty-game winners:

1961–63, New York Yankees: Whitey Ford, Ralph Terry, Jim Bouton
1965–66, Minnesota Twins: Mudcat Grant, Jim Kaat (Dave Boswell and

COURTESY OF THE NEW YORK YANKEES.

Johnny Sain

Jim Perry won twenty soon after Sain left)
1967–69, Detroit Tigers: Earl Wilson, Denny McLain (Mickey Lolich won twenty after Sain left and said he could not have done it without him)
1971–74, Chicago White Sox: Wilbur Wood, Stan Bahnsen, Jim Kaat (Sain cut the Sox' team ERA from 4.54 to 3.12; the club rose from last to fourth)

All of these, including Ford, never won twenty games before Sain took over and would not win twenty after he left.

Sain has taken other teams' castoffs and made them into stars. McLain, Perry, and Wood are the best examples.

In thirteen years of coaching, including one year at Kansas City, teams coached by Sain won five pennants. Strangely, however, never did one of his teams lead the league in team NERA.

Pitchers love the down-home, tobacco-spitting Arkansan, and managers hate him. Sain wins pennants for them, but he cannot get along with them. Before long there is a clash, and Sain must find another club to lead to a pennant.

The former auto mechanic from Walnut Ridge was a largely self-taught pitcher who finally made it to the majors after World War II. He won fame briefly as Warren Spahn's pitching partner and ace of the 1948 champion Braves.

Ralph Houk hired Sain as pitching coach in 1961, Houk's first year as Casey Stengel's replacement. Sain brought along an armful of inspirational books and tapes (*Think and Grow Rich, How I Raised Myself from Failure to Success in Selling*) and a rapport with his fellow craftsmen.

Denny McLain later asked Sain how many games he thought a good pitcher could win. "As many as you want to," Sain replied. That year Denny went from seventeen victories to thirty-one. As Sain said, "Anything you can conceive or believe, you can achieve."

"Pitching coaches don't change pitchers," he said, "we just stimulate their thinking. We teach their subconscious mind so that when they get on the mound and a situation arises, it triggers an automatic physical reaction that they might not even be aware of." Sain compares pitching to trap shooting. It must be so well learned that it does not require conscious thought, just a physical reaction.

Sain did teach Ford to throw a hard slider (the "slurve") and pitched him with three days' rest instead of the four or five that Casey Stengel had been using. "That made me a twenty-game winner," Ford said. (It actually made him a twenty-five-game winner—and twenty-four two seasons later.)

He did not try to make pitchers into carbon copies of Johnny Sain. The first thing he would do was hit fungoes to a new pitcher to see how he threw the ball back. "That generally will be his natural way of throwing and the way he should pitch."

"I adjust to their style, both as pitchers and people." He dressed with the players, not with the coaches, and liked to spend a lot of time just talking with the staff about whatever they were interested in; Denny McLain liked flying, for instance, and Sain, a former navy pilot, helped him study for his instrument exam. "You know when to lay off him, when to minimize his tensions and also when to inspire him." Sain taught his boys everything from how to put on sanitary socks to how to negotiate a contract.

Under Sain, Mickey Lolich told Pat Jordan, "Pitching takes on new shades and nuances. . . . Sain loves pitchers. He doesn't maybe love baseball so much, but he loves pitchers. He believes pitchers are unique, and only he understands them."

Pitching breaks down to velocity, rotation, change of speed, deception, and control, Sain said. And everything should be simplified. "The pitcher should always be thinking of how to make everything simpler."

To teach spin, Sain drilled holes in balls and inserted rods through them to illustrate better how each pitch rotates in flight.

One thing most pitchers appreciated was that Sain did not make them run. He said most coaches run their pitchers so they will not have to spend the time showing them what they need to know. "Doesn't it make more sense to practice the mechanics of pitching than it does to run?" he asked. "When you've abused your body pitching eight or nine innings, you need three days to recover." Dave Boswell, however, wondered if that was not a weakness of the Sain method, pointing out that both he and Kaat came up with sore arms at Minnesota.

Sain did not agree. "An arm will rust out before it wears out," he said.

Sain would not second-guess a pitcher; he told the hurler to throw what he thought best and if the batter hit it, well, he might have hit something else even farther. "That was a hell of a pitch," he would say; "he never should have hit it." As for the next hitter, "Throw him whatever you think best. You're the judge." Sain rarely visited the mound.

Despite all his success, Sain was always being fired. Houk was named Manager of the Year in 1961, thanks largely to Sain's pitching staff, but their relations cooled. "Houk hogged all the credit," Ralph Terry told Peter Golenbock. "But it wasn't Houk. It was Sain and [batting coach Wally] Moses. . . . They always tried to give the credit to the player, to the boy, and they were wonderful men." But, Terry said, Houk was afraid they were going to try to take his job. Two years later, when Yogi Berra succeeded Houk, John Sain was dismissed. "What general likes a lieutenant that's smarter?" Jim Bouton asked.

Manager Mayo Smith of Detroit was also cool to Sain. Sain was teaching lefty Mike Kilkenny to get left-handers out by coming at them sidearm. Smith told Kilkenny to "take that goddam pitch and shove it up your ass." When Sain took a day off, Smith had the pitchers running in the outfield. Angry, Sain demanded, "Is this the pitching staff that led all baseball in complete games last year?"

Mayo admitted that it was.

"Well," Sain asked, "are we going to follow a formula that I used last year or one that hasn't been successful here for twenty-five years?"

Mayo agreed they would use the successful formula. But it did not make Sain any more popular with the boss, who finally canned him.

When the Twins cast Sain off too, Kaat personally went to the front office and begged them to keep him.

Before he met Sain, Dave Boswell said, a baseball was just a ball. "But after Sain put that ball in your hand, you didn't see it the same any more. It had possibilities you never dreamed of."

Roger Craig and the Tigers

The Detroit Tigers may have won the 1984 World Series because Roger Craig, best known prior to that year for two horrible seasons with the New York Mets, taught the Tigers' staff to throw the split-finger fastball. Jack Morris, Dan Petry, Dave Rozema, and Milt Wilcox all improved their records under Craig.

The father-son relationship between Craig and Petry was often remarked on by television commentators during the Series. Petry admitted he had been winning in the past

Roger Craig

just because the Tigers got him a lot of runs. But "Roger kept pushing me, and I finally realized that I couldn't just rear back and throw."

Said manager Sparky Anderson gratefully: "The man is a genius. I could drop dead tomorrow, but if we lose Roger Craig, we've got problems." And they did. Craig went on to manage the Giants and to teach his pet pitch to Houston's Mike Scott.

The Flip Side

Not all pitching coaches are magicians, and not all pitchers revere and love them. "A lot of coaches would make good prison guards," Bouton wrote acidly.

Bouton's *bête noire* was Sal Maglie of Seattle. Sal yelled at one pitcher to forget the runner, concentrate on the hitter; when the runner stole home, Maglie exploded, "Dammit! You know you've got to pitch from the stretch." "Mother Maglie" was always fighting with Mike Marshall over whether Marshall should develop a screwball or not. Not until midseason did Maglie make his first useful suggestion to Bouton, showing him how Hoyt Wilhelm had gripped the knuckleball. He was full of other helpful hints, such as: throw three straight strikes knee-high over the outside corner. In one clubhouse meeting, Bouton said, Maglie's advice on the tough hitters was "pitch around them." In all, he told the hurler to pitch around five different hitters. "So according to Sal, you start off with two runs in and the bases loaded."

But no matter what Maglie said, "I agreed with him 100 percent," Bouton said.

"You don't make ball clubs arguing with pitching coaches."

Jim Turner of the Yankees was another Bouton target. Turner would yell to a pitcher to keep the ball down. If the pitcher got the man out with a high fastball, Turner would say lamely, "The boy's fastball is rising." If the batter hit it for a homer, Turner would scold, "See what happens when you get the ball up?" In Cincinnati, Bouton said, Turner fastened himself onto Sammy Ellis when Ellis won twenty games. "That son of a bitch," catcher Johnny Edwards told Bouton, "he knows how to take a winner and ride him to his next job. But when Ellis started going bad, Turner wouldn't even talk to him."

Art Fowler of the Yankees was not a bad pitching coach, Sparky Lyle said; even pitchers who scoffed at him as Billy Martin's crony and spy would ask him for advice. Fowler followed Martin wherever he went, ending his career with Billy in Oakland. "Art was one of the funniest men I've ever known," Oakland's pitcher Matt Keough said. Added Brian Kingman: "Billy was like the dad, chewing us out all the time, and Art was like the mom, telling us he really didn't mean it."

Two O's Coaches

In 1977 pitching coach George Bamberger left the Baltimore Orioles to manage the Milwaukee Brewers and the New York Mets (where he was a disappointment). Earl Weaver brought in Ray Miller to replace him. It is interesting to compare the two coaches' records with Weaver:

	Years	Flags	NERA Leaders	20-Game Winners	Cy Young Awards
Bamberger	10	5	4	17	4
Miller	5	1	2	6	2

No one has yet suggested a connection between the departure of Miller to manage

Texas in 1985 and the plunge of the Orioles to last place in 1986.

THE CATCHER

"A catcher is the wife of the battery couple," Waite Hoyt once said. "He must humor the pitcher and jolly him along to make him think he is the big cheese."

Some pitchers have been known to wax so lyrical about the communion between themselves and their catchers that it is hard to tell if they are describing a colleague or a lover. Said ex-Senators' pitcher Walt Masterson: "When a catcher signals exactly what a pitcher is thinking throughout a ball game—that's exact communication, that's beautiful."

"Pitching is a lonely business," Sandy Koufax wrote. "When John [Roseboro] is catching, I have a feeling that I have someone on my side. . . . John and I have been together for so long and can fall into such a complete rapport that [it's] as if there were only one mind involved."

Rick and Wes Ferrell, baseball's best brother battery, once went through an entire game without any signals at all. Wes pitched a two-hitter.

Lefty Grove, on his great batterymate Mickey Cochrane: "Funny, before I'd even look at him, I had in mind what I was going to pitch, and I'd look up and there'd be Mickey's signal, just what I was thinking. Like he was reading my mind."

No question about it—the pitcher and catcher function as a unit—a battery—to attack the batter (although, strangely, they are part of the *defensive* team). When the vibes are right, the pitcher throws not to the batter but *through* him to his other half, playing what ex-catcher Tim McCarver called "an elevated game of catch."

Pitcher and catcher occasionally have spats, just as other couples do. McCarver recalls one fight he had with Steve Carlton early in Lefty's rookie year over what pitches to call. But "once a pitcher trusts you . . . he doesn't have to worry about making the decisions; he can concentrate on pitching." Once, after they were on different teams, Carlton was knocked out of the box and asked Tim to meet him after the game and tell him what he was doing wrong. That, McCarver said, "is when I knew I had his confidence."

Jim Palmer preferred to pitch to Andy Etchebarren, a banjo-hitter, rather than to Elrod Hendricks, who might have produced a few more runs. Andy "calls exactly the game I want to pitch . . . but it bothers my concentration shaking off Elrod so much." (Worst catcher of all for Palmer was the slugging but moody Earl Williams, who once tipped his mask and stuck his tongue out at Jim!)

How can a catcher help a pitcher? "By hitting twenty-three home runs," Earl Weaver said. "They're all good receivers, that's why they're out there." Weaver let his pitchers call their own games, and when catcher Rick Dempsey protested, Weaver told him, "You're a catcher, not 'an executive receiving engineer.'"

Ex-catcher Joe Garagiola agreed. "You know what makes a good catcher?" he asked, picking a bat from the bat rack. "This!" And the lifetime .261 hitter gave the bat a good shake.

Not everyone agrees with Earl and Joe. Gaylord Perry went over to Cleveland from the National League in 1972 and immediately won twenty-four games with the fifth-place Indians. "I never could have done it without Ray Fosse," Gaylord said.

"A smart catcher like Al Lopez can be a big help to the manager," Chuck Dressen wrote. "In fact, I've seen smart catchers carry a bad manager. They would help him work with his pitching staff, and they would call all the pitches and even help him rotate his staff.''

McCarver believes writers have no conception of a catcher's value. Writing in *Sport* magazine, he said writers look on catchers simply as hitters who catch. Take these two championship seasons with the Cardinals:

Year	BA	ERA	ShO	CG
1967	.295	3.05	17	44
1968	.253	2.49	30	63

In 1967 Tim came in second in the MVP vote. The second year his batting average went down, but the Cardinals' pitchers were far better than before. Tim thought he was much more valuable to the team the second year, yet he did not get a single vote for MVP.

Not every catcher is a wizard. Moe Berg could speak a dozen languages, said Ted Lyons, but could not call a decent game in any of them. Warren Spahn seemed to regard catchers somewhat as Casey Stengel did (''if you don't have a catcher, you'll have a lot of passed balls''). ''Catchers have been designated as geniuses,'' Spahn told us, ''but I don't think that's the case. No one knows the rigors of pitching other than a pitcher.'' The strategy on each batter is a result of ''a meeting of the minds'' between the pitcher and catcher before the game, Spahn said. Indeed, some successful backstops regularly asked the pitcher what he wanted to throw in each situation, figuring the pitcher knew best where his confidence lay, then called for those pitches in the game. Paul Richards was reserve catcher for the 1933 champion Giants. ''I tried to let the good men pitch their own games by calling for the pitch I thought they wanted,'' he said. ''I don't recall Hubbell ever shaking me off.''

Catchers can steal strikes for their pitchers. One way is to distract the hitter with chatter. Biz Mackey, top catcher of the Negro leagues (better defensively than Josh Gibson) was a master at this, as were Bill Dickey, Gabby Hartnett, Clyde McCullough, Walker Cooper, and Yogi Berra. Even Ted Williams would break his concentration on the pitcher to turn back and tell Berra to go to hell.

Another way to steal a strike is to receive the borderline pitch in such a way that it looks better than it is, and by building rapport with the umpire. Always catch it in the strike zone, Birdie Tebbets advised. Mackey knew how to make a close pitch look good. But Dickey could not catch a low ball without blocking the ump's view, said Spud Chandler; it cost the Yankee hurler critical strikes now and then.

Berra cost his pitchers strikes by arguing with the umps; Yogi would commit the cardinal sin of turning his head, getting the fans up in arms against the arbiter and making an enemy of the ump. Tebbets ruffled no feathers, umpire Jim Honochick said; Birdie would merely say softly, ''Bring that pitch down a little, Jim,'' and chances are the next close decision would go his way.

Giving signals is another art. Pumping two fingers forcefully and confidently sends a far different message to the pitcher than putting two fingers down hesitantly and weakly.

But weak or strong, a catcher's signals must be protected from prying eyes. Ted Williams said he was on first one day when Berra ''got kind of careless with his right knee,'' and Ted was flashing all of Yogi's signs to first-base coach Del Baker, perhaps the all-time great sign stealer himself. Next time Ted came up, Yogi fumed to him, ''Boy, what dumbass pitchers we've got. Baker knows what they're going to throw every time.''

Catchers also have to be diplomats. Cardinals' manager Johnny Keane once ordered McCarver to go to the mound to slow Bob Gibson down. "He doesn't want me out there," Tim warned. When Keane said he did not give a damn, McCarver went halfway out, trying to appease both. "Keep your ass away from me while I'm working!" Gibson snarled.

In addition to everything else, a catcher must throw out base runners, catch foul pops, block low pitches, and even be teachers, like Paul Richards, who taught Hal Newhouser the slider. No wonder so many pitching coaches are former catchers.

How important is the catcher? Except for the pitcher, he is the most important man on the team.

The Pitchers' Catchers

Who were the top pitchers' catchers of all time? Based on the number of NERA crowns their staffs won (compared to the total years they caught), the top eleven are:

Catcher	Years	NERA Crowns
Elrod Hendricks	3.5	3
Mike Scioscia	6.5	4
Steve Yeager	10.0	6
Lou Criger*	5.0	3
Chief Meyers	7.0	4
Mickey Cochrane†	11.0	5
Bill Killefer	9.0	4
Johnny Kling	12.0	5
Thurman Munson	10.0	4
Bubbles Hargrave	8.0	3
Tim McCarver	8.0	3

*Twentieth-century years only.
†Hall of Fame.

NERAs include league titles through 1968 and division titles through 1969. A year is 100 or more games caught; half-years are 50 to 99 games.

One of the first things to strike you about the list may be: Where are the Hall of Fam-

ers? Mickey Cochrane is the only one on it. Where are Yogi Berra, Roy Campanella, Bill Dickey, Ray Schalk, Roger Bresnahan, Gabby Hartnett, Ernie Lombardi, Al Lopez, and Rick Ferrell? Or potential Hall of Famers Johnny Bench, Bob Boone, Carlton Fisk, Gary Carter, and Lance Parrish? All these immortals have been shouldered aside by lesser-known men who would appear to be better handlers of pitching staffs.

Elrod Hendricks

Elrod Hendricks was Baltimore's top receiver for only three years, 1969 to 1971. In each of those years the Birds won the pennant and the NERA crown as best staff in their division.

One could argue that Hendricks was fortunate to have some great pitchers—and a great manager—who gave him such an amazing record. Yet Baltimore has always had great staffs and other great catchers during the Weaver regency, but none of them produced a record like Ellie's.

In his three years, Dave McNally, Mike Cuellar, Jim Palmer, and Pat Dobson all won twenty games a total of nine times. They all did it together in 1971, making Hendricks only the second catcher in history to handle four twenty-game winners in one year (Ray Schalk was the other, in 1920).

Before Ellie took over, Baltimore had finished second. Hendricks lost his job in 1972, and the Orioles fell to third.

Chief Meyers

Chief Meyers spent only six years as catcher for the New York Giants, 1910–15, but his pitchers won three NERA titles, something his predecessor, Hall of Famer Roger Bresnahan, never accomplished even once.

When Meyers moved to Brooklyn in 1916, the Robins cut half a run off their ERA and jumped from third place to their first pennant.

Unfortunately, the Chief did not reach the majors until he was twenty-eight and played only nine years, one short of Cooperstown's requirements. But the Hall of Fame has made exceptions for others; perhaps one should be made for Meyers.

Mickey Cochrane

No catcher has ever won more NERA crowns than Mickey Cochrane has, and only Jim Hegan has caught more twenty-game winners. Before Cochrane joined the Philadelphia A's, they were a fifth-place club with a 4.39 ERA. In Cochrane's first year, 1925, the pitchers took half a run off their ERA, and the A's jumped to second place. The next year, John Thorn and Pete Palmer say, the A's may have fielded the best pitching staff of all time, winning twenty-four more games than could have been expected from an average staff.

In Cochrane's last year at Philadelphia, 1933, the team finished third. The year after he left, they fell to fifth. The Athletics would never win another pennant in Philadelphia.

Cochrane moved to Detroit and in his first two years lifted the Tigers from fifth to their first pennants in twenty-three years.

Bill Killefer

With a lifetime batting average of .238, "Reindeer Bill" Killefer may never make the Hall of Fame. Yet Grover Cleveland Alexander just might not be there without him.

Bill joined the Phils in 1912, Alex's second year, and together the pair won twenty, twenty-seven, twenty-seven, thirty-one, thirty-three, and thirty games.

Was Bill just lucky to be handling the great Alexander? In 1919 the two were traded to the fifth-place Chicago Cubs. Alexander was drafted into the army, but Killefer and the Cubs won the pennant without him. They also won Bill his third NERA crown.

Killefer and Alexander had left the Phils in second place; as soon as they were gone, the Phils sank to sixth.

Some day, perhaps, Cooperstown will recognize Bill Killefer as the other, and equal, half of the Alexander–Killefer battery. When they do, we suggest they put Bill's plaque on the wall opposite Alexander, where he can grin back at Alex, just 60 feet, 6 inches away.

Johnny Kling

No one has ever suggested a connection between those great Cubs' staffs of the early days of this century—Mordecai Brown, Ed Reulbach, and the like—and the almost invisible man in the face mask who caught them. Chances are not one fan in 100 even knows who Johnny Kling was—certainly the Cooperstown electors do not seem to.

In nine years, 1901 to 1908 and 1910, Kling's staffs won four pennants, finished second once and third twice.

They led all clubs in NERA five times, and no catcher has ever topped that, though Cochrane tied it. For two amazing seasons, 1906 and 1907, they posted team ERAs of 1.76 and 1.73.

On a park-adjusted basis, the early Cubs had three of the top five ERA staffs of all time. Johnny Kling caught all three of them.

In 1909 Johnny held out for more money and missed the entire season. The Cubs fell from first to second. He returned in 1910, and they went back to first. Kling was released that winter. The Cubs would not win another flag for eight years.

Tim McCarver

We think of Tim McCarver as the Svengali to Steve Carlton's Trilby. Actually, McCarver handled some fine pitchers in addition to Carlton. For example, even manager

Johnny Keane could not make a twenty-game winner out of Bob Gibson, but Bob won twenty games four times after Mc-Carver went behind the bat.

As a first-time regular in 1963, McCarver took over a sixth-place Cardinals' team and lifted them to second. The next year they were world champs, as Ray Sadecki won twenty games for the only time in his career. The Cards would win two more pennants, 1967 and 1968, with Tim behind the plate. In the latter year Gibson enjoyed a sensational season with a 1.12 ERA.

These were also Carlton's first years in the majors. In three-and-a-half seasons with McCarver, Steve won forty-seven and lost thirty-four, with a 2.71 ERA. When Mc-Carver was dealt away, Steve fell to 30–28 and added almost one run to his ERA.

In 1972 Tim caught half of one of the greatest pitching years ever recorded, Carlton's twenty-seven-victory season with the last-place Phils. (John Bateman handled the other half, after Tim was traded. Bateman has never received the credit he deserves.)

McCarver came back to the Phils in 1975 as Carlton's special catcher. In the next six seasons Steve won 116 and lost 55. Actually his winning percentage with Tim was only slightly higher than with his other receivers. In fact, after McCarver left, Carlton's wins went up from eighteen in 1979 to twenty-four in 1980 with Bob Boone.

Still Carlton and McCarver will always be linked in baseball lore. "When Steve and I die," Tim said, "we're going to be buried 60 feet, 6 inches apart."

Jim Hegan

Jim Hegan owns a record that will probably never be broken, at least as long as the five-day rotation lasts: He caught eighteen twenty-game winners, more than any other man who ever wore shin guards.

From 1946, when Jim joined the team, through 1957, his final year, Cleveland produced perhaps the finest pitching staff of the lively ball era—Bob Feller, Bob Lemon, Gene Bearden, Early Wynn, Mike Garcia, and Herb Score. Three—Feller, Lemon, and Wynn—are in the Hall of Fame. The pitchers got the publicity; all Jim got was broken fingers.

"Hegan was by far the best defensive catcher I ever pitched to," Feller said. In Jim's first season, 1946, Feller struck out 348 men. The Indians finished sixth, but they were a fourth-place team with Hegan behind the bat (45–43) and a seventh-place club without him (21–43).

In his final year, 1957, the Indians won more games, 111, than any team in the history of the American League.

Hegan obviously did not improve the club all alone. But the Indians' great pitching years exactly coincided with Jim's years on the team.

Billy Sullivan, Sr.

Ty Cobb once called Billy Sullivan the best catcher "ever to put on shoe leather." Sullivan and Big Ed Walsh were the big duo on the White Sox' "Hitless Wonder" teams of the early 1900s. Billy was behind the plate in 1901, when the Sox won the first pennant in American League history. He was there again in 1906, when the Sox upset the great Cubs, winners of 116 games, in the World Series, four games to two. And he was calling the signals again in 1908 when Walsh won forty games and just fell short of winning a third pennant.

Sullivan missed the 1903 season, and the Sox fell from fourth to seventh. He came back in 1904, and they rebounded to fourth again. He missed half of the 1909 campaign and all of 1910, and the Sox fell from third to sixth, while Walsh dropped from thirty-nine victories to fifteen. When Billy came back in 1911, the White Sox climbed to fourth and Big Ed returned to form with twenty-six wins.

Billy's son, Bill Jr., incidentally, became a fine catcher with the Browns and Tigers in the thirties and forties.

Roger Bresnahan

For six years, from 1903 to 1908, Roger Bresnahan handled the great Giants' pitchers Christy Mathewson and Joe McGinnity. He should have been the perfect catcher, having started out as a pitcher (he was 4–0 in 1897) and in fact once caught and pitched in the same game in 1901, probably the only man ever to do that.

Bresnahan joined the last-place Giants, along with manager John McGraw, from Baltimore midway through the 1902 season. The next year the two Irishmen lifted the Giants to second, as Mathewson jumped from eight wins to twenty-nine and McGinnity from fourteen to thirty-two. The next year they won the pennant.

Roger supposedly invented shin guards, one of the rationales for electing him to Cooperstown. Actually, they had been worn by Negro league infielders, such as Bill Monroe and Pop Lloyd, several years before Bresnahan first put them on. Bresnahan also claimed to have been born in Tralee, Ireland. Actually, he came from Toledo, Ohio.

Yogi Berra

Yogi Berra was, by all odds, the most famous catcher of all time, appearing on television year after year in the World Series.

Berra won the first-string catching job on the Yankees in 1949, Casey Stengel's first year as manager. It may not be a coincidence that that year the Yanks rose from third place to the pennant, beating Boston on the final day. It was the first of thirteen pennant-winners and three NERA champs Yogi would catch.

Three times Yogi was elected MVP. Yet in 1958 the Yankees played 25–8 ball without him. We are not sure how to explain that.

Because of the way he turned a phrase, some people regarded Yogi as a sort of comic figure, but Ted Williams, among others, thought he was a smart receiver. "He knew the little things that make the pitcher great," Ted wrote in *My Turn at Bat*. "Berra had it. He knew how to work with the pitcher."

Elston Howard

It took Elston Howard several years of waiting, but at the age of thirty-one he finally beat out Berra for the first-string catching job. The Yanks, who had finished third in 1959, Berra's last year, won the pennant in each of Howard's first five years.

Howard was fortunate that his tenure coincided with Johnny Sain's presence as pitching coach. The Sain–Howard combination brought the Yanks three pennants; after Sain left, Howard handled two more championship staffs without him.

(But it must also be noted that Howard was the regular catcher during the Yankees' slide from the pennant in 1964 to tenth in 1966.)

In 1967 Howard moved to the Red Sox and lifted a ninth-place staff to the pennant in "the Unforgettable Dream" summer— his sixth flag in eight years.

Roy Campanella

Roy Campanella called the signals for the 1957 Dodgers, whom Thorn and Palmer call the best staff in the history of the National League. In ten years he won three MVP awards, handled three NERA champion staffs, five pennant winners, and ten twenty-game winners.

The year he suffered his accident, 1958, the team ERA shot up more than a run a game, and the club plummeted from third to seventh.

Catchers Unaccounted For

Several noteworthy catchers did not win enough NERA crowns or catch enough twenty-game winners or catch on enough pennant-winning teams to make any of the top-ten lists. Nevertheless, we feel they deserve to be recognized.

Gus Mancuso

Like Bill Killefer and Lou Criger, the euphonious Gus Mancuso played with a hurler so brilliant that no one noticed who his catcher was. The hurler was Carl Hubbell. It is conjecture that Carl would have become known as the King if Gus had not helped.

When Gus Mancuso joined the Giants in 1933, they had just finished sixth and Hob had just won eighteen games. "Gus had a lot to do with Hubbell developing his screwball," said Gus' brother Frank. "It was all in his thumb, the way he'd spin the ball backwards." The two drilled it and drilled it; that year Hubbell blossomed into a star with twenty-three victories, and the Giants won twenty-one games or more every year, and the Giants won three flags.

In 1938 Gus was demoted to backup catcher. New York fell from first to third, and Hubbell's victories fell from twenty-two to thirteen. He never won twenty games again.

Six years later brother Frank joined the St. Louis Browns as catcher—and the Browns won their only pennant. Frank is now campaigning to get Gus into Cooperstown.

Jerry Grote

Nolan Ryan called Jerry Grote "the most complete catcher" he ever pitched to. Most Mets' pitchers from 1966 through 1976 would agree.

Tom Seaver scored five twenty-victory years in his career, four of them with Grote calling the pitches. Jerry Koosman posted his only twenty-win year with Grote. The three of them brought pennants to New York in 1969 and 1973.

Johnny Roseboro

John Roseboro was rushed behind the plate after Roy Campanella's accident in 1958, and both he and the Dodgers had a disastrous year at the grotesquely shaped Coliseum. The team finished seventh. But the next year they won the pennant.

Thereafter John teamed with Sandy Koufax, Don Drysdale, and manager Walter Alston to give the Dodgers some of the best pitching ever seen. They won four flags in an era of abysmally weak offense.

Koufax was a wild young lefty when John took over. By 1963 Sandy was a twenty-five-game winner, and his entire period of stardom came during Roseboro's tenure.

Moving to Minnesota in 1969, Roseboro helped the Twins come in first, his fifth flag in twelve years.

Carlton Fisk

Mostly famous for his prayerful 1975 World Series home run, Fisk won no NERA titles, but in his rookie year he lifted the Red Sox from third to second. He moved to the White Sox in 1981, and the team jumped from fifth to first in two years.

Darrel Porter

Over almost fourteen years, Darrel Porter's pitchers won twenty games seven times and division titles five-and-a-half times.

When Kansas City let him go in 1981, the Royals dropped from first to fourth. The Cards, who picked him up, rose from fourth to first.

Bob Boone

Bob Boone is a puzzle. When he joined the Phils in 1973 and the Angels in 1982, both clubs' ERAs went up. When he left the Phils in 1981, the club ERA went down. This would suggest that Boone was not an asset to the pitchers.

On the other hand, in Bob's first year at California, the Angels immediately rose from fifth to first. In all, he guided his staffs to six division flags and three NERA titles. He also caught three of Steve Carlton's six twenty-victory seasons, twice as many as Tim McCarver did.

MANAGERS

Johnny Keane

Bob Gibson said he liked some managers better than others, but he did not let it affect his pitching either way. Do not believe a word of it. If there was one man who gave him the confidence to be a big-league star, Gibson wrote in *From Ghetto to Glory,* it was Johnny Keane.

Keane had studied for the priesthood. His approach was "soft and fatherly," and by great good luck he was manager of Omaha in 1957 when twenty-one-year-old rookie Gibson reported for his first professional assignment. In his first game, Gibson was not getting the high strikes, then panicked, and pretty soon the other club had scored three runs and Keane was walking to the mound.

"That's pretty good for a first time," he said softly. "We'll get back to you later."

Keane worked with Bob on the sidelines, helping him get his pitches down, and with improvement, confidence grew.

In two years Gibson was with the Cardinals under Solly Hemus, who managed with a chip on his shoulder, Gibson wrote. When Hemus lost, which was often—the Cards finished seventh that year—he blamed everyone but himself. Gibson and Hemus did not hit it off at all, and Gibson rarely got into a game. On one of the few times that he did, Gibson walked a man, center fielder Bill White misjudged a fly, and Hemus came steaming to the mound, "ranting and raving," with the hook in his hand.

Gibson was 3–6 that year, 3–6 the next, and 2–6 in 1961 when, midway through the season, Hemus himself got the hook, and Johnny Keane was called up to replace him. Gibson felt like a prisoner released from jail.

"From now on you're in the regular rotation, Hoot," Keane said. Over the rest of the year Gibson won eleven and lost six and finished with the best ERA of any right-hander in the league. The next year he won fifteen, tops on the Cardinals' staff. "Pitching regularly made all the difference."

Bad Vibes

Not all manager–pitcher relationships are of the Gibson–Keane variety. Inevitably, some are more of the Gibson–Hemus kind.

Rarely, however, do they get quite as bad as Burleigh Grimes' relationship with his manager at Pittsburgh, Hugo Bezdek. One night on a Pullman the two battled each other, punching, biting, gouging, and choking, until the players, disappointed that neither one seemed able to murder the other, pried them apart.

Ty Cobb

The quintessential bad pitchers' manager was Ty Cobb, says SABR's Larry Amman, who has made a study of Cobb's career. Cobb managed the Tigers for six years, 1921–26, and his staffs were below average in ERA every year. There was no pattern to his rotation, Amman says—he might pitch a man with five days' rest or with one. He would warm up two or three starters and decide which to use minutes before game time. Cobb told young Carl Hubbell he would never be a pitcher. Ty wore a path from the outfield to the pitcher's mound, giving advice. Or he would whistle with his fingers and give hand signals to the pitcher and catcher, embarrassing both.

Once, according to Amman, Ty went to the mound and humiliated Howard Ehmke by going through an exaggerated lesson in pitching mechanics while the crowd looked on. Ehmke and Cobb came to blows over it. Ehmke was 13–14 and 17–17 under Ty, then moved to Boston and won twenty with the last-place Red Sox under Frank Chance, the man who had made the 1907–10 Cubs into the greatest pitching staff of all time.

When Cobb left the team in 1927, George Moriarty took over and cut almost half a run off Detroit's team ERA.

Mike Marshall's Quest

Mike Marshall, the great relief pitcher, was just too intelligent. He intimidated Mayo Smith of the Tigers (where Mike was 1–3 with ten saves), fought with Seattle coach Sal Maglie, who would not let him throw a screwball (3–10, no saves), and continued the battle with manager Harry Walker of Houston (0–1).

Not until Marshall joined Montreal in 1970 did he find the right manager for him, Gene Mauch, who told Mike to follow his own rules and work out his own training program.

Mike was 3–7 in 1970, then 5–8 with twenty-three saves, 14–8 with eighteen saves, and 14–11 with a league-high thirty-one saves. "I never did manage Mike Marshall," Mauch said. "His kind doesn't need a lot of managing."

Bill Lee's Gripes

In his book *The Wrong Stuff,* Bill Lee charged that the Red Sox' skipper Eddie Kasko, a political conservative, lost the 1972 pennant because he refused to use Lee, who sported a T-shirt saying, "Lick Dick in '72." Lee won only seven games that year, and the Red Sox lost by half a game. "My T-shirt may have cost us the pennant," Lee wrote.

Darrell Johnson, Dick Williams' ex-pitching coach, finally brought the Sox the pennant in 1975 but lost the stirring World Series to the Reds in seven games. Again Lee was critical. He thought Johnson left starters in too long and did not establish an order in the bull pen, going with whomever he felt was hot.

In the Series, the Sox were behind three games to two. It was Lee's turn to pitch the sixth game, but Johnson elected to go with Luis Tiant, who had three days' rest but had already pitched two complete games. Tiant got knocked out, though Carlton Fisk won the game with his homer in the tenth. Lee started the seventh game and lost 3–2. He insists that he could have won the sixth game and that Tiant, with an extra day's rest, could have won the seventh. No one will ever know.

Don Zimmer presided over the famous 1978 collapse, when the Sox raced to a thirteen-and-a-half-game lead, then lost the division crown to the Yankees in a one-game playoff. Lee called him a "cute, puffy-cheeked gerbil." In 1977, Zim's first year, Lee charged that he overworked Bill Campbell "to a state of collapse" and alienated Rick Wise because Wise wanted to grow a beard. According to Lee, Ferguson Jenkins thought Zimmer "didn't know diddly about pitching" and derisively tagged him "Buffalo Head," after "the dumbest animal in creation." By midseason Zimmer was not talking to half his pitching staff.

Lee said one factor in the 1978 collapse was that Zimmer simply would not give Lee a start in spite of his good record against the Yanks. In the famous Boston Massacre, when the Yankees whipped the Sox four straight to take the division lead, Lee pitched only once, after the game was out of control. He went seven innings and gave up only one earned run. Still he stayed in Zimmer's dog house.

In the playoff Zimmer went with Mike Torrez, though Lee begged pitching coach Al Jackson for the assignment. Torrez pitched well, but he tired and Zimmer left him in until he threw the famous home-run ball to Bucky Dent. Insisted Lee ruefully, ''That was my game to win.''

Pitchers' Managers

Considering that 40 percent of each big-league roster is made up of pitchers, and that pitchers are often the most intelligent men and the strongest personalities on a team, it is a mystery why so few go on to become managers. Christy Mathewson and Walter Johnson tried their hands at managing briefly but without notable success. Clark Griffith, Burleigh Grimes, Bob Shawkey, Freddy Fitzsimmons, Ted Lyons, Fred Hutchinson, Bob Lemon, Ed Lopat, and Tom Lasorda are others, plus oldtimers Al Spalding and John Montgomery Ward.

There is definitely a class of managers who might be called ''pitchers' managers,'' as opposed to such ''hitters' managers'' as Dick Williams, Sparky Anderson, and Casey Stengel. Some pitchers' managers are ex-catchers: Wilbert Robinson, Steve O'Neill, Al Lopez, and Paul Richards. However many ex-catchers were not pitchers' managers: Ralph Houk, Herman Franks, Yogi Berra, Bill Killefer, and Luke Sewell. Some pitchers' managers were former infielders: Earl Weaver, Walter Alston, John McGraw, Miller Huggins, Joe McCarthy, Jimmy Dykes, Frank Chance, Jimmy Collins, and Bobby Cox. Very few are ex-outfielders—only Billy Southworth and Fred Clarke come to mind.

Whoever they are, these are the men who know how to build and use a good staff. They are also usually the men who win the most pennants.

Tom Lasorda

An ebullient ex-pitcher, Lasorda's Dodgers average an NERA title every year and a half, which is perhaps the biggest reason why they also average a division championship every other year.

The most important part of managing, Lasorda told us, is psychological. ''The first thing I'd do is bring a couch into my office and put them on the couch. This''—tapping his forehead—''controls everything. To be successful, you got to believe in yourself.''

Lasorda believes in himself. When he replaced Walter Alston, he inherited a Dodgers' team that finished ten games back in 1976. Under Tom in 1977 they finished ten games up and drew almost three million record-breaking customers. Tommy John, Burt Hooton, Rick Rhoden, and Charlie Hough all had their best years.

It is true that Lasorda produced only two twenty-game winners in his first eleven years—Tommy John and Fernando Valenzuela. This is more probably a result of the five-day rotation now prevalent.

John worshipped Lasorda and wrote that he was more likely than Alston to understand a pitcher's problems. He was also ''better equipped to bring peace to the locker room''—in fact, ''just about the most lovable guy anyone ever worked for—full of fun, full of sympathy and understanding, full of enthusiasm.''

One of Lasorda's first acts on being named manager was to go to John and tell him, "Tommy, I need you. You are going to start, and you are going to win for us." Wrote John gratefully: "In all my career, I had never had a coach or manager express such confidence in me." Tommy did win for Lasorda—the only twenty-victory season in his career. "I give Tom Lasorda most of the credit," John said. Lasorda was willing to stick with him "when I was having a bad moment or two." John's eleven complete games that year were a tribute to Lasorda's "willingness to go the extra mile with me."

In contrast, Don Sutton and Lasorda never got along. Sutton had enjoyed his only twenty-victory year under Alston the year before Lasorda took over and never won twenty again. He campaigned openly for Jeff Torborg to get the manager's job instead of Lasorda. Thereafter, Don said, his conversations with his skipper tended to be loud and get louder, "like two people trying to see who can out-yell each other without listening."

Lasorda's choice of adjectives is as limited as Babe Ruth's, and he can be curt and snide to those who he feels cannot help him. But Sutton's seems to be a minority view. Most Dodgers love Lasorda and his rah-rah "Dodger blue" loyalty. (Even God, to Lasorda, is "the big Dodger in the sky.")

Lasorda loved practical jokes. He once dropped in on Tommy John's family, romping with the kids and telling them, "Uncle Tommy loves you." While John and three other players there fidgeted about being late to the park, Lasorda told them not to worry, that he would drive them. They finally left the house much too late and arrived after batting practice had begun. He fined them each $50. "Never trust the person driving to get you to the park on time," he told them sternly.

Earl Weaver

The antithesis of the bubbly Lasorda, Earl Weaver's driving, abrasive generalship has made him probably the second greatest pitchers' manager of all time. But, as with Lasorda, in private, Weaver's real personality is often just the opposite of his public persona.

In a career of seventeen years, Earl produced six Cy Young winners, a record (runner-up Walter Alston needed twenty-three years to produce five). Earl also averaged about one NERA title every other year.

"The only thing Weaver knows about pitching," Dave McNally once quipped, "is that he couldn't hit it."

"One thing I know about it," Earl retorted, "is who to put out on that mound and how to use them against the right club at the right time."

In his first full season at Baltimore, 1969, Weaver and pitching coach George Bamberger produced two twenty-game winners, three more the next year, and three more after that, plus their first Cy Young winner, Mike Cuellar.

Cuellar, a journeyman with Houston, was spotted and picked up by Baltimore. The O's gave him a Spanish translator, catcher Elrod Hendricks, and Mike immediately became a star. He, McNally, and Jim Palmer helped bring Earl three pennants in his first three years.

Both Weaver and Bamberger were lifelong minor-league players, but together they produced champions. "What the pitchers needed, that was my job," Weaver told us. "If he's missing [lacking] a pitch, I'd tell Bamberger to work on it: 'George, you got to teach him to turn that fastball over.' George could do that, teach them how, and to a lesser extent, so could Ray Miller [who followed Bamberger]. But what they needed, that was my job."

Earl Weaver's shouting matches with Jim Palmer throughout fifteen symbiotic years sum up the love–hate relationship that brought both of them greatness. "I can't throw the dumb pitches Earl wants me to and still be effective," Palmer complained. "Earl doesn't know the difference between a slider and a curve-ball."

But Weaver always apologized after he cooled off, Palmer said. "That's why you really can't stay mad at him. . . . Earl and I are actually quite a bit alike—which doesn't mean he's endearing, only that I understand him. Both of us like to win, we're emotional, we're stubborn, and we speak our minds. I like Earl, I really do. He's a pussycat when he's not overemotional. And when he is, he's too silly, too juvenile, to dislike. He's not vicious or spiteful, he just gets frustrated and needs outlets for it, like umpires."

Weaver preferred a player who let it all hang out rather than bottling feelings up. "Jimmy likes to help me manage," he wrote in his book, *It's What You Learn After You Know It All That Counts*. Actually, he admitted, Jim "has said many things over the years that have been valuable."

Interestingly, Palmer and Weaver give almost identical accounts of the same in-cidents, something that rarely happens in really vindictive fights.

In his book Weaver said he once over-heard Palmer say, "Weaver's the most optimistic man I ever saw. He programs his outlook and transmits it to you."

We asked Weaver if he and Palmer were really friends underneath. "Only one other combination stayed together as long as Palmer and I did," he nodded—"Alston and Drysdale." Ruefully, he smiled that he did kind of like "the underwear salesman."

Weaver and Palmer liked to needle each other in a way they could not have done if they were not basically friends.

After Weaver had been arrested for drunk driving, Palmer prefaced his banquet speeches with: "I'd like to apologize for Earl Weaver not being here tonight, but the Maryland State Police are conducting a drivers' education class."

Weaver's diminutive height was the subject of Orioles' jokes. "Did you ever notice," Palmer asked, "that when Earl comes to the mound, he always stands on the highest part of it?" (Pitcher Mike Flanagan was accused of telling six-foot jokes—they were over everyone's head. But with Weaver, he said, he only had to tell five-foot-seven jokes.)

Weaver was one of the first managers to study pitcher–hitter match-ups. He kept three-by-five cards on every combination the Orioles faced (his second baseman, Davey Johnson, would later extend the idea, putting these data on a computer when he became manager of the Mets). Weaver and Bamberger met over pinochle or at the hotel bar and went over the cards, then Earl taped the relevant ones to the dugout wall before each game. Not only did he know how each hitter did against each Baltimore pitcher, he could announce, "This guy is nine for twenty-seven against the fastball; throw him a curve."

Weaver was also a motivator (and hypnotist). As the awards piled up, Bamberger could tell a prospect, "Look, if you don't want to win twenty, it's all right. If you do, that's all right too. There are a number of guys who do want to win twenty, though." That usually got attention.

Four pitchers—Cuellar, Mike Torrez, Pat Dobson, and Steve Stone—came from other teams and enjoyed their only twenty-win seasons under Earl. With Torrez, Weaver wrote, it was a matter of teaching him a slow curve and how to set up a hitter.

Rookie Wayne Garland was another who had a celebrated feud with Earl. He chafed in the bull pen, complaining that he was pitching entire games out there without ever getting the chance to show his stuff in a game. Weaver said he was bringing the kid along gradually, teaching him a screwball and working on his move to first base. The only place for a rookie was long relief, he believed, since the rookie year is a learning time for both him and the manager. If he performs well there, then a spot is cleared for him in the starting rotation the next year.

Garland simply did not understand this. But when he got his chance in 1976, he too joined the Orioles' twenty-game club. Still, he complained that Earl had mishandled him and said he would not sign in 1977 unless Rochester's manager Joe Altobelli was brought up to replace Weaver. Then Garland jumped to the Indians for a million-dollar contract. "Mishandled!" Weaver sneered. "I wish someone would mishandle me like that."

To replace Garland, Weaver brought up Mike Flanagan, who quickly went to 2–8. Weaver gave him no encouragement, Mike charged; fellow starter Jim Palmer did. "Hell," Weaver retorted, "I thought the fact that I kept him in the rotation should have told him enough about my confidence in him." Flanagan was 13–2 the rest of the year. "Earl's been good to me," he admitted later; "he stuck his neck out for me." In 1979 Flanagan added another Cy Young award to Baltimore's growing trophy case. He would win fifty-seven games in his first three years under Weaver.

Steve Stone, a lifelong journeyman, arrived in Baltimore in 1979 and, like Palmer and Garland, had his shouting matches with Weaver. "You're not only an egomaniac," Steve bellowed, "you're a stupid egomaniac."

"And you're a loser," Weaver hollered back. "You'll always be a loser until you're willing to do things the right way." But he never lost faith that Stone could be a star. He never stopped preaching positive thinking, telling Stone his curve was just right for Baltimore, where the great Bird infielders could gobble up ground balls. But he also tried to instill Steve's confidence in his fastball.

Slowly, Stone began to listen. "I was 0 for 3 in arguments with the manager," he said. "If Earl wants you on his team," he finally reasoned, "it's because he's so sure of his own judgment of your ability. He's the best evaluator of talent in the majors, so his confidence rubs off on you." In his next start Stone struck out ten and won the game 12–1. He ended 1979 with five straight victories. The next year he won the Cy Young plaque.

The other clubs hated Weaver even more than the Orioles did. "He's always trying to intimidate you and intimidate the umpires," Sparky Lyle of the Yankees said. Weaver constantly hollered at the opposing pitcher, trying to upset him. Lyle complained, "Boy, he's a bastard. That's one reason he wins."

"Yelling," Weaver said sheepishly, "is just a way of communicating loudly. . . . I'm famous for three things: arguing with umpires, battling with players, and winning ball games. Well, you can't have the latter without the first two."

In 1982 Weaver announced he was quitting at the end of the year and just missed another division flag when the aging Jim

Palmer was bombed by the Milwaukee Brewers in the final game. Long after the game, the capacity crowd milled around the Baltimore dugout, chanting "We Want Weaver, We Want Weaver," until the little manager finally reappeared and acknowledged their salute with an embarrassed wave of his cap. It was a tribute we have never seen accorded to any other manager.

Paul Richards

Ex-catcher Paul Richards is a surprise so high on the list. He never won a pennant or was associated with great individual pitchers, except Hoyt Wilhelm. But there he is, ahead of Earl Weaver, Walter Alston, Joe McCarthy, Connie Mack, John McGraw, and other more famous managers of history. A great teacher and innovator (the oversized catcher's mitt for knuckleballers), he deserves his rightful place on the list of great pitchers' managers.

Billy Southworth

Billy Southworth has also been too long overlooked. He not only produced great pitchers (Mort Cooper) and three pennants with the Cards, he moved to the Boston Braves and did it again in 1948 with an entirely different club. It was easy to win with Spahn and Sain, but the "two days of rain" was the mark of Southworth's genius.

Billy Martin

Dipsomaniacal, pugilistic, profane, and lovable, Billy Martin enlivened the nation's sports pages and cut a swath through the American League, strewing pennants and angry general managers behind him wherever he went.

In ten years Martin averaged a twenty-game winner a year and a championship every other year. There is probably a direct connection between those two numbers. It is known as "Billy Ball." Martin worked his hot pitchers until their arms dropped off. They won flags for him by doing it. But when Martin left, the arms were gone, and so were the flags.

Among modern managers, he is second only to Earl Weaver in the percentage of twenty-game winners he produced per year. But Weaver's pitchers thrived under his direction; Martin's collapsed. Martin's victims numbered Mickey Lolich, Joe Coleman, Fergie Jenkins, Catfish Hunter, Ron Guidry, and others.

But Billy undoubtedly had hit on a winning formula, although it did not endear him to his bosses. He won the division title with the Minnesota Twins and was fired, won again with the Detroit Tigers and was fired, lifted the Texas Rangers to second and was fired, made the Yanks world champs and was fired (and brought back and fired again and brought back and fired yet again), raised the Oakland A's from last to second and was fired. Billy's problem (one of them, anyway), as Sparky Lyle observed, was that Billy could not fire the owners/general managers but they could fire him.

But some of the players loved him. He fought with them, drank with them, and became close to them.

He liked Oakland's pitcher Matt Keough, who said he "was just crazy enough to sit down and laugh at him when he was yelling at people." Keough once set fire to Martin's shoelaces. Billy replied by cutting up Keough's street clothes. "It was fun," Matt said.

But Brian Kingman, whose wrecked career he blames on Martin's regimen, said, "From day one we were motivated by fear. Billy wasn't just a manager, he was a tyrant. Nobody was sure of his job. Anybody could be replaced. It seemed as if your career depended on every play."

A Billy Martin team was a winning team, and a Billy Martin player was a winner. But he exacted a high price from his pitchers and paid a high price himself.

Wilbert Robinson

Uncle Wilbert Robinson was a cherubic, avuncular old catcher who had played with John McGraw on the famous old Baltimore Orioles and later understudied McGraw as coach of the Giants. It was Robbie who did so much to save Rube Marquard's career there. Later, as Brooklyn manager, Robbie gave a job to Dazzy Vance after everyone else had given up on him. Robinson put Vance on a five-day rotation, almost unheard of in those days, and saved his career.

"Robinson was the guy made a pitcher out of me," Hall of Famer Burleigh Grimes said. Burleigh had been 3–16 with Pittsburgh in 1918 when he was traded to the Dodgers. In his first year with Robbie, Grimes cut his ERA from 3.53 to 2.13, and his victories shot up from three to nineteen. Grimes won twenty-three in 1920 and led the Robins to the pennant.

Robinson was accused of being too lackadaisical, of not holding his players on a tight rein. Vance, his favorite pitcher, was leader of the "0-for-4" club, whose motto was "Do anything, but don't get caught." That usually meant staying out after curfew.

On one occasion, when a player began banging his bat on the dugout steps to get a rally started, Robbie put his fingers to his lips and whispered to him to tone it down; he did not want to waken pitcher Jess Petty.

Rube Foster

Rube Foster is often called "the black McGraw." He was a brainy, innovative pitcher, manager, owner, and league czar. His great Chicago American Giants' teams

of the 1920s were built around pitching and speed, and in an era of high-scoring sluggers, an American Giants' game was usually a tight pitching classic that ended with a score of 2–1 or 1–0.

Foster's greatest pitching find was Dave Brown, an ex-convict who many oldtimers say was the best black left-hander ever. (His career was short; Dave murdered a man in a New York bar and fled the law, never to pitch big-time ball again.)

Another of Foster's protegés was Frank Wickware, "the red ant" from Walter Johnson's home town of Coffeyville, Kansas. Wickware once beat Johnson 1–0.

Another was Webster McDonald, the softspoken submarine-baller who compiled a 14–3 lifetime record against barnstorming white big leaguers. The Giants had only two hitters, Cristobal Torrienti and Jim Brown. The rest of the lineup played the bunt-and-run game. "But you had to listen to what Rube said," McDonald emphasized. "He was good to you, but you had to learn, or you'd find yourself with one of the weaker clubs in the league." Foster told McDonald, "On the 3 and 2, you better break something; you better break that curveball, and you better break it over the plate, and not over the heart of the plate either."

When a pitcher did not follow orders to walk superstar Oscar Charleston, Foster spit in his face and fined him $150. "When I tell you to walk a man, walk him!"

Rube's younger half-brother, Lefty Bill Foster, rebelled against his autocratic older brother. Rube simply left him in the game to take his punishment until Bill finally agreed to listen. "Rube was a shrewd man," Bill grinned half a century later. "The more I think of it, the older I get, I can see Rube's point of view on a lot of things. And whatever he told me stuck." After Rube suffered a nervous breakdown, Bill became a star for

"The Baltimore Elites had five pitchers who could pitch in any league—*any* league," their catcher, Roy Campanella, once said. "There was Robert Griffith, Andrew Porter, Bill Byrd, Jim Willis, and a left-hander, Tom Glover. I would take those five pitchers, put them right on the Dodgers, and all of those fellows would be starters in the big leagues. And that was just part of the pitching staff in the colored league when I was there."

The man most responsible for this stellar staff was manager and ex-infielder George Scales.

Campy did not even mention Joe Black, who tried out at shortstop until Scales made a pitcher out of him and the Dodgers snatched him away. (Another Scales pupil: second baseman Junior Gilliam.)

Rube's successor, Dave Malarcher, and, many say, replaced Dave Brown as the best black lefty ever.

The Twenty-Victory Test

In addition to NERA titles, one could also calculate the manager's years per twenty-game winners. This method of evaluation is less satisfactory because it also encompasses the team's offensive support, which enabled the pitchers to win twenty. It also favors the older managers, who were in the game before the advent of the five-man rotation. Nevertheless, this rating system reveals some managers worth noting: Fred Clarke, Clark Griffith, and John McGraw.

Fred Clarke

Over nineteen years, from 1897 to 1915, Fred Clarke produced no less than twenty-five twenty-game winners. Only Al Lopez

even approached that, with sixteen over seventeen years. Clarke's top Pirates' pitchers were:

Pitcher	W–L	ERA
Jack Chesbro	196–131	2.68
Sam Leever	195–102	2.47
Jesse Tannehill	194–118	2.79
Babe Adams	194–140	2.76
Deacon Phillippe	186–109	2.59
Howie Camnitz	132–106	2.75

Only one, Chesbro, is in the Hall of Fame, though their records suggest that three or four of the others are as deserving as he was.

Clark Griffith

No one has yet suggested a connection between Clark Griffith and the sudden phenomenal of success of Walter Johnson that directly followed Griff's appointment as Washington's manager in 1912.

Griff was a foxy old pitcher himself, and in his first year as a pitcher-manager, 1901, his White Sox won the first pennant in the new American League. He helped himself by winning twenty-four games. It was the only pennant he would win in twenty-one years.

With the Yankees in 1904, Jack Chesbro won forty-one games for him but lost the pennant on a wild pitch on the last day.

Then came Washington and Walter Johnson.

To be sure, Johnson was already a fine pitcher before Griff arrived—he had won twenty games in each of the previous two seasons. But in 1912, he exploded with thirty-two wins. In his second year under Griff, Johnson had probably the greatest season enjoyed by any pitcher of any time. He won thirty-six games and lost only seven, with an ERA of 1.09 and a splendid opposition on-base average of .216, some 60 percent better than the league norm.

John McGraw

John McGraw's New York Giants won pennants ten times in thirty-three years, and five times they led the league in team NERA. But McGraw's greatest claim to pitching fame lay in the thirty-five men who won twenty games or more during his thirty-two years of leadership. More than one-third of the thirty-five were posted by one remarkable pitcher, Christy Mathewson.

Hall of Famer Burleigh Grimes pitched for Mac only one year and then only at the end of his career, but in that one year, Grimes says, "I learned more baseball than I had in all the years up to that point." Grimes told Anthony J. Connor (*Voices from Cooperstown*) that in five minutes McGraw taught him a whole new theory of curveball

pitching. Right-handers were hitting his spitter into right field, advancing the base runner on first to third base. McGraw told Burleigh to throw his curve over the plate in that situation, making the right-handers pull it to left. That way the runner either got doubled up or, at worst, had to stop at second. "It was a simple adjustment—took five minutes. Only problem was, I'd never thought of it before, and neither had any of my managers. I won nineteen games that year and twenty-five the next." Grimes figured he could have been a 300-game winner if he had met McGraw ten years sooner.

McGraw was undemonstrative toward his men. In 1914 Rube Marquard was suffering through his first bad year—his year-end record would be 12–22—and struggled to a twenty-inning 3–1 victory. McGraw did not even shake his hand. "Mac never complimented me," Rube said. "It was my job, period."

The 1911 Giants' staff: Marquard, Tesreau, Matty, Wiltse, Crandall

Mathewson made McGraw famous and probably put him in the Hall of Fame. But Mac and Matty were opposites on the field—McGraw, pugnacious and brash; Matty, phlegmatic and gracious—while close friends off the field. McGraw did not pick favorites among his staff, however, Giants' historian Fred Stein reported. On one train hop when there were not enough lower berths to go around, McGraw told all the players to draw lots. Matty drew an upper. "Let him sleep in one," McGraw shrugged. "I don't have any privileged characters on my ball club, and he's no better than anyone else."

The Non–Pitchers' Managers

Connie Mack, John McGraw, Casey Stengel, Bucky Harris—all are in the Hall of Fame as great managers. Dick Williams and Sparky Anderson will almost surely join them some day. They were all fine managers—their records prove that. But they were not particularly fine pitchers' managers. Whitey Herzog and Ralph Houk might fit in this category as well. One wonders how great they might have been if they had paid as much attention to their pitchers as they apparently did to the hitters on their clubs.

Charlie Dressen

Charlie Dressen, who took over as Dodger manager in 1951, was a star of the Three-I league ("I," "I," and "I," as columnist John Lardner put it). Dressen had managed Cincinnati during the Depression years, then understudied Leo Durocher as a Brooklyn coach before he finally got his chance to run the team. And when his big chance came, Durocher's Giants snatched the glory away, overtaking the Dodgers in the great 1951 stretch drive and playoff.

Dressen's reputation will forever be shaped by that historic playoff, in which he completely mismanaged his staff. He left Don Newcombe in too long in the dramatic final game, then brought the wrong man, Ralph Branca, in to relieve him with disastrous results.

There were hundreds of "ifs" in that unforgettable season. Erv Palica had won thirteen games for Burt Shotton, Dodgers' manager in 1950 and, Clem Labine told Golenbock, "had the best stuff of any pitcher that I've ever seen." But Dressen embarrassed Palica in front of the team, and Palica ended up winning only two games in 1951. A little more tact by Dressen and one more win by Palica, and there would not have been a playoff at all.

Bud Podbielan had won five games and saved one for Brooklyn in 1950 but, inexplicably, was hardly used by Dressen, though he was especially effective against the Giants. Podbielan won only two games in 1951 and did not even get into the playoffs.

In 1952 Dressen finally emerged from his mentor Durocher's shadow, beating Leo (sans Willie Mays) by four-and-one-half games. He owed his victory to rookie Joe Black, who won fifteen games, highest on the staff, and saved fifteen more in relief.

In the Series that fall, the Dodgers almost overturned the Yanks. They took a 3–2 game lead into the final two games at Ebbets Field. Carl Erskine, who had had a sore arm earlier in the year, had fully recovered and was straining to get into action, but Dressen refused to use him. Instead he pitched Billy Loes and a tired Joe Black and lost two close games and the world championship.

The next year Dressen insisted that Black learn a screwball or forkball, but Joe was physically unable to grip the ball. (Pitching coach Ted Lyons was frustrated at having all his advice ignored.) Black ended up winning six games and never won another in his life. But the Dodgers repeated as champs, mainly because Erskine finally won twenty games. Carl was 5–4 at midseason, so Charlie took him fishing "to change his luck," and it worked.

Casey Stengel

Casey Stengel was a disciple of John McGraw, for whom he played on the Giants. But before Casey became a genius as manager of the Yankees, he went through the hell of managing the old Brooklyn Dodgers and Boston Bees for nine years. He finished fifth twice, sixth twice, and seventh five times. After one of his many losses, he climbed wearily into a barber chair and asked for a shave. "But don't cut my throat, I may want to do that myself later."

Then, called out of retirement in 1949 to manage the Yanks, Stengel suddenly achieved greatness. He won ten pennants— five in his first five years—and six of his champs were ERA champs too. He produced seven twenty-game winners, and the most dramatic pitching feat of all time, Don Larsen's perfect World Series game.

Casey nurtured young Whitey Ford as a rookie in 1950, not letting him pitch in Fenway Park and building his confidence.

Stengel was generally loved by his players. After Ralph Terry threw a home-run pitch to Bill Mazeroski to lose the 1960 World Series, Stengel merely asked gently, "What were you trying to throw him?" Terry said he had been trying to keep it low. Casey replied, "As long as you were trying to pitch him the right way, I'm going to sleep easy at night."

THE UMPS

Pitchers and umpires get along, in Ron Luciano's quip, about like the Christians got along with the lions.

Even back in 1908 Christy Mathewson was calling umps "a necessary evil . . . like the odor that follows an automobile."

"They all could use improving," Jim Palmer said tersely.

Players make errors, umpires make mistakes, Mathewson said charitably. Bob Gibson agreed: "They just make more than everybody else . . . and when they die, I know where they're going."

An umpire has to bear down on some 250 calls every nine-inning game. The pressure on him never lets up. The players go to the dugout between innings; the ump gets no respite. Of course he will call some of those 250 wrong. "A lot of calls are guesses," Luciano admits. "Every major-league pitch moves some way or other. None go straight, not even the fastballs."

Every umpire has a different strike zone, and great pitchers—and hitters—study each ump as carefully as they study the opposing batters or pitcher.

Some umpires, such as Al Barlick, Bill Summers, and oldtimers Bill Dinneen and George Pipgras, are hitters' umps with narrow strike zones (surprisingly, Dinneen and Pipgras were former pitchers). Others, like Ed Sudol and Bill Kincannon, are pitchers' umps with wide zones. Kincannon told Larry Gerlach he calls a lot of strikes, especially on outside pitches, because it forces the hitter to swing, and the fans like to see a lot of action.

Some are high-strike umps, and some are low-strike umps. Pitchers feel that tall umps call more high strikes. The American League has traditionally been the high-strike league, probably because the larger chest protector AL umps wear prevents them from crouching as low as the NL arbiters. The Yankees' Spud Chandler was a low-ball pitcher and got a lot more low strikes from NL umps in All Star games than he got in the regular season. In contrast, Bob Gibson was a high-ball pitcher and always thought he would have done better in the American League. Palmer was another high-ball pitcher, and if he did not get the high strike, he was in trouble. Steve Palermo would refuse to call borderline strikes, Palmer charged. One year Jim lost three games with Palermo behind the plate. When he complained, he said, Palermo retaliated by ignoring obvious strikes.

Of course umpires have favorites. "Red Ormsby was a stinko," Chandler said heatedly. "He ran me crazy. I couldn't get a strikeout, I don't care where I threw the ball. I don't know why, he took a dislike to me."

The umpires considered Sam McDowell and Nolan Ryan complainers; McDowell started arguing before the ball left his hand, and Ryan even complained the night he struck out nineteen men, saying he could have gotten more if the umpiring had been better. Nolan got few breaks from the umps after that.

It works the other way too: Umpires can dislike hitters as well as pitchers. Roy Weatherly of the 1940 Indians, for example, was a crybaby; umps enjoyed calling close ones against him.

Pitchers complained that Ted Williams got four strikes, and the umps admit it. Ted always made it a point to be friendly with the umpires. He never argued with them, and at the end of every season visited their dressing room to thank them for their hard work all year. But the umps counter that great pitchers get "reputation" strikes too. Pitchers like Palmer felt they had spent a lifetime earning those reputation strikes and have no compunction about accepting their due on borderline calls.

Grover Alexander also cultivated the umpires. When rookie ump Beans Reardon called a few questionable balls, Alex asked him, "Young man, what's wrong with those pitches?"

"Not a thing, Mr. Alexander," Reardon replied. "I know I missed them. I'm just nervous."

"Don't worry about it, son," Old Pete said. "Settle down. I'll get the next one over."

"I never missed another one on him," Beans told Larry Gerlach.

Rich Gossage can intimidate umpires as well as he intimidates batters. Said Terry Forster: "They know he's fast, and they know his ball moves and rises, so they call a lot of strikes."

A pitcher with good control, like Ron Guidry or Catfish Hunter, will get more close strikes than a wild man like Ed Figueroa, who is all around the plate.

Gaylord Perry found that working fast not only kept his infielders on their toes, it made the umpires happy. "Then," he wrote, "they were giving me the outside corners."

Gerlach has made a study of umpires who worked no-hitters and reports that Frank "Silk" O'Loughlin—"the autocrat of umpires," Mathewson called him—worked seven no-hitters, more than anyone else. Dinneen called six, and Bill Klem five. Incidentally, Gerlach says, former pitcher Al Orth ("the Curveless Wonder" of the old New York Highlanders) was behind the plate for the Toney-Vaughn double no-hit game. And Dinneen is the only man both to pitch a no-hitter and umpire one.

Umpires and pitchers should have an affinity, not a rivalry, Luciano said. "With the possible exception of catchers and clinical analysts, umpires understand pitchers better than anybody in the world." He added that "only umpires and some pitchers really understand baseballs." When a pitcher called for a new ball, Ron sometimes slipped the old one into his pocket and put it back in play the next chance he got. "Jim Palmer was the only pitcher who consistently rejected the same baseballs," he said. It's somewhat like Ted Williams hefting two bats and telling which was half an ounce heavier. On the other hand, Dennis Eckersley would reject a ball, get the same one back, and pitch with it.

Only rarely does a pitcher show compassion for an umpire. Luciano said a fan once threw a soda bottle at him in New York, and Tommy John came running out of the dugout, "a look of deep concern on his face." When Luciano assured him that he was fine, the bottle had missed him, John turned away sadly.

8

The Pitches

This is a book about pitchers, not about pitching. We do not tell the youngster how to choose a delivery, grip the ball, condition his arm, build his stamina, or regulate his diet. That sort of book has been done many, many times since Henry Chadwick penned *The Art of Pitching* in 1885, and several outstanding instructionals are available.* And yet—while we focus on the men who throw the pitches rather than on the pitches themselves, it is said that a man *is* largely what he *does*: We cannot examine the pitcher apart from his pitching, or pitching apart from the pitch.

THE FASTBALL

You begin with the fastball. Thrown over the top, three-quarters, sidearm, or underhand, it is the pitch nature equips us all to throw, untutored, with strength and effort separating the speediest pitcher from the slowest. Yes, a fastball can be made faster through improved mechanics of the delivery (Tom Seaver said he pitches basically with his legs; Lefty Grove said, "I don't throw with my arm or shoulder, but with the base of my spine") and it can be made to sink, sail, or "back up" by varying the grip across the seams—but a live arm and a rising fastball that defies gravity are gifts; they cannot be learned.

Baseball's primal pitch remains its prime one. Even though boys experiment with curves and sliders at ever younger ages, it is still the fastball that draws the attention of the scouts. They may say that every major-league batter is a fastball hitter, but they weren't talking about Walter Johnson's fastball, or Bob Feller's, or Nolan Ryan's. As Kirby Higbe, the Dodgers' fireballer of the 1940s, said, "There's nobody out there on that field with as much confidence as the pitcher who can throw the real good fastball. You know that when you're right you can just overpower those hitters and that's all

*We would recommend particularly: Bob Shaw's *Pitching* (1972), Jim Palmer's *Pitching* (1975), Pat Jordan's *Pitching* (1976), and Tom Seaver's *Art of Pitching* (1984).

there is to it. Greatest feeling in the world, to rock back out there and fire that thing in. . . .''

Confidence in the high hard one can make it effective even when it is not in the Johnson–Feller–Ryan class. Robin Roberts had a great fastball in the early 1950s when he starred for the Phillies, but at the end of the trail, toiling with such teams as Baltimore and Houston, his speed was just a memory. Nonetheless, he went out and challenged hitters with what remained of his fastball and found it was still good enough. By the standards of major-league hitters, a fastball of 85 m.p.h. or under can be hit, but those in excess of 87 m.p.h. provide genuine difficulty. If you think the fastball of a ''junkballer'' like Stu Miller or Scotty McGregor is a creampuff to hit, go to the local batting range and step in against an 80-m.p.h. pitching machine.

Tom Seaver has said that every pitch has three components that make it difficult to hit—speed, movement, and location. Of these, speed is least important for retiring a batter. All the same, it is speed—pure blazing speed—that captures the imagination. Who was the fastest pitcher? Seaver in his prime threw 94 to 95 m.p.h. as measured by the JUGS gun, a radar device, but was never officially timed. Ryan had his fastball clocked at 100.8 m.p.h. in 1974; Feller's registered 98.6 in 1946; and measured by a more primitive device, Johnson's heater came in at 99.7 in 1914. Other notable clockings include J. R. Richard's 100 m.p.h. in 1978, Jim Maloney's 99.5 in 1965, Goose Gossage's 99.4 in 1980, and Lee Smith's 99.0 in 1984.

But surely these measures are not the whole story. Smokey Joe Wood was timed at 94.5 m.p.h. in the same year as Johnson, yet Sir Walter once said, ''No one throws faster than Joe Wood.'' The legendary Steve Dalkowski, said by many to be the fastest of all, was timed at ''only'' 93.5 m.p.h. in 1958 (he may have been exhausted by the time he finally threw a pitch over the plate where it could be measured). And Sandy Koufax's best measured fastball was only 93.0 m.p.h., one mile per hour less than Bob Turley's, if you can believe that.

So, finally, we are thrown back on the rocks of subjectivity if we are to answer the question, ''Who was the fastest?'' Today's players and fans would go overwhelmingly for Nolan Ryan. But speed is in the eyes of the beholder. Billy Herman, who starred in the 1930s and 1940s, voted for Van Lingle Mungo. Ted Lyons, Charlie Gehringer, and Wes Ferrell, among others, thought Lefty Grove was faster than Bob Feller. So did Grove, who thought that Rapid Robert was nowhere near as fast as Walter Johnson, and no faster than George Earnshaw. Feller, like Johnny Mize, thought Rex Barney was at least as fast as he was, but didn't have the same hop on the ball. Walter Johnson— whose fastball was described by Ty Cobb as ''a watermelon seed that, as it passed by, hissed at you''—when pressed to answer, had to admit that he believed he was faster than Grove or Feller. The modest Johnson allowed, however, that their fastballs, because they were delivered overhand, may have been harder for the batter to pick up than his own, which was slung to the plate from a low sidearm position. Many Negro leaguers say that Satchel Paige, before he hurt his arm in the late 1930s, was faster than anyone.

A telling opinion is that of Connie Mack who, because his major-league career began in 1886 and continued through 1950, saw them all. ''Amos Rusie was the fastest, without a doubt,'' Mack said. ''Maybe that's because I had to hit against him. They looked like peas as they sailed by me. All I saw of them was what I heard when they went into the catcher's mitt.'' Because Mack batted against the Hoosier Thunderbolt before 1893 as well as after, he had the terrifying task of standing in against a pitch that, while it may not have been truly as fast as Ryan's or Feller's, may well have *arrived at the plate in less time.* If we credit Rusie with a 95-m.p.h. fastball, it crossed the plate in 1892, having traveled fifty feet from the point of release, in 0.36 seconds. Ryan's 100-m.p.h. fastball of 1974, having traveled fifty-six feet from the point of release, crossed the plate in 0.38 seconds. Food for thought.

THE CURVE

One of the national pastime's most venerable disputes has been whether a curveball curves and, if the break is not simply an optical illusion, when that break occurs. The deviousness of the curve—and, indeed, all pitches, including the fastball—is a result of gravity, aerodynamics, and the limits of perception. Can a fastball rise? Certainly. If thrown with sufficient force and backspin, the ball can overcome the natural gravitational pull downward, just as an airplane makes selective use of variable air resistance and pressure, and generates lift: More pressure on the bottom, less on the top, and the object—airplane or fastball—rises. That rise is steady but appears sudden—the explosive hop of a Koufax fastball, for example—because the pupil of the eye is incapable of focusing fast enough to follow it.

That rise—and in general, the struggle of the pitch against gravity and air resistance—is aided by the elevation of the pitching mound. The height was limited to 15 inches in 1903 (presumably some groundskeepers created little Everests before then) and, in the wake of the Year of the Pitcher in 1968, was reduced to 10 inches.*

Similarly, the lateral spin applied to the ball for a curve, slider, or screwball will create greater air resistance on one side than on the other, and the ball will deflect from a straight path in the path of the lesser resistance. A curveball does curve, but it does not break ''late''—it begins to stray from the linear path as soon as it leaves the pitcher's hand, but as with the fastball, the eye does not see the break right away—hence the seemingly explosive curve of a Koufax or a Camilo Pascual, or the last-minute wrinkle of a Valenzuela screwball. The break of a breaking ball depends more on spin than speed: The more revolutions per minute, the tighter the spin; the tighter the spin, the greater the break.

The origin of the curveball is a mystery even hoarier than that surrounding its habits. Did Candy Cummings invent it in the mid-1860s, thus meriting his plaque in the Hall of Fame? Probably (see his own story in the accompanying box). But the contesting claims have merit, and one of them— the Fred Goldsmith version—continues to be pressed by his heirs. Since an entire book has recently been devoted to the curve (*The Crooked Pitch,* Martin Quigley, 1984), we will limit ourselves to a synopsis of the turmoil of the 1860s and 1870s.

---

*When did the raised mound first appear, and who is to be credited for its invention? SABR researchers, notably John Schwartz, have been pursuing this matter for years. Only in December 1986 did we stumble upon the answer in the archives at Cooperstown: John Montgomery Ward came up with the idea *before the creation of the pitcher's slab in 1893.* At a time when pitchers were still working out of a box, no later than 1883, but perhaps earlier, Ward ''conceived the idea that a pitcher would have an advantage if he could be slightly higher than the batter, so he and his teammates elevated the pitcher's mound.'' These are the words of Ward's nephew, John M. Fleming, to whom he told the story years later.

HOW I CURVED THE FIRST BALL
By William Arthur "Candy" Cummings

I have often been asked how I first got the idea of making a ball curve. I will now explain. It is such a simple matter, though, that there is not much explanation.

In the summer of 1863 a number of boys and myself were amusing ourselves by throwing clam shells (the hard shell variety) and watching them sail along through the air, turning now to the right, and now to the left. We became interested in the mechanics of it and experimented for an hour or more.

All of a sudden it came to me that it would be a good joke on the boys if I could make a baseball curve the same way. We had been playing "three-old-cat" and town-ball, and I had been doing the pitching. The joke seemed so good that I made a firm decision that I would try to play it.

I set to work on my theory and practiced every spare moment that I had out of school. I had no one to help me and had to fight it out alone. Time after time I would throw the ball, doubling up into all manner of positions, for I thought that my pose had something to do with it; and then I tried holding the ball in different shapes. Sometimes I thought I had it, and then maybe again in twenty-five tries I could not get the slightest curve. My visionary successes were just enough to tantalize me. Month after month I kept pegging away at my theory.

In 1864 I went to Fulton, New York, to a boarding school, and remained there a year and a half. All that time I kept experimenting with my curved ball. My boy friends began to laugh at me, and to throw jokes at my theory of making a ball go sideways. I fear that some of them thought it was so preposterous that it was no joke, and that I should be carefully watched over.

I don't know what made me stick at it. The great wonder to me now is that I did not give up in disgust, for I had not one single word of encouragement in all that time, while my attempts were a standing joke among my friends.

After graduating I went back to my home in Brooklyn, New York, and joined the "Star Juniors," an amateur team. We were very successful. I was solicited to join as a junior member the Excelsior club, and I accepted the proposition.

In 1867 I, with the Excelsior club, went to Boston, where we played the Lowells,

---

Cummings' account places the creation at about 1864. But in the early 1900s Alphonse "Phonnie" Martin, a pitcher for the New York Mutuals and contemporary of Cummings, claimed that he had used a drop ball and "in-curve" (screwball) from 1864 to 1872, and that Cummings, Tommy Bond, and Terry Larkin acquired the "outcurve" by imitating his style. In any event, Martin continued, such pitches were illegal until 1872, when the prohibition against the wrist snap was removed. One J. Mc-Sweeney attempted to pitch a curve in an 1866 game against the Unions of Morrisania, but was expelled by the umpire for employing a throw rather than the mandated pitch (straight arm, straight wrist).

According to Martin, there is no evidence

the Tri-Mountains, and Harvard clubs. During these games I kept trying to make the ball curve. It was during the Harvard game that I became fully convinced that I had succeeded in doing what all these years I had been striving to do. The batters were missing a lot of balls; I began to watch the flight of the ball through the air, and distinctly saw it curve.

A surge of joy flooded over me that I shall never forget. I felt like shouting out that I had made a ball curve; I wanted to tell everybody; it was too good to keep to myself.

But I said not a word, and saw many a batter at that game throw down his stick in disgust. Every time I was successful I could scarcely keep from dancing from pure joy. The secret was mine.

There was trouble though, for I could not make it curve when I wanted to. I would grasp it the same, but the ball seemed to do just as it pleased. It would curve all right, but it was very erratic in its choice of places to do so. But still it curved!

The baseball came to have a new meaning to me; it almost seemed to have life.

It took time and hard work for me to master it, but I kept on pegging away until I had fairly good control.

In those days the pitcher's box was six feet by four, and the ball could be thrown from any part of it; one foot could be at the forward edge of the box, while the other could be stretched back as far as the pitcher liked; but both feet had to be on the ground until the ball was delivered. It is surprising how much speed could be generated under those rules.

It was customary to swing the arm perpendicularly and to deliver the ball at the height of the knee. I still threw this way, but brought in wrist action.

I found that the wind had a whole lot to do with the ball curving. With a wind against me I could get all kinds of a curve, but the trouble lay in the fact that the ball was apt not to break until it was past the batter. This was a sore trouble; I learned not to try to curve a ball very much when the wind was unfavorable.

I have often been asked to give my theory of why a ball curves. Here it is: I give the ball a sharp twist with the middle finger, which causes it to revolve with a swift rotary motion. The air also, for a limited space around it, begins to revolve making a great swirl until there is enough pressure to force the ball out of true line.

I get a great deal of pleasure now in my old age out of going to games and watching the curves, thinking that it was through my blind efforts that all this was made possible.

to support Cummings' use of a curve against Harvard at Jarvis Field in 1867, and Bobby Mathews was the first to throw an out-curve within the rules, in 1869.

Fred Goldsmith asserted that he threw a curve in the mid-1860s while a boy in New Haven, Connecticut, and passed his secret pitch on to Hamilton Avery, pitcher for Yale. Word of the New Haven *wunderkind* reached New York, and Goldsmith gave an exhibition of his twisting pitches that was reported in the *Brooklyn Eagle* by Henry Chadwick:

Yesterday, at the Capitoline grounds, a large crowd assembled and cheered lustily as a youth from New Haven, Conn., named Fred Goldsmith, demonstrated to the satisfaction of all that a baseball could be so manipulated and controlled by throwing it from one given point to another as to make a pronounced arc in space. The test was made by drawing a chalk line on the ground a distance of 45 feet from one extremity to the other. An eight-foot pole was driven in an upright position at each end. Another pole was set in the same manner halfway between the two end poles, planted directly upon the line.

Now, everything was set for the test. Goldsmith was placed on the left side of the chalk line near the end pole facing the pole at the other end. The purpose of this was that the ball delivered from the thrower's hand was to cross the line, circle the center pole and return to the same side of the line from which it was thrown, before reaching the far pole. This feat was successfully accomplished six or eight times and that which had up to this point been considered an optical illusion and against all rules of philosophy was now an established fact.

This same sort of experiment was performed by John Ward on the Penn State campus in 1875, and by Tommy Bond and Bobby Mitchell at Cincinnati in 1877. Goldsmith went on to pitch in the International Association in the late 1870s, where he taught the curve to Larry Corcoran and Mickey Welch. Still, even as late as 1880, the curve was an oddity and most pitchers continued to rely upon the fastball, drop, and a change of speed—remember, the curve had to be delivered underhand and so was nothing more than the roundhouse curve with a purely lateral break that schoolboys still begin with. The underhand curve was not difficult to throw—Cummings pitched several at an Oldtimers' Game in Boston in 1910 when he was sixty-two, and a sportswriter noted that "a prettier or wider curve I never saw." However, the batters of the early 1880s found that the wide curve was not difficult to time, and the curve was beginning to fall into disuse.

Then the restrictions on the delivery were eased, first from the hip to the shoulder level in 1883, then to "anything goes" in 1884. The overhand drop and curve of Boston's Charlie Buffinton and the inshoot, or screwball, of Charlie Sweeney became the sensations of baseball, much as the split-finger fastball is all the rage today.

Who had the greatest curve ever? This enters an even more subjective realm than the parallel question about the fastball. We have talked with a lot of veteran players and observers, and the names that come up repeatedly are: Mordecai Brown, Dazzy Vance, Jughandle Johnny Morrison, Tommy Bridges, Hal Newhouser, Camilo Pascual, Sam Jones, Carl Erskine, Sandy Koufax, and Bert Blyleven.

THE CHANGE

No matter what date you assign to the debut of the curveball, the change of speeds was invented earlier. Credit most often goes to Harry Wright, who in his playing days was principally an outfielder but occasionally appeared as a "change pitcher"—the early days' relief pitcher, who had to trade positions with the pitcher because substitution from the bench was not allowed. Harry Wright—the Cincinnati Red Stockings' change pitcher behind the speedy Asa Brainard—threw a lollipop pitch, called a "dew drop," that proved surprisingly deceptive.

In the east at this time batters were puzzled by the tantalizingly slow pitches of Phonnie Martin. His celebrated drop started with a slight arc upward and descended at the plate as if it had suddenly lost its forward impetus. The ball was not hard to hit, but hard to hit safely: Batters would almost invariably lift the ball into the air. In a game Martin pitched for the Eckfords against the Powhatans in Brooklyn in 1869, twenty-six outs were recorded on fly balls and only one on a groundout. But Martin was basically a slowball pitcher, not a fastballer who mixed in a change of pace.

The first of the early pitchers to realize the benefits of keeping a batter off balance by delivering his slowball and his fast one with the same motion was Al Spalding, the most accomplished hurler prior to 1880: Combining his records in the National Association in 1871 to 1875 with his short tenure in the National League, Spalding compiled an astounding won-lost mark of 255–669 for a never equaled percentage of .787. Spalding never bothered with the new-fangled curve, and with those results one can see why. (Later pitchers who flourished in the majors without a breaking pitch notably were fastball pitchers like Johnson and Grove, neither of whom learned to throw a curve until late in their careers; perhaps the outstanding exception was Al Orth, "The Curveless Wonder" who won more than 200 games simply by changing speeds off a none-too-fast fastball.) Another outstanding pitcher of the nineteenth century who relied upon changing speeds was Tim Keefe of the Giants, whose change was a sort of palmball controlled, strangely, through pressure from the base of the thumb.

Today the palmball is one of the pitches used as a change; the others include the Paul Richards "slip pitch," the cut fastball, the split-finger fastball, and, rarely, a knuckleball or knuckle curve. Rarer still is the floater brought into popularity by Indianapolis' Bill Phillips (formerly of Cincinnati) and later revived as the blooper pitch of Pittsburgh's Rip Sewell, the folly floater of the Yankees' Steve Hamilton, and LaLob of the Yanks' Dave LaRoche. In most cases, the change is achieved simply by thrusting the ball as far back in the hand as possible so that the knuckles rather than the fingertips provide the pressure, creating more resistance and less speed.

What Al Spalding realized in the 1870s was a truth that eludes many major-league pitchers today: Speed is relative, and the use of an off-speed pitch makes the fast one look faster. When he was the Boston Red Sox' pitching coach, Al Jackson said, "Pitching is just an illusion. You're dealing with a man's eyes. Make him think he's getting one thing, and give him another and you've got him." Today, when an 85-m.p.h. fastball is the major-league norm, pitching coaches advise their charges to develop a change-up—either straight or curved—that is at least 15 m.p.h. slower. If the change is only 7 to 8 m.p.h. slower, it will not sufficiently disrupt the rhythm of the hitter who is looking for the fastball: To him, the 78-m.p.h. change-up is just an appetizing fastball.

One of the reasons Fernando Valenzuela is so effective despite an only average fastball is his ability to change speeds with his screwball. He can throw one scroogie at 77 to 80 m.p.h. and another at 64 to 70 m.p.h. Any pitcher who, with one motion, can vary the speeds of his pitches by 23 m.p.h. is going to be a star. (Other pitchers who rely upon changing speeds and pinpoint control are the two expatriate Red Sox, John Tudor of the Cardinals and Bob Ojeda of the Mets.)

Who in this century are the masters of changing speeds? The names most often mentioned are Al Orth, Eppa Rixey, Grover Alexander, Eddie Plank, Herb Pennock, Ted Lyons, Eddie Lopat, Johnny Podres, Stu Miller, and Scott McGregor. Of the pitchers we've seen in action, Podres was the change-up champ.

THE SLIDER

Cy Young called it a nickle curve, and called his contemporary Clark Griffith a "dinky-dinky pitcher" for throwing it along with other assorted "junk." But when Denton True Young's speed was no longer cyclonic and those in the know whispered that he was on the way down, he added the despised nickel curve to his wide breaking one and became a greater pitcher after age thirty than he was before. But Old Cy never called his pitch a slider; in later years, when other pitchers talked about their sliders, he would scoff that it was nothing new.*

But it was. The slider is gripped differently than the curve, and is thrown with a different wrist action; unlike the curve, it is more effective the harder it is thrown (and more damaging to the arm as well, which is why some organizations frown on its use by developing pitchers).

The slider is not a pretty pitch, like the curve. It is not difficult to learn. It just gets batters out. Masquerading as a fastball until it is upon the batter, it breaks little but "late" and it may be the most devastating weapon in the average pitcher's arsenal. Its discovery is most often credited to George Blaeholder of the St. Louis Browns in the late 1920s, but George Uhle said that he invented it while with Detroit in 1929: "Harry Heilmann and I were just working [on the sideline to catcher Eddie] Phillips. It just came to me all of a sudden, letting the ball go along my index finger and using my ring finger and pinky to give it just a little bit of a twist. It was a sailing fastball, and that's how come I named it the slider. The real slider is a sailing fastball. Now they call everything a slider, including a nickel curve."

Indeed they do. The rather tame slider of Uhle, Blaeholder, and in the early 1940s, Al Milnar and Johnny Sain bore little relation to the vicious hard slider of the 1970s, made famous by Sparky Lyle and Steve Carlton.

Walt Masterson of the 1940s Senators said that the slider was invented by Pete Appleton, the latter being heretofore more famous for having pitched seven years in the big leagues as Pete Jablonowski (record: 17–22), being sent down, and returning two years later as Pete Appleton and going 14–9. The pitch "started out as a flat slider," Masterson recalled in 1982; "now they throw one that goes down, and that's the devil."

That devilish delivery is one that Ty Cobb and Babe Ruth never had to face. Whitey Ford rejuvenated his career in 1961, just as he was losing his speed, by learning the slider from new pitching coach Johnny Sain. Ford said, "Ted Williams told me that he had only two pitches to worry about when he started—fastball and curveball. And the pitchers knew he could hit fastballs, so his guessing was narrowed to curveballs. Later they started throwing sliders, Ted said, and really had him guessing. It's got to be one of the reasons for lower batting averages these days."

THE SCREWBALL

Inshoot, indrop, whisker-trimmer, fadeaway, corkscrew—the ball that a right-handed pitcher breaks in to a right-handed batter—was thrown for years before Carl Hubbell christened it a screwball, but no one before King Carl threw it as often or with such a pronounced break. The pitch that Fernando Valenzuela, Mike Marshall, Bill Campbell, and Tug McGraw have made their bread-and-butter pitch in recent years descends directly from Hubbell and Warren Spahn, not from such pioneers as Christy

*As late as 1955, John Lardner doubted its existence, writing, "The slider? It's possib'. there is such a thing as the slider and, this being so, that it helps the pitcher. Or it may be that the slider is one of those national illusions that professional groups are sometimes able to foist off on the public, such as the idea that building all passenger automobiles in the shape of cockroaches represents artistic and mechanical progress."

Mathewson, Tully Sparks, Virgil Garvin, Bill Dinneen, and Rube Foster.

A reverse curve, or inshoot, was thrown occasionally by several early pitchers, including Sweeney and Radbourn of the 1884 Providence champions, and Mickey Welch of the Giants, who said in later years, "I had a fadeaway, although I didn't call it that. I didn't call it anything. It was just a slow curveball that broke down and in on a right-handed hitter."

Although it has frequently been written that Mathewson learned the fadeaway from (a) Rube Foster, the great black pitcher who served informally as John McGraw's pitching coach in the first decade of the century; (b) Nat Kellogg, his manager at Taunton in the New England League; or (c) Virgil Garvin of the Cubs, known as "Navasota Ned, the Texas Twister" for his peculiar pitches; Matty himself credited a more obscure player, lefty pitcher Dave Williams. Matty and Williams, who had a three-game trial with the Red Sox in 1902, were teammates on the Honesdale, Pennsylvania team of 1898, and later with Taunton. In fact many lefthanders had fooled with the pitch in the preceding two decades, and those who could mix an inshoot with the outshoot and drop were given the sobriquet "phenomenal."

Matty's development of the fadeaway— which he used as a change-up no more than ten to twelve times a game because of the arm strain—was enhanced in 1900 when he pitched in Norfolk. There he came under the tutelage of manager John Francis Smith, known in his heyday as "Phenomenal Smith" for his assortment of left-handed slants, and Matty's record in twenty-two starts was 20–2.

This story bears a striking similarity to Hubbell's. A Detroit Tigers' farm hand with Oklahoma City in 1925, Carl admired the sinking fastball of a young hurler named Lefty Thomas, who later that year would have a two-game cup of coffee with the Washington Senators. "Every time he needed an out pitch," Hubbell recalled, "Lefty threw that sinking fastball on the outside corner for a two-hopper to the short-stop and a double play. I told myself, 'That's for me.' But when I started working on the sinking fastball, I got to turning my wrist over more and more. I found if I gave it a good wrist snap, it would break more and more away from a right-handed hitter. I don't know if I invented the pitch, but Wolgamot [his catcher] and I invented the name. We had to call it something, so we called it a screwball."

The Tigers were concerned that the weird pitch would damage Hubbell's arm (they were right: today, when his arms relax at his sides, his left palm is turned to the outside) and barred him from throwing it. Without the screwball Hubbell was just another pitcher, and the chain let him go to the Giants. The rest is history: The twenty-four straight wins over two seasons, the five straight twenty-win seasons, and the famous five straight strikeouts in the 1934 All Star Game (equaled by his comrade in arms, Valenzuela, who was not, however, up against the likes of Ruth, Gehrig, Foxx, Simmons, and Cronin).

And who taught Valenzuela the pitch? No one as obscure as Dave Williams or Lefty Thomas, but another lesser light: Bobby Castillo, who teamed with Fernando in the Arizona Instructional League in 1979. The portly Mexican quickly mastered the "new" pitch (he had never heard of Hubbell or Mathewson) and, beginning in September of 1980, took the National League by storm. In eighteen innings of relief for the Dodgers he allowed no earned runs; then, to open 1981, he threw five shutouts in his first seven starts so that his major-league ERA to that point was 0.22. He went on to win the Cy Young award in that strike-abbreviated season and is one of the game's "franchise pitchers." And the screwball that made him is not likely to break him, because his motion is fluid and, now that every batter looks for the scroogie, his fastball has become his out pitch.

THE KNUCKLER

Everyone, pitcher or player, has fooled around with the knuckler. Mickey Mantle prided himself on having a pretty good one for purposes of the pregame warm-up toss. But few are the men who have rested their fortunes on the erratic, unpredictable butterfly, which, more than any other pitch, has a mind all its own. Phil Niekro, the knuckleball's most famous practitioner this side of Hoyt Wilhelm, said nearly a decade ago, "It's taken me twenty-seven years and I still don't know why the ball does what it does. If a man asks me to throw it down and in, I say he's talking to the wrong man."

Why is the pitch so unpredictable? Because the weather changes. Wind, humidity, and temperature affect all breaking pitches but none more than the rotationless (or nearly so) knuckler, which practically invites the air to have its way with it. The butterfly breaks in response to pressure exerted by air currents on the ridges raised by the stitches.

Those susceptible ridges have put many observers in stitches as they watched Niekro's batterymates flop around trying at least to knock down his dipsy-doodles. How do you catch a pitch that is so ill-behaved? Bob Uecker's celebrated answer was, "Just wait until it stops rolling, then pick it up." Charlie Lau said, "There are two schools of thought on catching the knuckleball. Unfortunately, neither of them works."

Okay, if you can't catch it, how do you throw it? Originally, with the knuckles, as the name implies, but ever since the 1910s, with the first two fingertips. The knuckler came into being in the summer of 1905, on the Augusta club in the Sally League. While Augusta centerfielder Ty Cobb drew most of the attention that year, the team's pitchers, Eddie Cicotte and Nap Rucker, were inventing a new pitch. Cicotte's efforts earned him the nickname "Knuckles," but he was to win greater fame in later years for his "shine ball" and infamy for tanking two starts in the tainted 1919 World Series. This is how Rucker described their invention:

> The knuckleball is held tightly by the thumb and little finger and the knuckles of the other fingers are closed, the ball resting against it. When the ball is pitched it is sent spinning on a horizontal axis. The downward thrust of the hand as the ball leaves, causes the ball to make a spin toward the box artist instead of against him. If this ball could be thrown fast enough, pitchers who have used it say, it would curve upward—something, however, impossible. In its efforts to climb, however, it slows up as it reaches the plate and then shoots quickly as the spinning motion dies, to one side or the other.

Detroit's rookie Ed Summers watched Cicotte throw the knuckler and in 1908 produced the fingertip version of the pitch, which he rode to forty-three victories in his first two years. The knuckler was little used in ensuing years, until the spitball, shine ball, emery ball, mud ball, and the like were banned in 1920. Then interest renewed, notably with the Philadelphia A's underrated Ed Rommel, who in 1922 won an awesome twenty-seven games, losing only thirteen, for a seventh-place club.

Other knucklers of the 1920s and 1930s included Lyons, who picked it up from an article about Rommel. Emil "Dutch"

Leonard was another knuckleball artist who got no respect despite a twenty-year career that continued through his forty-fourth year. In 1945, when Dutch went 17–7 for Washington, he was part of a starting rotation that consisted of *four* knuckleball pitchers—Roger Wolff, Mickey Haefner, Johnny Niggeling, and Leonard. The Senators were nosed out for the pennant on the final day and their valiant catcher, Rick Ferrell, may have made the Hall of Fame on this accomplishment alone.

But Leonard's most important contribution to the game was to give it, indirectly, Hoyt Wilhelm. The ace of North Carolina's Cornelius High, Wilhelm despaired of a big-league career because his fastball wasn't much; then, in 1939, he read an article about Leonard (as Lyons had about Rommel) and began his long climb through the bush leagues, finally hooking on with the Giants in 1952. There he made a splashy debut, hitting a home run his first time at bat (and never again in his twenty-one-year career), going 15–3 with eleven saves, and finishing second in the National League's Rookie of the Year balloting to another freshman reliever, Joe Black.

Wilhelm's next two decades saw him bounce back and forth between the leagues, leaving a trail of brokenhearted catchers in his wake. The National League's record for passed balls in one inning is four, achieved by Ray Katt in 1954; the American League record is three, held by Gus Triandos, Joe Ginsberg (both 1960), Charlie Lau (1962), and Joe Azcue (1969). The pitcher on all these occasions? You guessed it.

Dutch Leonard had wafted his knuckleball to big-league hitters at age forty-four. Wilhelm went him three years better. And at this writing, the incredible Phil Niekro is preparing for his twenty-fourth campaign at the age of forty-eight. Is it possible that what Ponce de Leon came upon in Florida was not the Fountain of Youth but a grapefruit league lesson in knuckleball pitching?

THE FORKBALL

The forkball was thought to have been invented by the Yankees' Ernie Bonham in the 1940s, was made famous by Roy Face, the Pirate fireman, in the 1950s, and made "new" by reliever Bruce Sutter, then of the Cubs, in the late 1970s (he called it a split-finger fastball rather than a forkball, but it is simply a forkball thrown a bit harder). Sutter took that pitch to St. Louis, then rode it to Atlanta prior to the 1985 season, having negotiated the largest contract ever signed by a pitcher.

The forkball, or split-finger fastball, has become *the* pitch of the 1980s. Detroit's coach Roger Craig taught it to his staff, and they used it to win the 1984 world championship; he went on to spread the gospel to San Diego and San Francisco, and other coaches picked up the pitch for their hurlers.

Yet former Red Sox' coach Al Jackson called it a pitch "for physical freaks only." The ball is wedged in between the index and middle fingers and thrown with a strong wrist snap. It is thrown with the motion of a fastball, comes in with the speed of a change-up, and at the last second drops like a spitter.

Just how it breaks depends on how it is held: how far apart the fingers are, how deep in the palm it is held, how much pressure is provided by the thumb. Sutter can make it break like a curve or like a screwball.

Sutter found his Jewel, as he calls the pitch, in 1973, when he injured his elbow while a kid in the low minors with the Cubs' organization. Surgery left his arm twisted, which he thinks may add to the odd rotation of the ball. The Cubs' roving minor-league pitching coach Jim Martin suggested he try the forkball.

Martin held it off-center and threw it with a rigid wrist. Sutter, whose hands are huge, holds the ball on center, his long index and middle fingers spread so that they grip the ball about one-third of the way down, something impossible for an average man to do. At release, the thumb pushes up as if snapping, or popping, the ball out.

By 1985 Sutter was using the pitch 90 percent of the time and had climbed into second place on the all-time saves' list. The hitters know what's coming, and still they can't hit it. For a change-up Sutter throws a fastball (!), which he sends in with the same motion, of course.

The paternity of the pitch actually goes back much farther than Bonham in the forties to Chattanooga in about 1905, when outfielder Mike Lynch, who had had a cup of coffee with the White Sox a few years before, experimented with the pitch and found he could get "astonishing" breaks. But the style tired his fingers, and he could not control it.

Three years later, playing with the Tacoma Tigers, he taught it to pitcher Bert Hall, who experimented with it in secret for about three weeks, learning to control it. Finally, on September 8, 1908, he sprang it on the unsuspecting Seattle club and shut them out on four hits. BERT HALL HAS NEW FANGLED BALL WORSE THAN SPITTER, the local paper headlined. That day the pitch—and the name *forkball*—were both born.

It did not seem to help Hall. He got a tryout with the Phillies in 1911 but pitched only seven games and had an 0-1 record. Hall and his miracle pitch both disappeared.

It was thirty years before another hurler used the pitch in the majors. Ernie Bonham had a fine 21–5 record for the Yanks in 1942 and won 103 big-league games in all using the pitch.

In 1953 Roy Face joined the Pirates possessing only a fastball and a curve, and he was unable to change speeds with either. He had no business being in the major leagues, but then again, these were the Pirates, who had lost 112 games the previous year. In spring camp of 1954, Branch Rickey sent Face—who had been a Pirate all through 1953—down to New Orleans to learn a change-up. Joe Page, himself trying to make it back to the big show, taught Face the forkball. With it Face led the NL in saves three times and in the charmed year of 1959 he won his first seventeen decisions, finishing an incredible 18-1.

Dodgers' pitcher Roger Craig was impressed. He tried Face's strange pitch, and though his record with it was disastrously bad, that's mainly because he soon became the workhorse of the new Mets.

In 1978 Craig was teaching the pitch to Little Leaguers. When he joined the Tigers as pitching coach, he started showing major leaguers how to throw it. "It's a devastating pitch," Craig told them, "and you can throw it with maximum arm speed without hurting yourself. It comes in like a fastball and then falls off the table."

Milt Wilcox was his first convert. "All I had was a fastball and a slider," Wilcox said, "and my slider wasn't that good." The new pitch cut one run off his ERA. He was soon throwing it 70 percent of the time.

Jack Morris was next. Although he had won forty-seven games in three years, he thought his fastball was deserting him, so he gave Craig's pitch a try, and it made him a star. In one game he had the White Sox chasing the funny fastball out of the strike zone and ended up no-hitting them.

Dan Petry was next to try it and won nineteen games for the world champs with it.

Mike Scott of the Mets was hanging on, the tenth man on a ten-man staff at the age

NATIONAL BASEBALL LIBRARY, COOPERSTOWN, N.Y.

Mike Scott

of thirty, when he went to Craig to learn the split-finger. A man with huge hands, Scott mastered the pitch quickly. By 1986 he was striking out 306 men, the oldest pitcher ever to go over 300. He won eighteen games, including a division-clinching no-hitter, captured the 1986 Cy Young award, and beat the Mets twice in the league playoffs, once with fourteen strikeouts, the second time on three hits. It is said that the Mets had to win the championship in six games because they were terrified of facing Scott again in the seventh. "He could make a cue ball dance," complained Mets' manager Davey Johnson, who thought Scott had to be scuffing the ball, though the charge was never proved. Marveled umpire Doug Harvey: "It's a fastball that just explodes like a bomb!"

Scott's catcher, Alan Ashby, said that, unlike the knuckler—or a scuffed ball—the split-finger is very predictable to catch—it just reaches home plate, then falls through an invisible hole in the air. There are few passed balls with it. But, while catchers can catch it, hitters cannot hit it.

Craig happily predicts that it will be "the pitch of the eighties," and we can foresee the day when almost every pitcher will be throwing the split-finger, or trying to. When we do, it may revolutionize baseball as profoundly as the change in pitching distance in 1893, Babe Ruth's home runs in 1919, and the relief revolution of the 1970s. Ted Williams believes the slider, which came on the scene in the late 1940s, ended the era of .400 hitters. The split-finger could end the era of the .300 hitter. If it ever does become widespread, Ashby warns, we may see batting championships won with .210 averages.

THE BLOOPER

John Chapman, a celebrated 1860s outfielder who never pitched in the majors, is credited with inventing the blooper.

But the most famous exponent of it, Truett "Rip" Sewell, claims it was born on December 7, 1941, the day Japan bombed Pearl Harbor. Sewell, who had just led the league with seventeen losses for the fourth-place Pirates, was out hunting and accidentally was shot in the foot.

"I had to learn to walk all over again," Sewell said. He had to walk with his right big toe up, both feet pointing straight ahead Indian style. And he had to learn to pitch on his toes, without a contortionist windup, straight overhand like the Australian crawl stroke in swimming. "I learned to pitch with my body, not just my arm," he said. "I can pitch all day without getting tired."

The blooper ball was born. Other pitchers, who turn their shoulders toward the plate, cannot control the blooper. And they cannot hide the ball as well either, Sewell said.

Sewell lobbed it into the air like a mortar round, to arch slowly down over home plate. Most batters could not hit it at all, and very few hit it with power.

Sewell called it the blooper. Others called it the Eephus. Hitters called it the #$%&*! Eephus.

Sewell also threw normal pitches, which seemed all the more effective after the blooper. "He's not fast," the hitters would mutter, "but, doggone, he's sneaky."

"By the grace of God, and by being shot, I became a better pitcher," Rip insisted. The next year he turned his record around to 17–15, the most games he had ever won in his life. He followed that with seasons of 21–9 and 21–12.

For the first three years, he said, "No one ever came close to hitting a homer off the blooper. I could go out there today and throw that Blooper to Reggie Jackson and Dave Winfield and all those guys who are supposed to be great hitters, and I doubt they could hit it out of the park."

The closest batters came to hitting it was a triple by Stan Musial. Then came the 1946 All Star game and Ted Williams. Ted hit it for one of the most famous home runs in history.

Sewell gets asked a lot about the pitch now, as he travels around Florida giving inspirational talks to civic groups. After leaving baseball he had both legs amputated below the knees, the result of a mishap. But he does not consider himself handicapped, does all his own driving, and even plays golf three times a week. When Williams comes down to Sarasota every spring with the Red Sox, Rip drives over to sit on the bench and chin about The Pitch.

That one pitch made Rip eternally famous. Some may remember who was pitching when Roger Maris hit his 61st home run; others will recall the victim of Henry

Aaron's 715th. But everyone with a sense of baseball history knows who was pitching when Ted hit the blooper.

"I'm happy he hit it," Sewell said from his retirement home in Plante City, Florida. "I'm not a bit embarrassed. If I had struck him out, you'd never have heard anything about it. But he hit it, and that made me as famous as Ted."

In recalling the day now, Sewell dropped his voice and confided: "We don't talk about it much in public, but Ted, myself, and [umpire Larry] Goetz know it's true. Ted was two-and-a-half feet out of the batter's box when he hit that ball. Goetz said, 'Ted, if it had been a game that meant anything, I'd have had to call you out.'"

Williams nodded and grinned. "Yeah, I know it," he said. "I was this far out of the box," and he sheepishly held his hands apart as if measuring a fish.

DIRTY TRICKS

Pitchers discovered early that changing the cover of the ball would make it do things Isaac Newton would have thought impossible. The principle behind all foreign-substance or doctored-ball pitches is the same: The spit (mud, a nick, whatever) increases air resistance on that side of the ball, thus making the ball, in its flight through the air, veer the other way—the path of least resistance, be it up, down, or sideways. These aerodynamic principles are, of course, in effect on every pitch, legal or not. But with a legal pitch, a hurler must rely on his own ability to direct the ball by pressure and placement of the seams or apply pressure unevenly with his fingers or make the ball rotate this way or that. A trick pitch gives pitchers a little boost.

Stepping outside the law may not be ethical, but it *is* effective. As Orioles' coach

George Bamberger told Ross Grimsley in the middle of one bad jam: "If you can cheat, I wouldn't wait one pitch longer."

The Emery Ball

One of the dirtiest tricks in the pitchers' book is the emery ball, that is, scuffing the cover with sandpaper to make it dip and flit in a way that a smooth, round ball does not.

Some people think Clark Griffith, "the Old Fox," invented this nasty bit with Chicago—Pop Anson's Colts and later, upon his dismissal, Orphans—in the 1890s. Griff used to hit the ball against the heel of his shoe, and when the batters complained, he replied innocently that he was just knocking the mud off his spikes. Griff won twenty games for seven out of eight years, 1894–1901. Did he or didn't he? Only his shoemaker knew for sure.

Another theory is that the emery ball was the product of technological progress. When the old wooden grandstands were replaced by concrete, pitchers soon learned that a foul ball that hit the new stands was "mellowed" on the spot where it hit and would do funny things when pitched. The only thing wrong with this theory was that pitchers had long known how to take advantage of a soft spot in the ball to create a sharper-breaking ball.

Some say the emery ball was discovered by accident by a semipro pitcher in Denver named Russ Ford.

"He was pitching to his brother one day," in the early 1900s, long-time friend William Green recalled. "They were using a stone wall for a backstop, and a few pitches would get away and bounce off the wall. After a while the ball got scuffed up.

"Russ discovered that if he held the ball a certain way, it would really break sharply." So Ford began experimenting. "He found that if he took a bottle cap and scuffed the ball up a little more, the break would be even sharper. He kept working on it, and he got so good his brother could hardly catch it."

Like most players then, Ford cut the leather out of the pocket of his glove. He taped some emery paper around his middle finger, slipped his finger through the hole in the pocket, and scuffed up the ball.

Russ used the pitch with such impressive results that the New York Highlanders signed him in 1910. He won twenty-six games his first year up, as the Highlanders finished second, and twenty-one more the next year, though the team slipped to sixth.

The pitch was eventually outlawed—but not eliminated. There are a dozen ways to put a nick on the cover. But, as knowledge of the emery ball spread, the umps watched the pitchers like hawks, and it was hard for a pitcher to scratch the ball. So a confederate usually did it for him.

Shortstop Leo Durocher performed the role for Dizzy Dean of the Cardinals. He filed his belt buckle, and when the Gashouse Gang got into a tight spot, where they needed a strikeout, Leo would nick the ball, hand it to Dean, and say, "It's on the bottom, buddy." If Diz left it on the bottom, Leo said in *Nice Guys Finish Last*, "he'd throw three-quarters, and the ball would sail—vroooom! If he turned it over so the nick was at the top, it would sink." With Diz's natural ability, that little extra edge made it no contest.

Don Sutton hints that he may have scuffed a ball up once or twice. Once, meeting Gaylord Perry, Sutton said, "he gave me a jar of Vaseline. I thanked him and gave him a piece of sandpaper."

Rick Honeycutt of Seattle was caught redhanded in one game with both a piece of sandpaper and a thumbtack taped to his index finger. He was banished from the field, of course, and absentmindedly wiped his

Whitey Ford won more World Series games than any other man. But he takes a great deal of glee in recalling perhaps the most important money pitch he ever made, in the All Star game of 1961.

As Ford told it in *Whitey and Mickey*, he and his partner in mischief, Mantle, had lost a $200 side bet on the golf course to Horace Stoneham, owner of the Giants. Stoneham magnanimously offered to go double or nothing if Ford could get Willie Mays out in the upcoming All Star game. At first, Ford said, Mantle would not have anything to do with the deal—"he knew Mays was like nine for twelve off me lifetime." But Whitey finally cajoled his pal into it. "Now all I had to do was get Willie out."

Ford knew that under All Star rules, he would probably get only one shot at Mays. He got two strikes on Willie, "and now the money's on the line." So Whitey did what any red-blooded American boy would have done: "I loaded up the ball real good. . . . And then I threw Willie the biggest spitball you ever saw." The ball came in chest-high, then dropped as if a hole had opened under it. Willie just stared in disbelief as the umpire cried strike three, and in from center field galloped Mantle, jumping in the air as he ran "like we'd just won the World Series." Probably none of the 60,000 people in Candlestick Park knew what all the excitement was about.

"It was a money pitch, that's why," Ford said. "We'd just saved ourselves $400."

hand across his brow—almost putting his eye out.

Yankees' catcher Elston Howard sharpened a buckle on his shin guard and rubbed the ball on it before throwing it to the pitcher, Jim Bouton said in *Ball Four*.

Whitey—"they don't call me Slick for nothing"—Ford used what he calls "the ring." Ford had a jeweler friend make him a ring with a small file rasp welded onto it. He disguised it with a flesh-colored bandage, "and I had my own toolbench out there with me."

Whitey would flap his glove to warn Howard what was coming, "and it worked like a charm."

When umpire Hank Soar became suspicious, Ford replied innocently that it was his wedding ring.

Umpire John Stevens finally caught him, Bouton said. "Whitey," Stevens ordered, "go into the clubhouse. Your jock strap needs fixing. And when you come back, it better be without that ring."

The Mud Ball

Ford looks injured when accused of dirty tricks. That's a little strong, he said. " 'Tricks' might be a better word." Besides, he insisted, he only used them at the end of his career, when he really needed them.

One of his tricks was rubbing the ball's seams in mud to change its balance and hence its flight. When thrown like a fastball, it would drop like a cut ball, he says.

When Bo Belinsky pitched against Ford, Bo used to race to the mound at the start of his inning to grab Ford's ball before the umpire got to it. "The first pitch was a beauty," he said. But if it was fouled into the stands and he was given a new, clean ball, he was done for.

Doc White of the old White Sox said Jim

Whitey Ford

gloved hand. The sixth time, he would have the ball in his bare hand and get some resin, dirt, and spit on it all in one move. It was a great pitch, he says, when you needed a ground ball to get you out of the inning.

The Gunkball

The gunkball (a term coined by Whitey Ford in his *mea culpa*, "Confessions of a Gunkball Artist") is just the opposite of a spitter.

His problem, he says, was not trying to make the ball slippery, but trying to get a better grip on it. So he concocted some "gunk"—turpentine, baby oil, and resin, and mixed them into a "magic elixir" that he hid inside a roll-on deodorant bottle. The gunk was flesh colored and practically invisible. Between innings he lathered up his fingers.

Ford's secret would have lasted forever if it had not been for Mickey Mantle and Yogi Berra. Berra was an inveterate moocher, so Mantle, the gagster, put Whitey's "deodorant" where Yogi could not miss it coming out of the shower. Yogi did not miss it, and a few minutes later he was running around the locker room howling with his arms glued to his sides. They had to cut his hair to get him free.

THE SPITTER

The earliest dated account we have of a pitcher with mischief on his mind and moisture on his fingertips is 1868, when sixteen-year-old Bobby Mathews of the Lord Baltimores loaded one up against the Kekiongas of Fort Wayne. A player who saw the game—Alphonse "Phonnie" Martin, one of the umpteen claimants to invention of the curveball—recalled that "it was a revelation to us." Mathews brazenly spit on the ball, then served it underhand with a stiff wrist, as the rules then required. The ball made

Scott of that club invented the mud ball. If so, Scott used it to keep his ERA down around 2.00 and win twenty games with the fifth-place Sox in 1913.

Second baseman Frankie Frisch used to help load the ball with mud for the Cardinals in the thirties. According to Durocher, Frisch would spit tobacco juice in his hand, scoop up a little dirt, and twist the ball in his hand just enough to put a little smear of mud in the seam. "The ball would sail like a bird," Leo said.

Ford's technique was to go to the resin bag four or five times with the ball in his "a decided outcurve" at times, and at other times it curved in and dropped. "You may not believe it," Martin wrote in later years, "but I know I am right, for I saw it."

Mathews—a fine pitcher who, counting his National Association record of 1871–75, won more games than any pitcher not in the Hall of Fame—was a "wonderful little man," in the words of a contemporary. How little is a matter of dispute, with some records listing him at 5 feet, ½ inch and 110 pounds, others at a more robust 5 feet, 5½ inches and 145 pounds. In either case it seems that guile rather than power must have been the key to his success. Although he never was "a spitball pitcher" in the sense that Ed Walsh was, he kept the pitch in his repertoire throughout his long career, which culminated in three straight thirty-win seasons for the Philadelphia Athletics of 1883–85. "Mathews used to cover the palm of his left hand with saliva and rub the ball in it," pitcher (and later umpire) Hank O'Day said. He twisted the ball around "until there was a white spot on it as big as a silver quarter." (Remember, back then an entire game would be played with one or two baseballs, even if they were blackened early in the game.)

Mathews retired in 1887, and the mysterious sinking pitch went with him. Some reports indicate that it resurfaced at Bridgeport in the Eastern League around 1900, and Tommy Bond has been given credit for it. This would be plausible, inasmuch as Bond was the ace Boston pitcher of the late 1870s, when Mathews was in his prime, and was involved in the Bridgeport management with his former teammate Orator Jim O'Rourke.

Another tale names Elmer Stricklett of Sacramento in the Pacific Coast League as the inventor and passer of the torch to Ed Walsh and Jack Chesbro in 1904. Most stories, however, credit Frank Corridon, a

COURTESY OF JOHN THORN.

Bobby Mathews

pitcher who went on to some success as a spitballer with the Phils, as the man who taught the pitch to Stricklett, who had somewhat less success with it as a Dodger.

Still another tale, and probably the one to be believed, credits outfielder George Hildebrand, a Brooklyn Dodger for all of eleven games in 1902 and later an American League umpire. Hildebrand claims he discovered the spitball for himself while with Providence of the Eastern League in 1901. It had rained that day, and the grass was wet as he and Corridon warmed up together. Corridon's tosses were acting strangely, and Hildebrand had an inspiration. He took the ball from Corridon, spit on it, and threw it. The ball dipped so sharply that Corridon's eyes popped. He began experimenting and a month later struck out nine Pittsburgh Pirates in five innings with it.

When Hildebrand was traded to Sacramento, he taught the pitch to sore-armed Elmer Stricklett, and Stricklett won eleven straight games and a ticket to the White Sox in 1904. That spring he reportedly showed it to Jack Chesbro of the New York Highlanders.

Spit between the seams, Stricklett said, and hold the ball with the fingers between the seams, not across them, and the fingertips on the wet spot, thumb underneath. Throw with a normal fastball motion and let the ball slip out without friction and almost without spin. It moves as fast as a fastball, but when it gets to the plate, it suddenly goes crazy. It might dip sharply to the right one time, to the left the next—even Stricklett did not know where it would go. Batters swore the ball was "haunted."

Chesbro gave Stricklett credit for controlling the spitter more than any of his predecessors, but Jack maintained that he had been experimenting with a moistened ball long before the term spitball was coined. Chesbro wrote that he "repeatedly succeeded in curving the ball further than I had anticipated." He realized, however, that "there was always in evidence the chance of a wild pitch."

Chesbro not only began throwing it, he taught it to Al Orth, the "curveless wonder" who joined the team from Washington later that year. An underhander, Orth was one of the few men who could make the pitch break up, or seem to. Orth, who had lost twenty-two games the year before, was 11–6 after joining New York. Chesbro won

forty-one games, the most in this century, and worked 454 innings. Together they almost pitched the Highlanders to the pennant in one of the most exciting pennant races ever. But saliva, which was the team's salvation, was also its undoing. Chesbro threw one spitter too many, and it sailed over the catcher's head on the last day of the season, sending in the run that beat New York out of a chance to win the pennant in the next game.

But Stricklett's greatest student was not Chesbro. He was a strapping coalminer's son with five years of formal schooling, a striking, handsome man with jet black hair who could "strut standin' still." His name was Big Ed Walsh.

Ed Walsh

In the spring of 1904 Walsh was a twenty-three-year-old rookie who had had a few undistinguished years in the minors. White Sox manager Fielder Jones assigned him to be Stricklett's roommate and told Elmer to teach the kid the new pitch. Ed mastered the technique, and depending on his grip, could make the ball break four ways: down and in, straight down, down and out, and up (the last was thrown underhanded like Orth's). Walsh usually kept the ball at knee level. Tigers' veteran Sam Crawford, recalling Walsh at his peak, shook his head and said all he could see was the spit going by.

But Ed struggled to control the pitch. In 1904 he won only six games; in 1905, eight. Then, midway in 1906, control suddenly came. "I could hit a tack on a wall," he said. Till then Walsh had had a mediocre season; so had the Sox—they hit .223 that year, last in the league. But in August both Walsh and the White Sox took off. The team went on a nineteen-game winning streak, and Walsh won seven of them, including four shutouts and two one-run games. Four of his victims were Chesbro's Highlanders, whom the Sox went on to beat out for the pennant.

In the World Series, Walsh twice beat the mighty Cubs, winners of a record 116 games, shutting them out in the third game and striking out twelve, a mark that would stand for twenty-three years.

Afterward, National League president Harry Pulliam denounced the pitch as "unclean" and a "freak" that prevented good fielding and scientific batting, and he demanded that it be banned.

Unsanitary? Heck no, Walsh said. "You don't use a big glob." Just enough to wet two fingers. He did not even need spit; perspiration would do. Ed used the pitch only two or three times to each batter; the rest of his pitches were fastballs, which he threw with the same motion.

The 1908 season would be the biggest of Walsh's life. Using a Don Larsen sort of no-windup delivery, he won 40 games and saved 7 more, hurling a stunning 464 innings, with 269 strikeouts. Big Ed almost pitched the punchless (.224) Sox to the pennant again. They finished one game out.

(Note that the only two men to win forty games in this century, Chesbro and Walsh, were both Elmer Stricklett's pupils. Stricklett's big-league record was only 35–51, but as a teacher he was a Hall of Famer.)

Over the next season, the hitters finally found a way to stop Walsh's spitter. Ed actually licked the ball, rather than spit on it, so the A's smeared a little horse manure on it. "I vomited all over the place," he recalled. Walsh was so mad, he fired beanballs at every hitter who came up. "Nobody tried that trick on me again," he said.

In 1910 Walsh had a remarkable ERA of only 1.27, the best of a career that would leave him the game's all-time ERA champ with a mark of 1.82. Finally, however, the overwork caught up to him; some say it was Fielder Jones' fault for wearing him out in the City Series against the Cubs in October 1912. After winning twenty-seven in 1912, he won only thirteen more over the next five years.

The end came too soon. The new Federal League offered him $75,000 to jump to them—a staggering amount of money then—but he could not accept: His arm was gone. Still, Walsh won 195 games and a plaque in Cooperstown. He credited 90 percent of his victories to the spitter.

Doak, Grimes, Coveleski

Soon other pitchers picked up the new pitch. Bill Doak of the Cards won twenty games with it twice. He counseled keeping the wrist rigid to make the ball float, the same delivery used for the knuckler.

Stan Coveleski (dubbed "the greased Pole" by the *New York Times*) won twenty games four years in a row, 1918–21, and again in 1925. He helped pitch the Indians to the 1920 pennant with a 24–14 record. Supposedly washed up, he led Washington to the flag in 1925 with a record of 20–5.

The Indians faced the Brooklyn Robins in the World Series of 1920. The Robins had surged from fifth place the year before, largely on the strength of twenty-three games won by another spitballer, Burleigh Grimes, one of five twenty-game seasons Grimes would enjoy with the pitch.

One of Burleigh's problems was deception. Like Walsh, he held his glove to his mouth on every pitch, whether he actually spat on the ball or not. The Robins could not understand how the hitters seemed to know when he spit and when he did not. At last someone noticed: Grimes' cap was too small, and when he really spit, the bones in his temple twitched just enough to make the hat move slightly. So the Robins gave him a new, larger cap, and the sign stealing stopped.

In the Series, Coveleski won the first game 3–1, Grimes won the second 3–0, and Coveleski the fourth 5–1; the teams then moved to Cleveland for game five. It would be Grimes against Cleveland's thirty-game winner, Jim Bagby. Lady luck immediately deserted Burleigh. In the first inning, the Indians loaded the bases on three bleeding infield hits, bringing up Elmer Smith, their cleanup man and an excellent fastball hitter. Grimes had retired him with spitters in game two.

Unfortunately, Robins' coach Jack Coombs, a former American Leaguer, told Burleigh that Smith could not hit a fastball. Also unfortunately, the Indians were reading Grimes' spitter again. This time the culprit was Robins' second baseman Pete Kilduff. A fan had noticed in game two that Kilduff scooped up some dirt when the spitter was coming and tossed it away if the fastball was called. Forewarned, Smith laid off the spitter and waited for the fastball. When Grimes finally threw it, Smith slammed it over the wall for the first World Series grand slam in history.

Coveleski came back in the seventh game (it took five to win that year) and shut the Robins out 3–0. He had given up two runs in three Series victories, the finest World Series pitching performance since Christy Mathewson's three shutouts in 1905.

That was enough for the rule makers. The next year they outlawed the pitch, though permitting Doak, Grimes, Coveleski, and fourteen others who had pitched spitballs legally in the years before and were so designated by their teams, to continue to use it legally. Coveleski went on to win 214 with it, and Grimes 270. They both rode the pitch to the Hall of Fame.

When Grimes retired in 1934, he was the last man to throw the spitball legally in the major leagues. But he was not the last man to throw the spitball, not by a long shot.

Preacher Roe and Other Illegal Spitballers

In 1952 Cincinnati Reds' manager Luke Sewell accused Sal Maglie of the Giants and Preacher Roe of the Dodgers of throwing the spitter. Roe was "a cheating son of a gun," the irate Sewell fumed. Dodgers' manager Charlie Dressen laughed it off.

Then in 1955 came the bombshell: Roe, who had retired the year before, publicly confessed that he had indeed been throwing the spitball as his "money" pitch and had won ninety-three games in seven years with it.

Roe came from Ashflat, Arkansas, and entertained city writers with such down-home phrases as, "It was rainin' as hard as

Preacher Roe

NATIONAL BASEBALL LIBRARY, COOPERSTOWN, N.Y.

a cow pissin' on a flat rock." He also had a good fastball and led the league in strikeouts with the Pittsburgh Pirates in 1945. That winter he was punched at a basketball game in Arkansas and was unconscious for seven hours. When he reported to the Pirates in 1946, he was still having dizzy spells, and his fastball was gone. He won three and lost eight. The next year he was 4–15, and the Pirates sent him home. His career was over at the age of thirty-three. He had only two choices, he said, quit the game or develop a new pitch. He did not want to quit.

In 1948 a suddenly rejuvenated Roe hooked up with the Brooklyn Dodgers, went 12–8, and cut his ERA in half. In 1949 he was 15–6 and pitched a 1–0 shutout over the Yankees in the World Series. The next year he was 19–11, and in the ill-fated 1951 season Preach had a sensational 22–3 record. Roe was 11–2 in 1952 and beat the Yanks again in the Series. He was 11–3 in 1953.

Before the spitter, Roe had been 34–47. After it, he was 95–38, including the World Series.

How did Roe do it? Dressen said later that Roe spit on the back of his glove just after delivering the ball. Everyone was watching the pitch and did not see him rub his pitching fingers on the glove.

Roe's 1955 confession set off an explosion of sanctimonious piety. Some indignant editorialists wanted to strip his ninety-three spitball victories from the record books. "The game is in a sorry state if success is based on willful violation of the rules," *The Sporting News* preached. What effect would this have on impressionable young boys? columnists asked. Ladies will stop coming to games, others warned.

The assault took Roe aback. The pitch was mostly a decoy, he insisted; he actually threw it only once or twice a game. "I told my story with just one point in mind," he explained, "to show that the spitball isn't a dangerous pitch, and in the hope that maybe I could help bring it back as a legal pitch." The hitters already had too many advantages, he believed. Besides, nobody thinks it is immoral to steal signs, so why make a fuss about the spitball?

"I didn't sin against God," Preacher insisted.

Catcher Roy Campanella was a big help to Roe in his deception. If the ump asked to see the ball, "Campy would toe the ball, sly like, as he bent over to pick it up, and that would roll it dry. He's one of the big reasons I never got caught." Campy did not need a sign for the pitch; he had caught so many of them in the Negro leagues that he knew how to handle them.

Roe was not the only sinner, Campy agreed. "I've hit against more spitballs than I've caught," he chuckled.

Soon the fingers began pointing, and the list of those named as spitballers was almost as long as the list of those not named: old-timers Dave Danforth, Urban Shocker, George Earnshaw, and Fred Frankhouse were accused. So were Claude Passeau, Virgil Trucks, Bob Lemon, Marv Grissom, Art Fowler, Larry Jansen, Harry Brecheen, Red Barrett, Ellis Kinder, Steve Gromek, Murry Dickson, Johnny Schmitz, and Joe Page.

The main suspect, however, was Lew Burdette of the Braves, and he enjoyed the role. He loved to make an elaborate show of spitting on his fingers, then an elaborate fake wipeoff. When the ump called for the ball, he rolled it to him. One team kept a movie camera trained on him every minute. He threw 60 percent spitters that night, he said, and the camera did not spot one of them. He was spitting between his teeth, Gaylord Perry later said. "Lew washed his pants with a lot of soap," outfielder Tommy Holmes said. "He was wiping his hands on his pants and getting the soap. Three-fourths of his pitches were wet.''

Whatever Lew Burdette was doing, it worked. He always said that having the hitters worried about a spitter was as good as actually throwing it. Lew had two twenty-victory years, 1957 and 1958, and pitched the Braves to the pennant both times. In the 1957 World Series, he beat the Yankees' Bobby Shantz 4–2 in game two, Whitey Ford 1–0 in game five, and Don Larsen 5–0 in the seventh game.

Harry Walker of the Astros always claimed Jim Maloney threw his no-hitter against Houston with a spitter. Phil Regan was caught once personally by National League president Warren Giles, who nevertheless cleared him, ''because he's a Christian man, and I didn't think he would cheat.''

A lively debate raged over the topic: To spit or not to spit? On one side were those who thought pitchers needed more help; on the other, those who thought the offense needed strengthening. Commissioner Ford Frick came out for the spitter. So did AL president Joe Cronin. The debate was still raging without resolution when the greatest spitballer of modern times stepped onto the stage.

Gaylord Perry

On May 31, 1964, Mets' fans saw the longest game in baseball history, a rare Mets' triple play—and Gaylord Perry throw his first major-league spitball.

''I was the eleventh man on an eleven-man pitching staff,'' Perry wrote in his rollicking apologia, *Me and the Spitter*. He was twenty-five years old, had won a total of six big-league games, and was earning $9,500 a year, when Giants' manager Al Dark sighed and waved him into the game in the thirteenth inning.

''I was a power pitcher with almost enough power,'' Perry said. So he had been secretly working on a spitter under the old maestro, Bob Shaw. This was at last the moment to use it. The first pitch, to Chris Cannizzaro ''dipped into the dirt like a shot quail.'' Cannizzaro missed the next by a foot. While Mets' manager Casey Stengel hollered ''Spitter!'' and ''Spread out the rain tarp under him!'' Perry walked Cannizzaro, but the next man, Galen Cisco, hit into a double play, and first baseman Orlando Cepeda rolled the ball back to the mound. In the dugout Haller was laughing: ''Reduce the load of juice, Gaylord,'' he said, ''Sudol [the umpire] is getting suspicious of that splashing sound in my mitt.''

Perry went on to win the game in the twenty third inning, his first spitball victory. History had been made.

It was easy to load up, he wrote. In fact, some pitchers were too obvious about it. ''Slobberers,'' Perry called them haughtily. ''We true masters had little respect for them.'' Perry himself was a slobberer at first, he admitted shamefully. You could see the spit flying off the ball in flight, and Haller was getting a drenching behind the plate. But Perry gradually learned to cut down on his load until he became a true master too. The reduced friction counts, not the amount of spit; in fact, less spit gives better control, he wrote.

The true masters wet their fingers, which was then legal, and followed with a fake wipe-off. Perry's trick was to wet the back of his thumb while wetting his first two fingers; he then wiped off the fingers, but flicked them over the thumb while he looked in for his sign.

Unlike the fastball, which spins backward toward the plate, the spitter rotates forward, if at all. Perry applied very delicate pressure with two fingers on top of the ball and hard pressure with the thumb from below, letting the ball slip off the lubricated fingers with reduced spin. He compared it to squirting a wet watermelon seed from the fingers. The farther out on the ends of his fingers he could grasp the ball, the more it sank.

Umpire Chris Pelekoudas said the spitball is thrown like a fastball, with the same velocity. "But it comes in with no spin, then it sinks and breaks down. . . . Hard slider, my foot! A slider spins. A forkball spins a little bit. The spitball comes in dead."

A great spitter is a thing of beauty. Leon Wagner once was fooled by a Perry spitter and tried to check his swing so violently that he missed the ball but fouled off his helmet.

A good spitball pitcher needs a glue-fingered infield. The Giants' infielders had to learn to throw the spitter and were soon throwing better ones to first than Perry was throwing to the plate. A good catcher is also indispensable, someone who can block low pitches and keep his thumb on the league president's signature when handing the ball to the ump.

The decoy is as important as the pitch itself, Perry wrote. He practiced his by the hour in front of a mirror. He eventually included six in his repertoire. With many decoys mixed in to confuse the hitter, Perry was having a ball with his new "dewdrop" pitch, the "super sinker." A simple (and innocent) tug at the cap would send hitters into a frenzy. Once, while Hank Aaron looked for a spitter, Gaylord threw a roundhouse curve "as dry as a Baptist wedding." Hank, who actually hit .307 against Perry lifetime, developed the habit of stepping out of the box on every pitch, figuring that would give the ball time to dry. He once flipped Gaylord a ball before a game with a big *X* on it and the words, "Spit here, Gay."

Fooling the coaches was harder but worth the effort. Perry liked to give them an obviously fake wipe early in the game, so they would flash the spitter sign to the batter, who obediently swung a foot below the pitch. Thereafter the leery hitters refused to believe the coaches' signs. Perry says Don Drysdale faked a spitter once and almost took Dick Dietz's head off with a fastball. "Dietz didn't want to guess any more."

To keep the saliva flowing, Perry chewed slippery elm or Wrigley's Spearmint. He particularly liked to use the latter against Wrigley's Cubs. Slippery elm, a cough medicine, came from the corner drugstore and cost twenty-nine cents a box, three cents a game. Sea moss also worked, Perry reported, but it tended to foam "and made you look like a mad dog."

Leo Durocher, as manager of the Cubs, complained long and loud—until his own Cal Koonce developed a good one; then Leo quieted down considerably. It was Durocher, Perry said, who actually made 1967 "a big spitball year." Leo called for the umps to check the ball so often that a new rule was introduced that limited the number of balls that could be thrown out. That meant pitchers could keep a soiled ball in the game longer than before. (The trick was to "eat" the ball somehow at the end of the inning so the other team would have to start with a new one.)

Another rule also revolutionized the art of spitball pitching: Pitchers were no longer allowed to bring their hands to their mouths at all. But every technological challenge calls forth a technological response. Pitchers now began to use everything *but* spit; the grease ball was born.

"Anyone who had money in petroleum jelly stocks must have made some quick profits," Perry wrote. He himself started with Vaseline, and frustrated opponents sneered that a thirty-nine cent tube made Perry into a $100,000 pitcher. A thin coating on the face and neck blended right in with his sweat and was "more slick than spit." Teammates would give Gaylord a military-style inspection before every game. If they could see their faces reflected in his forehead, he had used too much. One touch of his forehead would last for two pitches, and best of all, the hitter would not be expecting the second one.

Perry put the grease on his neck, forehead, wrist, ear, pants, cap, shirt, shoe, and belt—he'd have put it on his hair if he had any.

Perry made sure he had at least two caches at all times, in case he was ordered to wipe one off. But usually he had plenty of time to hide the evidence before the umpire reached the mound, especially if the manager ran out to argue.

Perry even carried a tube in his hip pocket. Once, he says, he slid into home on a close play. The catcher went one way, he went the other, and the bat boy dived in between them to catch the tube before the umpire saw it.

Once Pelekoudas ordered Perry not to touch his hair during the game. Gaylord obeyed. Walking off the field together, Perry handed Pelekoudas a towel. Inside was a tube of Vaseline. Pelekoudas still has it in his trophy case at home.

Perry began a long, scientific search for the perfect substance, something invisible, odorless, and effective. Baby oil was good, as was suntan lotion. He borrowed some of Sandy Koufax's Capsolin, which eased the pain in Sandy's arm by making him sweat. Perry's family doctor recommended vaginal jelly, which also worked well, except that it was not as long-lasting as the others. "If I had a long inning, my K-Y reserves could run pretty low. I had to give up vaginal jelly."

The perfect substance turned out to be just plain sweat. "Sometimes," he said innocently, "it may even get on the ball." But a rule cannot be passed against sweating, and luckily, "the Good Lord blessed me with oily skin."

The National League umpires heaved a sigh of relief when Perry—and Bill Singer of the Dodgers—were traded out of the league. As a going-away present, Pelekoudas presented Gaylord with a one-pound jar of Vaseline, which Perry lifted up triumphantly for the crowd to see.

Billy Martin of Detroit was the first AL manager to complain of Perry's greaser. He even brought a bloodhound trained to sniff Vaseline to the park. Oakland's manager Dick Williams demanded that Perry change his shirt. Gay happily complied—he had just taken off a greasy shirt the inning before and now put it back on. Was Perry teaching his illicit secrets to the other Indians? Other teams began calling the Cleveland staff "The Great Slime."

By year's end Perry won twenty-four and lost sixteen (eight of the losses were by one run). He was the first man to win twenty in both leagues since Cy Young and, appropriately, won the Cy Young award.

The debate over the spitter intensified. Martin's Tigers, and later his A's, were widely accused of throwing it. Earl Weaver set up a television camera to study how Perry did it so he could teach it to his Baltimore farm hands. Rick Honeycutt got caught. Jim Merritt did not, but he trapped himself when he admitted using some of Perry's K-Y jelly. It cost him a $250 fine, and was worth every penny in publicity, Perry said.

So the debate still rages. Frankly, we think baseball ought to sanction the pitch. The fans do not mind it—attendance has never been higher, and most know the spitter is

THE MAN WHO PITCHED
ON ONE LEG

An ex-minor-league pitcher, Lieutenant Bert Shepard was shot down on a strafing mission over Germany in 1944 and woke up in a POW camp with his right leg amputated. Repatriated, and wearing an artificial leg made by a fellow POW, Bert won a tryout with the 1945 Washington Senators. "I was lucky it was my right leg," said left-hander Shepard; the left leg is more crucial, because a lefty drives off it. "You need the back leg for balance." Coming down on the artificial right leg "doesn't hurt a thing."

Bert pitched three hitless innings against the Brooklyn Dodgers in a war-bond exhibition game before giving up three hits and two runs in the fourth. He also faced Yogi Berra's navy team and gave up one run on three hits in five innings. Berra met Bert on crutches several years later. "Too bad about your leg," Yogi said. "I had it off back then, Yogi," Bert smiled. Berra's eyes popped. "You're *kidding*!"

At last, on August 14, Shep pitched an official American League game. The Red Sox had pounded the Washington starters for twelve runs in the third inning when Shepard came in. He struck out George "Catfish" Metkovich (.260) to end the in-

ning and win an ovation. He pitched five more innings, gave up three hits, a walk, and one run, for an ERA of 1.69. He struck out two.

The Senators did not invite him back in 1946, but that fall Bert toured with Bob Feller's all-stars. Stan Musial went 0 for 4 against him. Third baseman Bob Lemon struck out three times. He always said, "Shepard's the one who made a pitcher out of me."

(Corporal Lou Brissie almost had his right leg amputated in Italy. Unlike Shepard, Brissie was a right-hander, who pushed off the right leg. Wearing a steel brace, he pitched several years for the Athletics, winning fourteen games in 1948 and sixteen in 1949. In one of his first games, Ted Williams lashed a drive back to the box that bounced off the brace with a resounding thonk. "Damn it, Williams, pull the ball!" Brissie yelled. Williams did pull the next one for a homer. "I didn't mean that much," Brissie shouted.)

At the age of sixty-five, Bert Shepard lives in San Diego, walks thirty-six holes of golf in under five-and-a-half hours, and campaigns for his own design for artificial limbs. He says he never could have pitched with the present ones.

used. It takes as much skill to throw the spitter as the knuckler, and both pitches behave similarly. If one is legal, both should be. And Perry is a prime example of how the pitch adds a decade to a pitcher's longevity. Like Prohibition the ban on the spitter does not work, it merely makes lawbreakers of otherwise law-abiding folks and hypocrites

of the rest. Even the hitters do not really complain. In fact, many a batter has been heard to mutter of Nolan Ryan: "Why doesn't he throw a spitter like everyone else?"

Bring back the spitter? It never went away.

9

Strategy

Baseball is like church. Many attend, but few understand.
　　　　　　　　　　　　—Wes Westrum

The beauty of baseball—the very heart of the game—is in its minute details, its layer upon layer of largely unseen complexity. Like art and literature, it affords simple pleasures on the surface, and more delicious, complex satisfaction for those who perceive the inner levels. No part of the game is apparently more straightforward but actually more labyrinthine than the path of the pitched ball.

A great artist such as Carl Hubbell could bring even the enemy bench alive in appreciation of the mental chess match between pitcher and batter. Billy Herman said his Cubs used to leave their seats and stand on the dugout steps to watch Hubbell at work, mixing up his screwball, curve, fastball, change-up, screwball again. "He didn't have overpowering stuff," Herman said, "but he was a marvel to watch."

Sadly, the beauty of this mental game is lost on at least 45,000 out of the 50,000 persons in a stadium. You cannot enjoy, or even comprehend, it from a seat in the up- per left-field stands. You must get a seat in the lower stands, behind home, and keep careful tally of each pitch on your scorecard to uncover the artistry of what is happening. A great television announcer—Joe Garagiola, Tim McCarver, Vin Scully, for instance—can double or triple your enjoyment at home.

Even many sportswriters are oblivious to what used to be called, in the first decades of this century, the "inside game"—they feel it is not news, will not be appreciated by their editors, and seems more "technical" than the average fan or they themselves can comprehend. So they report on only the externals—a fly to left, a great stop at third, a dramatic strikeout, and spice things up with a locker-room observation on the order of "I saw the ball real good today." Why was the hitter allowed to pull the ball to left? Why had the third baseman been shaded over toward short? Why did the curve produce a strikeout in that situation? The writer presumes that his readers will not care and so closes his eyes to the sublime aspects of baseball.

The inner game, the mental game between pitcher and hitter, is infinitely complex. Its strategy consists not of one pitch, but a whole palette of pitches. Said Warren Spahn: "It depends on the hitter, the experience prior to this time at bat, the situation—whether you're pitching for a double play, or trying to keep him from hitting behind the runner." Spahn could have added: the shape of the park, the direction of the wind, the score of the game, the umpire's personal strike zone, what the hitter hits best, what the pitcher throws best, what the hitter expects, what the pitcher thinks he expects, what the hitter thinks the pitcher thinks he expects, and so on.

Strategy will always be a human, subjective art, even when based on the most sophisticated objective data. Each ball game offers hundreds of crossroads that require a player's, coach's, or manager's judgment. The pitcher's approach to strategy "keeps the game always new, always tantalizing," Tommy John said. "It may tire your brain, but it will never anesthetize it."

PITCHER'S MEMORY

The first time up perhaps the batter went out on a change-up. The next time he is looking for it again. Do you cross him up with something different? Scott McGregor said, "The real chess match begins in his last time at bat, when the game's on the line. You throw the first pitch out of the strike zone [Ray Miller wouldn't approve] to see what he's looking for. Maybe he's hungry for an outside fastball and he's leaning over the plate. So you jam him. It's a game of adjustments, and the guy who keeps adjusting survives. He never gets in a pattern, or if he does, he sees it and breaks it."

A pitcher must not only know how he retired each hitter in this game, said Ed Lopat, he must know how he handled him last month. If he cannot remember, he should keep notes and review them before every game. "It's part of the business," Lopat said.

As Phillies' catcher Benny Culp put it, speaking of Schoolboy Rowe: "He wouldn't pitch a game, he'd *weave* one."

THE COMPUTER AGE

While pitching will always remain an art, it is also a science, and increasingly so. We can remember, not too many years ago, asking each major-league front office how its batters did against right- and left-handed pitching. Except for data on switch-hitters Mickey Mantle and Pete Rose, not one of them knew—or, apparently, had even wondered! Since the 1890s they had been religiously taking left-handed hitters out and putting in right-handed pinch-hitters because that was "the book." They believed in "the book" without ever knowing what the book really was. Not until the 1970s did the Elias Sports Bureau begin to record and supply "situational stats" to the clubs.

Johnny Sain kept charts on all his pitchers. Each chart contained a diamond with lines showing where each hitter hit the ball, red for base hits, green and blue for flies and grounders. The chart also showed what pitches the hitter hit, what pitches he went out on, when he stole, and the like. Usually the man scheduled to pitch the next day kept the chart. Nolan Ryan said it was a good way to concentrate on the upcoming game and see how your teammate is getting them out.

When he was with Kansas City, lefty Larry Gura used a home computer. He kept 13 disks, one for each opposing team, and for every hitter he could flash on the screen a replica of Sain's chart.

Several clubs have also moved into the computer age, replacing Earl Weaver's famous three-by-five cards with floppy disks. "No one's ever had this level of information before," said Dick Cramer, who designed the Edge computer system used by the White Sox, A's, and Yankees. "We can just ask all sorts of questions no one's been in a position to ask before." For instance, the A's say that fourteen of Davey Lopes' fifteen home runs in 1983 came on fastballs. How many pitchers or their catchers were aware of that?

THE BOTTOM LINE: SOME RULES OF THE GAME

What then does it all add up to? How do the great artists work?

"A good pitcher's main job," Sal Maglie once observed, "is not to give up the first run." And the best way to prevent that first run—or any run—is to get that first man out every inning and to get the first pitch over.

"The whole idea is to throw the ball over the plate," said George Bamberger. "Throw the ball down the middle, but don't throw the same ball twice. Change the speed."

As Bamberger's successor at Baltimore, Ray Miller, put it, pitching strategy boils down to three rules: "Throw strikes, change speeds, work fast."

Or, as Warren Spahn said, "Hitting is timing; pitching is upsetting timing."

A basic tenet of pitching—"Let him hit it; you've got fielders behind you"—was implied back in 1845 in the rules devised by Alexander Cartwright. The early rules specified three strikes but had no provision for called balls, presuming that a pitcher would

permit the ball to be struck and put into play. Christy Mathewson preached this practice, as did Jim Palmer; Bob Gibson lived by it, and Sandy Koufax believed it as well: "I became a good pitcher when I stopped trying to make them miss the ball and started trying to make them hit it."

Should a pitcher go with his best pitch, or should he pitch to the batter's weakness? The pitching fraternity is almost unanimous on this point: They would rather throw their best pitch with confidence, even if it means challenging the hitter's strength, than throw their second-best pitch in deference to the batter.

The cat-and-mouse game can get tremendously complicated. Ty Cobb deliberately used to look bad on a pitch early in the game, in hopes the pitcher would throw it later, when the game was on the line. Pitchers do the same thing. Jim Palmer sometimes held his best pitch back, refusing even to show it to the hitter until the late innings, when he really needed it.

Low or high? The traditional wisdom is to keep the ball low and avoid the potentially dangerous long fly. As mentioned earlier, manager Eddie Stanky of the White Sox used to offer pitchers a free suit of clothes for pitching twenty ground balls a game. But Earl Weaver preached that most hitters are low-ball hitters, and the fastball is much tougher to hit high in the strike zone. In a hit-and-run situation, said Nolan Ryan, the high ball is best, because it is harder to hit on the ground into the hole.

The First Strike

Data show "how important it is to throw the first strike in there," Dick Cramer said. It reduces the number of walks, of course. It also gives the pitcher the option to work on the batter, to use a pitch off the plate to set up the one he wants the batter to chase.

"You don't worry much about a hitter's weakness until you get ahead of him," Don Drysdale said. "First you concentrate on getting your good pitches over, to put him in a hole."

Certainly, the hitter may smash a strike out of the park, but the risk is small compared to the reward. Cramer found that the batter hits the first pitch safely well under 10 percent of the time. The other 90 percent he either takes it, misses it, fouls it, or goes out. So the odds are all with the pitcher in throwing the first pitch over. "Even if the batter swings," Cramer said, "he's got to hit .350 to .360 before it takes away the advantage to the pitcher to get that first strike in."

Pete Palmer did a study involving more than 2,500 at-bats and also concluded that getting the first pitch in for a strike is a big advantage to the pitcher. The average hitter in Pete's study hit .259. But after the pitcher got the first strike in, the batter suddenly lost nineteen points on his average and became a .240 hitter. If the pitcher missed with the first pitch, however, the batter's eventual batting average for that time at bat rose eight points, to .267.

In fact, Pete's study, detailed in *The Hidden Game of Baseball*, demonstrates that the eighth-place hitter with a 1–0 count is more dangerous than the cleanup man with an 0–0 count. Moreover, three out of every four walks come after missing the plate with the first pitch.

Palmer's study followed 2,545 hitters through every count. Here's what he found:

PERFORMANCE BY BALL-STRIKE COUNT

Strikes		Balls			
		0	1	2	3
0	Samples	2,545	3,091	1,070	336
	BAT	.259	.267	.260	.250
	SLG	.388	.415	.416	.321
	OBA	.317	.371	.477	.750
	RUNS	.002	.035	.085	.205
1	Samples	3,196	2,689	1,450	583
	BAT	.240	.243	.265	.285
	SLG	.347	.365	.418	.457
	OBA	.273	.306	.389	.600
	RUNS	−.031	−.010	−.044	.150
2	Samples	1,208	1,733	1,322	750
	BAT	.198	.195	.208	.199
	SLG	.279	.283	.310	.309
	OBA	.221	.239	.309	.479
	RUNS	−.076	−.065	−.022	.065

Before computers came to baseball, Dodgers' statistician Allan Roth kept this kind of data for the Dodgers, and every pitcher closeted himself with Roth in the spring to go over the previous year's stats.

In 1960, Sandy Koufax learned, he gave up a collective .209 average to all the hitters he faced. But on the first pitch, all batters hit Koufax at a .349 clip (that is, on all first pitches hit fair—about four-fifths of all first pitches are either taken, fouled off, or missed). That was better than Dick Groat, the league's leading hitter that year at .325.

So Koufax concentrated on that first pitch, with the following results:

FIRST PITCH

Year	Bat. Avg.	W–L	ERA	SO	BB
1960	.349	8–13	3.91	197	100
1961	.312	18–13	3.52	269	96
1962	.243	14–7	2.54	216	57

Presumably these are batting averages only for balls put in play. The batting average for all pitches (including balls, strikes, and fouls) would be considerably lower.

In 1984, David Driscoll of Toronto reported, Dave Stieb's first-pitch batting average was .379. But remember, that means only .379 of the balls put into play. Of all strikes (or pitches that the hitter thought were strikes and swung at), Stieb's BA was .102. Of all total pitches, including balls, it was about .050. Koufax's figures were probably down around there too.

Driscoll analyzed 3,741 plate appearances and reported the results in Bill James' 1985 *Baseball Abstract*. After subtracting called balls and counting only called strikes or swings, Driscoll's figures show that the hitters hit the first pitch safely almost exactly ten percent of the time (.099). Counting all pitches, they hit it 5 percent of the time.

Cliff Johnson's batting average was .058; Garth Iorg's was odds for the hitters. And, as James commented, those are not batting averages, those are really on-base averages. If pitchers could give an OBA of .099 all the time, every game would be a shutout.

"The first pitch is the key," Red Sox' coach Bill Fischer agreed. "It should be your best stuff. If you could get everyone to hit the first pitch, you'd get twenty-seven outs."

However, there is one important caveat. According to SABR's Keith Sutton, three

pitchers—Tommy Bridges, Billy Pierce, and Milt Wilcox—all lost perfect games when the twenty-seventh batter hit the first pitch for clean hits.

During the 1983 playoffs and World Series, John Holway studied what happened when the batter swung at the first pitch. He found that such a hitter had to be sure to get a good piece of the ball. If he hit it fair, he became an instant .400 hitter, but if he fouled it off or missed it, his eventual batting average for that time at bat would plummet to .100.

Ted Williams instinctively knew the odds, even in the precomputer age, and preached to batters never to swing at the first pitch— at least against a new pitcher. Ted liked to look it over and refresh his memory on what the pitcher threw. It is better to say, "Gee, he's faster than I remember," while digging in for the next pitch than it is to say it while walking back to the dugout after popping up.

Oddly, a day-by-day study of Williams' .406 season reveals that he often did swing at the first pitch, so his theory must have developed later, just as his theory of hitting with dead wrists also came gradually. We have a letter from Ted dated 1942 in answer to a youthful request for batting tips. Live clean, he said, and get plenty of snap in your wrists. Which Ted Williams are we to believe—the young Ted Williams who had just hit .400, or the older Ted who remembered how he had?

From the old-time Negro league slugger Louis Santop to the modern Roberto Clemente, many hitters habitually take the first pitch. Charlie Gehringer thought he got careless swinging at the first strike and was a more careful batter after he had a strike on him.

The Third Pitch: 1–1

This is a crucial count for both pitcher and hitter. A strike at 1–1 is also worth 100 points in the final OBA: if the pitch is a strike, the OBA goes down about eighty points; if it is a ball, it goes up twenty.

The Third Pitch: 2–0

The 2–0 pitch has always been considered the hitter's pitch. But the data show that that is not the case.

It is, nevertheless, a big pitch for the pitcher. When he is behind 2–0, he must get the third pitch over. If he does, he can cut the on-base percentage almost 100 points (from .477 to .385). If he does not, he is now in a hole 3–0, and the chances are three to one (.750) that the hitter will wind up on base.

Billy Martin must have realized this: He demanded that his pitchers throw a fastball on the 2–0.

Oddly however, the batting average does not change on the 3–0. In fact, it actually goes down on the 3–0 (from .260 to .250) and up slightly on the 2–1 (to .265). If Mike Schmidt is at bat with men in scoring position, and a pitcher can afford a walk but not a hit, this is a good time to see if Schmidt will go fishing for a bad pitch. If he does not bite, he will probably walk, but so what?

The best count for the hitter is the 3–1 pitch, which is no surprise. Next best is the 2–1. It is surprising, however, that the 2–0 is not the hitter's pitch it was reputed to be.

Hitters did a bit better on the 1–0 and 2–1 counts.

Palmer found the eventual on-base average (hits plus walks and hit batsmen) to be: for the 3–1, .600; for the 2–1, .389; for the 2–0, .477; for the 1–0, .371.

Two Strikes, You're Out

The best count for the pitcher, of course, is any two-strike count. The hitter has one chance out of five of hitting it safely, so you can give 4–1 odds on that pitch and eventually win enough money for a trip to the World Series. Allan Roth's data showed that Jackie Robinson was the best two-strike hitter he found, and Robinson's best two-strike averages were only in the .270s. Ted Williams might have been the best two-strike hitter of all. He choked up on the bat and just tried to meet the ball.

Today Boston's Wade Boggs is surely the premier two-strike hitter. In 1985 half of his 200 hits came with two strikes. "He never swings at the first pitch," said Baltimore pitcher Ken Dixon, "so you're up one strike. Then he fouls off the second, and you're up two. That's when he does his best hitting."

The 0–2 count is an interesting one. In the old days the wisdom was to waste a pitch on the 0–2 or, better yet, knock the batter down on it—but above all, do not give him anything good to hit. Giants' manager Mel Ott once fined pitcher Bill Voiselle $500 for letting a hitter hit the 0–2. Voiselle's salary that year was $3,500, but Ott said he would fine him again if he ever put another 0-2 pitch over the plate. In one game the umpire shot his arm up in the air, signifying a strikeout on the 0–2. "That was a ball!" the alarmed Voiselle hollered. "What are you trying to do, ruin me?"

Nowadays, however, many pitchers and managers believe in going for the kill on the 0–2. "If you have a batter at your mercy, why let up on him?'' Tommy John asked. ''Get him out with three pitches if you can,'' agreed Bamberger. ''I've seen too many cases where it's 0–2, you waste one, and pretty soon it's 3–2.''

Bob Gibson could not understand the logic of wasting a pitch on the 0–2. ''What are you accomplishing if you throw the ball a foot over the batter's head?'' he asked. ''What are you setting him up for when you do that? He's not going to swing at it. All you have done is waste a pitch. When I get 0–2 on a hitter, I like to get him out with the next pitch. I throw a lot of pitches as it is, I don't need to throw any extra ones.''

The 0–2 ''should be the pitcher's pitch,'' said Nolan Ryan. ''Use it to set up another pitch, or make a hitter hit *your* pitch.''

THE MASTER STRATEGISTS

Clark Griffith

Clark Griffith was called ''the Old Fox.'' He was the brainiest, most cunning pitcher at the turn of the century, and years after he quit pitching to become owner of the Senators, he could sit in the stands and predict 97 out of 100 pitches that the man on the mound would throw.

He was also one of the slowest workers in history, delaying, stalling, tantalizing, then delivering the pitch the hitter never expected. He taunted the batters—''You big stiff, you couldn't hit this with a board''— then pitched high and wide and made them swing wildly. When the hitter was tensed to the breaking point, Griff would smile and say, ''Hit this, you big bloat,'' then toss the ball underhanded while the desperate batter fell to his knees swinging.

Rube Foster

Andrew ''Rube'' Foster pitched for the black Cuban X Giants at the same time Griffith was pitching for the White Sox. Foster

Clark Griffith

got his nickname by beating Rube Waddell of the Athletics. Frank Chance, manager of the Cubs, wistfully called him ''the most finished product I've ever seen in the pitcher's box.''

Writing in Sol White's *Negro Baseball Guide* of 1906, Foster counseled pitching with the head more than the arm. He liked to throw the curve on the 3–2, knowing that most hitters would not be expecting it. The real test comes when the bases are filled: ''Do not worry. Try to appear jolly and unconcerned. I have smiled often with the bases full with two strikes and three balls on the batter. This seems to unnerve them.''

THE OLDEST BIAS IN BASEBALL

When Hank Aaron sent his 715th home run soaring over the wall in 1973, it marked the triumph of one man over decades of discrimination and prejudice. For baseball has discriminated against Aaron and dozens of other innocent hitters who have had to overcome an accident of birth over which they had no control. Jackie Robinson, Roy Campanella, Josh Gibson, Ernie Banks, Willie Mays, Monte Irvin, Jim Rice—all have had to overcome a handicap not faced by Ty Cobb, Babe Ruth, Ted Williams, Roger Maris, Willie Keeler, or George Brett.

Yes, all have been victims of discrimination because they had the misfortune to be born right-handed.

Basketball discriminates against short men, football against light men, and horse racing against heavy men. Baseball discriminates against right-handed men.

The bias knows no racial barriers. It strikes at whites just as unfairly as it has hit blacks. From Honus Wagner to Mike Schmidt, it has numbered among its victims Rogers Hornsby, Jimmy Foxx, and Joe DiMaggio and has bestowed its benefits on Reggie Jackson, Willie Stargell, and Rod Carew.

And, if baseball discriminates against right-handed hitters, then it must also discriminate against left-handed pitchers, since most hitters are right-handed and therefore have an advantage when batting against left-handed pitching.

Pete Palmer confirms it. He analyzed 143,000 American League plate appearances from 1974 to 1978 and found that right-handed pitchers yield batting averages four points less than do lefties (.266 to .270), or about 1.5 percent. Presumably, that is because most hitters are right-handed and have the advantage over lefty pitchers. The average right-handed batter hits twenty points less than the average lefty (.261 to .281), or about seven percent less.

This has been ascribed to the extra step advantage lefties have in beating out infield hits, to somewhat shorter right-field fences, and above all, to the fact that most pitchers are right-handed. Palmer, however, feels the major reason is that lefties play the power positions, first base and outfield, while the good-fielding but weak-hitting shortstops usually hit right-handed. But this does not explain why power spots are usually reserved for left-handers.

Larry Lynn and John Schwartz of SABR have studied this phenomenon in detail. Lynn found that true lefties—those who both bat and throw with their left hands—are superior batters compared to all other combinations. (Babe Ruth was a true lefty, Ty Cobb was not—he threw with his right hand.) Psychologists say it has to do with the right and left sides of the brain and the fact that batting requires the coordinated use of both hands. Lynn has not studied pitchers, but believes that since pitching is a primarily one-handed activity, the advantage for true lefties would be less pronounced.

The highest batting average, Pete found, is the left-handed hitter against the right-handed pitcher. He is liable to slug the hurler for a .291 average. When two right-handers oppose each other, the chance of a hit is .255.

Palmer's data from 277 American League players from 1974 to 1977 look like this:

PERFORMANCE BY LEFT-RIGHT COMBINATIONS

| | Pitcher | | | | | | | | | | | |
| | Right | | | | Left | | | | Total | | | |
Batter	PA*	BAT	SLG	OBA	PA*	BAT	SLG	OBA	PA*	BAT	SLG	OBA
Right	59	.255	.375	318	32	.274	.409	.342	91	.261	.387	.326
Left	29	.291	.450	.361	14	.261	.375	.322	43	.281	.425	.349
Switch	6	.264	.368	.354	3	.266	.370	.335	9	.265	.368	.347
Total	94	.266	.397	.334	49	.270	.397	.336	143	.268	.397	.334

*Plate Appearances, in thousands.

If Wade Boggs had been able to hit lefties better, he might have hit .400 in 1983. Wade hit .398 against righties, but could hit only .281 against lefties, bringing his overall average down to .361.

By contrast, consider Ted Williams. In 1941 he hit .396 against righties, about the same as Boggs did. But against lefties Ted hit .461! He himself was surprised to be told this. His only explanation: Against lefties he did not try to pull the ball, but merely hit it up the middle. The statistics seem to bear this out: Of his league-leading thirty-seven homers that year, only one came against a southpaw, Lefty Gomez.

Lefties made Ted a .400 hitter. In fact, two lefties put him over—Gomez and Marius Russo, both of the Yanks. Against Gomez Ted got ten hits in twelve at-bats; against Russo he was seven for ten. Without them he would have gone down in history as the last of the .398 hitters. (One wonders: if he had hit up the middle against right-handers too, he might have ended up hitting over .500!)

Joe DiMaggio was another exception to the rule. During his hitting streak, he hit .324 against lefties but .423 against righties. However, unlike Williams, DiMaggio hit the same-side pitchers with power—fourteen homers against the righties and only one against the lefties.

Paradoxically, Pete Palmer and his computer have come up with the information that in the first eighty-four years of this century, left-handed pitchers as a group scored lower ERAs than right-handers about 72 percent of the time. And the left-handed dominance is growing. In the first decade, 1901–10, the two sides were even—lefties led five years and righties the other five. But since 1945 the breakdown has been:

	L	R
1945–54	10	0
1955–64	9	1
1965–74	7	3
1975–84	8	2

We're not sure why this is so. Right-handers easily outnumber lefties in the population at large (estimates on this vary widely, from 4:1 to 20:1). How can a minority outperform the majority so over-whelmingly? Are right-handers inherently inferior to lefties as baseball players? Our sense of justice and our belief in the God-given equality of our fellow man rebels at the very suggestion.

Even if this were true, one would expect both sides to be even, since managers would add lefties who are progressively less good until lefties and righties balanced each other in effectiveness.

So we do not yet know why lefties have an advantage in yielding runs; we only know that they do. The only way to erase this bias is to divide the two leagues into an all-righty league and an all-lefty league and let the two champions play each other in October.

This left-handed bias is slowly beginning to sink into the psyches of baseball's best thinkers. Palmer reports that the number of left-handed pitchers has been growing slowly but steadily since 1901, from about 20 percent of all pitchers to about 30 percent at present.

And, as Bill James points out, over a recent ten-year span, first-division teams had a total of 2,535 lefties on their staffs, while second-division clubs had only 1,758. James adds that Dick Williams habitually loads up with left-handers every time he moves to a new club. He is the only manager in history we are aware of who does that.

On the other hand, there is the mystery of the Toronto Blue Jays. For four years in a row, 1981–84, they failed to get a single victory from a left-handed starting pitcher. Is that why they failed to win a pennant in that stretch?

Maybe Dick Williams is onto something.

Christy Mathewson

Christy Mathewson was a master at the game within the game. Against the Cubs' Joe Tinker, who choked up on the bat, Matty used curves low and outside and consistently got him out—until Joe tried a long bat and stood deeper in the box. When Matty threw his first curve, Joe practically jumped across the plate and smote it to right field for a double. If Matty pitched inside, Joe was in position to hit that one too. "Then," Matty admitted, "he had me. From that day on, Tinker [a lifetime .263 hitter] became one of the most dangerous batters I ever faced."

Cy Seymour also murdered Matty's curve, and though Matty tried to mix his pitches up, Cy would wait for the curve. So Matty tried nothing but fastballs "around the neck." Seymour, still waiting for the curve, struck out four times that day.

But in the World Series of 1911 Frank Baker of the A's outguessed Matty. Christy figured Baker would not hit a low curve over the outside corner, since Baker, a left-hander, was a dead pull hitter. Matty fed him one, but the umpire called it a ball (Matty always insisted the ump missed the call). That put Matty down 2–1 on the count. He had to lay the next one over the plate, and Baker walloped it for a home run, winning the nickname that would follow him the rest of his life, Home Run Baker.

Chief Bender

Ty Cobb considered Chief Bender of the A's the "brainiest pitcher" he ever saw. In the 1911 World Series, Cobb said, Bender waved the outfield around to the right against the Giants' catcher, Albert "Chief" Meyers. A .332-hitting right-hander and a good fastball hitter, Meyers naturally expected a curve on the outside. Instead he got

Chief Bender

a fastball down the middle, which he took in amazement for strike three. Sighed Cobb in admiration: "Pure skulduggery."

Grover Alexander

How did Old Pete Alexander strike out Tony Lazzeri in the 1926 World Series? "Alex pitched to Lazzeri's strength," sec-

ond baseman Frankie Frisch said, "something neither Tony nor the other Yankees expected. Just before the third strike, Lazzeri hit a long ball that was barely foul. But that didn't bother Alex. He threw one down Tony's alley again and surprised him right out of there. He won that one with his head—and that razor-sharp control."

Ted Lyons

The White Sox' Ted Lyons urged getting by on three pitches—fastball, curve, and either a knuckler, screwball, or slider— "take your pick." Sometimes, he warned, a pitcher tries to have too many pitches. He himself, Lyons told us, had a "good slow curve. That's the best pitch to a big strong left-hand hitter; they like you to throw hard so they can hit it hard."

Lyons was a tough pitcher, and in every match-up, he became tougher. The more he faced you, the better he became at playing "those little pitcher–batter thinking games," Ted Williams wrote in *My Turn at Bat*. Lyons was sneaky fast, spotted his curve well, and mixed in a change and a knuckler. "The only thing you can't do," the veterans told young Williams, "you can't guess with the son of a gun. . . . He'll usually outthink you." Williams got the better of the game his rookie year, but the next year Lyons "struck me out twice on fastballs in situations where I thought he would not dare throw a fastball, and he knew I was thinking he wouldn't, so he threw it anyway. Put a little extra on it. Out I went, still looking for a curve. Lyons was a smart pitcher."

Murry Dickson

The Cardinals' Murry Dickson had eight pitches—fastball, slider, sinker, screwball, knuckleball, curve, a change on the fastball, and another on the curve. Catcher Joe Garagiola had to take off his mitt to give the signals. And Murry threw them overhand, three-quarters, sidearm, or submarine, making thirty-two possible varieties. The only pitcher we can think of who comes close would be Juan Marichal—and perhaps Joaquin Andujar on one of his more playful days.

Dickson once struck the Dodgers' Carl Furillo out with eight straight curves on a 3-2 count. After Carl fouled the first seven, Garagiola asked him, "What do you think you're going to get next?"

"Another curve," Furillo guessed.

"Right," Joe said, "but neither one of us knows from what angle." It was overhand, and it was slow, and Furillo did not touch it.

Jim Bouton

A pitcher's strategy is heavily influenced by his ammunition. Bouton, a knuckleballer after he had lost his fastball, started every hitter off with a knuckler and stayed with it until the count reached 3-0. To heavy hitters such as Harmon Killebrew or to anyone in a game-winning situation, he would even throw it on the 3-0. "I'd rather walk the guy with my best pitch than let him beat me with one swing at my worst."

Against Pete Rose once, Bouton remembers, he was two runs ahead, two men on, and two outs. He threw two knuckleballs for balls. Catcher Bruce Edwards signaled for a fastball; Bouton shook him off. "Rose is just going to rip my fastball. I know it." So he threw a knuckler for a strike, another for a foul strike, and a third for strike three "and strutted off the mound."

Robin Roberts

Robin Roberts won 286 games with one simple formula and only two signs—fastball and pitchout. Up until late in his career, when he added a curve, he relied on control

and a fastball that moved. He did not study hitters; rather, he threw to everyone in the same way—low and away and high and tight, the classic pattern; when he added the curve it always had to be below the belt. "That's the whole story of pitching," he summed up. "Keep your life and your pitching real simple, and you'll get along."

Nolan Ryan

After he had lost a couple miles an hour off his fastball, Nolan Ryan called his curveball the key to his strategy. "Whenever you see me with high strikeouts in a game, I've got my breaking ball working. I might strike out five or six guys on fastballs the first time through the lineup. But not later. The curveball's got to be there to set them up. And if you get behind in the count, you can't set anybody up."

TED CONS SPAHN

Sometimes the hitter can con the pitcher. Warren Spahn tells of chatting with Ted Williams in spring training one year. "That's a pretty good fastball," Ted told him. "You ought to use it more often."

Spahn was puzzled. "I always thought my curve was my best pitch."

The next summer they faced each other in the All Star game in Griffith Stadium. "This is the spot to use my fastball," Spahn thought, and Ted blasted it into the center-field bull pen. As Ted jogged around second base, Warren turned and shouted, "You conned me into that pitch last spring, didn't you?"

Ted just smiled and kept on jogging.

As pitcher Bob Veale once observed, "Good pitching always stops good hitting, and vice versa."

Tim McCarver, the Thinking Man's Catcher

"It's much easier to work a good hitter than a poor hitter," catcher Tim McCarver wrote in *Sport*. "Poor hitters have no idea what you're going to throw to begin with, so why try to outthink them? You go after them with stuff, rather than with pitch selection. But there's beauty in working a good hitter."

(Joe Garagiola said he was once struck out on three straight pitches and stomped off the field, fuming, "You could at least have *worked* on me!")

McCarver believes pitchers should start more hitters off with breaking balls, to "keep the fastball fresh." Get ahead in the count, he advises, and use the fastball to push the hitter back, which gives the outside of the plate back to the pitcher.

It is essential to be able to throw the curve over the plate if you are going to make it your first pitch, and even more essential when you are behind in the count, to prevent the hitter from waiting for the fastball. It is a skill few of the oldtimers had but is more and more common among today's hurlers.

10

Wins

Cy Young had 510. Old Hoss Radbourn had 60 in one year. Rube Marquard had 20 in a row.

Baseball pays off on wins. But what is a win? Is a win with the world champions equal to a win with the tail-enders, for example? Of course not.

OFFENSIVE SUPPORT

Take the case of two men pitching on the same day. One allows four hits and one run and wins the game 2–1. The other also allows four hits and one run, and loses 1–0.

Fernando Valenzuela began the 1985 season with an ERA of 0.00 after his first four games—not one earned run in thirty-three straight innings. Yet his won–lost record was 2–2, as errors and poor support cost him two defeats. Fernando felt like Rich Gossage when he was with the White Sox: ''You had to pitch a shutout to tie.''

Back in 1946 Tex Hughson of the Red Sox always seemed to draw Bob Feller and Hal Newhouser as opponents. On one west-

Charles Radbourn

ern swing, he beat Feller 1–0 when Bobby Doerr scored from third on a 110-foot foul pop-up. Four days later he beat Hal Newhouser 1–0 on a bases loaded walk in the ninth. Tex clinched the pennant the following month on another 1–0 victory over Cleveland. He was the Sox' stopper—when they began to stumble, he stopped the losing streak. But, given the support he got, he was lucky to win twenty games while losing eleven.

Meantime Hughson's teammate Dave "Boo" Ferriss was giving up a hit an inning, a high total that usually characterizes a sub-.500 hurler. But the powerful Boston bats—Ted Williams, Bobby Doerr, Rudy York, John Pesky, Dom DiMaggio—were pasting the other pitchers. Boo once gave up

thirteen hits and won 15–4, though generally he was winning by scores of 9–6 or 8–4; he coasted to a 25–6 season.

In the Mets' pennant-winning year of 1973, Jon Matlack had the third-lowest ERA in the league but was dead last in offensive run support. He finished with a 13–15 mark.

Bill James has discovered that the differences in run support can be huge, over three runs per game average for a year in some cases.

Nine pitchers in 1985 had TRAs (total runs allowed) of 3.7 or 3.8. But their won-lost marks varied widely, from the Yankees' Ron Guidry's 22–6 to the Giants' Mike Krukow's 8–11. The difference was that Guidry got 5.4 runs per game from Yankees' batters; Krukow got only 2.9 from Giants' hitters:

Pitcher	Team	Runs	TRA*	W–L
Ron Guidry	New York Yankees	5.4	3.7	22–6
Mike Scott	Houston Astros	5.0	3.7	18–8
Joaquin Andujar	St. Louis Cardinals	4.9	3.8	21–12
Tom Browning	Cincinnati Reds	4.8	3.8	10–9
Steve Trout	Chicago Cubs	4.8	3.6	9–7
Dan Petry	Detroit Tigers	4.0	3.7	15–13
Charlie Hough	Texas Rangers	3.6	3.7	14–16
Kevin Gross	Philadelphia Phillies	3.4	3.8	15–13
Mike Krukow	San Francisco Giants	2.9	3.7	8–11

*Total Run Average, includes all runs, earned and unearned.

In 1984, according to the *Elias Baseball Analyst,* Dodgers' pitchers cut their collective ERA, but Dodgers' hitters cut their run support even more—down to about half a run per game. As a result, the Dodgers lost

eighteen games more than they had lost in 1983. Fernando Valenzuela and Rick Honeycutt were particularly hurt (Honeycutt's 1983 record includes both Texas and Los Angeles):

	1983				1984			
	Runs	TRA*	ERA	W–L	Runs	TRA*	ERA	W–L
Valenzuela	4.83	4.39	3.75	15–10	3.12	3.76	3.03	12–17
Honeycutt	4.53	3.41	3.03	16–11	3.54	3.53	2.84	10–9

*Total Run Average, includes all runs, earned and unearned.

In an even more dramatic example, at one point in 1985 the Cardinals' John Tudor and Joaquin Andujar had almost identical ERAs. Yet Tudor had a 1–7 won–lost record, while Andujar was 7–1. The difference was run support.

Some men, mysteriously, do better than they would be expected to, given the difference between their runs received and runs allowed. In 1984 Eric Show of San Diego was given 3.66 runs per game and gave up 3.83, total. That looks like the formula for a losing season, yet Show was 15–9. On the other hand, why did Jerry Koosman and Dennis Eckersley do so poorly?

	Runs	*ERA*	*W–L*
Koosman	4.5	3.82	14–15
Eckersley	4.5	3.32	10–8

What we do not know yet is when those offensive runs were received. Perhaps they came in big bunches, say eight or nine in a game three times a year, while the rest of the time the pitcher might have had only two or three as support.

James does have those data on one man, Bud Black of the 1984 Kansas City Royals. His won–lost record was 17–12, not too impressive considering that the Royals were division champs. But in his twelve losing games, Black gave up only 3.8 runs per nine innings, the lowest figure for losing contests

that year. The Royals averaged only 1.3 runs in those games, however, also the lowest in baseball that year. In five games Black and the bull pen held the opponents to three runs or less five times, yet Black was charged with all five losses. With any luck, he might have ended up with a 22–7 record.

(Black's bull pen hurt him twice, when he departed after giving up only three runs but the Royals went on to lose 4–3 and 6–5. Those could also have been victories, which could have made his record for the year 24–5.)

The next year poor Bud again ended with one of the worst batting support marks, only 3.9 runs per game. That is the biggest reason for his 10–15 record with the world champion 1985 Royals' team.

Five pitchers switched lists between 1983 and 1984, proving perhaps that the breaks do even out eventually. Valenzuela and the Braves' Craig McMurtry went from the lucky list to the unlucky, and their records reflected it: Val fell from 15–10 to 12–17; McMurtry, from 15–9 to 9–17. Three went from unlucky to lucky: Houston's Bob Knepper, Cleveland's Burt Blyleven, and Seattle's Matt Young. Knepper's record improved from 6–13 to 15–10, and Blyleven's from 7–10 to 19–7 (Young's improvement was minimal, from 11–15 to 6–8).

According to Bill James, the luckiest and unluckiest pitchers in 1985, in terms of offensive support, were:

AMERICAN LEAGUE, 1985

Luckiest Pitchers	*Team*	*Runs*	*TRA*	*W–L*
Dennis Martinez	Baltimore Orioles	6.2	5.5	13–11
Bruce Hurst	Boston Red Sox	6.0	4.8	11–13
Ed Whitson	New York Yankees	5.9	5.7	10–8
Bill Krieger	Oakland A's	5.5	5.7	9–10
Ron Guidry	New York Yankees	5.4	3.6	22–6

Unluckiest Pitchers	Team	Runs	TRA	W–L
Danny Darwin	Milwaukee Brewers	3.4	4.6	8–18
Charlie Hough	Texas Rangers	3.7	3.7	14–16
Danny Jackson	Kansas City Royals	3.8	4.1	14–12
Bob Ojeda	Boston Red Sox	3.8	4.2	9–11
Bud Black	Kansas City Royals	3.9	4.9	10–15

NATIONAL LEAGUE, 1985

Luckiest Pitchers	Team	Runs	TRA	W–L
Bryn Smith	Montreal Expos	5.4	3.4	18–5
Mike Scott	Houston Astros	5.0	3.7	18–8
Kurt Kepshire	St. Louis Cardinals	4.9	5.2	10–9
Joaquin Andujar	St. Louis Cardinals	4.9	3.8	21–12
Dwight Gooden	New York Mets	4.9	1.7	24–4

Unluckiest Pitchers	Team	Runs	TRA	W–L
Jose Deleon	Pittsburgh Pirates	2.3	5.1	2–19
Mike Krukow	San Francisco Giants	2.9	3.7	8–11
Dave LaPoint	San Francisco Giants	3.0	4.3	7–17
Bill Laskey	San Francisco Giants/ Montreal Expos	3.2	5.5	5–16
David Palmer	Montreal Expos	3.4	4.0	7–10

The Giants' Krukow made the unluckiest list three years in a row, 1983–85. Dan Petry of Detroit made it twice, 1983 and 1984, and almost made it again in 1985. He won nineteen, eighteen, and fifteen in those three years. Imagine how he would have done if the Tigers had given him some runs to work with.

Talking about bad luck, Pete Palmer said Mets' reliever Skip Lockwood gave up only seven runs in 1979—yet lost five games. In 1963 Diomedes Olivo of St. Louis yielded nine runs, and they cost him five ball games. The all-time tough luck pitchers on Palmer's list:

Pitcher	Club	Lg	Year	Runs	Losses	Runs/Losses
Skip Lockwood	NY	N	1979	7	5	1.40
Diomedes Olivo	StL	N	1963	9	5	1.80
Steve Howe	LA	N	1983	15	7	2.14
Jim Brewer	LA	N	1972	16	7	2.29
Lee Smith	Chi	N	1983	23	10	2.30
Rollie Fingers	SD	N	1978	33	13	2.54
Darold Knowles	Was	A	1970	36	14	2.57
Al Worthington	Min	A	1964	18	7	2.57

MORE LOSSES THAN EXPECTED

Player	Runs For–Agst	W–L Actual	W–L Expected	Diff.	No. of Std. Dev.
Bert Blyleven	1,499–1,191	176–160	202–134	– 26	3.34
Red Ruffing	2,688–2,117	273–225	303–195	– 30	3.24
Dave Koslo	820–740	92–107	107–92	– 15	2.60
Harry Howell*	1,186–1,103	131–145	147–129	– 16	2.48
Eddie Smith	752–816	73–113	87–99	– 14	2.39
Dizzy Trout	1,385–1,166	170–161	188–143	– 18	2.38
Denny Lemaster	835–778	90–105	103–92	– 13	2.32
Otto Hess*	660–664	70–90	82–78	– 12	2.20
Warren Spahn	2,684–2,016	363–245	375–233	– 12	1.16

MORE WINS THAN EXPECTED

Player	Runs For–Agst	W–L Actual	W–L Expected	Diff.	No. of Std. Dev.
Tom Seaton	621–614	93–65	80–78	13	2.52
Joe Coleman, Jr.	1,082–1,202	142–135	126–151	16	2.34
Togie Pittinger*	869–982	115–112	101–126	14	2.22
Casey Patten*	822–1,069	105–128	91–142	14	2.18
Wes Ferrell	1,565–1,382	193–128	178–143	15	2.05
Mike Torrez	1,458–1,469	184–155	168–171	16	2.05

*These four pitchers of the dead ball era had their runs-allowed data estimated from known data on earned runs allowed.

James' data are so revolutionary that it is a shame they are not available for every pitcher in history. We urge present and future historians to make offensive support a part of every pitcher's stats. (We also think that TRA, total run average, is more indicative than ERA, earned run average.)

It is not clear yet exactly why teams distribute their support erratically among men on the same pitching staff. Is it just luck, a short-term statistical quirk? It could have something to do with the opposing pitchers. Some pitchers draw the opponents' aces. Teams always used to save their best arms for when the Yankees came to town, and Casey Stengel used to hold out Allie Reynolds and Whitey Ford and spot them against the contenders' aces. So these Yankees' pitchers, in spite of the hard-hitting teams behind them, may have deserved their wins as much as anyone else.

Expected Lifetime Wins

No long-range study of actual run support has been done yet, but Palmer has made a study of pitchers' presumed lifetime run support, based on their teams' average runs scored each year. He then compared that number to the known runs that each pitcher gave up.

For example, Red Ruffing gave up a total of 2,117 runs over his career, or 4.08 runs per game (that is, total runs; his ERA was 3.80). Meanwhile the Red Sox and Yankees scored an estimated 2,688 runs—4.39 per nine-inning game—behind him. Given the number of games Ruffing pitched, with that kind of batting support, Palmer says he should have won 303 and lost 195. Instead, he won only 273 and lost 225, or 30 less wins than expected.

By contrast, Joe Coleman, Jr., gave up 6.35 total runs per game, while his clubs supported him with an estimated 5.71. With those numbers, Palmer says, Coleman should have been 126–151; he actually was 142–135, 16 wins more than expected.

It is not clear why Ruffing won thirty games less than he should have and Coleman sixteen more. One hypothesis is that Red was unlucky and Joe was lucky. But the Ruffing data tend to confirm a suspicion voiced by oldtimer Joe Judge that Red was deliberately trying to lose in his early years with the Red Sox in an attempt to force the Sox to trade him. If so, the plan worked, and Ruffing ended up with the champion Yankees, where he began winning twenty games instead of losing twenty.

Palmer identified nine starters over the years who lost significantly more games than would be expected given their run support and their runs given up, and six who won significantly more than expected.

DEFENSIVE SUPPORT

Tom Ferrick was a journeyman right-hander in the 1940s, posting such records as 8–10 and 2–5. In 1947 his ERA of 3.15 was wasted on the seventh-place Senators, who "supported" him to a 1–7 record. In 1950 Ferrick started the year with seventh-place St. Louis, where he went 1–3. Moving to the first-place Yanks that summer, he was 8–4. The writers were amazed at the improvement. Improvement! His ERA had been 3.88 with the Browns, 3.79 with the Yanks. "I'm not doing anything different," Ferrick tried to tell them. "With the Browns, a ground ball was a hit; with the Yankees, it's an out or possibly two."

Still, many a twenty-game winner can thank a fast outfield and a tight infield. As pitcher Bill Lee of the Red Sox points out, not only do great fielders like Luis Aparicio save runs, they save arms by cutting down the number of pitches needed to get twenty-

seven outs, thus also saving runs that a tired pitcher might give up in a later inning.

A high-ball pitcher needs a great outfield to run down the fly balls he gives up. Lefty Gomez's secret of success was "clean living and a fast outfield." Lefty says he made a star of Joe DiMaggio. He never saw Joe's face, Lefty says; all he saw was his uniform number as Joe ran back after long drives.

A sinkerball pitcher needs a great infield to gobble up the grounders. Earl Weaver believes the Baltimore infield of the late sixties and early seventies—Brooks Robinson, Mark Belanger, and others—made stars out of Steve Stone and other curveball pitchers who had never been big winners until they came to the Orioles.

Stone was the first to agree. In 1977, he recalls, he led the White Sox with fifteen wins, in spite of a shortstop who committed forty errors and a second baseman "with a Teflon glove."

BULL-PEN SUPPORT

Let's look at those twin brothers again. One departs in the eighth inning with men on first and second. Goose Gossage strolls in from the bull pen and gets the side out to preserve the victory—"cleaning up the garbage," as Sparky Lyle put it. But the other brother is not so lucky. His reliever gives up a walk and a single, both runners score, and he loses the game.

Lefty Gomez owed many victories to his reliever, Fireman Johnny Murphy; Lefty said he could pitch as long as Murphy's arm held out. In 1984 Ron Guidry suffered the worst won–lost record of his career, 10–11. Yet, he says, he left six or seven games with leads that the bull pen failed to hold. Denny McLain lost his thirty-second win in 1968 because his bull pen could not hold a lead in the ninth.

Phil Erwin of the *Baseball Insight* newsletter reports that bull-pen support varies as much as hitting support. He compiled his own list of lucky and unlucky starters based on the ERAs of the relievers who came in to rescue them. In 1985 Ron Romanick of the California Angels topped the lucky list; his relievers gave up 1.97 earned runs per inning after he left. Neal Heaton of the Cleveland Indians led the unlucky list, with bull-pen "support" of 6.54. That year the pennant-winning St. Louis Cardinals' "No Name" bull pen gave great support to Danny Cox (2.13) and Joaquin Andujar (2.29). But on the Los Angeles Dodgers support varied widely. The Dodgers' pen gave Bob Welch a 2.50 effort and Orel Hershiser 2.80, but Fernando Valenzuela watched his relievers yield 5.36 runs, more than twice as many.

Erwin's two lists, as printed in *Sports Illustrated*, follow:

Lucky Pitchers	Team	W–L	Support
Ron Romanick	California Angels	14–9	1.97
Danny Cox	St. Louis Cardinals	18–9	2.13
Dave Palmer	Montreal Expos	7–10	2.15
Britt Burns	Chicago White Sox	18–11	2.25
Joaquin Andujar	St. Louis Cardinals	21–12	2.29

Unlucky Pitchers	Team	W–L	Support
Neal Heaton	Cleveland Indians	9–17	6.54
Ray Fontenot	Chicago Cubs	6–10	5.69
Fernando Valenzuela	Los Angeles Dodgers	17–10	5.36
Mike Boddicker	Baltimore Orioles	12–17	5.33
Ted Higuera	Milwaukee Brewers	15–8	5.32

One observation we have is that a reliever's ERA is sometimes completely misleading. It is how well the new pitcher does in shutting the door on inherited runners that counts. If he comes in with men on second and third and gives up a single to score both runners, the runs are charged to the starter and do not show up in the reliever's ERA. The fireman was paid to put out the fire and did not do it. Seventy years ago, the inherited runners were charged to the reliever if they scored. Baseball today does not yet have a stat to measure how well a reliever does his job (although, as mentioned earlier, the Orioles and Phillies have devised the hold/squander stat).

Our own Solomon-like decision: The run of any inherited runner who scores should be charged, fifty-fifty, to each man, the pitcher who put him on and the pitcher who let him score. This will mean some half-runs in the box scores, but so what? And if an inherited run leads to a loss, then each pitcher, the starter and the reliever, should be charged with half the loss. This is the fairest system we can devise, and if anyone has a better suggestion, we would be happy to hear about it.

Moreover, wins and losses are assigned arbitrarily anyway. Consider this scoring in justice: A National League pitcher hurls a beautiful game and goes into the eighth tied 0–0. Reluctantly, the manager lifts him for a pinch-hitter. An inning later his mates score a run and win the game, only the win is not attributed to him; he gets a no-decision. (Nowadays he would probably get a quality start.)

Another example: The long reliever usually gets nothing for his efforts. In the 1984 World Series, the San Diego Padres' bull pen did a magnificent job holding the Tigers after the starting staff was pounded early in the game. Dave Dravecky and his mates in many ways were the most effective hurlers in the Series, yet they got nothing for it, not a win, not a save, not even a loss.

Often the fate of both starting pitchers is taken out of their hands by the relievers. As an example, consider the Astros–Phillies' game in 1985 in which Nolan Ryan started against Steve Carlton. Both starters pitched beautifully and retired after six innings with Carlton ahead 1–0. At that point Carlton had a victory and Ryan a loss. Reliever Kent Tekulve of the Phils came in and gave up a tying run. That took Ryan off the hook—he could no longer lose it. But it also robbed Carlton of a well-deserved win. Both men were in the locker room taking their showers when they got the bad, or good, news. (In a final irony, the Phils scored a run in the eighth, and Tekulve, who had cost Carlton a win, got the win for himself.)

Why not give both Carlton and Tekulve a win? Both contributed to the victory. (We would even give a victory to every player on the winning team, period. You find out some amazing things that way—.330 hitters who are not missed a bit and .220 hitters who seem to spark their clubs to victory when they are in the game but watch them lose when they are on the bench.)

In 1983 Joaquin Andujar was 6–16 by the traditional count. But, according to Ron Lewis' *Book on Starting Pitchers* (Research Analysis Publications), the club won another ten games after he left. Andujar got ten no-decisions, but the team's real won-lost record in games that Andujar started was 16–18. Quite a difference.

Storm Davis of the Orioles had a 13–7 record in 1983. But his team had a 21–8 record in his games. Davis had kept them close enough so the bull pen could win eight out of nine after he left.

In 1984 Davis was 14–8. His teammate, Mike Boddicker, was 20–11. But the Orioles actually won seven and lost two games after Davis left, so their record in games he started was 21–10. Their record in Boddicker's starts was 22–12. In Davis' case, the bull pen picked up wins; he must have left with the score tied or a run or two behind. In Boddicker's case, the bull pen picked up saves; he must have left when he was ahead in the score. Or, to put it another way, the O's scored early for Boddicker and late for Davis. We might call these extra victories "Total Games Won and Lost."

THE PARK FACTOR

The home stadium is another big factor in a pitcher's record. Certainly the home crowd's cheering, plus the last bats, give an advantage. But some pitchers seem to like home cooking even more than we would expect. Bob Shirley and Tommy John both cut more than four runs off their ERAs in 1984 just by coming home. Bill Gullickson loved Montreal, Bill James reports. In five years, 1981–85, he was 42–20 three, while only 26–41 on the road.

In 1985, James adds, Yankee's and Indian's pitchers could not wait to come home. Some figures:

	Home		Road	
	W–L	ERA	W–L	ERA
Ron Guidry	13–2	2.87	9–4	3.77
Dave Righetti	9–1	2.24	3–6	3.38
Bob Shirley	5–1	1.86	0–4	3.92
Neal Heaton	7–5	3.55	2–12	6.63
Curt Wardle	5–1	4.54	2–5	9.20

Neal Heaton had pulled a big switcheroo. According to Lewis, in 1984 he had cut four runs from his ERA when he played away from Municipal Stadium.

In 1984 and 1985, Joaquin Andujar was actually a losing pitcher in his home park, Busch Stadium, with a 17–20 record, but a big winner at 24–6 when on the road.

Grass vs. Turf

One of the biggest differences between parks is use of grass or Astroturf. Grass slows up ground balls, so fielders can get to them easily. Visiting teams in Wrigley Field complain that the grass always seems long when Steve ''Rainbow'' Trout, a sinkerball pitcher, pitches.

Andujar's problem at Busch was that he hated Astroturf. His two-year record on grass was 14–2, while he was 7–24 on Astroturf.

But Jay Tibbs of the 1985 Cincinnati Reds was definitely a turf pitcher, with an 0–7 record and a 5.03 ERA on grass and a 10–9 record and 3.51 ERA on turf. Tibbs was in the right park, the carpeted Riverfront.

The Mound

Dodger Stadium in Los Angeles has a higher mound than do other parks. And the lights are said to be just a shade dimmer. Neither of those factors hurt Sandy Koufax, Don Drysdale, Don Sutton, and Fernando Valenzuela.

Bob Feller liked the high mound in Cleveland's Municipal Stadium: He could ram the ball down the hitters' throats. It was so high that if you fell off it, you would break a leg, Indian owner Bill Veeck laughed. Ed Lopat, the Yankees' junk dealer, liked a low mound. So when Lopat came to town to face Feller, guess what kind of mound the Cleveland groundskeeper prepared for the game.

Eighty years ago groundskeepers used to soap the dirt around the mound so that, when the pitcher reached down for a hand-

ful of dirt to dry his hands, he was actually making them more slippery—how Gaylord Perry would have loved that! But the Giants' Bugs Raymond did not, so he put some resin in his back pocket. The idea caught on, and the resin bag was born.

The Fences

Veeck revealed another secret. In 1948 the Cleveland stadium had a wire fence cutting down the immense distances to the original bleacher walls. But the fence posts could easily be moved in or out. When the Yankees' sluggers came to town, they were moved out. When weak-hitting teams arrived, they were moved in to help the Indians, unless the visitors had some right-handed power, in which case the right-field fence came in but the left-field fence stayed deep.

Baltimore's Memorial Stadium has deep power alleys. A high-ball pitcher, such as Jim Palmer, who gave up a lot of fly balls, can expect that most of them will stay in the park to be caught. The background in Baltimore is also notorious around the league. The scoreboard is situated exactly where it can camouflage a right-hander's delivery as he releases the ball. The row of houses visible from home plate does not help either.

Short power alleys in left field in Boston's Fenway Park make that park infamous among left-handers. It hurts them not only physically but psychologically. Bill Lee said he felt as if he was scraping his knuckles on the so-called Green Monster and feared that it might fall down and kill the shortstop. The Red Sox have always had plenty of right-handed power hitters—Jimmy Foxx, Rudy York, Jim Rice, Tony Armas—aiming at The Wall. Whitey Ford was one of many lefty pitchers who were kept from pitching in Fenway because of it. (Yet Boston's Lefty Grove and Mel Parnell won there.)

Likewise lefty Warren Spahn did not want

to pitch in Brooklyn's Ebbets Field, with its friendly left-field stands. The Dodgers also used to load their lineup with right-handed sluggers—Gil Hodges, Roy Campanella, Andy Pafko, Jackie Robinson—because of the short power alleys. Then they went to Yankee Stadium, with its distant left-field fence, for the World Series and were consistently beaten. But it was their park that beat them as much as the Yanks. The predominantly right-handed Red Sox used to have the same trouble on the road, especially in Yankee Stadium, which is why they did not win more pennants.

Conversely, the short porch in Yankee Stadium's right field penalizes right-handed pitchers facing lefty sluggers such as Babe Ruth, Lou Gehrig, Yogi Berra, Mickey Mantle, Reggie Jackson, and Don Mattingly. But lefties liked to let right-handers pull the ball into "Death Valley" in left. Southpaws Lefty Gomez, Whitey Ford, Ed Lopat, and Ron Guidry have all found the stadium congenial. Joe DiMaggio complained about the home runs he lost there, but by pulling the ball to left, he was playing right into the pitchers' hands.

A park can scar a pitcher long after he leaves it. Earl Weaver believes the high fastball is one of the best pitches in baseball— Jim Palmer had a great one. But Baltimore's Memorial Stadium is big enough to contain most of the mistakes that get hit into the air. When Steve Stone first joined the Orioles, he refused to throw a high fastball—his years in Wrigley Field, Chicago, where the wind carried fly balls over the wall, made him stick to his curve, which the batters hit mostly on the ground. Weaver was convinced that a high fastball would make Stone's curve even more effective. Several shouting matches later, Steve agreed to try it and won twenty-five games for the only time in his career.

Nolan Ryan has been accused of setting his records in pitchers' ball parks, the Astrodome in Houston and Anaheim Stadium. But it's not yet clear what effect those parks have on power pitchers. If Ryan fogs the ball past the batters, the park dimensions suddenly become irrelevant.

"I don't make adjustments to the ball park," Ryan told John Holway. "I pitch down anyway. If you pitch down, you don't have to worry about short fences as much."

The new parks—Pittsburgh's Three Rivers, Cincinnati's Riverfront, St. Louis' Busch—are almost identical. Traditionalists like Bob Bluthardt, head of SABR's parks committee, scoff at them as "toilet seats," and pitcher Jim Kaat compares them to a woman's breasts—"you've seen one, you've seen the other." But at least they have introduced some consistency into interpark statistics.

Pete Palmer's Park Adjustment

Pete Palmer has devised a way to remove the park bias from batting and pitching stats. He determines what he calls the "park factor" for each park (see chapter 12, *Stats*).

In 1980 Don Sutton of Los Angeles was the nominal ERA champ in the National League with a 2.21 figure, compared to 2.34 for Steve Carlton of Philadelphia. But when the Dodger Stadium advantage was removed, Palmer found, Sutton was 57 percent better than the average pitcher in the league, but Carlton was 67 percent better.

An excellent pitcher helps make his park a "pitchers' park" and thus hurts himself in the park-adjusted ERA. It works the other way too, of course. And there is no way yet to isolate the park's influence on lefties versus righties, fly-ball versus low-ball hurlers, power hitters versus singles hitters, and so forth. But until a better system comes along, Palmer's adjusted data are superior to the raw, unadjusted numbers.

STARS OF THE MOUND

In 1976 Oakland's owner Charlie O. Finley hired an astrologer, a gorgeous redhead named Laurie Brady, to do daily charts on all his players. Manager Chuck Tanner promptly threw them in the waste basket. Perhaps he should have read them—the A's finished out of the playoffs that year for the first time in six years.

Curious, we checked into all 206 ERA champions since 1876. The average should be seventeen ERA champs for each of the twelve signs. But we found that Pisces have won twenty-eight, while Aquarius has won only eight each. What are the odds on this happening by chance? Statisticians say anything over 20:1 is "significant." Pete Palmer says the odds on ERA kings is 200:1.

The list, with representative pitchers, follows:

Sign	Dates		Titles
Pisces	Feb. 19–Mar. 20	28	Grove, Alexander, Vance, McCatty
Aries	Mar. 21–Apr. 19	27	Young, Joss, Walters, Kremer, Sutton
Scorpio	Oct. 23–Nov. 21	20	Johnson, Seaver, Gooden, Gibson, Feller
Libra	Sep. 23–Oct. 22	20	Palmer, Ford, Waddell, Capra, Podres
Cancer	Jun. 21–July 22	19	Hubbell, Coveleski, Stieb, Honeycutt
Leo	July 23–Aug. 22	19	Mathewson, Clemens, Wilhelm, Blue
Capricorn	Dec. 21–Jan. 19	16	Koufax, Wynn, Lyons, Leever, Keefe
Virgo	Aug. 23–Sep. 22	16	Guidry, Chandler, Faber, Boddicker
Taurus	Apr. 20–May 20	13	Spahn, Newhouser, Walsh, Scott
Sagittarius	Nov. 22–Dec. 20	12	Tiant, Gomez, Carlton, Swann, Friend
Gemini	May 21–Jun. 20	9	Chance, Parnell, Cicotte, Pfiester
Aquarius	Jan. 20–Feb. 18	8	Doak, Ryan, Ruth, Hammaker, Reynolds

NIGHT AND DAY

Night games also affect pitchers' records. Night ball is perhaps the biggest reason for the fall in batting averages over the last forty years. Yet some pitchers, primarily power pitchers, benefit from the dark more than others. Others defy the odds and find it easier to get the hitters out in the sunshine.

Some 1985 "day" pitchers, as researched by Bill James, all Oakland A's, are:

	Day		Night	
	W–L	ERA	W–L	ERA
Chris Codiroli	9–1	3.77	5–13	4.81
Jay Howell	3–1	1.59	6–7	3.52
Bill Krueger	6–5	3.79	3–5	5.35
Don Sutton	8–1	3.28	7–5	4.32

Rick Sutcliffe of the Cleveland Indians was one of the best nighttime pitchers in baseball and was also a better pitcher on Astroturf than on grass. In 1984 he moved to the Cubs' Wrigley Field, where all home games are played on grass during the day. Sutcliffe won sixteen and lost one, winning the Cy Young award.

OTHER FACTORS

The ball, of course, has an effect, but it should affect a pitcher's ERA, not his won–lost record. ERA is a pitcher-versus-hitter yardstick. In a dead ball era and in a large park, the ERA goes down. With a lively ball or a small park, it goes up. But won–lost data are pitcher-versus-pitcher stats. There

The peaks are Pisces and Aries—late winter and early spring. Midwinter (Aquarius) and late spring (Gemini) are worst. We hasten to add that the data surprised us, confirmed skeptics that we were.

We asked Pete Palmer to do a readout on the birthdays of all 4,212 men who pitched in the major leagues from 1909 to 1981. Skeptical, as we had been, he found that the best time to be born if you want to grow up to be a big-league pitcher is, appropriately, summertime, especially from the All Star game through the World Series (Leo through Libra). The worst times are winter and spring.

Palmer even plotted aggregate ERAs and won–lost data for each sign. Scorpios turned out to be best in both categories. Geminis had the worst ERAs and Cancers the worst W–L records.

Among strikeout pitchers, Scorpio also predominates, with four of the top-ten lifetime leaders: Walter Johnson, Tom Seaver, Bob Gibson, and Jim Bunning.

Bob Feller, Fernando Valenzuela, and Dwight Gooden are also Scorpios.

We also did a study of biorhythms but found absolutely zero correlation between performances and ups, downs, and crossing days.

As far as we know, only one big-league pitcher has ever used astrology in his pitching: Wes Ferrell, the terrible-tempered but talented hurler who won twenty games five different years with mediocre teams in the 1920s and 1930s. He told the *Washington Post*'s Shirley Povich that astrology ruled his life. Povich reported:

> On the days the stars say they are in his favor he will be the picture of confidence on the pitching mound. He says that several years ago when he was with Cleveland he had his horoscope read and a re-check of his season's victories revealed that he had won ball games on days when the stars were favorable and had lost games when, according to the horoscope, the days were due to be "bad."

will always be one winner and one loser in every game, whether the score is 1–0 or 11–10. In a 162–game schedule in the American League, there will be exactly 1,134 victories a year and 1,134 defeats. How they are divided reflects the pitchers' battle among themselves. Denny McLain did not win his thirty-one games because 1968 was a pitchers' year; he won them in spite of the fact that it was a pitchers' year. He had to beat some hot pitchers to win thirty-one.

Every successful pitcher also needs the right manager, who gives him enough starts to win twenty. And what about the pitching coach who shows the pitcher a new weapon? Or the catcher who calls a great game and keeps him calm in the pinches?

A PROPOSAL

All the factors mentioned in this chapter contribute in varying degrees to making a winner. At the very least, all future encyclopedias should include a note in parentheses on each line of a pitcher's record. For example, examine the following pitching data:

1899	St. Louis	26–15
1900	St. Louis	20–18
1901	Boston	33–10

These stats do not give us many tools for judging this pitcher. However, when we add a quick parenthetical note to show how the team behind him did in the league standings, we suddenly see things more clearly:

1899	St. Louis	(5)	26–15
1900	St. Louis	(6)	20–18
1901	Boston	(2)	33–10

Now we can see instantly why Cy Young suddenly went from a twenty-game winner to a thirty-three-game winner.

Even better would be a note on a pitcher's offensive support. Until actual figures are compiled, we can at least note how his team ranked in batting that year. Instead of team standing, we might include team BA standing, thus:

1899	St. Louis	(6)	26–15
1900	St. Louis	(2)	20–18
1901	Boston	(4)	33–10

Now we begin to wonder why Young could win only twenty games with the second-best hitting team in the league but thirty-three with the fourth best. (Our guess: The new American League was an easier league to win in.)

Some reference books use asterisks to indicate background information, such as 1945, military service; 1946, jumped to Mexico; 1948, sore arm. This is helpful but still does not reveal the real issues. Someday perhaps some encyclopedia will provide the really essential information, such as for the following mythical pitcher:

1923   19–10 (rookie of the year)
1924   9–16 (July, twin brother killed in auto accident)
1925   21–9 (May, met most wonderful girl in the world)
1926   27–8 (June, married)
1927   17–10 (August, hurt shoulder, out six weeks)

1928   14–15 (March, took $5,000 pay cut)
1929   9–18 (July, daughter diagnosed leukemia)
1930   6–12 (February, bank fails, lost $6,000 life savings)
1931   4–9 (January, began drinking heavily)
1932   1–5 (January, wife left him)
1933   0–1 (April, given unconditional release)

WINNING:
THE ULTIMATE GOAL

Winning is what the game is all about, and the pressure pitcher who can reach back for the big pitch when the game is in the balance deserves all the credit he can get. Other stats are fancy, but nothing is as fancy as a victory.

Sandy Koufax broke a raft of strikeout records. But he lost the game in which he broke Christy Mathewson's single-season record. He lost the game in which he broke his own record. He lost the game in which he set a record with forty-one strikeouts in three straight games. He lost when he struck out his thousandth man. He lost again when he struck out number 1,500. "Those records will kill you," he wrote.

Or, as Robin Roberts said, "There's a fine line between winning a game and putting on a show."

Here, then, are the big winners in history and some background on how they won their games. For the era 1901–20, we use the won–lost records compiled by Frank Williams of SABR. Williams made a painstaking search of all box scores and score sheets to locate and correct many inaccuracies that crept into the record keeping back then; his findings were published in *The National Pastime* of 1982.

Let's start, appropriately, with Cy Young.

Young's 510

The two records that everyone says are unbreakable are Joe DiMaggio's fifty-six-game hitting streak and Cy Young's 510 lifetime victories. Everyone may be right.

Young's mark may be broken sometime in the twenty-first century, but the game will not then be baseball as we know it. In fact, when Young set the record, the game was not baseball as we know it either.

Cy played twenty-two years and started 816 games. That's close to forty starts per year, year in and year out, in a steady four-day rotation with no time off for injuries. In fact, Young once started forty-nine games in one year, almost one-third of his team's total games.

Today pitchers do not start more than thirty-five games a year. If they tried it, they would quickly find themselves outpitched by stonger, better-rested arms. Even assuming that someone can win twenty-five of the thirty-five, he must do it for twenty solid years before he reaches 500.

When Young pitched, he could pace himself. He averaged almost a hit an inning. Today that would be a formula for disaster. Young could afford to coast, let a man or two hit the ball. No 1901 version of Bucky Dent was going to hit a ball over the fence and beat him out of a pennant. When the Dents did come up, they lifted easy flies well in front of the fence. Today's pitchers do not have that luxury. Ask Mike Torrez of the 1978 Red Sox.

Cy did have a little luck too. He had been a fine pitcher in the National League in the 1890s, but by 1900 he was thirty-three and his victory total was down to twenty, the lowest number he had ever won. It looked like the usual pattern of the old body running down. But Young was saved from that fate. The next year baseball expanded, from eight teams in the 1900 National League to

COURTESY OF JOHN THORN.

Cy Young

sixteen in the new two-league lineup. The talent was diluted by a factor of two—half the batters he faced would have been in the minors the year before, and half the pitchers he had to beat would also have been minor leaguers in 1900. And, to improve matters further, Cy wound up in the junior league, which did not have the talent the older National League had, in spite of the raids on it. It made Cy young again. In 1901 he suddenly zoomed up to thirty-three wins, his best season in five years.

(Larry Lajoie was having the same heady

DID CY YOUNG WIN 510 OR 511?

Most record books show 511 victories. But in 1907 Cy received credit for a win in relief that, under modern scoring rules, should have been given to the man who preceded him, Ralph Glaze. Glaze left the game after eight innings on the losing end of a 4–1 score. The Sox rallied in the top of the ninth for five runs, so that when Young came in to pitch the ninth, he had a 6–4 lead. Cy pitched the final inning and got credit for the win, one of nineteen he won that year.

Frank Williams of SABR thought that was unfair to Glaze and went before the rules committee to argue for justice, but he was turned down. "If I hadn't been dealing with an immortal like Cy Young," Williams says, "I think I probably would have gotten the switchover to Glaze."

However, we think he makes sense. We give Cy 510.

WALTER JOHNSON—416 OR 417?

Walter Johnson's case is the opposite of Cy Young's. His Cooperstown plaque says he won 416 games, including 16 in a row in 1912. Frank Williams says they cannot have it both ways—Sir Walter either won 417 or he did not win 16 in a row, because one of the 16 is disputed.

The game in question came on August 5 at Chicago, right in the middle of Johnson's streak. Walter came in in relief of Jay Cashion in the eighth with his team behind 7–1 and pitched the last 2⅓ innings—he even knocked in the winning run himself in the tenth. Some contemporary newspapers and record keepers gave Johnson credit for the win; others, probably through honest accident, gave it to Cashion. Of course, today there would be no question about it—Johnson would be given the victory.

But somehow, over the years, baseball was trapped in a contradiction. It acknowledged Johnson's August 5 victory as part of his streak but not as a game won otherwise, either in his total for the year, 32, or his lifetime total, 416.

---

experience. He leaped from .337 in the 1900 NL, to .426 in the new, diluted 1901 AL. Poor Honus Wagner wasn't nearly as smart. He stayed in the tougher NL. If he had jumped to the AL, he probably would have out-Cobbed Cobb.)

Young followed his thirty-three wins with thirty-two more in 1901 and twenty-eight in 1902. And the oldster, who had pitched one no-hitter before jumping to the AL at age thirty-four, now pitched two more at the ages of thirty-seven and forty-one!

Eventually the American League did catch up to the National League in talent, but it took about two decades to occur. In the meantime, Young basked in his fountain of youth. He won 226 games after the age of thirty-three and ended up with 510 in all, a total that will never be equaled.

Walter Johnson's 417

Walter Johnson came into the American League as a nineteen-year-old rookie in 1908, and for the next twenty-one years, through 1927, proceeded to win 417 games, the second highest total in history. Could he have done it in the National League? We doubt it.

Much has been made of the fact that Sir Walter had a weak club behind him. He owns the all-time record for both winning shutouts (110) and losing them (65). He

Johnson had more trouble beating the records committee than in beating opposing teams. He lost three shutouts to the committee when it discovered that he had pitched less than nine innings. All three were lopsided victories, and Walter was removed because the manager wanted to rest him, not because he was in trouble. But rules are still rules, so instead of 113 shutout victories, the record books give him 110, still far ahead of anyone else.

PLANK, CHESBRO: STILL WINNING GAMES

Pete Palmer discovered that in 1911 someone had carelessly forgotten to count a complete game victory by Eddie Plank.

Jack Chesbro was the victim of a careless mistake in 1906, when someone counted one of his wins as a loss. Two other victories were posthumously given to Chesbro, so that the latest *Macmillan Encyclopedia* carries his new lifetime totals as 199–128, instead of the former (and incorrect) 196–131.

When these errors were called to the attention of the records committee, they were rectified.

DIZ DID NOT WIN THIRTY

In *The Dizziest Season,* G.H. Fleming pointed out that Dizzy Dean did not win thirty games in 1934. One of his "victories" was assigned to him in violation of all rules, in those days or these. Diz came in as a reliever with the Cardinals already in the lead, yet he was given the win for what was obviously a save. It happened in midsummer, so it was not done just to give Diz thirty victories. His total is a phony thirty, and we give him twenty-nine.

Without those 30 wins, it is doubtful that Diz would be in the Hall of Fame today; his lifetime 158 wins is not of Cooperstown caliber. However, if Diz had not foolishly sat out several starts that year in a puerile dispute over a few hundred dollars of his brother Paul's salary, he would have won thirty with ease.

also leads in winning and losing 1–0 games (thirty-eight wins, twenty-seven losses). Walter had to scratch for his wins as no other top pitcher ever has. In 1908 he won three shutouts in four days, yet the best he could do was 14–14, as the Senators finished seventh. In 1909 Johnson lost five shutouts in one month and ended the year with a 12–25 mark. In 1918 he had to battle eighteen innings to win a shutout.

In 1910 Johnson was shut out ten times, a record. He only lost seven other games all year and won twenty-four, with a splendid 1.35 ERA. Again the Senators finished seventh. To show what he was up against, one of the losses came when his third baseman threw an easy ground out into the stands. Today it would be a two-base error; under the rules then, however, the batter was allowed to score.

The Senators finished either seventh or eighth for the first five years Johnson was with them. (That's why, he said, he got a job with them so early.) In 1909 the team finished last, winning only forty-two games, almost as bad as the infamous 1962 Mets, and poor Walter won thirteen and lost twenty-five; ten of those losses were shutouts. The next year, in a magnificent performance, he won twenty-five and just about singlehandedly lifted the team out of the cellar to seventh. He did it again in 1911.

Walter Johnson

Then the hangdog Senators moved. They finished second in 1912 and 1913, and Johnson moved with them, winning thirty-two the first year and thirty-six the second. In 1912 he lost two more by 1–0. The first one came on a rainy day, and the decision to play was made at the last minute, leaving him no time to warm up. He gave up a home run to the first man he faced, Harry Hooper (who hit only two the entire year). Johnson lost the second one in ten innings on one scratch hit. "I doubt if I ever pitched a better game in my life," he said.

Thereafter the Senators were a respectable club, not a champ but not a doormat either, and Johnson was a steady twenty-game winner with them. He had some off years, 1920–23, but then he finally got the moment of glory he had been waiting for: The Senators broke through and won a pennant for him in 1924 and again in 1925. Johnson responded with two more twenty-win seasons, the last two of his life.

Johnson's 417 victories are the closest anyone has come to catching Cy Young. How many more might he have won with just a little better support from his mates?

Mathewson's 373

Christy Mathewson was the Tom Seaver of great-granddad's day—the all-American boy next door, the clean-cut Ken doll with the golden arm. Matty had everything, from good looks to the good fortune to play for the most consistently successful club of his day, the New York Giants.

"It's great to be young and a Giant!" second baseman Larry Doyle exclaimed, and that was just what the handsome Matty was.

Except for the first two years of Mathewson's career, when they finished seventh and eighth, the Giants won five pennants and never finished lower than fourth from 1903 through 1914.

Of course, we do not mean to suggest that he was getting a free ride for all those years. He was perhaps the biggest reason the Giants won all those pennants. Still, no other great pitcher has been so blessed with the support of so many championship players behind him. Matty would have been great with any team—as a twenty-year-old rookie in 1901, he won twenty games, even though the Giants struggled in seventh. The next year they fell to last, and he fell to fourteen wins.

But in 1903, when they climbed to second, Matty climbed to thirty. The next two years the Giants were champs, and so was Matty, posting thirty-three and thirty-one wins each season. In the best year of his life, 1908, he was heroic, giving them thirty-five victories as they just missed winning the flag on the final day, when the Cubs beat him in the replay of the Merkle game.

Over fourteen years, from 1901 to 1914, Matty won twenty games or more each year except 1902. In 1915 the once golden arm was finished. Matty could give them only eight victories, and the team plunged to last place. He quit in 1916 with 373 total wins.

Matty would die young. A captain in the chemical corps in World War I, he was gassed and never fully recovered; he died in 1925 at the age of forty-five.

It had been quite a career: 439 complete games, 373 wins, and only 188 losses.

Grover Alexander Misses 400

Actually, Matty ended his career, and went to his grave, thinking he had won 372 games. Grover Alexander ended his career thinking he had beaten Matty by one. Then, in the 1930s, someone discovered that Matty had won a game in 1902 that was inadver-

tently not credited to him, and Mathewson's career total was upgraded to 373, tying him with Alex. "Under today's rule, Matty definitely would have gotten the victory," Frank Williams agrees.

But what about Alex? He could have hung on a bit longer to get one more victory to beat Matty if he had known he needed it. As he said when the total was changed, "Well, I can't do anything about it now. I've been retired. I can't go back and get another win." (On the other hand, Mathewson could not go back and win one more either. Records always favor the pursuer, not the pursued.)

So Alexander and Mathewson both finished with 373. But if it had not been for World War I (not to mention the bottle),

Grover Alexander

Alex would certainly have had 400 wins. And with better teams behind him, who knows how high he could have gone.

Alex did not break in until he was twenty-four, in 1911, and he was an immediate sensation, with twenty-eight victories to lead the league with the fourth-place Phils. The Phils finished fifth, second, and sixth over the next three years, and Alex posted nineteen, twenty-two, and twenty-seven wins.

Then came the pennant-winning year of 1915. (Researcher Al Kermisch points out that a filly won the Kentucky Derby that year. A filly—and the Phillies—would not win again until 1950.) Playing for a champion was fun, and Alex responded with thirty-one victories.

The Phils finished second the next two years, and Alex gave them two more thirty-victory seasons. He was thirty years old, coming off three straight thirty-win years, with ERAs well under 2.00, when he was traded to the pennant-bound Cubs. If ever a pitcher was poised for greatness, Alex was in 1918. A fourth straight thirty-victory season seemed assured.

Instead, he won exactly two games.

Alex spent most of the year in France with General Pershing's American Expeditionary Force and did not get back to the Cubs until 1919 was half over. He won sixteen games. Just to show what he could have done, he won twenty-seven in 1920 with a second-division team behind him.

Alex brought back a new problem from France, alcoholism. Some days he could not even shake hands without taking two or three stabs at it. But, amazingly, he pitched pretty good ball in spite of it—ask Tony Lazzeri of the Yanks in the 1926 World Series. In 1927, with the second-place Cards, Alex won twenty-one games at the age of forty, sixteen more with the world champs the year after that.

But those two wartime years did him in. He won only eighteen in those two seasons and, conservatively, could have been expected to win at least twice as many, probably up to twenty-five or thirty more than he actually did. If so, he would certainly have surpassed the 400-win mark and might have come close to Johnson's 417 as well.

Could Feller Have Made 400 Too?

No one thinks of Bobby Feller as a 400-game winner. He did not even come close to 300, ending up with 266 at the age of thirty-seven. But World War II stole almost four big years out of his career, right at its peak.

Bob had just turned twenty-three when Japan bombed Pearl Harbor in December 1941. He had already won 108 big-league games, more than any kid his age in history. At that age Walter Johnson had scored fifty-seven, but Cy Young and Grover Alexander had not even won their first games.

Feller won twenty-four, twenty-seven, and twenty-five games, 1939–41, with a club that finished third, second, and fourth. If ever a young man was ready for greatness, it was twenty-three-year-old Bob Feller in 1942.

At twenty-three Denny McLain won thirty-one; Rube Marquard won a record twenty straight. At age twenty-six, Feller's last year in the navy, Ed Walsh won forty. In between, during ages twenty-three through twenty-six, Young, Johnson, and Mathewson all won thirty games—twice. For the four-year period, Johnson won 119, Mathewson 110, and Young 104. Feller won exactly five, all at the end of 1945.

"I estimate that if there had been no war, I could have struck out 1,200 men and won 100 games," Feller said objectively.

Unlike many other soldier-athletes, Feller did not spend the war playing baseball in Honolulu or running a physical-training program in the States. "I have eight battle

COURTESY OF JOHN THORN.

Bob Feller

Feller ended up with 297 complete games, 266 wins, and 159 losses.

And eight battle stars.

Spahn's 363

Wonderful Warren Spahn ended his career with 363 major league victories, the most ever by a left-hander. He too spent three years in the war, 1943–45, as a sergeant in the engineers and was wounded while helping to repair the famous Remagen Bridge, the Allies' first bridgehead across the Rhine. It is difficult to say how many games the war cost him. He had had a short tryout with the Braves before he entered the service at the age of twenty-two, and he won only eight for the Braves after coming out in 1946. But if he had won only eleven games in the three wartime seasons, it would have been enough to give him 374 victories, putting him ahead of Matty and Alex.

Spahn finally quit playing at the age of

stars,'' he said proudly. ''I was there the day we shot down 400 planes off Saipan, protecting the landing in the Marianas.''

So let's give him at least 100 games to go with the 266 he actually did win. That makes 366, only eleven shy of Alexander and Mathewson. Feller spent the last few years of his career sitting in the bull pen watching Bob Lemon, Early Wynn, and Mike Garcia do all the pitching for the Indians.

''If I'd had a record in reach, I might have hung around like Pete Rose and Gaylord Perry,'' he said. ''I definitely could have beaten Mathewson and Alexander. Johnson is more debatable.''

To judge a pitcher, Bob said, ''ask if he completed more games than he won and if he won 100 more than he lost.''

Warren Spahn

forty-four. Spahn's teammate, Gaylord Perry, thinks he could have gone on another year or two. He was losing games by scores of 2-1 and 3-2, Perry said; it was a shame they did not let him keep pitching.

Grove's Minor-League Captivity

Lefty Grove ended his career with exactly 300 victories and struggled to get the last one at the age of forty-one. It was not the military that made compiling victories tough for Grove—he managed to play his entire career between the two major wars of the century. But he might have had another twenty to thirty wins if he had left the minors three years earlier.

Grove was twenty-five when he signed with the Philadelphia A's. He spent five years with Baltimore in the International League before the draft, when minor-league teams could keep their players as long as they wanted to. Quinn had bought Lefty for $3,000, the price of a new fence for the Martinsburg, West Virginia, club. For five years he hoarded Grove, who won 108, lost 36, and struck out 1,020 hitters. Lefty won twenty-seven games twice, not even including several victories in exhibitions over big leaguers. SABR's Bob Gill says Grove shut out the New York Giants on three or four hits with eleven or twelve strikeouts. Al Kermisch adds that in 1924 Lefty beat the White Sox, striking out fourteen, then blanked the Athletics without walking a batter. That was when Connie Mack of the A's decided to meet Baltimore's price—$100,600. (The extra $600 was put in to break the old record of $100,000, which the Yankees announced they had paid Boston for Babe Ruth.)

Grove joined a second-place A's club in 1925. If he had arrived three years earlier, he would have found them in seventh place. Still, ten extra victories a year for three years is not an unreasonable guess, and Lefty very well might have attained more than that.

Then he was suddenly sold to the Red Sox and promptly had the worst season of his career, 8–8, as injuries threatened to end his career. There he was, at the age of thirty-five, with his fastball gone, the notorious Green Monster behind him, and a patsy-hitting club to support him (the Sox were last in homers in 1934). What did he do? He bounced back, developed a curve, and won twenty games in 1935. In eight years with the Sox, he would win 105 games, to end at exactly 300.

THE MODERN WINNERS

Thanks to the baseball draft system, a variety of military deferment systems, and modern sports medicine, the 1980s have seen a rash of 300-game winners—Steve Carlton, Tom Seaver, Gaylord Perry, Phil Niekro, and Don Sutton—all of whom played out their long and splendid careers without the impediments that had curtailed the careers of many great stars of the past.

Phil Niekro

Phil Niekro is six years older than Jim Palmer. Yet he was still pitching winning baseball several years after Palmer gave up his toe plate for a microphone. Niekro is only four years younger than Sandy Koufax. Yet he was still winning ball games twenty years after Koufax won his last one. He has won 311 major-league games in all and was still pitching at the end of 1986. He owes this phenomenal staying power to the knuckleball.

Niekro would have won more if he had played with the Yankees during his first eighteen years instead of toward the end of his career. The Braves went through eleven losing seasons while Phil was with them; they finished last six times, four of them in a row. Niekro led the league in defeats four years straight, a record, with totals of twenty, eighteen, twenty, and eighteen. The wonder is that he could win twenty games at all. But he did, three times.

Phil Niekro had stamina, and he had heart. He did not win his first big-league game until he was twenty-six. He did not have his first twenty-victory season until he was thirty. He had his third at the age of forty. He led in complete games four times, with a high of 23 in 1979, and pitched more than 300 innings four times, a rarity in modern baseball. He saved twenty-nine games in relief. We can safely say that our children will probably never see his like in their lifetime.

And Phil achieved it all in a notorious hitters' park, Atlanta. It did not affect his W–L record, since presumably the park affected his opponents as much as it did him. But it did affect his ERA and his home runs allowed. Four times he led the league in tossing gopher pitches.

At the end of 1986, when he was forty-eight years old, Niekro was seventh on the all-time strikeout list, fifth in innings pitched, fifth in walks, and first in wild pitches—he once threw four in one inning. He led the league in wild pitches twice and in hit batsmen once.

Niekro learned the knuckleball from his father while in grade school. He did not play Little League ball, "so there was nobody to tell me not to throw it."

It was Niekro who changed Dale Murphy into an outfielder. Dale, then a catcher, required knee surgery after being hit by Niekro's knuckler. Murphy should have listened to another Niekro catcher, Bob Uecker, whose secret of catching the knuckleball was "let it stop rolling, then pick it up." This technique had definite advantages, Ueck said: "I got to meet a lot of important persons. They all sit behind home plate."

Phil won more than 300 big-league games with the pitch and one without it. The one without it was win number 300, in October 1985. Earlier that summer he had sat on the Yankee bench and watched Tom Seaver beat New York for Tom's 300th victory. "I was thinking with him on every pitch," Phil said. "I was throwing pitches with him, breathing with him every inning. He showed me the way."

On the last day of the season, the Yankees faced the Toronto Blue Jays, who had just clinched the division title the day before. Niekro's father was hospitalized in intensive care the morning of the game.

Before the game Niekro told catcher Butch Wynegar he was not going to throw any knucklers because he was tired of hearing people say he could not get people out without the pitch. So Niekro threw sinking fastballs, curves, screwballs, and bloopers, but not one knuckler. "I was making them use their muscles," he said. "I was keeping them off balance." Phil gave up only one hit in the first six innings. He gave up another, a double to his old Atlanta teammate Jeff Burroughs, in the seventh.

Then, in the ninth, with two out and Niekro leading 6–0, Toronto's Tony Fernandez cracked a pinch-hit double. That brought Burroughs up again. Phil's brother Joe, also a Yankee starter, went to the mound to ask if Phil wanted to pitch to Jeff. Phil said he did.

This was the spot for the knuckleball, and Phil threw three of them to strike Burroughs out swinging. Jeff tipped his batting helmet and bowed toward the mound, as 44,000 Toronto fans stood and applauded. "I decided if I was going to win the 300th, I should finish it up with a knuckleball," Phil said.

Gaylord Perry: Me and My Spitter

What the knuckler was to Niekro, the spitter surely was to Jackson Gaylord Perry. Without it, he could not have pitched nearly as long as he did, nor won 314 games.

Gaylord Perry

Perry was even more unlucky than Niekro, for in twenty-two seasons he played for only one division champ, the San Francisco Giants of 1971.

Like Niekro, Perry was a workhorse, with five years of 300 innings or more.

Fans may have mixed emotions about the spitter, but we feel it kept a great artist in

the big leagues for several additional years, adding some fine performances and a lot of laughs. What could be wrong with that?

Tom Seaver: Everything Roses

Like Christy Mathewson in great grandpa's day, Tom Seaver was the all-American hero, and he enjoyed a storybook career. He received the adulation of the New York press and its fans, got an early start on his career, took excellent care of his body, and pitched without serious interruption for nearly twenty years.

But like Johnson, Alexander, and Young, he played for sub-.500 teams over his career (total) and might well have won 300 games years before he actually did in 1985. He is arguably the greatest modern pitcher.

Steve Carlton: In the Wrong Park?

Steve Carlton has won 323 games through 1986, but there is no telling how many he might have won in another park. Data for two years, 1983–84, indicate that Carlton pitched better on grass—it was worth 1.4 runs off his ERA the first year and almost one run the second. Yet he pitched his entire career in St. Louis and Philadelphia, both of which had stadiums carpeted in Astroturf.

It is also a shame that Carlton could not have stayed with St. Louis for one more year. He was traded to the last-place Phils in 1972 and won twenty-seven games for them. How many could he have won with the Cards, who batted twenty-four points higher than the Phils?

Don Sutton: 310, But Only One 20

Much has been made of the fact that Don Sutton has won 310 games in his lifetime but has had only one twenty-victory season. Chalk that up to the modern five-day pitching rotation. On the other hand, does the extra day of rest lengthen careers? A lot of oldsters are still winning games into their forties now—Sutton, Seaver, Perry, Niekro.

Sutton might have had more twenty-victory seasons if he had come up two decades earlier on a shorter rotation. On the other hand, he might have retired sooner. Which system produces the better career totals? We may never know.

NOT QUITE 300

Ruffing Misses 300

Red Ruffing's two years in the army at the end of his career may have cost him the twenty-seven games he needed to go over the 300-victory mark. He won fourteen before going in and seven after coming out at the age of forty.

But what really hurt Red were the five years he spent with the wretched Red Sox at the beginning of his career. His victories with them totaled nine, six, five, ten, and nine, and his losses were a sky-high twenty-five and twenty-two.

Was Ruffing the victim of a horrible team? Or did he bring it on himself? "We always thought Red was dogging it with the Red Sox," old-time first baseman Joe Judge said. Ruffing's ERA was well over four per game with the Sox, well under that with the Yanks.

Ferguson Jenkins: 284, but No Pennant

What if Ferguson Jenkins had played with a champion, say the Cardinals or Dodgers?

He won twenty games for each of the first five years of his career with the Cubs, yet never reached the World Series. The Cubs finished third three times and second twice. Imagine where they might have finished without him.

Jenkins could blame his failure to reach 300 wins on his trade from the Cubs to Texas. Jenkins was a much better pitcher in the daytime—in 1984 alone he added four runs to his ERA under the lights—and pitching in lightless Wrigley Field might have added a couple dozen victories to his lifetime total.

In addition, Nolan Ryan pointed out, Jenkins was a low-ball pitcher, and the NL umpires gave him the low strikes, while the AL umpires did not.

Sandy Koufax: Too Soon for Surgery

If Sandy Koufax had been born a decade later, after modern sports surgery had been perfected, he might have been a 300-game winner. Sandy was at the height of his career at the age of only thirty when bone spurs in his elbow stopped him abruptly at 165 victories. Nowadays, he says, a doctor could operate to remove the spurs and have him back on the mound within a few weeks. In 1966, however, such a procedure was unknown.

Eight years later, another great lefty, Tommy John, had won 117 games at the age of thirty-one, when he faced a similar decision because of a torn ligament in his pitching arm. A medical miracle, plus faith in God, put Tom back on the mound after a year of recuperating, and he went on to win 141 more games in the next nine years.

If Sandy could have won 141 more, it would have given him 306 for his career.

Jim Palmer—268 Plus ???

If the Los Angeles Dodgers could have won even one game in the 1966 World Series, Jim Palmer might have retired with 300 big-league victories instead of 268.

Jim was a cocky twenty-one year old that October when he shut out the great Sandy Koufax for the Orioles' second victory in a row. The Dodgers never scored another run and went meekly down to defeat in four straight. But Palmer had pitched with an injured arm. "If I'd had to pitch again in the Series, I couldn't have done it," he told us.

In that case, the Orioles would have rushed him to the hospital over the winter, and he would have been ready to pitch in 1967. Instead, Palmer tried to pitch the next year with the arm problem still unsolved, could win only three games, and was sent down to Rochester, then Miami, and then Elmira. ("If my arm hurts in Baltimore, it's going to hurt in Elmira," he said, but the Orioles were not listening.) In two years in the minors, Jim was repeatedly on the disabled list and won a total of one game.

When an operation finally cured the arm problem, Palmer went back to Baltimore. He had won fifteen games in 1966 before the troubles began and sixteen, including a no-hitter, in 1969, after they were resolved, in spite of losing the entire month of July to more injuries. He then ran up four straight twenty-victory seasons. Could he have won at least sixteen games in each of the two missing seasons? That would have been enough to give him 300 for a career.

Jim Kaat: 283 (Shhhh)

One of the best-kept secrets in baseball is that Jim Kaat retired with 283 major-league victories, more than the totals of half the pitchers in the Hall of Fame.

"I've never craved center stage," Kaat said. Jim just missed the big bonus money as a rookie and the big free-agent money as a veteran and shrugged that "you don't get rich pitching for Minnesota." You do not even get known. If he had been a Yankee, he would have been a star. Instead, he smiled, he was the only pitcher who could win a game without anyone knowing who pitched for the winning team. Not even the Hall of Fame electors.

Ted Lyons: 260, Plus

Ted Lyons was another whose wartime service may have cost him. Lyons was forty-two when he answered the call in 1943, and although he was not in his prime, he was rolling along, winning twelve to fourteen games a year, as the White Sox' Sunday pitcher. He could have added another twenty victories to his final total of 260 he ended up with.

The biggest anchor around Lyons' neck was his team, the White Sox, though he would never admit it. From the year he

Ted Lyons

COURTESY OF JOHN THORN.

joined them in last place in 1924 until 1936, the Sox staggered around in the second division—usually deep in the second division. Even so, he gave them three twenty-victory years, including twenty-two wins in 1930, when the club finished seventh.

But Lyons, the courtly southerner from Louisiana, loved the big city up north and looks back on his career there with fondness. "I won 260," he reasoned. "How many more could I have won with another team?" (A 400 total was possible, Yankees' manager Joe McCarthy once declared.)

Lyons hurt his arm after his twenty-two win season in 1930. He won only four the following year and never did regain his star status. But he remained a quick-witted, intelligent pitcher, as gentle as he was powerful. ("When he grabbed you," Ted Williams once said, "you stayed grabbed.")

Nolan Ryan—Why Not More?

His critics say Nolan Ryan should win twenty games a year just by throwing his glove on the mound. Yet he has won twenty only twice, and by the end of 1986 had won "only" 253 games. Are his critics right? Is Ryan just a showman who can dazzle with no-hitters and high strikeout games, but when it comes to the bottom line, cannot put those games in the victory column for his team?

To start with, 253 victories is a pretty good total—seventeen more than the renowned Whitey Ford has, for instance. It is only fifteen less than Jim Palmer has, and Palmer pitched for the Orioles in their championship heyday, and only three or four per year less than Tom Seaver's total.

Nolan expects to pitch at least through the 1987 season, by which time, barring accidents, he should be up around the 265 mark.

Second, Ryan has seldom had really good teams backing him up. In twenty years his teams have been division or league champs only five times. They finished last twice and next to last five times. Perhaps more important, they finished last in team batting three times and were usually down near the bottom in league average. In addition, rarely did they boast strong bull pens who could save his games without letting the other club tie or win after Ryan left. Ryan throws hard, and when he departs, he usually leaves his team in contention. "My job is to give my team an opportunity to win the ball game. I have no control over how many runs we score."

Whitey Ford and Korea

Few persons realize it, but Whitey Ford is another who lost two years to the army, during the Korean conflict. He averaged seventeen wins a year after coming out, so he might have added about thirty-five more to the 236 victories with which he ended his career. Even with Korea, Ford won more games than any Yankee in history.

At first glance, you cannot feel sorry for Whitey, not with all those great Yankee teams behind him. But, Mickey Mantle reminds us, manager Casey Stengel used to hold Ford out of series against the weak clubs in order to spot him against the contenders. If Stengel had pitched him in a regular four-day rotation, there is no telling how many times Whitey would have won twenty.

Perhaps Ford's major piece of bad luck was that he did not meet Johnny Sain until he was thirty-two years old. Ford had never won twenty games, even when backed by so many pennant winners. In 1960 he won only twelve for the American League champs. Then Casey Stengel left and Sain arrived and increased Whitey's victories, mainly by giving him ten extra starts a year. If Whitey and Johnny had met a decade earlier—well, who knows what they could have done together?

CUBAN STARS

The Cuban winter leagues produced not only great native players but both blacks such as Martin Dihigo, who could not play in the white majors in the States, and whites such as Adolfo Luque, who became a star in Cincinnati. It also starred U.S. Negro leaguers, who played there in the winter, and U.S. white major leaguers—Fred Fitzsimmons, Johnny Allen, Max Lanier, and others. Cuban baseball was a fast league.

The first U.S. big leaguers arrived in Cuba almost eighty years ago. Here is how they did in games on the island:

Year	Team	W–L
1908	Reds	4–7
1909	Tigers*	4–8
	All Stars	2–2
1910	Tigers*	7–4
	A's	1–5
1911	Phils	5–4
	Giants*	9–3
TOTAL		32–33

*Pennant winners.

One of the 1908 Reds' losses was a one-hitter to José Mendez. One of the 1909 losses was an eleven-inning no-hitter by Eustaquio Pedroso. The 1909 All Stars included pitchers Mordecai Brown (26–9), Howie Camnitz (24–6), Addie Joss (13–14), and Nap Rucker (13–19). The A's only victory in 1910 was by Chief Bender over Pedroso, 2–1. One of the Giants' 1911 losses was by Christy Mathewson to Pedroso and Mendez, 9–6. Manager John McGraw was so mad that he threatened to send his team home on the next boat.

Martin Dihigo Wins 244

Cubans regard Martin Dihigo, their big pitcher-outfielder-infielder as the greatest player the island ever produced, better than Dolph Luque, who won 193 big-league games, or Luis Tiant, who won 229.

Dihigo's lifetime victories, in the U.S. black major leagues and in Cuba and Mexico (where the best U.S. blacks were also playing during the winter) totaled 244. And he started out as an infielder-outfielder, not even playing as a pitcher until late in his career.

According to Jorge Figueredo, Cuban baseball historian, Dihigo leads all Cuban league players in lifetime victories with 107, one more than Luque.

Jorge Figueredo, Cuban baseball historian, says there is no truth to the oft-repeated story that Fidel Castro was a potential big-league pitching prospect. Even in college, Figueredo says, Fidel Castro did not do much pitching. However, Monte Irvin says young Castro, a great fan, used to hang around the stadium where the teams worked out. "If we'd known he wanted to be a dictator," Irvin said, "we'd have made him an umpire."

NEGRO LEAGUES

Who were the biggest winners in the Negro leagues?

Data are still incomplete, as scholars continue to delve into old newspaper box scores, but at latest count, Big Bill Foster, Rube Foster's younger brother, was the lifetime leader in wins, with 116 victories in the Negro leagues plus Latin America. (The black leagues played 50 to 100 league games a year; the rest were against white semipro teams.) The top winners tabulated so far are:

Pitcher	Years Played	W–L
Bill Foster	1926–36	131–83
Joe Rogan	1920–35	112–42
Webster McDonald	1925–39	84–42
Bill Drake	1920–30	83–60
Satchel Paige	1926–47	73–30
Nip Winters	1923–30	71–34
Ted Radcliffe	1927–46	49–33

Many great pitchers are not on the list. Smokey Joe Williams, voted the greatest black pitcher of all time in a 1952 poll of experts (Satchel Paige came in a close second), enjoyed his best years before the leagues were formed, and, even after, played with the independent Homestead Grays. Cannonball Dick Redding is another who was past his prime when the leagues were formed. The wins of others—Leon Day, Hilton Smith, Bill Byrd, Raymond Brown—who pitched in the 1930s and 1940s have not yet been tabulated.

Satchel Paige

Why is Satchel Paige ranked so low? Satch missed a chunk of playing time during the Depression, when the Negro leagues folded and Satch played with a white semipro team in Bismarck, North Dakota. When he did return to the league, with the Kansas City Monarchs in 1939, he usually pitched two or three innings almost every day to draw a crowd. Technically, then, he cannot be credited with many victories. His known stats follow:

Year	Team	(Rank)	W–L	ERA	SO	BB	IP
1926	Birmingham	(2)	8–2	—	—	—	—
1927	Birmingham	(5)	5–8	—	—	—	—
1928	Birmingham	—	14–5	—	—	—	—
1929	Birmingham	(6)	11–11	—	—	—	—
1930	Birmingham–Baltimore	—	12–5	—	—	—	—
1932	Pittsburgh	—	8–2	—	—	—	—
1934	Pittsburgh	(2)	7–2	—	—	—	—
1936	Pittsburgh	(1)	8–1	—	—	—	—
1944	Kansas City	(6)	4–2	0.75	47	5	48
1945	Kansas City	(6)	2–2	—	30	6	33
TOTAL			79–40				

Smokey Joe Williams

In 1952 a special panel of experts for the Pittsburgh *Courier* voted Satchel Paige the second-greatest black pitcher who had ever lived. First place was awarded to Smokey Joe Williams, the lanky, hawk-nosed half-black, half-Indian pitcher from Texas. Joe defeated six members of the Hall of Fame and yet has never been allowed to enter the hallowed halls of Cooperstown himself.

In frequent postseason games from 1908 to 1934, Joe wrote a 23–7 record against white big-league stars. His victims numbered Walter Johnson, Grover Alexander, Chief Bender, Rube Marquard (twice), and Waite Hoyt, five Hall of Famers. Paige was

THE CUBAN CONNECTION

For almost half a century, from 1913 to 1960, Cuba sent more men to the U.S. big leagues than all other foreign countries put together. Cuban pitchers alone numbered Dolf Luque, a twenty-seven-game winner in 1923; Luis Tiant, who won 229 big-league contests; Mike Cuellar, a Cy Young winner; and Camilo Pascual, whose curve ranked with Koufax's. In 1960 twenty-six Cubans were playing on U.S. major-league rosters.

Then suddenly that rich pipeline was cut off. When Tony Perez retired in 1986, the U.S. majors were without a Cuban player for the first time in seventy-three years. But surely the Cubans had not suddenly stopped playing great baseball. The communist boycott of the 1984 Los Angeles Olympics cost Americans the chance to see Cuba's best stars close up on television. But earlier Cuban Olympic champs in other sports—heavyweight fighter Teofilo Stevenson and runner Alberto Juantoreno—were the most devastating athletes at their events in their day.

Were there any pitchers who might have shone in baseball just as brilliantly if they had had the chance? Of course there must have been. Who, then, are these invisible Cuban Valenzuelas, Andujars, Sotos, Hernandezes—men who would be major-league stars but for the arbitrary bar of politics?

An example of how good the Cubans are is Barbaro Garbey, the only Cuban since 1960 to play in the U.S. major leagues. He was good enough to play on the 1984 world champion Detroit Tigers, but he was not good enough to make the first string of the Cuban national team.

The Cubans could probably beat many major-league teams in a short series, says California Angels' scout Preston Gomez. Second baseman Felix Issasi hit .429 in the 1972 Pan-Am games and was considered a second Joe Morgan. He was wooed by both the Reds and Orioles but turned them both down, saying he was worried about what would happen to his brother if he left Cuba.

Cuban-born scout Julio Blanco-Herrera, the discoverer of Dennis Martinez in Nicaragua, is one of the few Americans who has seen the Cuban teams in action. Now scouting for the Milwaukee Brewers, Blanco-Herrera regularly attends the international tournaments, which are usually won by the Cubans. Former pitcher Orlando Peña, also a native Cuban and a scout, is another who has watched Cuban baseball closely. Tony Oliva, the two-time batting champion, has also seen the Cubans perform, including his brother, pitcher Juan Carlos Oliva. Here are their scouting reports.

JOSE ANTONIO HUELGA

"The best pitcher they had," says Blanco-Herrera flatly. Huelga beat future Dodger Burt Hooton 3-1 in extra innings to win the 1969 world amateur championship in Bogotá. In the 1972 championships in Nicaragua, Huelga pitched a nineteen-strikeout no-hitter. Bruce Brown, writing in the *Atlantic*, says Huelga led the Cuban league in strikeouts seven times.

Huelga was killed in an auto accident while still a young man.

BRAUDILIO VINENT

Barbaro Garbey insists that Braudilio Vinent, the black fireballer, was the best

Cuban pitcher of the past quarter-century: "He had velocity, a good slider, excellent control, and he kept the ball down."

Peña adds that Vinent holds the Cuban post-Castro records in wins, strikeouts, innings pitched, and complete games. His won–lost record, according to Brown, was 118–52, and his ERA 2.03.

In the 1980 world amateur tournament in Japan, Vinent's fastball was clocked at 90 m.p.h., Blanco-Herrera says. Ex–big leaguer Conrado Marrero taught him the slider. "Marrero was teaching all those guys to throw a forkball and a slider."

Oliva took batting practice against Vinent in Havana in 1973. "He threw hard," Tony reports, "and he had a good breaking pitch."

In the Pan-Am games in the early seventies, Peña remembers, Vinent went twelve innings against Nicaragua before losing 1–0. "It was one of the most memorable games in the history of the Pan-Am games."

ROGELIO GARCIA

"The Cuban Smokey," right-hander Rogelio Garcia "had a very strong arm and an outstanding forkball," according to Blanco-Herrera.

Peña rates Garcia and Vinent as the two best he saw. Garcia was "a big, husky black guy," who stood 6 foot, 3 inches, and weighed about 190, Peña says.

"He's the guy who took them to victory (over the United States) in the last game in 1983." The Americans that year had nineteen high draft choices on their squad. Scouts watched enviously while Garcia fogged the ball in at 93 and 94 m.p.h.

PEDRO PEREZ-PEREZ

Pedro Perez-Perez was "big and black and reminded you of Bob Gibson" with his overpowering fastball, Blanco-Herrera says. In Mexico in 1975 Perez-Perez helped defeat the U.S. amateur team that included outfielder Steve Kemp, catcher Ron Hassey, and pitcher Scott Sanderson. Perez-Perez now coaches the Cuban national team.

JUAN CARLOS OLIVA

Tony Oliva's brother, Juan Carlos, pitched in the 1979 world amateur games. He threw a slider, a fastball, and a sinker, says Tony. He wasn't a hard thrower, says Blanco-Herrera, "but he was a smart pitcher."

* * *

The Mariel boatlift from Cuba to Florida in 1979 drew dozens of scouts to the Florida beaches, hungrily scanning the arrivals for Vinent, Garcia, and the others. Unfortunately none of them were on board. Perhaps, Peña speculates, the real motive for the 1984 Olympic boycott was that "some of the boys might want to stay here."

In 1985 the best-looking pitcher in the Caribbean tournament was right-hander Jose Aleman, who posted an ERA of 1.00 in the games under the coaching of the veteran Romero. Right-handers Luis Tissert and Costa, "a big lanky wiry black guy," plus lefty Jorge Valdez, were also impressive.

Blanco-Herrera says, politics or not, the Cubans can still play baseball. "They've got it in their blood, and they've got all the tools." But, he sighs, their government "won't even let them talk to scouts."

the sixth. His 1–0 victory over Johnson was called by one man who saw it the greatest duel he ever witnessed.

Two of Williams' defeats were by the score of 1–0, including a ten-inning no-hitter he reportedly pitched against the National League champion Giants in 1917. Two other losses came when he was past the age of forty.

Williams spent most of his career before the Negro leagues were organized, so no league records on him are available. But the records we do have are tantalizing hints at what Joe might have achieved if he had been given the chance.

TOPS IN THE MINORS

SABR's minor-league committee under Bob Hoie says the top lifetime minor-league win-

ner, Bill Thomas, won 383 games, yet he never pitched an inning in the big leagues.

The Old Orioles

Several excellent minor-league pitchers were barred from the major leagues by arbitrary and unfair practice: the right of independent minor-league owners to retain their top stars as long as they pleased. These were the stars of the great, then minor-league Baltimore Orioles' teams of the 1920s, along with the slightly younger Lefty Grove. The Orioles not only dominated the International League, they probably could have whipped half the teams in the so-called major leagues. Look at the records of their seven big pitchers as supplied by SABR's Bob Gill:

Pitcher	Years in Minors	W–L	WS*	ERA	Majors
Johnny Ogden	1920–27	191–80	9–4	3.50	25–34
Rube Parnham	1917–26	139–60	1–3	3.31	2–2
Lefty Grove	1920–24	109–36	3–8	2.96	300–141
Al Thomas	1921–25	105–54	4–4	3.34	—
Harry Frank	1919–23	93–36	0–1	3.50	—
George Earnshaw	1924–28	78–48	4–1	4.01	127–93
Jack Bentley	1916–22	48–9	5–0	2.13	46–34

*Little World Series.

Today, with numbers like those, all seven would be snatched up by the majors before Labor Day of their first season.

Parnham had had a tryout with the A's in 1917 and again in 1918, when, goodness knows, Connie Mack needed anyone he could get. It is not clear why Parnham did not stick. The inference is that Orioles' owner Jack Dunn offered him more than Mack could. At any rate, Parnham won thirty-three and lost seven with Baltimore in 1923; twenty of his victories came in a row, a minor-league record.

George Earnshaw was the same age as Lefty Grove. He joined the Orioles just as Lefty left and almost duplicated Grove's experience. In 1925 the Washington Senators reportedly offered $100,000 for him, but Dunn turned it down. Earnshaw finally reached the Athletics in 1927 at the age of twenty-seven. In his first three full seasons, he won twenty-four, twenty-two, and twenty-one games, as he and Grove led the A's to three straight pennants.

The virtually unknown Harry Frank had a won–lost record just a shade above

TWENTY WINS WITH A TAIL-ENDER

Anyone can win twenty games with a champion. Eight men have done it with last-place clubs:

Year	Pitcher	Team	W–L	ERA
1901	Noodles Hahn	Cincinnati Reds	22–19	2.71
1918	Scott Perry	Washington Senators	25–19*	1.98
1923	Howard Ehmke	Boston Red Sox	20–17	3.53
1924	Hollis Thurston	Chicago White Sox	20–14	3.80
1951	Ned Garver	St. Louis Browns	20–12	3.73
1972	Steve Carlton	Philadelphia Phillies	27*–10	1.97*
1974	Nolan Ryan	California Angels	22–16	2.89
1979	Phil Niekro	Atlanta Braves	21–20*	3.39

*Led league.

Four—Perry, Ehmke, Thurston, and Garver—never won twenty again, though Thurston and Ehmke pitched with some good clubs (Ehmke of course pitched for the great A's team of 1929). They had the misfortune to have their best years at the worst possible times. If they had been with halfway decent teams, Pete Palmer calculates, Ehmke might have won twenty-six and Thurston twenty-four instead of the twenty they actually did win. And with a pennant winner, who knows?

Note poor Scott Perry. In 1918 he came up to the American League, with the woeful A's. He pitched more innings and more complete games than anyone else and had an excellent ERA of 1.98. With just an average team, his 21-19 record could have been 26-14, Palmer estimates. But the next year Perry was 4-17 and the year after that 11-25, and that was just about the end of his career.

MULLIN: TWENTY LOSSES FOR THE CHAMPS

Is it harder to win twenty games with a cellar team or lose twenty with a pennant winner? George Mullin of the 1907 pennant-winning Tigers succeeded in achieving the latter feat, with a 20–20 record.

THE 20–20 CLUB

Phil Niekro is the latest of eight men who have won twenty and lost twenty in the same year. Two of them—Ironman McGinnity and George Mullin, did it twice.

It is quite an accomplishment to lose twenty games. It either means the manager has faith in you, or he does not have anyone else to put in in your place. It used to be fairly common to lose twenty in the early years of this century, but this is rarely tolerated now. Here is the list:

20–20

1901	Joe McGinnity	Baltimore	26–21
1902	Bill Dinneen	Boston (A)	21–21
1903	Joe McGinnity	New York (N)	31–20
1905	George Mullin	Detroit	21–20
1906	Irv Young	Boston (N)	20–21
1907	George Mullin	Detroit	20–20
1913	Jim Scott	Chicago (A)	20–20
1916	Walter Johnson	Washington	25–20
1973	Wilbur Wood	Chicago (A)	24–20

Phil Niekro

Grove's. Why he never reached the majors is a mystery.

Johnny Ogden joined the Orioles in the same year Grove did, but it took him three more years to escape. As a result, he holds

---

Frank Shellenback won 295 games in the Pacific Coast League, a record for that circuit. Shell probably could have been a big-league star, but he was the victim of bad timing. A spitball pitcher, he had won eleven games for the White Sox in 1918 and 1919 but was not in the league when the spitter was banned in 1920 and thus not among those allowed to continue to use it in the majors. So he had no choice but to stay in the minors, where he carved out a pretty good career. Too bad—after the Black Sox scandal decimated the Chicago staff, they could have used Shell.

---

the all-time International League record for victories. His brother, Curley, pitched for the A's and Senators at a young age, but Johnny was thirty before he finally got a shot.

THE JAPANESE

Masaichi Kaneda

Across the Pacific, Masaichi Kaneda won 400 games and lost 298, pitching most of his career with the lowly Swallows. The Swallows usually won about fifty-five games a year, and Kaneda often won half of them. He holds the all-time professional record for strikeouts with 4,121, making one wonder how he (and world home-run king Sadaharu Oh) might have done in the States.

Kaneda won twenty games or more fourteen years in a row. His 944 games were more than Cy Young's 906, though less than Hoyt Wilhelm's 1,070. His 82 shutouts would rank him just below Christy Mathewson's 83, in fourth place internationally.

Whatever Became of Mashi Murakami?

Masanori Murakami, known as "Mashi" to San Francisco fans in 1965, was the only Japanese to play in the U.S. majors. He had a record of 5–1 with nine saves in two partial years. Then the Japanese demanded him back, rupturing baseball relations between the two countries until commissioner Ford Frick promised not to sign any more Japanese.

Murakami dutifully returned home but had a mediocre record and soon dropped out of the game.

THE RUSSIANS ARE COMING!

Name the only Russian-born pitcher to win 300 professional games. The answer is Victor Starfin, who won 303 games in Japan after emigrating there as a child after the Bolshevik Revolution. In 1939 he won forty-two of the Tokyo Giants' sixty-six victories.

Starfin is an enigmatic example of what we might expect someday if the Soviet Union ever gives up its native game of lapta and adopts the quaint American version known as baseball. How many more Star-fins could they produce?

WINNING STREAKS

The longest major-league winning streaks in a single season are:

Year	Pitcher	Team	(Rank)	Games
1912	Rube Marquard	New York Giants	(1)	20
1888	Tim Keefe	New York Giants	(1)	19
1884	Hoss Radbourn	Providence Grays	(1)	18
1890	John Luby	Chicago White Stockings	(2)	18
1885	Mickey Welch	New York Giants	(2)	17
1936	Carl Hubbell	New York Giants	(1)	17 (incl. World Series)
1936–37	Johnny Allen	Cleveland Indians	(4)	17
1959	Elroy Face	Pittsburgh Pirates	(4)	17 (all in relief)
1968–69	Dave McNally	Baltimore Orioles	(1)	17
1886	Jim McCormick	Chicago White Stockings	(1)	16
1912	Walter Johnson	Washington Senators	(2)	16
1912	Joe Wood	Boston Red Sox	(1)	16
1931	Lefty Grove	Philadelphia A's	(1)	16
1934	Schoolboy Rowe	Detroit Tigers	(1)	16
1947	Ewell Blackwell	Cincinnati Reds	(5)	16
1962	Jack Sanford	San Francisco Giants	(1)	16
1983	LaMarr Hoyt	Chicago White Sox	(1)	16 (incl. playoff)

Rube Marquard's Twenty

To the end of his life, Rube Marquard swore he won twenty games in a row, not the nineteen for which the record books give him credit. We think he was right.

Early in his streak Rube came in to relieve Jeff Tesreau in the top of the ninth, with the Giants losing by a run. In the bottom of the ninth New York scored twice to win the game, but the official scorer gave the victory to Tesreau. Under today's rules, of course, Marquard was technically the winner, which would have meant twenty straight instead of nineteen.

The question is: Should we accept the scoring rules of 1912 or apply the scoring rules of today?

Frank Williams (and historian David Voigt) argue that today's generation should not tamper with the way things were done in the past. In fact, Williams says, the 1912 rule was superior to today's rule, and Tesreau logically deserved the win more than Marquard did. If the rule makers of 1912 gave Marquard nineteen straight—and Marquard himself accepted it at the time—then we have no more right to undo it than our grandchildren will have, let's say, to throw out all our save statistics and impose their own stats on Hoyt Wilhelm, Rich Gossage, and Rollie Fingers.

Rube Marquard

Our own arguments:

First, we sympathize with Tesreau, whose great effort deserved to be rewarded even more than did Marquard's.

Second, if one wants to compare men of different eras (which is exactly what we are doing), one must establish one standard for all. Therefore, arbitrarily, let's use today's standards.

Third, why not let our grandchildren use a better way if they have one? We will not be around then anyway.

Therefore, Marquard won twenty games in a row.

Actually, Rube won his last game in 1911, so some claim he really won twenty-one in a row. (On this two-season basis, Dave McNally won twenty-four straight, as did Carl Hubbell.) However, he was beaten in the World Series that fall when Home Run Baker unloaded a homer to win his immortal nickname, so Rube will have to be content with twenty straight.

Johnson and Wood Both Win Sixteen in 1912

The year 1912 was a vintage year for streak pitchers. Marquard won twenty straight, and in the American League, Walter Johnson and Smoky Joe Wood each won sixteen.

Johnson started first, on July 3; Wood began his streak five days later. Picking up three victories in relief, Johnson notched his fourteenth straight, a shutout over fourth-place Chicago, on August 16, to tie Jack Chesbro's American League record, while Wood had just scored his ninth.

Johnson made it fifteen straight with a 4–2 win over fifth-place Cleveland and sixteen straight with an 8–1 triumph over sixth-place Detroit. He was finally stopped when he came in to pitch in relief with two men on base. He let both score, which lost the game, and under the scoring rules of the time, the reliever was charged with the loss. (Today, of course, the man who put the runners on base would be responsible. However, Walter lost his next game fair and square anyway, so the question is moot.)

Wood meanwhile kept gaining on John-

Walter Johnson and Smoky Joe Wood

Wood goes for his sixteenth straight win

son with a magnificent string of wins—8–0 over St. Louis, 6–0 over Detroit, 8–1 over Cleveland, 3–0 over Chicago, 1–0 over last-place New York. He had now won thirteen in a row, six of them shutouts, with a series against the Senators coming up. Boston and Washington were running one–two in the American League, so both teams yielded to the clamor of the fans and agreed to match their two aces, Johnson and Wood, to see if Walter could stop Joe's bid to break his new record.

The two met in Boston on Friday, August 20, and they gave the overflow crowd a splendid duel. Neither side scored for five innings until Wood's roommate, Tris Speaker, the batting champ with .383, hit a double into the crowd standing on the field (an out any other day?) and scored on a single by Duffy Lewis (.284) that just missed Danny Moeller's glove. It was all Smokey needed, and he won the game 1–0 to pull within two of Johnson's mark.

Wood won a sloppy game against Chicago 5–4, then defeated St. Louis 2–1 for number sixteen. Could he pass Sir Walter?

His next game was against the Tigers, a team he had beaten three times in his streak by scores of 1–0, 4–1, and 6–0. But this time he just did not have it, issued four walks in a row, and was bombed off the mound. Joe claimed that he could have won if it had not been for an error on an easy pop fly. The Sox had already clinched the pennant, and the regular shortstop, Heinie Wagner, was being rested, while rookie Marty Krug played in his place. The pop-up hit Krug on the belt buckle and three runs came in. Wood and Johnson had to share the record.

Both went on to win more than thirty games that year. Johnson was 33–12 and led the league with a 1.39 ERA and 296 strikeouts. He also saved three games. Wood was 34–5 and added three more victories in the World

Series over Marquard's Giants. He was only twenty-two, and the world lay at his feet.

The next spring Wood slipped on the wet outfield grass, injured his leg, and his world fell apart. He won only nine games in 1913 and never did regain his form. But, like Roy Hobbs, the fictional "Natural," Wood came back several years later as a hitter and carved out a second career for himself. Bernard Malamud knew his baseball history.

Grove Sixteen, Just Misses Twenty-seven

Lefty Grove tied Johnson's and Wood's record of 16 in 1931. With a little luck, he might have made it twenty-seven—if Al Simmons had not taken a day off and gone home to Milwaukee.

A rookie, Jim Moore, took Al's place in left. Grove was facing the fifth-place Browns in St. Louis, and he and Dick Coffman were tied 0–0 for seven innings. With two out in the seventh and a man in scoring position, a Brownie lifted a fly to left. Moore, unfamiliar with Sportsman's Park, started in and the ball fell behind him to score the run that beat Lefty 1–0.

If Grove was famous for one thing more than his fastball, it was his temper. And Lefty let it all out in the clubhouse afterward, punching lockers, ripping uniforms, throwing bats, kicking water buckets, and, above all, cussing Al Simmons.

Four days later he had gotten it out of his system and went on to start a new streak of eight in a row. Without the 1–0 defeat, that would have been twenty-seven.

Hubbell's Seventeen— Or Was It Twenty-four?

Some record books give Hubbell only sixteen straight, the number he won in the regular season, but we add a seventeenth which he won against the Yankees in the World Series. The Yanks finally beat him in his second start.

Some purists don't count the Series. In that case, Hub won twenty-four straight, his last sixteen in 1933 and his first eight in 1934.

Carl's sixteen in 1933 were remarkable, because they sparked the Giants to the pennant. The team was in fifth place, playing exactly .500 ball, when the streak began in mid-July. With Hub leading the way, they won fifty and lost twenty-one the rest of the way to win by five games. He also saved three games during the streak.

Hubbell might have made it seventeen straight if he had not lost 1-0 on an error four days before his streak began. Carl himself is philosophical. Since the Giants couldn't score, "the best I could have got was a tie."

SHUTOUTS

The most shutouts, lifetime, were racked up by Walter Johnson, 110. The top twelve leaders in shutouts were:

SHUTOUT LEADERS, LIFETIME

Rank	Pitcher	Number of Shutouts
1	Walter Johnson	110
2	Grover Alexander	90
3	Christy Mathewson	83
4	Cy Young	77
5	Eddie Plank	69
6	Warren Spahn	63
7	Tom Seaver*	61
8	Ed Walsh	58
9	Three Finger Brown	58
10	Don Sutton*	58
11	Pud Galvin	57
12	Bob Gibson	56

*Through 1986 season; still active.

Johnson is far and away the leader in 1-0 victories, with thirty-eight. The closest man to him, Grover Alexander, has less than half.

Bradley, Alex: Sixteen in a Year

The record for total shutouts in a season belongs to Grover Alexander and George Washington Bradley, each with sixteen. Bradley pitched back in 1876, the first year of the National League, when teams played less than half as many games as they do now.

Next come Jack Coombs and Bob Gibson, both with thirteen.

Incidentally, Alexander also shares the minor-league shutout record, fourteen, according to SABR's *Minor League Stars*, edited by Bob Hoie. Alex shut out his fourteen in 1910 with Syracuse of the New York State league. Two men had set the record just one year before: Vean Gregg of Portland and Ulysses Simpson Grant "Stony" McGlynn of Milwaukee.

SCORELESS INNING STREAKS

Chesbro, White, Coombs

In 1904 Happy Jack Chesbro started off with forty-one scoreless innings. That was the year Chesbro won forty-one games and lost the pennant in the last weekend on a wild pitch.

Later that year Doc White of the hitless-wonder White Sox topped him with five straight shutouts, a total of forty-five innings.

In 1910 Colby Jack Coombs went fifty-two straight scoreless innings on his way to thirty-one victories.

Johnson's Fifty-six Straight

In 1913 Walter Johnson made the record fifty-six. He gave up a first-inning run to the New York Highlanders (.273), then shut them out the rest of the game and added five complete shutouts after that. He held the last-place Browns (.237) scoreless for three more innings in the next game before his string was ended. It was fifty-five years before the mark was broken.

Drysdale's Fifty-eight

In 1968 Don Drysdale broke Johnson's mark for the most consecutive shutouts, six, and the most consecutive shutout innings, fifty-eight. (Some books say 58.2, but we count only whole innings—the job is not over until the third man is out.)

Big Don was coming to the end of his career that May, when he shut out the Cubs 1–0 on two hits and started an amazing string:

Date	Opponent	(Rank)	BA	Score	Hits
May 14	Chicago Cubs	(3)	.242	1–0	2
May 18	Houston Astros	(10)	.231	1–0	5
May 22	St. Louis Cardinals	(1)	.249	2–0	5
May 26	Houston Astros	(10)	.231	5–0	6
May 31	San Francisco Giants	(2)	.239	3–0	6
June 4	Pittsburgh Pirates	(6)	.252	5–0	3

The Giants' game, which tied the record of five straight by White and Johnson, was a heart-stopper. For the third time in the streak, Don loaded the bases in the ninth with no outs, then hit batter Dick Dietz (.272) on the arm—but the umpire ruled that Dietz had deliberately tried to get hit and called him back with the count now 3–2. Drysdale got Dietz on a short fly, Ty Cline (.223) on a grounder, and Jack Hiatt (.232) on a pop-up to nail down the shutout.

He then went out on June 8 and pitched three more scoreless innings to pass Johnson's consecutive-inning mark with fifty-eight.

In spite of these heroics, Drysdale ended the year with only a 14–14 record, and the next year he called it quits.

Kaneda's Sixty-four

Once again, it was a Japanese who set the world record for scoreless innings. In 1958 Masaichi Kaneda broke all marks with sixty-four shutout innings in a row. That year he won thirty-one and lost fourteen, with an ERA of 1.30.

11

No-Hitters

PERFECTION

According to the record books, only twelve men have pitched perfect games in 118 years of trying, since 1869. That is about one every ten years.

But fifteen other men (including Pud Galvin twice) have been even more perfect than all the first twelve, except Harvey Haddix. They faced twenty-eight or more men in one game without giving up a hit or a walk. Twelve had their fielders boot one or more balls behind them. We feel this is even better than perfect. Not only must they keep their cool in spite of the errors, they must pitch from the stretch—always more difficult than with a windup—and they have to get an extra out—sometimes more—than the other perfect pitchers did not have to get. It just does not seem fair that, when a shortstop makes a sensational play to rob a batter of a sure hit, the pitcher is given a perfect game, but if another shortstop boots an easy grounder, the pitcher is penalized.

Waite Hoyt pitched eleven perfect innings

J.L. Richmond

sandwiched between hits in a thirteen-inning game.

Four other pitchers retired twenty-seven in a row—the last twenty-seven—after giving up hits to the leadoff men.

So our perfect-game list contains thirty

names (twenty-nine games) not found on other such lists. Here then are all thirty-one in order of the number of consecutive batters they faced without giving up a hit or a walk:

Year	Pitcher	Batters	Opponent	(Rank)	BA	Notes
1959	Harvey Haddix	36	Pittsburgh	(2)	.265	(12 innings)
1919	Waite Hoyt	34	Yanks	(3)	.267	(2nd–13th inning)
1880	Pud Galvin	33	Worcester	(5)	.231	(6 errors)
1884	Charlie Buffinton	32	Providence	(1)	.241	(5 errors)
1971	Rick Wise	32	Chicago	(3)	.258	(2nd–12th inning)
1908	Nap Rucker	30	Braves	(6)	.239	(3 errors)
1885	John Clarkson	29	Providence	(4)	.220	(3 errors, 1 DP)
1970	Bill Singer	29	Philadelphia	(5)	.238	(2 errors, both his own)
1883	Hoss Radbourn	28	Cleveland	(4)	.246	(1 error)
1884	Pud Galvin	28	Detroit	(8)	.208	(1 error)
1905	Christy Mathewson	28	Cubs	(3)	.245	(2 errors, one DP)
1910	Tom Hughes	28	Cleveland	(5)	.244	(1 error)
1920	Walter Johnson	28	Red Sox	(5)	.269	(1 error)
1967	Joel Horlen	28	Detroit	(2)	.243	(1 error)
1974	Dick Bosman	28	Oakland	(1)	.247	(1 error, his own)
1880	J. L. Richmond	27	Cleveland	(3)	.242	
1880	J. M. Ward	27	Buffalo	(7)	.226	
1904	Cy Young	27	Philadelphia	(5)	.249	
1906	Lefty Leifield	27	Cubs	(1)	.262	(8 innings, 3 errors)
1908	Addie Joss	27	White Sox	(3)	.224	
1922	Charlie Robertson	27	Detroit	(3)	.305	
1956	Don Larsen	27	Brooklyn	(1)	.252	
1964	Jim Bunning	27	Mets	(10)	.246	
1965	Sandy Koufax	27	Cubs	(8)	.238	
1968	Catfish Hunter	27	Minnesota	(7)	.237	
1981	Len Barker	27	Toronto	(7)	.226	
1984	Mike Witt	27	Texas	(7)	.261	
1954	Robin Roberts	27*	Cincinnati	(5)	.262	
1980	Jerry Reuss	27*	San Francisco	(5)	.244	
1981	Jim Bibby	27*	Atlanta	(4)	.243	
1917	Ernie Shore	26†	Washington	(5)	.241	

*Retired last twenty-seven batters in a row after giving up a hit to leadoff man.

†Starter Babe Ruth walked the first man and promptly slugged the umpire in the jaw and was banished; Shore rushed in from the bull pen, got the runner on a steal attempt, and retired the next twenty-six.

Note: Hooks Wiltse in 1908 and Lew Burdette in 1960 missed perfection because each hit a batter, with Wiltse hitting the *last* batter—the opposing pitcher—with an 0-2 count.

Of all the perfect games, which was the most perfect?

Harvey Haddix: The Perfect Twelve

The greatest game ever pitched was thrown by a thirty-three-year-old Ohio farm boy named Harvey Haddix, in 1959.

Haddix had bounced around the minors until he was twenty-six years old. In one game, in Columbus of the American Association, he had thrown ten consecutive hitless innings. It won him a job with the Cardinals, where, in his first full season, 1953, he almost had another no-hitter, giving up his first hit in the ninth, one of twenty games he won that year. But Harvey never seemed to fulfill that early promise. By 1958 he was down to eight wins.

On May 26, 1959, the sky was threatening, lightning flashed, and a stiff wind blew as Haddix warmed up for the game in Milwaukee against Lew Burdette and the

Harvey Haddix

hard-hitting Braves—Hank Aaron (.355, thirty-five home runs that year), Ed Mathews (.306, forty-six), Joe Adcock (twenty-five homers), and the rest.

Early in the game, Harvey remembered later, he hung a curve to someone, he could not remember who, "but I got away with it." He struck out Eddie Mathews on "the best fastball he [Haddix] has ever had," Mathews said. Adcock went down swinging twice on a high slider.

For eight innings Haddix did not give up a hit, or even a walk.

In the last of the ninth, Haddix set the Braves down again 1-2-3, striking out two of the three men to face him. He had registered a rare perfect game, and his Pirate teammates mobbed him as he came back to the dugout.

Unfortunately, they had not scored any runs off Burdette. Haddix's roommate, Bob Skinner, had hit a long drive to center, but the wind had held it up and sent the game into the history books.

Haddix admitted that he was tense as the game wore on, but "more tired than nervous." When catcher Burgess came out to ask how he felt, Harvey told him, "Smokey, your horse out there is getting tired."

In the tenth Haddix once more set the Braves down 1-2-3. He did it again in the eleventh. And the twelfth. It was the longest perfect game ever pitched, but still Haddix could not win it.

In the thirteenth Haddix got two strikes on leadoff man Felix Mantilla, a right-hander hitting only .215, then threw what he thought was the third strike over the plate. "I thought we had Mantilla struck out," Burgess said. But umpire Smith called it a ball. Mantilla then hit to third baseman Don Hoak, who threw wildly to first, giving Milwaukee its first base runner after thirty-six straight outs.

Next Mathews sacrificed, Aaron was walked intentionally—now the perfect game really was ended, though it is questionable whether Aaron would have walked if Hoak had thrown straight.

Then Haddix threw a slider to Joe Adcock. "I was tired," he admitted. "I wanted a low pitch and came in high with it." "He struck me out twice with that same kind of pitch," Adcock said. But this one he slammed over the fence. The no-hitter—and the game—were gone.

Nevertheless, Harvey Haddix had made history. He had done something no other pitcher had ever done before or has ever done since. He had pitched twelve innings of perfect baseball. He hoped to cash in on his fame, and indeed a television quiz show offered him $300 for an appearance, which he had to decline. Ironically, Haddix ended the year with only a 12–12 record for the fourth-place Pirates.

Burdette gave up twelve hits, and he likes to point out that "I'm the guy who won the greatest game ever pitched."

Waite Hoyt: Thirty-four Straight

In 1919 Boston's nineteen-year-old Waite Hoyt pitched nine perfect innings against the Yankees, retiring thirty-four straight batters in one game. That places him second only to Haddix. Yet his name appears in no record books. He gave up one hit in the first three to open the second, and one in the twelfth, and was absolute perfection in between.

Pitching against the Yankees in the Polo Grounds, Hoyt, the Brooklyn schoolboy, got the Yanks out 1-2-3 in the first. But in the second, three straight singles scored a run. Hoyt then got the last three men to end the inning, and for the next ten innings the Yankees never touched first base.

Hoyt would have lost 1–0 if his teammate

NATIONAL BASEBALL LIBRARY, COOPERSTOWN, N.Y.

Waite Hoyt

Babe Ruth had not smashed the longest home run ever seen in the Polo Grounds— clean over the right-field roof. It was the Babe's twenty-eighth of the year, breaking Ed Williamson's thirty-five-year-old record of twenty-seven and sending the game into extra innings.

Still tied 1–1, Hoyt got the first man out in the thirteenth, thus retiring thirty-four straight hitters. Then Wally Pipp (.275) smashed a mighty drive to the wall in faraway dead center for a triple, and Del Pratt (.292) lifted a fly to Ruth, scoring Pipp.

Not until Haddix, almost forty years later, would anyone match Waite's feat.

The *New York Times* revealed what it thought of the achievement in its headline the next morning:

RUTH WALLOPS OUT HIS 28TH HOME RUN
TERRIFIC CRASH OVER THE POLO GROUNDS
STANDS SETS NEW WORLD'S RECORD.

Hoyt's feat was buried far down in the story and has languished virtually unknown to historians ever since.

Charlie Robertson: Some Are More Perfect than Others

If perfection can be divided into more perfect and less perfect, then perhaps the most perfect game was pitched by Charlie Robertson against the Detroit Tigers in 1922.

In the ten-year period of 1924 to 1933, the lively ball era was at its liveliest. Baseball saw .400 hitters come along almost every other year. Only six pitchers overcame that handicap and hurled no-hitters during that period.

By contrast, look at 1969, when batting averages were deflated. Six men hurled no-hitters in that year alone.

That is what makes Robertson's game the toughest no-hitter of all. He hurled it against Ty Cobb and the Tigers, a club that hit .305 as a team that year. No other man has ever thrown a no-hitter against so powerful a lineup, and Robertson's game was a perfect one—he did not give up even a walk. And he did it in the second major-league game he ever pitched.

The opposition included Cobb, the living legend who was about to hit .401, Harry Heilmann (.356), Bobby Veach (.327), Lu Blue (.300), and Topper Rigney (.300). Cobb loaded the lineup with left-handers, including himself, and an overflow crowd stood on the outfield fringe.

The Tigers protested that Robertson was throwing an illegal pitch (the spitter had been outlawed two years earlier), and umpire Dick Nallin threw several balls out. Was Robertson really doctoring the ball? Or was this Cobb's form of psychological warfare against the rookie? (On the other hand, was it Robertson's psychological strategy against Cobb?)

In the second, left-fielder Johnny Mostil went back to the fence to catch a long drive by Veach. And Harry Hooper made a great catch on Bobby Jones (.257) on the dead run. Otherwise, Robertson breezed by the Tigers' sluggers. He never even got in a hole on the count.

The crowd grew quiet in the ninth, as the last batter, pinch-hitter Danny Clark (.292), swung viciously at the first pitch and missed. He took the next one for a strike, and Cobb came charging out of the dugout, demanding that the ump look at the ball. Nallin not only inspected the ball, he carefully inspected Robertson's entire uniform. Apparently satisfied, Nallin went back behind the plate. Clark took another strike, a fastball, for strike three.

Perfect, Minus

Five men have come within one pitch of perfection, losing their perfect games with two out in the ninth. Should they go on the list? Why not? After all, Shore is credited with a perfect game, though he faced only twenty-six batters. They are: Hooks Wiltse, Tommy Bridges, Billy Pierce, Milt Pappas, and Milt Wilcox.

Of the five perfect games spoiled with two out in the ninth, only one has been broken up by a base on balls. (Hooks Wiltse's was spoiled on July 4, 1908, when, on an 0–2 count, he hit the last batter—the opposing pitcher!) It happened to Milt Pappas of the Cubs in 1972.

The umpire was Art Froemming, then in his second year in the National League. Pappas was in his sixteenth, and next-to-last, season in the majors.

Milt was having the best season of his career. He was the best control pitcher in either league, with only 29 walks in 195 innings. "He could spot the ball very well that year," his catcher, Randy Hundley, said.

He was scheduled to face the last-place San Diego Padres at Wrigley Field on September 2, a cold, windy day. He woke up with a bad cold and considered asking manager Whitey Lockman to give him the day off, but his wife urged him to go to the park and pitch.

In the first, Milt went to three balls against Leron Lee, a left-hander who hit .300 that year, but Lee grounded out. No other Padre would draw three balls against Pappas until the ninth.

"He couldn't get his change-up over, so he was throwing a straight fastball and a quick-breaking slider," Hundley said. "There wasn't that much difference, so I suggested we take something off the slider to get an off-speed pitch. Ordinarily you don't hear of taking something off a slider, but he got a lot of outs with a change-up slider."

Pappas' biggest scare came from Enzo Hernandez (.195), who dropped a beautiful bunt down the third-base line and beat it out—just before the ball rolled foul by inches. Hernandez then struck out. In the fifth, Nate Colbert (.250) hit a one-hopper into the hole, where shortstop Don Kessinger made a "superplay" on the wet grass.

Hundley, meanwhile, was having problems. He swung on a perfect pitch and flied weakly to center and, as he trotted back to the dugout, made a disgusted gesture. "Do that once more, and you're out of the game," Froemming snapped.

The crowd was on its feet for the ninth inning as Pappas prepared to face right-handers John Jeter (.221) and Fred Kendall (.216), and a pinch-hitter for the pitcher.

Jeter missed a strike, took a ball, and flied to center, where Bill North slipped, fell, and lost the ball in the sun. But left-fielder Billy Williams dashed over and made the catch.

The first pitch to Kendall was a slider, which Pappas hung in the strike zone. Kendall lined it down the first-base line—foul. On the next pitch he grounded out.

The last man up was pinch-hitter Larry Stahl, a left-handed veteran hitting .226.

He missed the first pitch, strike one.

The next one was outside, ball one.

Stahl swung and missed the third pitch, for strike two. Pappas, the best control pitcher in baseball, had to get just one more strike.

On the fourth pitch he threw a slider— low. Ball two.

Hundley signaled for a fastball, which cut the corner of the plate. Froemming called it a ball. This was the first time Pappas had gone to three balls since the first inning. It all came down to one last pitch. Pappas had to get this one over.

Hundley put down one finger for another fastball. Froemming went into his crouch, and Pappas into his windup. The pitch was close, but Froemming called, "Ball four."

Pappas was philosophical after the game. "I was lucky," he said. "I got away with several hanging sliders, and I had three or four scares."

As for the last three balls: "They were so close, I don't know how Stahl could take them. I was just hoping Froemming might sympathize, since it was a perfect game. But he couldn't be expected to do that.

"The pitches were balls. They were borderline, but balls. Froemming called a real good game."

Froemming insisted at the time that the perfect game "never entered my mind. The pitch is either there or it isn't. It's a ball or a strike. Those last three pitches weren't there. They weren't even borderline. They were 'shoe shiners,' well below the knees."

Hundley disagreed: "The 3-2, I wouldn't argue on that one so much. But I go back to the 2-2 pitch. That pitch was good enough to call a strike. I was surprised, and I really think Larry Stahl was surprised when he wasn't called out on the 2-2 pitch. Froemming could have called that a strike and nobody would have said anything about it."

Froemming had another point. "The key to the whole thing," he said, "was that Hundley never said a word on either pitch. And Hundley's aggressive that way, he'll argue with you." It may be that Froemming's earlier threat to eject Hundley was a factor in his silence.

Don Larsen—Perfect in the Series

The most famous no-hitter ever pitched— and next to Haddix's gem, perhaps the greatest—belongs to Don Larsen, who tossed it in the 1956 World Series against the Brooklyn Dodgers.

Like Harvey Haddix, Larsen, twenty-seven, had been a journeyman toiling in obscurity. He had started with the wretched St. Louis Browns in 1953, winning seven and losing twelve. The Brownies moved to Baltimore the next year and lost 100 games, 21 of them by Don, who could win only 3. But two of the victories, fortunately, were against the Yanks, and that winter New York decided to snatch him from the Orioles.

In 1955 the Yanks shipped him to Denver, but he came back in time to win eight of his last nine to help New York win the pennant again. However, he lost one in the World Series against the Dodgers that fall.

Like most of the Yanks, Larsen liked to party. "Sleep," said Mickey Mantle, "was his mortal enemy." In spring training with the Yanks in 1956 Don banged his car into a telephone pole at 4 A.M. "He was probably mailing a letter," Casey Stengel theorized.

In his first full season as a Yank, Don

The last pitch of Don Larsen's perfect game

started off shakily and was knocked out in five of his first seven games. Then manager Casey Stengel taught him a no-windup delivery that Casey had learned from the old Kansas City Monarch star Bullet Joe Rogan almost forty years before. It must have helped, because Don recovered to win his last four games, one of them a two-hitter against the Red Sox. He finished with an 11-5 mark as the Yanks won the pennant again and prepared for another showdown with the Dodgers.

Whitey Ford, Johnny Kucks, and Tom Sturdivant were New York's big winners, but at least one astute student of pitching, Ted Williams, urged anyone who would listen to keep an eye on Larsen. The new delivery made him tough, Williams said, and the Yankee Stadium shadows in October made him even tougher.

Larsen made Ted look like a bad judge of pitching talent in game two in Brooklyn, when Larsen started, was cuffed for four runs, and was driven to the showers in the second inning. "I figured I had blown my chance," he said. Sure that Stengel would never give him another start, he went out for a few drinks with the guys.

But Stengel had not given up. The short fences in Brooklyn may have worried Don, Casey said. "He can pitch better. You'll see."

As usual, Don was out drinking before game five, but to his surprise, he took the mound the next day in Yankee Stadium against Sal "The Barber" Maglie, who had himself pitched a no-hitter in the regular season just a few weeks earlier.

On the first Dodgers' hitter, Junior Gilliam, a .300-batting switch-hitter, Larsen threw a beautiful curve over the outside corner for a called third strike. Umpire Babe Pinelli told himself, "Oh, oh, Larsen's got it today."

The second hitter, Peewee Reese (.257), worked the count to 3-2, and another Larsen curve broke over the plate for called strike three. It was the only 3-2 count against Larsen that day.

In the seventh, when the infamous Yankee Stadium shadows crept across home plate, the Bums still had not gotten a hit or even a walk. The superstitious Yankees froze in their dugout and bull-pen seats, afraid to move and bring bad luck. They could not even go to the bathroom. Don himself was nonchalant. He punched Mickey Mantle on the arm and pointed. "Look at the scoreboard, Mick. Two innings to go. Do you think I'll make it?" Mickey stared at him, dumbfounded.

Larsen went into the ninth still fresh—he had thrown only eighty-five pitches. The television camera kept dwelling on the scoreboard, showing the Yanks ahead 2-0 on Mantle's home run and the goose egg under HITS for the Dodgers. But superstitious announcer Mel Allen refused to break the old jinx against mentioning the no-hitter out loud. In the park itself, a thunderous silence reigned. Billy Martin called the infielders together and told them grimly, "Nothing gets through."

On the mound Larsen took several big breaths to relax, then concentrated on the first batter, Carl Furillo. Furillo fouled off two pitches, took a ball, high, then fouled off two more. He finally hit a soft fly to Hank Bauer in right, as the big crowd roared. Two outs to go.

Don took his cap off and wiped his brow. The next batter, Roy Campanella, pulled one deep into the left-field stands, as the crowd gulped. But the ball was foul. Then Campy slapped a grounder to Martin at second. Only one out to go.

Brooklyn manager Walt Alston sent up a pinch-hitter for Maglie—ten-year veteran

Dale Mitchell, a left-handed slap-hitter who rarely struck out. Obtained from Cleveland, where he had faced Larsen often, Mitchell had hit .292 in the pennant drive for the bums. His record as a pinch-hitter was 6 for 14. This would be his final at-bat in the major leagues.

Larsen prayed silently, "Help me get through this," then threw a fastball "a fraction outside," said Pinelli, who gulped and called it ball one. The next pitch was a called strike. Then a swinging strike. Ahead 1–2, Larsen took another deep breath, as an airliner roared overhead, then threw what Mitchell called "probably as good a ball to hit as anyone had all day"—a hanging curveball. Dale swung and fouled it off to left.

The stands were so quiet, Pinelli told Al Stump, that he could hear Larsen breathing. One more deep breath. The next pitch was another fastball, which Pinelli could not pick up until it was two-thirds of the way to the plate. "It was high and outside," Mitchell said. He started to swing, then held up. Ball two or strike three?

Pinelli shot his right hand up in the air, and the scene on the field became pandemonium. Catcher Yogi Berra raced to the mound and leaped on Larsen in a bear hug.

Was it really a strike? "It was not a strike," Mitchell insisted. He turned around to protest, "but there wasn't anybody to discuss it with." To some of us watching on television, and to others in the stadium, the pitch did indeed look a mite outside. Even to Mantle in center field, "it looked like a bad call." But it was Mitchell's job to protect the plate with two strikes. The ball was too close to take. There is not a fan in the world who would change the call.

"This," sighed owner Del Webb, "will set spring training back forever."

In the clubhouse later, one reporter asked Stengel if the game was the best he had seen Larsen pitch.

"So far," Casey replied.

MULTIPLE NO-HITTERS

Nolan Ryan's Five

Weak support and injuries have kept Nolan Ryan from the big twenty-victory years that the public demands of its great pitchers, but he is the toughest man to hit in the history of baseball.

All five of his no-hitters came against strong opponents. It is interesting that Ryan, a low-ball pitcher, pitched four of them in the "high-ball" American League:

Year	Opponent	(Rank)	BA	BB	SO
1973	Kansas City Royals	(2)	.262	3	12
1973	Detroit Tigers	(3)	.254	4	17
1974	Minnesota Twins	(3)	.272	8	15
1975	Baltimore Orioles	(2)	.252	4	9
1981	Los Angeles Dodgers	(2)*	.262	3	11

*Won division and league playoffs.

Ryan pitched his first two no-hitters within two months of each other, in 1973. On May 15 he blanked the second-place Royals.

On July 15 Nolan did it again, against the

third-place Tigers. He had better velocity and a harder curve, he says, and struck out seventeen. Ryan might have made it nineteen or twenty—he had sixteen after seven innings—but an eighth-inning batting rally by his team cooled his arm off, and he struck out only one over the last two frames. Even at that, Norm Cash (.262) came up with two out in the ninth—with a piano leg instead of a bat. It gave everyone a laugh, "but it didn't relieve any pressure for me," Ryan wrote. When the ump ordered Cash to get a regular bat, Nolan got him for the final out—"my favorite no-hitter."

Ryan almost pitched a third no-hitter in his next start, pitching seven hitless innings against the Orioles. Weak-hitting Mark Belanger (.226) spoiled it with a blooper into short center. "If [outfielder] Ken Berry had been playing me straight away, he catches that ball easily," Belanger said. (Belanger, a lifetime .228 hitter, hit over .300 against Ryan.)

Nolan missed another no-hitter the following month on another bloop single, this one by Thurman Munson (.301) of the Yanks. The ball fell just out of reach of shortstop Rudy Meoli and second baseman Sandy Alomar. "We both felt like we could have caught it," Meoli said later. "I came within four inches of catching it as it was."

Nolan pitched his third no-hitter, 1–0, the following year against the third-place Twins. He struck out 367 that year and won twenty-two for the Angels, who finished last.

No-hitter number four came in an off year for Ryan, 1975. He struck out only 186 and won only fourteen as the Angels finished last again. But he no-hit the Orioles 1–0, as usual getting hardly any help from his teammates. "I had more command of my three pitches—fastball, curveball, and change-up," Ryan wrote. The last strike of the game was on "a tantalizing change-up to Bobby Grich" (.260). "He didn't know I didn't have a fastball," Ryan said. "I got tremendous satisfaction out of it. It was pure pitching performance."

Ryan's record fifth no-hitter came after he moved to Houston in the NL, and he says it was the most satisfying of all, surpassing even number two in his estimation. It came late in the pennant race against the front-running Dodgers, and it came before millions on national television.

In the ninth, Ryan got switch-hitting pinch-hitter Reggie Smith (.200) on three straight strikes—he just fired them in against Smith, who was coming in cold off the bench. Lefty Ken Landreaux (.251) grounded to first.

That brought up Dusty Baker, a right-hander hitting .320, with Steve Garvey, another righty at .283, on deck. "I really wanted to get that curve over," Nolan said. "I was going to go 3-0 on Baker before I challenged him [with a fastball]. The guy I didn't want to face in that situation, pitching out of the stretch, was Garvey. He's hard for me with that little strike zone." Baker swung on the curve and hit an easy hopper to third for the final out.

That was the strike-shortened season, and Ryan won eleven and lost five, with the best ERA in the league, 1.69.

Sandy Koufax's Four

Sandy Koufax threw four classics—one a year, in 1962, 1963, 1964, and 1965. The last was a perfect game.

His four gems look like this:

Year	Opponent	Rank	BA	BB	SO
1962	New York Mets	(10)	.240	5	13
1963	San Francisco Giants	(3)	.258	2	4
1964	Philadelphia Phillies	(3)	.258	1	12
1965	Chicago Cubs	(8)	.238	0	14

Bob Feller's Three

One man belongs alongside Ryan and Koufax—Bob Feller. Even with his wartime service, Feller pitched three no-hitters.

Incidentally, Feller would have pitched five if it had not been for a guy named Bobby Doerr, who personally spoiled two of Bob's bids.

Johnny Vander Meer's Two in a Row

Johnny Vander Meer was a hard-throwing left-hander who could not stick with the Dodgers' organization because he could not get the ball over the plate, though he struck out 295 at Durham, North Carolina, in 1936. In the spring of 1938, Reds' manager Bill McKechnie gave the newly acquired rookie a few pointers on his delivery. They must have helped, because on June 7 John pitched a three-hitter against the Giants to bring his record to 5–2. The final hit came in the ninth by pinch-hitter Hank Lieber, who hit a blooper just over second base.

Four days later Casey Stengel's fifth-place Boston Bees came to town. They hit .250 that year. To everyone's amazement, including his own, Vandy shut them out without a hit. His control was fine, he walked only three, and his big catcher, Ernie Lombardi, picked two of them off, which meant Johnny could work from a windup instead of a stretch, with the bases empty.

"I had a pretty good sinker that day," Vandy told Walter M. Langford. "I wasn't real quick, didn't have my real good stuff, but it was one of my few days I had control. I think there were only about five fly balls in that game."

Four days later the Reds were in Brooklyn to play the Dodgers (.257), who would end up sixth that year. It was the first night game in Ebbets Field history. Some fans from Vandy's hometown in New Jersey

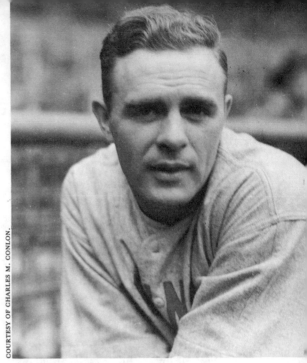

Johnny Vander Meer

were there to give him a watch in a pre-game ceremony, usually considered a sure jinx.

Vandy's curve was hanging, so he went to his fastball, which was in fine form. But he was wild, going to 3–2 often and in trouble in almost every inning.

In the ninth Brooklyn's Buddy Hassett (.293), a left-handed batter, hit the first pitch back to the mound. Vandy knocked it down and "had to scurry a little bit to pick it up and throw him out. That was probably the toughest ball to handle in either of the two ball games." But Johnny walked Babe Phelps, a .208-hitting catcher; he also walked the more dangerous Cookie Lavagetto (.273) and Dolph Camilli (.251) to load the bases.

Ernie Koy (.299) grounded to third, forcing Phelps at home. That left Vandy with one out to go and Brooklyn's manager Leo Durocher, a .219 slugger, up.

Lombardi went out to the mound and told him, "You're either going to give up a hit or you're not, so blaze that fast one in there." Vandy reared back and fired two strikes in on the Lip. Then he threw one that he says nicked the outside corner with two inches to spare. But, as he told writer Donald Honig, umpire Bill Stewart had trouble seeing over Lombardi and called it a ball. Instead of blowing up, Vandy kept his silence. The next pitch was outside. Leo lunged at it and hit a line drive down the right-field line, foul. On the next pitch, Durocher smacked a line drive to center, which Harry Craft caught at his shoe tops.

Vandy had done it—pitched the only back-to-back no-hitters in big-league history. And by a rookie at that.

The happiest man in the park was Bill Stewart. "I blew that pitch," he admitted. (Wondered John: Would he have said so if Leo had gotten a hit?)

In his next game, against the Bees again, Vandy threatened to make it three straight, until Debs Garms (.315) hit a 3–2 pitch in the fourth.

Vandy had gone twenty-one innings without giving a hit, almost a record. Cy Young is tops with twenty-four innings. But, Johnny points out, if he had not given that "sloppy" hit to Hank Lieber in the ninth inning on June 7, he would have gone 29 straight hitless innings, or more than the equivalent of three straight games.

OTHER NOTABLE NO-HIT ACHIEVEMENTS

Young's Twenty-four-Inning Hitless String

When Vander Meer went for his third straight no-hitter, one interested spectator was the great Cy Young, then seventy-one years old, who went to the stadium from his farm in Ohio to see if Vandy could break Young's record of twenty-four straight hitless innings set back in 1904.

Young was thirty-seven years old in the spring of 1904 and had already won 379 of his lifetime 510 victories. His string began with the last two innings he pitched on April 25. Five days later he went in in relief and pitched another seven without allowing a hit.

On May 5 Cy was matched against Philadelphia's great Rube Waddell, who had just beaten Boston on a one-hitter on his way to his third straight twenty-victory season. Ten thousand people were in the stands in Boston (a big crowd then) to see the two biggest drawing cards in the league hook up.

"I don't think I ever had more stuff," Cy would reminisce years later.

Boston's right-fielder Buck Freeman saved Cy with a diving catch of a pop-up in the third. In the seventh Patsy Dougherty crashed into the left-field fence to snare a long foul. Catcher Lou Criger almost went into the Boston bench to get a foul.

Finally Young was down to his last batter, Waddell (.122), as the Boston fans called for a pinch-hitter to make Cy earn his game. Instead, Connie Mack sent Rube up to hit for himself. Rube took two strikes and flied deep to center, as the fans mobbed Young and one old gentleman pressed a five-dollar bill into his hand (worth perhaps fifty dollars today).

Six days later—Cy was getting plenty of rest between starts—he faced the New York Highlanders, forerunners of the Yankees, who would duel Boston right down to the final game—that was the year New York's Jack Chesbro unleashed a wild pitch to lose the pennant. The New Yorkers were hitting .259, and Young held them hitless for six innings before a bloop single ended his string at 24, a feat that no man since has been able to match.

Eckersley Almost Matches Young

Seventy-three years later, in 1977, Dennis Eckersley tested Young's record, and he might have beaten it if he had not caught the flu.

The twenty-two-year-old Cleveland right-hander started his string May 25 with seven hitless innings against the woeful Seattle Mariners. Five nights later he added a nine-inning no-hitter against the California Angels.

On June 5 Eck was fighting a slight case of the flu as he warmed up in the Kingdome for another game against the Mariners. With two out in the sixth, Seattle's Ruppert Jones, who hit .263 that year, drove one over the center-field wall to break the string at twenty-one complete innings. One thing Young did not have to contend with, which Eck did, was a hopped-up ball. In Cy's day, Harry Davis led the league with ten homers.

Toney and Vaughn: The One-in-a-Million Game

What are the odds against two men pitching nine-inning no-hitters in the same game? Fred Toney and Jim "Hippo" Vaughn did it in Chicago on May 2, 1917.

Vaughn, of the host Cubs, was a right-handed strikeout artist. His nickname, "Hippo," seems misleading for a man who stood 6 feet, 4 inches tall.

Toney of the Reds was more of a finesse pitcher. Eight years earlier, when he was a twenty-one year old in the Blue Grass league, Fred had hurled one of the master-piece games of minor-league history, seventeen innings without a hit. He struck out nineteen and walked one.

For nine innings the two gladiators traded out for out. In the top of the tenth, Vaughn's luck ran out. Big Jim got Heinie Groh (.304) for out number one. But Larry Kopf (.255) hit a ground ball between first and second to break the no-hitter. After Greasy Neale (.294) flied out, Hal Chase (.277) lifted a fly

to center that outfielder Cy Williams dropped as Kopf raced to third. When Jim Thorpe, a .237 batter, hit a roller between the mound and first base, Vaughn hustled over and scooped it up. Realizing he had no play at first, he flipped the ball home—but the catcher let it bounce off his chest, and Kopf crossed the plate with the run that won the game.

Koufax Trumps Hendley

Sandy Koufax's perfect game was his fourth no-hitter, breaking Bob Feller's modern record. Sandy had to be perfect that night, September 9, 1965. His Dodgers were half a game behind in a tense pennant race with the Giants, and his opponent, Bob Hendley of the Cubs—a minor leaguer at the start of the season—was almost perfect himself, with a one-hitter. It was the only time in history that a no-hitter trumped a one-hitter.

Koufax was pitching in pain that year, and though he took a 21–7 record into the game, he had not won in his last five starts, Glenn Dickey points out in *The Great No-Hitters*. The Dodgers finished seventh in batting that year—a rally consisted of a walk to Maury Wills, a steal, an infield out, and a sacrifice fly. Koufax was so frustrated that he had thrown a rubbing table against the wall after being taken out in his last start.

But in Dodger Stadium the night of September 9, his elbow felt better than it had in weeks. His curve was snapping, and he set the Cubs down in order through the early innings.

Then, suddenly, "my fastball came alive, as good a fastball as I've had all year."

Koufax and Hendley battled 0–0 until the fifth, when the Dodgers finally scored, but without a hit. Lou Johnson (.259) walked, was sacrificed to second, stole third, and scored on the catcher's overthrow. (Two innings later Johnson would ruin Hendley's no-hitter with a bloop double down the right-field line.)

Koufax knew he was working on a no-hitter, he said later. But with a 1–0 lead, he was more worried about losing the game than the no-hitter. "I was trying to keep the ball low and away, because Chicago is a good hitting team."

In the bottom of the seventh, Sandy went to 3–0 against Billy Williams, the Cubs' best hitter at .315, with thirty-four home runs. "I tried to throw as hard as I could down the pike," Koufax said, "because if Williams walked, Ron Santo (.285, thirty-three home runs) was next up, and he could put it out of the park." He retired Williams to end the inning.

In the eighth, Sandy whiffed right-handers Santo, Ernie Banks (.265), and rookie Byron Browne.

In the ninth, another right-hander, rookie Chris Krug (.201) led off. Koufax struck him out. Righty Joey Amalfitano (.271), pinch-hitting for Don Kessinger, also struck out.

Now Harvey Kuenn, another right-hander, advanced to hit for Hendley. A slap hitter who rarely struck out, Kuenn was a lifetime .303 hitter, although he was nearing the end of his long career and hit only .233 that year. "But I have great respect for Harvey as a hitter," Koo said. His usual strategy against pinch-hitters coming cold off the bench was to fire fastballs, and this is what he did to Kuenn. "I gave him all fastballs, and I gave it everything I had." Kuenn went down swinging on three straight strikes, Sandy's sixth whiff in a row, to cap a perfect night.

He would end the year with 382 strikeouts, another record, and a 26–8 mark. The Dodgers won the pennant by two games and the World Series in seven, as Koufax threw two shutouts against the Twins. But it was the perfect game that secured his place in the Hall of Fame.

Hendley, the forgotten man of the evening, ended with a 4–4 record for the year and a 48–52 record lifetime.

No-Hit Brothers

Bob and Ken Forsch are the only brothers to pitch no-hitters.

Rick Ferrell (.297) almost broke up his kid brother Wes' no-hitter in 1931, but the scorer ruled it an error, and Wes got his claim to fame.

But Alex Gaston (.223) did break up his brother Milt's no-hitter in 1926, whacking the first pitch for a hit with one out in the ninth. Milt thought it was a dirty trick: "Alex never hit a first pitch before in his life."

Ehmke's Lucky Break

Howard Ehmke got a lucky break on his no-hitter in 1923. The opposing pitcher, Slim Harriss, hitting .066, slammed a two-base hit and was called out for not touching first.

Trucks: Five Wins, Two No-Hitters

Virgil "Fire" Trucks won only five games in twenty-four decisions in 1952, yet two of them were no-hitters and one was a two-hitter. He shut out the fifth-place Senators without a hit in a masterpiece that took only one hour and a half. He almost made it two in a row against the fourth-place A's until he gave up a single in the seventh.

Three months later he faced the mighty Yankees and no-hit them.

HOMETOWN ADVANTAGE: SCORERS AND STADIUMS

No one has yet done a study on no-hit official scorers, an unsung part of the no-hit team. There is probably no way ever to know how many no-hitters were made—or broken—by an official scorer's error.

At one time official scorers were appointed by—and paid by—the home team. They now get their pay from the league, but they are still selected from among the writers for hometown papers. Over the years no less than 71 percent of all no-hit games have been pitched at home, a suspiciously high figure.

Partisan scoring is not confined to pitching of course. In 1941 New York scorer Dan Daniel gave Joe DiMaggio two highly suspicious hits in Yankee Stadium to keep his hitting streak alive. Without those two calls, Joe would have been stopped at twenty-nine games, and no one would remember his streak at all.

Let's examine a few of the more notorious cases of questionable official scoring that turned hits conveniently into errors, so that a hurler could enter Valhalla.

1910: Addie Joss

In 1910 Addie Joss lost a chance at a third no-hitter because of what the *Cleveland Press* called a "doubtful" hit by .178-hitting Freddy Parent of the White Sox. That's right, the game was played in Chicago.

Ironically, it was the second time Parent had spoiled a no-hitter for Addie. He had broken up one on Labor Day 1908 as well.

It was a cold April day in 1910 when Parent beat out a slow roller to Cleveland's third baseman Bill Bradley. Most scorers gave Parent the benefit of the doubt and marked "hit" in their box scores. But as Joss piled up more hitless innings, seven Chicago writers and two Cleveland writers sought out the official scorer to demand that he give Joss the benefit of the doubt. Only then did they discover that White Sox owner Charlie Comiskey had been too cheap to pay an official scorer.

The writers agreed among themselves: Bradley had had a better than even chance to catch Parent. (Bradley magnanimously agreed with them later.) So, the writers decided, if no one else got a hit, they would change it to an error.

In the end, they erased Parent's hit and gave Bradley an error and Joss a no-hitter.

1917: Ernie Koob

On another "dark, dank and dismal day," this one in St. Louis in early May 1917, the Browns' Ernie Koob pitched a one-hitter for eight innings, then saw the one-hitter change, like Cinderella's pumpkin, miraculously into a no-hitter.

The second hitter of the game, Buck Weaver (.284), hit a ground ball to second-string second baseman Ernie Johnson, substituting for Del Pratt. Johnson fielded it with his chest, picked it up, cocked his arm, and dropped the ball over his shoulder.

The reporters in the press box set up a lively argument. The Chicago writers insisted it was a hit, and they finally won. The official scorer, J. B. Sheridan of the St. Louis *Globe-Democrat*, marked it a hit.

But as the hitless innings accumulated, Sheridan had second thoughts. He polled the players on the field, and the umps, and all agreed that it had been an error. Sheridan "yielded reluctantly" and changed his call to error. Koob got his no-hitter, but, sniffed the *St. Louis Post-Dispatch*, it was "stained with doubt."

1952: Virgil Trucks

Virgil Trucks' second no-hitter, against the Yankees in 1952, was a one-hitter for six innings before becoming a no-hitter. In the third inning shortstop Johnny Pesky could not get a ground ball out of his glove, and scorer John Drebinger of the *New York Times* ruled it a hit. As the innings piled up, Drebinger began to worry. Finally, in the ninth, he phoned Pesky in the dugout, and John told him, "I just messed it up." Drebinger then erased the hit and marked it an error. This is a rare example of a scorer changing his ruling to help a visiting pitcher.

1959: Sam Jones

In 1959 some 82,000 fans in the Los Angeles Coliseum thought Sam Jones pitched his second no-hitter. An infielder's throw pulled the first baseman off the bag. Ed Sudol had to call him safe, and the scorer called it a hit. "I personally thought it was an error," Sudol told Larry Gerlach, "but I'm an umpire, not a scorer."

1983: Bob Forsch

On another dreary April day in St. Louis, Bob Forsch either did or did not pitch a no-hitter against the pennant-bound Phils.

The Phillies' Garry Maddox (.275) drilled the first pitch in the eighth inning to Cardinals' third baseman Ken Reitz. Reitz lunged to his left, but the ball darted past his glove and into left field, as Reitz slapped his thigh in disgust and the crowd gave a collective groan of disappointment. But the groans turned to cheers when "E-5" flashed on the scoreboard. Said Reitz, "That's the first time I ever got a standing ovation for making an error."

The Phils set up a howl. The ball never touched Reitz's glove, insisted Mike Schmidt, himself a Gold Glove third baseman.

"The ball hit the webbing," insisted Reitz, who had set a record in 1977 for the fewest errors in a season by a third baseman. "I misplayed it. It was an error all the way. We get paid to catch those."

Even if he had caught it, Phils' manager Danny Ozark countered, there was no way Reitz could have caught the speeding Maddox.

"I have absolutely no second thoughts on this call," said scorer Neal Russo of the *Post-Dispatch*, a veteran of fifteen years scoring the games at a stipend of $50 a game. Russo conceded that it was "a somewhat difficult play," but insisted that "the ball went over Reitz's glove."

A half a century earlier, before the "hit" and "error" signs on the scoreboard, Russo might have been persuaded to change his call. But everyone in the park had seen it; it was too late to change.

A Proposal

It is long past time for baseball to scrap its archaic system of letting hometown writers score the games. Even if 95 percent of them are conscientious and competent, there remains that 5 percent who might be suspect. We do not let hometown umpires call the balls and strikes. Surely, with twenty-six one-million-fan teams today, baseball can afford to hire professional scorers, as it hires professional umpires, carefully screened to remove any possible hometown bias, to travel to every game, keeping score and being paid by the league.

NO-HITTERS AND PARKS

The most no-hitters have been thrown, surprisingly, in the most notorious hitters' park in baseball—Fenway Park. Ten hurlers have defied The Wall and stopped the opposition hitless there. Two other supposed hitters' parks, Wrigley Field and the Polo Grounds, each witnessed nine no-hitters.

The best park for no-hitters was Houston's old Colt Stadium, which hosted two in its three-year tenure as home of the National League Colt .45s (now Astros). Today your best bet to see a no-hitter is to buy a ticket to an Oakland, Milwaukee, San Francisco, or Kansas City home game.

The champion no-hit team this century was the Brooklyn Dodgers, with seventeen, in spite of playing in tiny Ebbetts Field.

By contrast, Pittsburgh's Forbes Field, home to the Pirates for sixty-four years, never witnessed a single no-hit game.

Griffith Stadium, Washington, witnessed only two in fifty-one years, even though it was a wide open pitchers' park and home of Walter Johnson. One would think the weak-hitting Senators would have been tempting victims for visiting stars.

Minnesota fans have seen only one in twenty-six years—in the now-defunct Metropolitan Stadium. Atlanta fans bought winning tickets in the no-hitter lottery only once in twenty-three years; that's 1,700 games, not very good odds. Atlanta is a hitters' park, but New York's Shea Stadium, a "pitchers' " park, has seen only two in twenty-three seasons (including two years when the Yanks were co-tenants).

Yankee Stadium has been another bad park, even though again it is considered a pitchers' park and has been home to many excellent Yankees' pitchers. Why some left-hander like Whitey Ford or Ron Guidry could not have used the park's "death valley" in left to help get him a no-hitter is a mystery.

No-Hitters and the Thermometer

Many no-hitters seem to be pitched on cold days in the early spring and fall. Ted Williams did not like to hit in cold weather and blames today's longer schedule as one reason for the drop in batting averages. Dick Cramer, father of the Edge computer, has tabulated all White Sox and A's games and agrees that hitting goes down with the temperature (or pitching goes up with it).

JINX

One of baseball's oldest superstitions is that mentioning a no-hitter will spoil it. So, naturally, teammates whistle and look nonchalant, and opponents go out of their way to shout the forbidden word.

Nolan Ryan said that, during the game (or in his case, games), his teammates will not even talk to him. The longer the game gets, the farther away they sit on the bench, "as if I've got the plague or something." Ryan appreciates it, because he likes to concentrate on the next inning anyway.

What of radio and television commentators?

When Bill Bevens of the Yanks was struggling to preserve his no-hitter in the 1947 World Series, announcer Red Barber (of the Dodgers, of course) made frequent references to it. Bevens lost both the no-hitter and the game.

Mel Allen of the Yankees and Waite Hoyt of the Tigers (a former pitcher himself) never would mention the hoodoo word.

When Don Larsen was working on his game, Bob Wolff used oblique language, such as "Larsen has retired twenty-four straight Dodgers. . . . Is it possible? Can it happen?" On television, the announcers said nothing but let the camera dwell silently on the scoreboard.

During Harvey Haddix's thirteen-inning classic, the Pittsburgh radio announcers kept their listeners informed that a perfect game was taking place.

Vin Scully of the Dodgers agreed with his predecessor, Barber, that he owed it to his listeners to inform them. In fact, if a pitcher went into the ninth with a no-hitter going, Scully taped the ninth, then gave it to the hurler as a souvenir. Sandy Koufax received four such souvenirs, so the jinx did not bother him.

Some pitchers scoff at the jinx. Larsen shocked Mickey Mantle in his Series classic by punching Mick on the arm and saying, "Gee, Mick, think I can do it?"

Jim Palmer had kidded Dave McNally and Mike Cuellar about choking after their no-hitters were broken up in 1969. When he was working on his own a few weeks later, he walked up and down the bench in the eighth inning, holding his fingers around this throat. Then he went out in the ninth and calmly finished the no-hitter.

During Tigers' Jack Morris' no-hit bid in 1984, a White Sox' fan kept yelling that he had better watch out for his no-hitter. Finally, Morris yelled back, "I know I'm working on a no-hitter, and you better keep watching, because I'm going to get it too." And he did.

ONE-HITTERS—WHEN ONE IS BETTER THAN NONE

Bob Feller threw three one-hitters before he pitched his first no-hitter, on opening day 1940. He always insisted he had more stuff in the one-hitters.

What is the difference between a no-hitter and a one-hitter anyway? As Bill James points out, we are inconsistent in the way we penalize and reward pitchers. For instance:

The batter hits a ground ball to the shortstop, who kicks it for an error, and the pitcher goes on to throw a no-hitter.

Another day, the same pitcher, the same ground ball, but a different shortstop: This time he is one step out of position, or one step too slow. He just misses the ball, and it goes through for a base hit. Why do we reward the first effort with a no-hitter and not the second?

Southpaw Bill Burns had two no-hitters spoiled with two out in the ninth. SABR's Al Kermisch says that in 1908 Germany Schaefer (.259) singled to center to spoil one. A year later Burns' old teammate Otis Clymer (.196) entered the game when a regular was tossed out by the ump and singled to spoil Burns' second attempt. Burns won the game anyway, 1–0 over Walter Johnson. He pitched a total of five years and ended with a 27–48 record.

Feller's Twelve One-Hitters

Bob Feller has pitched more low-hit games (no-hitters plus one-hitters) than anyone, including Nolan Ryan. Bob's twelve one-hitters are four more than any other man has pitched:

Name	No-Hit	One-Hit	Total
Bob Feller	3	12	15
Nolan Ryan	5	8	13 (through 1986)
Addie Joss	2	7	9
Hoss Radbourn	1	7	8
Jim Maloney	3	5	8
Mordecai Brown	1	5	6
Grover Alexander	1	5	6
Sandy Koufax	4	2	6
Tom Seaver	1	5	6 (through 1986)
Steve Carlton	0	6	6 (through 1986)
Don Sutton	0	5	5 (through 1986)

Four of Alexander's one-hitters came in one year, 1915, another record.

Feller's fifteen low-hit games were as follows:

Year	Opponent	(Rank)	BA	Broken up by	BA	BB	SO
1938	St. Louis	(7)	.281	B. Sullivan	.277	5	10
1939	Boston‡	(2)	.291*	B. Doerr	.318	6	13
1939	Detroit	(5)	.279	E. Averill	.262	3	13
1940	Chicago	(5)	.278	NO HIT	—	5	8
1940	Philadelphia‡	(7)	.271	D. Siebert	.286	3	13
1941	St. Louis‡	(6)	.266	R. Ferrell	.252	7	6
1945	Detroit	(1)	.256	J. Outlaw	.271	4	7
1946	New York	(3)	.248	NO HIT	—	5	11
1946	Boston	(1)	.271*	B. Doerr	.271	9	9
1946	Chicago‡	(5)	.257	F. Hayes	.233	3	5
1947	St. Louis	(8)	.241	A. Zarilla	.224	1	10
1947	Boston	(3)	.265	J. Pesky	.324	1	4
1951	Detroit	(5)	.265	NO HIT	—	3	5
1952	St. Louis‡	(7)†	.250	B. Young	.247	3	5
1955	Boston	(4)	.264	S. White	.261	1	2

* Led league.

† St. Louis finished seventh but at the time of this game was in first with a 7–1 record.

‡ Away.

Consecutive One-Hitters

The first man to pitch back-to-back one-hitters was one-handed Hugh Daily in 1884. Daily's lower arm had been blown off when a theatrical fireworks device exploded prematurely backstage, where the teenaged Daily worked. He rigged up a pad on the stump so he could knock batted or thrown balls into the air with it and catch them as they came down. Anyway, Daily pitched a no-hitter in 1883, then four one-hitters in 1884, including the two back to back. That year he won 28 and lost 30 while striking out no less than 483 hitters. He must have thrown his good arm out, because he never won more than four games in any year after that.

Tom "Toad" Ramsey did even better two years later, when he won 38 and lost 27 for the fourth-place Louisville club and struck out 496 men. Some authorities say his first one-hitter was actually a no-hitter. Then, pitching with only one day's rest, Ramsey followed that with a twelve-inning one-hitter. He was overpowering in both games, striking out sixteen men in the first and seventeen in the second.

Other double one-hitters were pitched by Charlie Buffinton (1887), Lon Warneke (1934), Mort Cooper (1943), Whitey Ford (1955), and Sam McDowell (1966).

World Series Near Misses

The ultimate frustration must be to miss a no-hitter in the World Series. There have been four:

Year	Pitcher	Opponent	BA	Spoiled by	BA
1906	Ed Ruelbach	White Sox	.230	Jiggs Donohue	.257
1945	Claude Passeau	Tigers	.256	Rudy York	.264
1947	Bill Bevens	Dodgers	.272	Cookie Lavagetto	.261
1967	Jim Lonborg	Cards	.263	Julian Javier	.281

The most poignant and dramatic of those lost no-hitters, of course, belongs to Bill Bevens of the Yankees, who came within one out of a no-hitter in the 1947 World Series against the Dodgers. It would have beaten Larsen to the punch by nine years. But even in failure, Bevens earned immortality.

Once again, the star, Bevens, was the last man you would have bet on to reach immortality. He had had a horrendous record of 7–13 with a club that won the pennant by twelve games.

The Yanks were leading two games to one when Bevens took the mound October 3 and began throwing toward the general direction of home plate. Sometimes he, even threw over home plate. He walked eight men in eight innings and threw one wild pitch.

In the fifth, Bevens walked the last two hitters in the order, Spider Jorgenson (.274) and pitcher Hal Gregg (.265). Eddie Stanky sacrificed, and when Peewee Reese hit a grounder to Phil Rizzuto, Jorgenson scored.

The Bums had a run but still had not gotten any hits. They came close: Joe DiMaggio caught Gene Hermanski's long drive in the fourth, and Tommy Henrich jumped and caught Hermanski's drive to the right-field wall in the eighth.

Then came the ninth, with Bevens leading 2–1. Bruce Edwards (.295) led off with a long fly to left, and again a Yankee outfielder—ex-pitcher Johnny Lindell—had to make a leaping catch. Carl Furillo (.295) walked, and Jorgenson flied out. Only one more out to go.

Pete Reiser (.309) hobbled to the plate on a sore ankle he had injured the day before. Al Gionfriddo, running for Furillo, took off for second as catcher Yogi Berra pegged the ball to the bag. Yogi had been having a bad Series, and once more his throw was late. If it had been on the money, the game would have been over.

Yankees' manager Bucky Harris next ordered an intentional walk to the left-handed Reiser, violating a cardinal rule: never put the winning run on base. It was Bevens' eighth walk of the game, a Series record—the old record by Jack Coombs had lasted since 1910.

Veteran Cookie Lavagetto, came in to bat for Stanky. The veteran Lavagetto, in his last year in the majors, was a .261-hitter who had done mostly pinch-hitting that year. In forty-one games he had been able to knock in only eleven runs.

"I had never faced Bevens before," Lavagetto said. All he knew was that Bevens was a fastball pitcher—and that he was wild. "Fastball pitchers pitch me up and in," Cookie said.

Bevens' first pitch was, surprisingly, in there. Lavagetto swung hard and missed.

Why weren't the Dodgers taking? It was clear that Bevens would probably get behind with a couple of balls and have to groove one. If he walked Cookie, it would bring Peewee Reese, hitting .284, to the plate. Nobody, apparently, was going by the book that day.

Bevens put his second pitch in there, and

Lavagetto hit it. The ball sailed into right, glanced off the short fence there, and both runners scored before Henrich could throw it in. In almost any other park, it would have been an out.

It was Cookie's last major-league hit. The following spring a sore arm ended Bevens' career after only forty victories and thirty-six defeats.

12

Stats

Statistics are like a girl in a bikini. They show a lot, but not everything.

—Toby Harrah

Experts and fans alike will always debate the best way to measure pitchers' effectiveness. Almost everyone agrees that the present systems are imperfect at best and unfair at worst. But no one agrees on how to replace them.

Wins and losses are the most honored yardstick and probably the worst. The pitcher with the pennant winner gets a whopping advantage over one with a tail-ender. The pitcher with a good-hitting club has a big advantage over one with patsy hitters backing him up. Ditto a good defensive club. The pitcher with a good bull pen who can leave his mistakes on base has a big advantage over one whose reliever gives up a base-clearing triple. ("Happiness," Bob Lemon said, "is good friends and a good bull pen.")

In fact, the entire system of allotting wins between starters and relievers was never good, and now, in an era of wholesale relief pitching, it is downright anachronistic. Even

more unlucky is the starter who has no bull pen and is left in the game to absorb a loss instead of being yanked while he is still ahead.

Another favorite indicator is strikeouts. But they are just another means of getting an out, probably the most wasteful means of all.

ERA is a better yardstick. But here again a good bull pen can cut a player's ERA and a bad bull pen can bloat it. A fast infield and outfield can reduce both hits and runs. And the park affects the average: Bill James claims that a 3.65 ERA in Atlanta is equal to a 3.11 in the Astrodome.

"The ERA is ridiculous," says George Sisler, Jr., son of the batting immortal. "It fools a lot of people. It doesn't really tell you anything at all—the type of park, who he's playing for. In many cases it is affected by the manager; a pitcher might work for a manager who tends to go too long with him."

Luis Tiant

PITCHING AVERAGE

In 1968 Cleveland's Cuban dervish, Luis Tiant, was the greatest pitcher of the past eighty-five years by vote of the only electors who count—the enemy hitters, who do their voting with their bats. That year Luis contorted himself into a dozen shapes on the mound, whirled, and uncorked a dozen dancing pitches. In all, 905 opposing hitters walked up to the plate to hit his dazzling deliveries (not counting walks, sacrifices, hit batsmen), and 753 of them trudged back to the dugout, dragging their bats and muttering.

That's a combined batting average of .168—we call it pitching average—and it is the stingiest any man has ever been in this century; the old record, Ed Reulbach's estimated .176 in 1906, was a full eight points higher. Since pitching averages are the mirror of batting averages, that makes Tiant the Rogers Hornsby of pitching (Hornsby has the highest single-season batting average in this century, .424 in 1924).

Even more impressive than Looey's splendid 1968 season was Walter Johnson's 1913 record. Walter held opponents to a .186 batting average, but when adjusted for his home park and for the league batting average that year, it was 45 percent better than average. Tiant's .168 in the Year of the Pitcher was 41 percent better than average. The best PAs of all time, on an adjusted basis, were:

Year	AL Pitcher	PA	% above average
1913	Walter Johnson	.186	45
1949	Tommy Byrne	.183	43
1968	Luis Tiant	.168	41
1956	Herb Score	.186	40
1917	Stan Coveleski	.193	39

Year	NL Pitcher	PA	% above average
1906	Ed Reulbach	.177	44
1980	Mario Soto	.187	44
1962	Bob Gibson	.204	36
1912	Jeff Tesreau	.206	36
1907	Carl Lundgren	.185	33

If Tiant is the Hornsby of pitching, then Nolan Ryan is the Ty Cobb. Ryan has won more PA titles, eight—five in the AL, three in the NL—than any other man, as Cobb won more batting titles. His lifetime PA of .204 is the best of any man since 1901. Sandy Koufax is next at .205. (However, if we adjust for parks, then Ryan won only four titles, and Koufax passes him as first on the lifetime list.)

Since a .200 PA is roughly equivalent to a .400 BA, Ryan and Koufax are amazing. Most pitchers never reach .200 even once in their lives, let alone over a full career.

Ed Reulbach

We have compiled PAs since 1968, including yearly leaders since 1901. Pete Palmer and his computer have corrected these pencil computations where necessary and greatly expanded them. Data before 1911 had to be estimated, since AB (at bats) for pitchers or BFP (batters faced by pitcher) were not compiled then. Pete multiplied innings pitched by about 2.8 and added hits, a formula he arrived at by comparing the result with the league's known offensive at-bats. If all outs were made by batters, the formula would be simply hits plus three times innings pitched; the difference is outs on the bases; this varies slightly from year to year.

Palmer also adjusted each mark to the league average, then adjusted again for the home-park factor (hitters' or pitchers' park). The result is the percent improvement over the average.

Pitching average is not the ultimate rating statistic, but it is another valuable tool at the service of anyone who wants to get a handle on who the toughest pitchers in the game are. While BAs have been religiously calculated and venerated for more than a century, PAs have been ignored, their very existence virtually unsuspected. Pitching averages can tell us a lot that other averages cannot. For instance, if we had had PAs in 1956, we would not have been surprised by Don Larsen's perfect World Series game. He had compiled a fine .204 average in the regular season, second only to Herb Score's .186.

In 1977 Jerry Koosman could have been excused if he had asked plaintively: "What am I doing wrong?" He yielded a PA of .232, fourteen points better than Rick Reuschel and almost the same as John Candelaria—yet they won twenty games and Kooz lost twenty.

Incidentally, only one man has ever won both a pitching average crown and a batting average title. Who was he? Babe Ruth, who posted a .189 PA in 1916 as a hurler for the Boston Red Sox and a .378 BA as a batter for the New York Yankees in 1924.

Lifetime leaders, unadjusted, follow:

LIFETIME PA LEADERS

Pitcher	AB	H	PA
Nolan Ryan*	14,664	2,990	.204
Sandy Koufax†	8,378	1,754	.209
Hoyt Wilhelm†	8,177	1,757	.215
Ed Reulbach†	9,614	2,117	.220
Addie Joss†	8,547	1,895	.222
Tom Seaver*	17,558	3,970	.226
Walter Johnson†	21,788	4,925	.226
Mordecai Brown†	11,736	2,708	.231
Bob Feller†	14,162	3,271	.231
Whitey Ford†	11,786	2,766	.235
Chief Bender†	11,260	2,645	.235
Don Sutton*	17,935	4,233	.236
Eddie Plank†	16,796	3,956	.236
Christy Mathewson†	17,822	4,216	.237
Steve Carlton*	18,872	4,487	.238
Bob Lemon†	10,655	2,559	.240
Gaylord Perry	20,397	4,938	.242
Rube Waddell†	10,890	2,640	.243
Warren Spahn†	19,739	4,830	.245
Grover Alexander†	19,618	4,868	.248
Early Wynn†	17,212	4,291	.249
Cy Young†	27,994	7,092	.253
Lefty Grove†	15,044	3,849	.256

AB = BFP – BB – HB – SH – SF
*Still active; stats through 1985.
†Hall of Fame.

The absolute lowest PAs we have found belong to Burt Hooton, .111 for seventy-two at-bats in 1971, Fernando Valenzuela, .136 for fifty-nine at-bats in 1980, and Andy Messersmith, .154 for eighty-one innings in 1968.

Relief PA and OOBA

Relief pitchers often break .200. But it is unfair to compare a reliever who throws hard for two innings to a starter who must pace himself over seven innings or more.

Best relief pitchers in pitching average (PA) and opponents' on base average (OOBA) lifetime (through 1985) and per season are:

BEST ADJUSTED RELIEF PAs

	Lifetime	
Pitcher	*BA*	*% above average*
Bruce Sutter	.223	19
Tom Hall	.211	17
Rich Gossage	.221	17
Hoyt Wilhelm	.216	15
John Hiller	.229	13

		Season		
Year	*Pitcher*		*BA*	*% above average*
1968	Vicente Romo		.154	54
1977	Rich Gossage		.170	53
1967	Ted Abernathy		.170	52
1983	Tom Niedenfuer		.170	52
1980	Bruce Sutter		.183	52

BEST ADJUSTED RELIEF OOBAs

	Lifetime	
Pitcher	*OOBA*	*% above average*
Bruce Sutter	.282	18
Dick Hall	.283	13
Don Mossi	.299	11
Hoyt Wilhelm	.290	10
Ted Wilks	.304	10

		Season		
Year	*Pitcher*		*OOBA*	*% above average*
1977	Bruce Sutter		.232	51
1964	Dick Hall		.228	42
1944	Joe Berry		.238	37
1981	Rollie Fingers		.236	36
1983	Tom Niedenfuer		.240	36

Now, at last, the baseball establishment has begun to take notice of pitching averages. Seymour Siwoff, using computers, has published complete PAs in *The Elias Baseball Analyst.* He not only gives PAs and OOBAs, he has filled in the heretofore missing dou-

bles and triples given up by every pitcher, so that for the first time a fan can know the slugging average each hurler yields.

Nor is that all. Siwoff has broken down all three averages based on a wondrous array of circumstances. For instance, you can learn that in 1985 Dwight Gooden's PA was .228 against right-handed hitters, .170 against lefties. Some other key PA figures for Gooden that year:

Factor	*PA*
Grass	.199
Turf	.210
Home	.192
Road	.213
Leadoff inning	.233
Bases empty	.190
Runners on	.219
Men on 2nd or 3rd	.226
Ditto, second out	.183
Late-inning pressure	.221

How did managers ever make moves in the old days without this knowledge? How did general managers ever make trades? Wouldn't it be exciting to have the same information on Walter Johnson? Ty Cobb? Babe Ruth? Without it, all we have to go on is biased ignorance.

Consideration of PAs might also make a difference in honoring each league's best pitcher with the Cy Young award. For example, in spite of all his PA crowns, Nolan Ryan has never won the writers' nod as Cy Young winner. By contrast, Steve Carlton has won the writers' vote four times but has earned the hitters' accolade only once. Jim Palmer has three Cy Youngs but no PA titles.

In 1977, while the hitters were down on the firing line facing Ryan's fastball, the writers, safe in their glass-enclosed press boxes, were electing Sparky Lyle the AL Cy Young winner. Lyle, the relief ace of the championship Yanks, had a PA of .257; Ryan's was .195.

In 1983 John Denny of the first-place Phils won five games more than Ryan did with the third-place Astros. His PA of .230 ranked sixth in the league, compared to Ryan's .195. Yet Denny won the Cy Young; Ryan got only a single third-place vote. That same year the AL PA king, Mike Boddicker, did not get even one vote for the Cy Young honor. His teammate, Scott McGregor, got three though his PA of .266 was three points worse than that of the average pitcher in the league.

Those were not even the scribes' worst goofs. In 1982 they had elected Pete Vuckovich, whose PA of .275 was eleven points worse than that of the average pitcher in the league! It made Pete the worst pitcher ever elected a Cy Young winner, replacing Lyle for that dubious honor.

From 1956 through 1986, the writers have named fifty-two Cy Young winners. Only twelve times have they picked the same men the hitters did: Sandy Koufax and Tom Seaver twice, plus Bob Turley, Don Newcombe,

Bob Gibson, Vida Blue, Ron Guidry, Fernando Valenzuela, Roger Clemens, and Mike Scott.

OPPONENTS' ON BASE AVERAGE

What about walks? In some of Nolan Ryan's wildest years, smart batters could go up to the plate without a bat and stand as much chance of getting on with a pass as with a hit. We try to quantify this in the opponents on base average (OOBA), which tallies hits, walks, and hit batters and divides them by total batters faced. (A walk is not equivalent to a hit; although many walks eventually become runs, rarely do walks bat in runs. If you factored in an "opponents' slugging percentage," you would get a closer approximation of the total runs actually allowed.)

The greatest OOBA belongs to Walter Johnson in that magnificent 1913 season. He held opponents to a .216 OOBA, an almost unbelievable 60 percent better than the other AL pitchers that year. Closest to him is Christy Mathewson, who was 39 percent better than average in 1909. The leaders are:

Year	AL Pitcher	OOBA	% above average	Year	NL Pitcher	OOBA	% above average
1913	Walter Johnson	.216	60	1909	Christy Mathewson	.230	39
1908	Addie Joss	.218	38	1965	Juan Marichal	.240	38
1978	Ron Guidry	.250	33	1966	Juan Marichal	.230	38
1968	Luis Tiant	.233	32	1970	Ferguson Jenkins	.265	38
1917	Stan Coveleski	.260	32				

In 1913 Johnson gave up just six hits and one walk every nine innings, for a total of 7.0 runners per game. No one else has ever been so stingy:

Year	AL Pitcher	Runners/Game	Year	NL Pitcher	Runners/Game
1913	Walter Johnson	7.0	1909	Christy Mathewson	7.5
1908	Addie Joss	7.3	1908	Mordecai Brown	7.6
1910	Ed Walsh	7.4	1908	Christy Mathewson	7.6
1905	Cy Young	7.8	1966	Juan Marichal	7.8

Young, Mathewson, and Babe Adams won the most adjusted yearly crowns, five apiece. Best adjusted lifetime OOBA marks through 1985 are:

Pitcher	OOBA	% above average
Walter Johnson	.279	16.3
Addie Joss	.261	15.6
Mordecai Brown	.279	15.4
Grover Alexander	.288	15.4
Urban Shocker	.302	15.3
Christy Mathewson	.276	14.9
Ed Walsh	.264	14.9
Sandy Koufax	.276	14.7
Noodles Hahn	.290	14.7
Tom Seaver	.282	14.6
Ferguson Jenkins	.289	14.5
Cy Young	.288	14.4
Joe Wood	.285	14.1
Carl Hubbell	.291	13.4
Juan Marichal	.278	13.2
Lefty Grove	.311	13.2
Babe Adams	.284	13.2
Deacon Phillippe	.287	12.9
Tiny Bonham	.289	12.8
Don Newcombe	.299	12.5
Harry Brecheen	.298	12.0
Gary Nolan	.287	12.0
Dizzy Dean	.298	11.9
Bert Blyleven	.298	11.7

Ryan's lifetime OOBA is .315, which is not too bad actually, better than Bob Feller's, Early Wynn's, and Bob Lemon's.

ERAs AND NERAs

A strong case can be made that the best single-season pitching performance of this century was Walter Johnson's superb 1913 season, when he won 36 games, over 346 innings, and held opponents to a 1.14 ERA. In their book, *The Hidden Game of Baseball*, John Thorn and Pete Palmer make that case.

They report that Johnson's ERA was 157 percent better than the league ERA (LERA) of 2.93, and after adjustment for the hitters' park he pitched in,* was 185 percent better, or almost three times as good! (It would have been even better if he had not goofed off in the final game of the season, a meaningless contest in which he threw soft pitches to let the other team have some fun. That bit of skylarking cost five points on his final ERA for the year.)

A year after Johnson's super season, Hub Leonard of the Red Sox scored an all-time low ERA of 0.96 which, when adjusted for his home park, was 184 percent better than the LERA; however, he pitched 121 fewer innings than Johnson and won 17 fewer games.

In 1906 the Cubs' Mordecai Brown had a 1.04 ERA, 153 percent over his league and, adjusted for a home park that favored hitters, 171 percent better. This is the third-best mark of the century.

Palmer and Thorn call this statistic—an ERA normalized to the league average and adjusted for home-park impact—the normalized, adjusted ERA, or NERA. In *The Hidden Game*, they posited a baseline of 100 (actually 1.00, but they dropped the decimal for convenience) for league average performance; thus they would state Walter Johnson's 185 percent superiority to the league as a NERA of 285 (2.85 times as good as the average). But be-

*As stated earlier, the computation of the park factor itself is complex, but suffice it to say that the key ingredient is the number of runs scored at the park in question by the visiting teams. If the park features 11 percent more scoring than the average park (defined as having a park factor of 1.00), then its park factor might be 1.11. This was in fact the park factor for Washington's National Park in 1913, when Walter Johnson had a 1.14 ERA compared to the league's 2.93. Dividing the latter by the former and multiplying the result (2.57) by the park factor, we get a normalized adjusted ERA for Johnson of 2.85. This is understood as 185 percent better than the average pitcher in the league, who would, in 1913, have had an actual ERA of 2.93 while pitching for a team whose home-park factor was 1.00.

cause both "185" and "285" are unfamiliar expressions of pitching prowess, we can express these in terms of the time-honored and thus more comfortable ERA.

Let's assume that from 1901 through 1986 the average ERA of all pitchers in all decades and in all parks was 3.66, which is indeed the norm for all major-league play since 1876. If 1913 had been that model year when the LERA was in fact 3.66 (indeed, if any year were chosen, it would have exactly the same LERA of 3.66), then Walter Johnson's superiority—185 percent better than the league average, or a NERA of 285—could have been expressed as an ERA of 1.28.* This normalized, adjusted earned run average—or NERA—has the same meaning as Palmer's NERA of 285, *but is expressed as an ERA rather than as a ratio.* Thus Hub Leonard's performance of 1914, when he had an actual ERA of 0.96, becomes a NERA of 1.29, the second best ever, and Brown's performance of 1906, when he had an actual ERA of 1.04, becomes a NERA of 1.35, the third best ever.

In modern times the best NERA was scored by Bob Gibson in 1968. His 1.12 was one of the lowest recorded, although he did it in the Year of the Pitcher, when the rules of the game had conspired with the evolutionary trend toward pitcher dominance to penalize hitters more than ever before. He was also fortunate to pitch in a park that slightly favored pitchers. Still, Gibson was 153 percent better than the average pitcher that year, and fourth place on the all-time single season NERA list would belong to him, with 1.45.

Of course we cannot really compare Johnson, Leonard, and Brown with Gibson. The competitive level is vastly higher today, given the population explosion and the generally superior athletes playing. The amazing improvement in Olympic records since, say, 1912, makes that clear. Walter Johnson could no more dominate today's major-league hitters than Jim Thorpe could defeat Carl Lewis in the long jump. Most of the high baseball percentages were achieved in the early years of the century, when competition was not so intense. The erosion of the percentages over the years does not mean pitchers have become worse than their fathers and grandfathers; it means the competitive level now is just too high for anyone to achieve the actual ERAs of such forgettable pitchers as Carl Lundgren or Jack Taylor, and too high for all but a handful—Dwight Gooden, Ron Guidry, Bob Gibson, and Whitey Ford—to dominate the league as thoroughly as Johnson, Alexander, or Mathewson once did.

But relating all ERAs to one standard—the 3.66 norm for all major-league play—is at least a step toward rationalizing the hodgepodge of annual ERAs that are virtually unrelated to those of decades ago and have long been misleading fans and historians. Microscopic actual ERAs achieved in the dead ball era are elevated; overblown ERAs attained in a hitters' period like the 1930s are deflated. Thus we see, for example, that Lefty Grove's 2.81 ERA of 1936 was a *better* pitching performance than Mordecai Brown's 1.47 ERA of 1908: Grove's adjusted ERA was 79 percent better than the league average that year and is expressed as an NERA of 2.04, while Brown's adjusted ERA was 78 percent better than his league's average and is expressed as an NERA of 2.06.

Using NERA, we can see ERAs in a more realistic perspective. The top ten NERA leaders in each league, based on an all-time league ERA of 3.66, follow:

*LERA of 3.66 divided by ERA of *x* equals NERA of 285; thus *x* equals 1.28, what Johnson's ERA would have been in a model year.

NERA LEADERS, TOP TEN IN EACH LEAGUE

American League

Year	Pitcher	ERA	LERA	% above avg.	NERA
1913	Walter Johnson	1.14	2.93	185	1.28
1914	Hub Leonard	0.96	2.73	184	1.29
1912	Walter Johnson	1.39	3.34	139	1.53
1918	Walter Johnson	1.27	2.77	136	1.55
1978	Ron Guidry	1.74	3.77	121	1.66
1919	Walter Johnson	1.49	3.21	119	1.67
1931	Lefty Grove	2.06	4.38	114	1.71
1908	Addie Joss	1.16	2.39	110	1.74
1958	Whitey Ford	2.01	3.77	104	1.79
1901	Cy Young	2.15	3.66	103	1.80

National League

Year	Pitcher	ERA	LERA	% above avg.	NERA
1906	Mordecai Brown	1.04	2.63	171	1.35
1968	Bob Gibson	1.12	2.99	153	1.45
1909	C. Mathewson	1.14	2.59	141	1.52
1915	G. Alexander	1.22	2.75	137	1.54
1985	Dwight Gooden	1.53	3.59	135	1.56
1907	Jack Pfiester	1.15	2.46	130	1.59
1905	C. Mathewson	1.27	2.99	129	1.60
1907	Carl Lundgren	1.17	2.46	126	1.62
1902	Jack Taylor	1.33	2.78	116	1.69
1905	Ed Reulbach	1.42	2.99	102	1.81

Johnson dominates the list, with four of the top six NERAs in the American League. Yet, magnificent as Johnson's NERA performances are, Sir Walter is not the finest NERA pitcher of all time. That honor belongs to Lefty Grove, whose career fell almost entirely inside the two worst lively ball decades ever, the 1920s and 1930s. Hits were never cheaper and ERAs never higher. But this masks Grove's greatness. On a park-adjusted NERA basis, Lefty won ten individual NERA titles, twice as many as Johnson. (Dazzy Vance is third, with four titles.)

And on a lifetime basis, Grove and Johnson are almost tied, each 46 percent better than the average pitcher over his career (Johnson, 1907–27; Grove, 1925–41). Grove just edges Johnson, 2.51 to 2.52, with reliever Hoyt Wilhelm two thousandths of a run behind. (It is a mistake to compare relievers to starters, as mentioned earlier, but we include Wilhelm here as a matter of interest.)

The best NERA starters lifetime are:

AL Pitcher	% above average	NERA	NL Pitcher	% above average	NERA
Lefty Grove	46	2.51	Mordecai Brown	43	2.56
Walter Johnson	46	2.52	Grover Alexander	36	2.69
Ed Walsh	44	2.54	Christy Mathewson	36	2.69
Addie Joss	41	2.60	Harry Brecheen	33	2.75
Cy Young	36	2.69	Sandy Koufax	32	2.77
Rube Waddell	33	2.75	Dizzy Dean	31	2.79
Whitey Ford	32	2.77	Carl Hubbell	31	2.79
Hal Newhouser	32	2.77	Tom Seaver*	29	2.84
Ron Guidry*	28	2.86	Bob Gibson	29	2.84
Stan Coveleski	28	2.86	Ed Reulbach	26	2.90

*Still active; figures compiled through 1986.

Pete Palmer issues one caveat with regard to the NERA, the park-adjustment factor, which is not constant but varies from year to year. It is based on a comparison of the batting averages for visiting teams compared to the league BA overall. But of course this changes as the home pitchers change. For example, historically, Fenway Park has been considered a hitters' park. "But something has happened to Fenway in the last few years," Palmer says—it has now become a pitchers' park. Of course, the Green Monster has not changed, but the Red Sox' pitchers have. In effect, the pitchers being rated have an influence over the park factor used in rating them. Palmer thinks that a three-year moving average—an average of the last three years, moving up each year to include the most recent date while dropping the oldest—would remove this danger. But meanwhile, his park factor is the best way yet devised to correct the bias of the unadjusted data that often penalizes some pitchers while it helps others.

RUNS SAVED

Using the NERA concept, Palmer can calculate how many earned runs Johnson probably saved the Senators, compared to what an average pitcher probably would have given up per nine innings if he had pitched as many innings as Johnson did, and he had pitched for Washington. This stat gives credit for effectiveness *and* durability. A pitcher with an ERA of 2.50 over 125 innings will have saved his team only half the runs of a pitcher with an ERA of 2.50 over 250 innings.

Most of us may be willing to take Pete's say-so, but for statisticians, the formula is:

$$LERA \times park\ factor \times (IP \div 9)$$
$$or$$
$$2.93 \times 1.11 \times (346 \div 9) = 125,$$

which is the earned runs a league average pitcher would be expected to yield if his home park was Washington. But Johnson gave up only 44, so

$$125 - 44 = 81$$

In other words, Johnson saved the Senators eighty-one earned runs that year. This is the most, of course, that any man has saved a team in a single season. The next best: Johnson's seventy-nine of the year before. The leaders:

RUNS SAVED LEADERS

Year	AL Pitcher	Runs Saved
1913	Walter Johnson	81
1912	Walter Johnson	79
1931	Lefty Grove	75
1944	Dizzy Trout	72
1901	Cy Young	69
1902	Cy Young	67
1932	Lefty Grove	67
1935	Lefty Grove	67
1973	Bert Blyleven	65
1971	Vida Blue	64
1978	Ron Guidry	64

MOST TITLES, AMERICAN LEAGUE

Pitcher	No. of Titles
Lefty Grove	7
Walter Johnson	6
Cy Young	3
Hal Newhouser	3

RUNS SAVED LEADERS

Year	NL Pitcher	Runs Saved
1915	Grover Alexander	70
1934	Dizzy Dean	69
1923	Dolph Luque	66
1924	Dazzy Vance	62
1930	Dazzy Vance	62
1905	Christy Mathewson	61
1939	Bucky Walters	61
1965	Juan Marichal	60
1966	Sandy Koufax	60

MOST TITLES, NATIONAL LEAGUE

Pitcher	No. of Titles
Grover Alexander	5
Christy Mathewson	3
Dazzy Vance	3
Carl Hubbell	3
Warren Spahn	3
Don Drysdale	3
Bob Gibson	3
Phil Niekro	3
Steve Carlton	3

WINS ABOVE LEAGUE, WAL

"The secret of success as a pitcher lies in getting a job with the Yankees," Waite Hoyt once said. How many extra games would Johnson's eighty-one runs saved win?

Pete Palmer says a pitcher gives up about ten runs for every game he wins (the actual figure varies from year to year, from nine to eleven). In 1913 the league required about nine extra runs—runs in excess of runs allowed—for every victory.

Thus Johnson gave the Senators nine victories more than Joe Average (a pitcher of league-average ability) would have won for them over the same number of innings.

We can call these nine victories wins above league, or WAL.

The best WAL pitchers in this century were:

Year	AL Pitcher	WAL
1913	Walter Johnson	9
1912	Walter Johnson	8
1944	Dizzy Trout	8
1918	Walter Johnson	7
1931	Lefty Grove	7
1945	Hal Newhouser	7
1971	Vida Blue	7
1971	Wilbur Wood	7
1973	Bert Blyleven	7
1978	Ron Guidry	7

Year	NL Pitcher	WAL
1915	Grover Alexander	8
1934	Dizzy Dean	7
1968	Bob Gibson	7

For a variety of reasons, including his relatively few innings pitched, Hub Lenord's heroic NERA of 1914 translated into only five wins above league.

Thanks to Johnson's exertions in 1913, Washington finished in second place with a 90–64, .584 record. Without Johnson, they would have had an 81–73, .526 record and a fourth-place finish—provided that they found an average pitcher who could give them 346 innings!

The biggest inequity in present won–lost records is that some pitchers hurl for pennant winners, while others toil for tail-enders. How would they do if they all pitched for the same team, a mythical average team playing exactly .500 ball. Call this mythical

team the Grays. An average pitcher on the Grays would win half his decisions and lose half. How would Johnson do on the Grays?

Johnson had forty-three decisions in 1913 (36–7), so if he were an average guy on an average team, he would probably have finished with a 22–22 record, or 21–21. Give the odd game to his win column and make him 22–21. But Johnson's nine WALs made him a far above average pitcher. So we add his WALs to his wins and subtract them from his losses, thus:

$$
\begin{array}{cc}
W & L \\
22 & 21 \\
+\ 9 & -\ 9 \\
\hline
31 & 12
\end{array}
$$

Using the same logic, we can pretend that all the best WAL pitchers in this century played on the Grays. This eliminates the effects of a good or bad team and reveals the following:

Year	Pitcher	WAL	Actual W–L	(Team Rank)	Grays W–L
1913	Walter Johnson	9	36–7	(2)	31–12
1912	Walter Johnson	8	33–12	(2)	31–14
1915	Grover Alexander	8	31–10	(1)	29–12
1944	Dizzy Trout	8	27–14	(2)	29–12
1918	Walter Johnson	7	23–13	(6)	25–11
1931	Lefty Grove	7	31–4	(1)	25–10
1934	Dizzy Dean	7	29–7	(1)	25–11
1945	Hal Newhouser	7	25–9	(1)	24–10
1968	Bob Gibson	7	22–9	(1)	23–8
1971	Vida Blue	7	24–8	(1)	23–9
1971	Wilbur Wood	7	22–13	(2)	25–10
1973	Bert Blyleven	7	20–17	(3)	26–11
1978	Ron Guidry	7	25–3	(1)	21–7

Most of the WAL-adjusted W–L records are expected. A pitcher with a good team (Dean in 1934) will lose some victories when he is "traded" to the average Grays, and a pitcher on a weak team (Blyleven in 1973) will gain some. But notice Dizzy Trout and

Bob Gibson: They do better on the Grays than they did on the *champion* Detroit Tigers and St. Louis Cards. Palmer points out that the explanation lies in their real W–L records. Both Trout and Gibson won less in real life than they should have. It can work the other way too. In 1972 Steve Carlton had a 27–10 mark with the last-place Phils. That works out to six WALs, but on the Grays, theoretically a better club than the Phils were, Steve would be only 25–12. Why? Palmer shrugs. In the real world, he says, unlike the mathematical one, balls take funny bounces.

Thirty Wins

It is almost impossible to win thirty games on the Grays. Most of the thirty-game win-ners in this century owed their success to their teams, not the other way around. In all, eighteen men have won thirty games or more since 1901. If they had all played with the Grays, only four would be left: Walter Johnson twice, Jack Chesbro, Joe Mc-Ginnity, and Ed Walsh.

If Denny McLain had pitched on the Grays instead of on the Tigers, he would have won twenty-three games, not thirty-one. Here's how they all fare on the Grays:

Year	NL Pitcher	Actual W–L	(Team Rank)	WAL	Grays W–L
1903	Joe McGinnity	31–20	(2)	5	31–20
1903	Christy Mathewson	30–13	(2)	5	27–15
1904	Joe McGinnity	35–8	(1)	6	28–15
1904	Christy Mathewson	33–12	(1)	3	26–19
1905	Christy Mathewson	31–8	(1)	6	26–13
1908	Christy Mathewson	37–11	(2)	4	28–20
1915	Grover Alexander	31–10	(1)	8	29–12
1916	Grover Alexander	33–12	(2)	4	27–18
1917	Grover Alexander	30–13	(2)	4	26–17
1934	Dizzy Dean	29–7	(1)	7	25–11

Year	AL Pitcher	Actual W–L	(Team Rank)	WAL	Grays W–L
1901	Cy Young	33–10	(2)	6	29–14
1902	Cy Young	32–11	(3)	6	28–15
1904	Jack Chesbro	41–12	(2)	6	33–20
1908	Ed Walsh	40–15	(3)	3	31–24
1910	Jack Coombs	31–9	(1)	5	25–15
1912	Walter Johnson	33–12	(2)	8	31–14
1912	Joe Wood	34–5	(1)	6	26–13
1913	Walter Johnson	36–7	(2)	9	31–12
1920	Jim Bagby	31–12	(1)	4	26–15
1931	Lefty Grove	31–4	(1)	7	25–10
1968	Denny McLain	31–6	(1)	4	23–14

The all-time leader in WAL is Cy Young.

THE BEST STAFF—EVER

We can use the same NERA technique to measure teams. Which had the best pitching staff of all time?

Connie Mack's Philadelphia A's of 1910–14—Bender, Plank, Coombs?

The Chicago Cubs of that same era—Brown, Reulbach, Pfiester, Overall?

The Philadelphia A's of 1929–31—Grove, Rommel, Earnshaw?

The Cleveland Indians of the 1950s—Lemon, Wynn, Feller, Garcia, Score?

The New York Yankees of the 1950s—Turley, Ford, Reynolds?

The Baltimore Orioles of the 1960s and 1970s—Palmer, McNally, Cuellar?

Thorn and Palmer say none of the above.

The best staff, at least for a single year, they say, played for the 1926 Philadelphia Athletics: Lefty Grove, George Earnshaw, Rube Walberg, and Jack Quinn. Still rebuilding from the disastrous 1915 break-up, the A's finished only third that year and finished next to last in team batting. In fact, the club lost fourteen games that a team of even average hitters would have won. On hitting alone—with an average pitching staff—the A's deserved to finish sixth.

But the hurlers were in super form; they gave the A's twenty-four victories more than an average staff that year would have been expected to win. The average American League pitcher that year posted a 4.02 ERA. But the A's gave up only 3.00, 34 percent better than average. After allowing for their ball park—Shibe Park was the best hitters'

park in the league that year—the Philadelphia hurlers were actually 54 percent better than average.

Thorn and Palmer say the A's hurlers saved their club a whopping 243 runs compared to an average staff, and that translates into an estimated 24 games, which is why the A's finished third instead of sixth.

Thorn and Palmer identified the 1957 Dodgers as the second-best staff of all time. Johnny Podres, Don Drysdale, Don Newcombe, and the others also pitched in the worst pitchers' park in the league, Ebbets Field. Even so, Podres led the league in ERA, even without a park adjustment, with Drysdale close behind. The Brooklyn pitchers probably won nineteen extra games on the strength of pitching alone and lifted the weak Brooklyn bats to third.

We present below the list of yearly team title holders, along with each staff's probable extra pitching victories and the names of the top four starters. We also give the name of the manager and catcher who handled each staff.

NL NERA TITLES (ERA, PARK ADJUSTED)

Year	Team	Rank	WAL	Manager	Catcher	Staff
1901	Boston	(5)	11	Selee	Kittridge	*Willis,* Dinneen, Pittinger, Nichols
1902	Chicago	(5)	10	Selee	Kling	*J. Taylor,* Lundgren, Menefee, Williams
1903	Pittsburgh	(1)	7	Clarke	Phelps	*Leever,* Phillippe, Doheny, Kennedy
1904	New York	(1)	11	McGraw	Warner	*McGinnity,* Mathewson, D. Taylor, Wiltse
1905	Chicago	(3)	14	*Selee/* Chance	Kling	Reulbach, Wicker, Brown, Lundgren
1906	Chicago	(1)	18	Chance	Kling	*Brown,* Pfiester, Reulbach, Lundgren
1907	Chicago	(1)	16	Chance	Kling	*Pfiester,* Lundgren, Brownv, Reulbach
1908	Chicago	(1)	9	Chance	Kling	*Brown,* Overall, Pfiester, Reulbach

Year	Team	Rank	WAL	Manager	Catcher	Staff
1909	Chicago	(2)	15	Chance	Archer	Brown, Overall, Reulbach, Pfiester
1910	Pittsburgh	(3)	8	Clarke	Gibson	Adams, Leifield, Cammitz, White
1911	New York	(1)	12	McGraw	Meyers	*Mathewson,* Marquard, Crandall, Ames
1912	New York	(1)	15	McGraw	Meyers	*Tesreau,* Mathewson, Ames, Marquard
1913	New York	(1)	9	McGraw	Meyers	Mathewson, Tesreau, Demaree, Marquard
1914	St. Louis	(3)	11	Huggins	Snyder	*Doak,* Sallee, Perritt, Grimes
1915	Philadelphia	(1)	12	Moran	Killefer	*Alexander,* Mayer, Rixey, Chalmers
1916	Brooklyn	(1)	9	Robinson	Meyers	*Marquard,* Pfeffer, Cheney, Dell
1917	Philadelphia	(2)	7	Moran	Killefer	Alexander, Rixey, Oeschger, Mayer
1918	Chicago	(1)	11	Mitchell	Killefer	*Vaughn,* Tyler, Douglas, Hendrix
1919	Chicago	(3)	11	Mitchell	Killefer	*Alexander,* Vaughn, Douglas, Martin
1920	Brooklyn	(1)	15	Robinson	Miller	Grimes, Cadore, Mamaux, Pfeffer
1921	Pittsburgh	(2)	11	Gibson	Schmidt	*Adams,* Glazner, Cooper, Hamilton
1922	New York	(1)	10	McGraw	Snyder	Douglas, Ryan, Nehf, J. Barnes
1923	Cincinnati	(2)	8	Moran	Hargrave	Luque, Rixey, Donohue, Benton
1924	Cincinnati	(4)	13	Hendrix	Hargrave	Rixey, Benton, Mays, Luque
1925	Cincinnati	(3)	10	Hendrix	Hargrave	*Luque,* Rixcy, Donohue, Benton
1926	Chicago	(4)	13	McCarthy	Harmett	Root, Bush, Kaufmann, Jones
1927	Brooklyn	(6)	8	Robinson	DeBerry	Vance, Petty, Elliott, McWeeny
1928	St. Louis	(1)	13	McKechnie	J. Wilson	Sherdel, Haines, Mitchell, Alexander
1929	New York	(3)	13	McGraw	Hogan	*Walker,* Hubbcll, Fitzsimmons, Benton
1930	Brooklyn	(4)	10	Robinson	Lopez	Vance, Elliott, Phelps, Clarke
1931	St. Louis	(1)	10	Street	J. Wilson	S. Johnson, Hallahan, Derringer, Rhem
1932	Chicago	(1)	6	*Hornsby/* Grimm	Hartnett	*Warneke,* Bush, Malone, Root
1933	New York	(1)	9	Terry	G. Mancuso	*Hubbell,* Schumacher, Fitzsimmons, Parmelee
1934	St. Louis	(1)	14	Frisch	Davis	*D. Dean,* Walker, P. Dean, Carleton

Year	Team	Rank	WAL	Manager	Catcher	Staff
1935	Pittsburgh	(4)	14	*Traynor*	Padden	*Blanton,* Swift, Hoyt, Weaver
1936	New York	(1)	6	Terry	G. Mancuso	*Hubbell,* Gables, Schumacher, Smith
1937	Pittsburgh	(3)	6	Traynor	Todd	Bauers, Brandt, Blanton, Swift
1938	Chicago	(1)	11	*Grimm/* Hartnett	Hartnett	*Lee,* Root, Bryant, French
1939	Cincinnati	(1)	12	McKechnie	Lombardi	*Walters,* Thompson, Derringer, Moore
1940	Brooklyn	(2)	13	Durocher	Phelps	Hamlin, Tamulis, Wyatt, Casey
1941	St. Louis	(2)	12	Southworth	G. Mancuco	White, Lanier, Warneke, Cooper
1942	St. Louis	(1)	12	Southworth	Cooper	*Cooper,* Beazley, Lanier, Gumbert
1943	St. Louis	(1)	14	Southworth	Cooper	*Lanier,* Cooper, Krist, Brecheen
1944	St. Louis	(1)	13	Southworth	Cooper	Cooper, Lanier, Wilks, Brecheen
1945	Chicago	(1)	12	Grimm	Livingston	*Prim,* Passeau, Wyse, Borowy
1946	St. Louis	(1)	11	Dyer	Garagiola	*Pollet,* Brecheen, Dickson, Brazle
1947	St. Louis	(2)	11	Dyer	Rice	*Brazle,* Dickson, Brecheen, Munger
1948*	Boston	(1)	9	Southworth	Masi	Sain, Voiselle, Spahn, Bickford
	Brooklyn	(3)	10	Durocher/ Shotton	Campanella	Roe Barney, Branca, Hatten
1949	St. Louis	(2)	13	Dyer	Rice	Staley, Pollet, Brazle, Brecheen
1950	Philadelphia	(1)	7	Sawyer	Seminick	Konstanty, Roberts, Simmons, Miller
1951	New York	(1)	6	Durocher	Westrum	Maglie, Jansen, Koslo, Hearn
1952	Philadelphia	(4)	10	Sawyer/ O'Neil	Burgess	Roberts, Drews, Simmons, Meyer
1953	Milwaukee	(2)	11	Grimm	Crandall	*Spahn,* Buhl, Antonelli, Burdette
1954	New York	(1)	11	Durocher	Westrum	*Antonelli,* Gomez, Maglie, Liddle
1955	Brooklyn	(1)	6	Alston	Campanella	Newcombe, Labine, Erskine, Podres
1956	Milwaukee	(2)	9	Grimm/ Haney	Crandall	*Burdette, Spahn, Conley, Buhl*
1957	Brooklyn	(3)	19	Alston	Campanella	*Podres,* Drysdale, Newcombe, McDevitt
1958	Cincinnati	(4)	8	*Tebbetts/* Dykes	Bailey	Haddix, Purkey, Nuxhall, Lawrence
1959	Los Angeles	(1)	5	Alston	Roseboro	Craig, Drysdale, Koufax, Podres
1960	Los Angeles	(4)	15	Alston	Roseboro	Drysdale, Williams, Podres, Koufax

Year	Team	Rank	WAL	Manager	Catcher	Staff
1961*	St. Louis	(5)	9	Hemus/ *Keane*	Schaffer	Simmons, Gibson, Sadecki, Jackson
	Cincinnati	(1)	9	Hutchinson	Zimmerman	O'Toole, Joy, Purkey, Hunt
1962	St. Louis	(6)	15	Keane	Oliver	Gibson, Broglio, Simmons, Jackson
1963	Chicago	(7)	9	Kennedy	Bertell	Ellsworth, Jackson, Buhl, Hobbie
1964*	St. Louis	(1)	11	Keane	McCarver	Gibson, Craig, Simmons, Sadecki
	Cincinnati	(2)	11	*Hutchinson/* Sisler	Edwards	O'Toole, Maloney, Purkey, Jay
1965	San Francisco	(2)	13	Franks	Haller	Marichal, Shaw, Herbel
1966	Los Angeles	(1)	13	Alston	Roseboro	*Koufax,* Sutton, Osteen, Drysdale
1967	St. Louis	(1)	13	Schoendienst	McCarver	Briles, Hughes, Gibson, Carlton
1968	New York	(9)	11	Hodges	Grote	Koosman, Seaver, Selma, Cardwell
1969	St. Louis	(4)	14	Schoendienst	McCarver	*Carlton,* Gibson, Briles, Washburn
	San Francisco	(2)	4	King	Dietz	Marichal, G. Perry, McCormick, Bolin
1970	Chicago	(2)	17	Durocher	Hundley	Holtzman, Jenkins, Hands, Pappas
	Cincinnati	(1)	5	Anderson	Bench	Simpson, Nolan, McGlothin, Merritt
1971	New York	(3)	6	Hodges	Grote	*Seaver,* Sadecki, Koosman, Gentry
	Los Angeles	(2)	4	Alston	Sims	Sutton, Downing, Osteen, Singer
	San Diego	(6)	4	Gomez	Barton	Roberts, Kirby, Arlin, Phoebus
1972	Pittsburgh	(1)	11	Virden	Sanguillen	Blass, Ellis, Moose, Briles
	Los Angeles	(3)	5	Alston	Cannizzaro	Sutton, Osteen, John, Downing
1973	Los Angeles	(2)	11	Alston	Ferguson	Sutton, Messersmith, John, Osteen
	Chicago	(5)	7	Lockman	Hundley	Reuschel, Hooton, Bonham, Jenkins
1974	Atlanta	(3)	14	*Mathews/* King	Oates	Capra, P. Niekro, Morton, Reed
	New York	(2)	6	Berra	Grote	Matlack, Seaver, Koosman, Parker
1975	Los Angeles	(2)	5	Alston	Yeager	Messersmith, Hooton, Sutton, Rau
	Pittsburgh	(1)	9	Murtagh	Sanguillen	Reuss, Rooker, Kison, Ellis
1976	Los Angeles	(2)	9	Alston	Yeager	Rau, Sutton, John, Rhoden
	Philadelphia	(1)	7	Ozark	Boone	Lonborg, Carlton, Kaat, Christenson

Year	Team	Rank	WAL	Manager	Catcher	Staff
1977	Los Angeles	(1)	10	Lasorda	Yeager	Hooton, John, Sutton, Rau
	Chicago	(4)	7	Franks	Mitterwald	Reuschel, Bonham, Krukow, Burris
1978	Los Angeles	(1)	8	Lasorda	Yeager	Hooton, Rau, John, Sutton
	Philadelphia	(1)	4	Ozark	Boone	Carlton, Ruthven, Christenson, Lerch
	Pittsburgh	(2)	4	Tanner	Ott	Blyleven, Candelaria, Robinson, Rooker
1979	Pittsburgh	(1)	10	Tanner	Ott	Kison, Candelaria, Blyleven, Robinson
	Atlanta	(6)	1	Cox	Benedict	P. Niekro, Matula, Solomon, Garber
1980	Philadelphia	(1)	8	Greene	Boone	*Carlton,* Ruthven, Walk, Lerch
	Houston	(1)	4	Virdon	Ashby	Ruhle, K. Forsch, Ryan, J. Niekro
1981	Los Angeles	(2)	5	Lasorda	Scioscia	
	San Francisco	(4)	5	Robinson	May	Blue, Alexander, Griffin, Whitson
	St. Louis	(1)†	8	Herzog	Porter	Sutter, B. Forsch, Sorensen, Martin
1982	Montreal	(3)	14	Fanning	Carter	*Rogers,* Lea, Sanderson, Gullickson
	Atlanta	(1)	2	Torre	Benedict	P. Niekro, Camp, Mahler, Walk
	Los Angeles	(2)	2	Lasorda	Scioscia	Valenzuela, Reuss, Welch, Stewart
1983	Los Angeles	(1)	10	Lasorda	Yeager	Welch, Pena, Reuss, Valenzuela
	Pittsburgh	(2)	5	Tanner	Peña	Rhoden, Candelaria, McWilliams, Tunnell
	Philadelphia	(1)	5	Owens	Virgil	Koosman, Denny, Carlton, Hudson
1984	Los Angeles	(4)	12	Lasorda	Scioscia	*Pena,* Hershiser, Honeycutt, Valenzuela
	New York	(2)	3	Johnson	Carter	*Gooden,* Fernandez, Darling, Lynch
1985	San Diego	(4)	6	Williams	Kennedy	Dravecky, Show, Hawkins, Hoyt
1986	Houston	(1)	13	Lanier	Ashby	*Scott,* Knepper, Ryan, Deshaies
	St. Louis	(3)	8	Herzog	Hurdle	Cox, Tudor, Forsch, Mathews

Note: Managers in *italics* managed the most games of the two listed.
Pitchers in *italics* are the individual NERA winners.
NL East and West leaders are listed from 1969 to 1985.
*Tie for best park adjusted pitching staff
†In 1981, all six NL East staffs had net negative WALs. St. Louis was – 0.20.

AL NERA TITLES (ERA, PARK ADJUSTED)

Year	Team	Rank	Pitchers' WAL	Manager	Catcher	Staff
1901	Detroit	(3)	8	Stallings	Beulow	Yeager, Miller, Siever, Cronin
1902	Boston	(3)	9	Collins	Criger	Young, Dinneen, Winter, Sparks
1903	Boston	(1)	11	Collins	Criger	*Young,* Dinneen, Hughes, Winter
1904	Boston	(1)	9	Collins	Criger	Young, Tannehill, Dinneen, Gibson
1905	Philadelphia	(1)	10	Mack	Schreckengost	*Waddell,* Oakley, Plank, Henley
1906	Cleveland	(3)	10	Lajoie	Bemis	Joss, Rhoades, Hess, Bernhard
1907	Chicago	(3)	5	Jones	Sullivan	*Walsh,* White, Smith, Altrock
1908	Cleveland	(2)	8	Lajoie	Clarke	*Joss,* Chech, Rhoades, Berger
1909	Philadelphia	(2)	12	Mack	Thomas	*Krause,* Morgan, Bender, Plank
1910	Philadelphia	(1)	12	Mack	Lapp	*Coombs,* Morgan, Bender, Plank
1911	Chicago	(4)	9	Duffy	Sullivan	Walsh, Scott, White, Lange
1912*	Washington	(2)	9	Griffith	Henry	*Johnson,* Groom, Hughes, Cashion
	Boston	(1)	10	Stahl	Carrigan	Wood, Collins, O'Brien, Bedient
1913	Chicago	(5)	9	Callahan	Schalk	Cicotte, Scott, Russell, Benz
1914	Boston	(2)	6	Carrigan	Carrigan	*Leonard,* Foster, Collins, Bedient
1915	Washington	(4)	10	Griffith	Henry	*Johnson,* Ayers, Gallia, Boehling
1916	Chicago	(2)	11	Rowland	Schalk	*Cicotte,* Faber, Russell, Williams
1917	Boston	(2)	12	Barry	Agnew	Mays, Ruth, Leonard, Shore
1918	Washington	(3)	13	Griffith	Ainsmith	*Johnson,* Haynes, Shaw, Ayers
1919*	Cleveland	(2)	6	*Fohl/* Speaker	O'Neill	Coveleski, Bagby, Morton, Myers
	New York	(3)	6	Huggins	Ruel	Mogridge, Thormahlen, Quinn, Shawkey
1920	New York	(3)	6	Huggins	Ruel	*Shawkey,* Mays, Collins, Quinn
1921	New York	(1)	6	Huggins	Schang	Mays, Hoyt, Shawkey, Collins
1922	St. Louis	(2)	10	Fohl	Severeid	Wright, Shocker, Vangilder, Kolp
1923	New York	(1)	9	Huggins	Schang	Hoyt, Pennock, Bush, Shawkey
1924	Washington	(1)	10	Harris	Ruel	*Johnson,* Zachary, Marberry, Mogridge

Year	Team	Rank	Pitchers' WAL	Manager	Catcher	Staff
1925	Philadelphia	(2)	7	Mack	Cochrane	Gray, Harriss, Rommel, Walberg
1926	Philadelphia	(3)	24	Mack	Cochrane	*Grove,* Walberg, Rommel, Quinn
1927	New York	(1)	9	Huggins	Collins	*Moore,* Hoyt, Shocker, Pennock
1928	Philadelphia	(2)	7	Mack	Cochrane	Grove, Quinn, Rommel, Walberg
1929	Philadelphia	(1)	12	Mack	Cochrane	*Grove,* Earnshaw, Walberg, Shores
1930	Washington	(2)	4	Johnson	Spencer	Liska, Crowder, Hadley, Marberry
1931	Philadelphia	(1)	13	Mack	Cochrane	*Grove,* Earnshaw, Walberg, Mahaffey
1932	Cleveland	(4)	12	Peckinpaugh	Sewell	Ferrell, Harder, Brown, Hudlin
1933	Cleveland	(4)	9	Peckinpaugh/ Johnson	Spencer	*Harder,* Brown, Hildebrand, Ferrell
1934	Boston	(4)	6	Harris	Ferrell	Ostermuller, Ferrell, Welch, Rhodes
1935	Boston	(4)	12	Cronin	Ferrell	*Grove,* Ferrell, Walberg, Ostermuller
1936	Boston	(6)	9	Cronin	Ferrell	*Grove,* Ferrell, Marcum, Ostermuller
1937*	New York	(1)	8	McCarthy	Dickey	*Gomez,* Ruffing, Hadley, Pearson
	Chicago	(3)	9	Dykes	Sewell	*Stratton,* Lee, Whitehead, Lyons
1938	New York	(1)	11	McCarthy	Dickey	Ruffing, Gomez, Hadley, Pearson
1939	New York	(1)	12	McCarthy	Dickey	Ruffing, Hadley, Gomez, Donald
1940	Chicago	(5)	17	Dykes	Tresh	Rigney, Smith, Lyons, Lee
1941*	Chicago	(3)	7	Dykes	Tresh	*Lee,* Smith, Rigney, Lyons
	New York	(1)	7	McCarthy	Dickey	Russo, Chandler, Ruffing, Donald
1942	Detroit	(5)	12	Baker	Tebbetts	Newhouser, Bridges, Benton, White
1943	Chicago	(4)	6	Dykes	Tresh	O. Grove, Deitrich, Humphries, Smith
1944	Detroit	(2)	14	O'Neill	Richards	*Trout,* Newhouser, Overmire, Gorsica
1945*	St. Louis	(3)	11	Sewell	F. Mancuso	Potter, Hollingsworth, Muncrief, Kramer
	Detroit	(1)	11	O'Neill	Swift	*Newhouser,* Benton, Hoyt, Overmire

Year	Team	Rank	Pitchers' WAL	Manager	Catcher	Staff
1946	Detroit	(2)	7	O'Neill	Tebbetts	*Newhouser,* Trout, Hutchinson, Trucks
1947	Philadelphia	(5)	6	Mack	Rosar	Fowler, Marchildon, McCahan, Flores
1948	Cleveland	(1)	13	Boudreau	Hegan	*Bearden,* Lemon, Gromek, Feller
1949*	Cleveland	(3)	12	Boudreau	Hegan	Garcia, Lemon, Feller, Wynn
	Detroit	(4)	13	Rolfe	Robinson	Trucks, Hutchinson, Newhouser, Gray
1950	Cleveland	(4)	9	Boudreau	Hegan	*Wynn,* Feller, Lemon, Garcia
1951	Chicago	(4)	8	Richards	Masi	*Rogovin,* Pierce, Dobson, Holcombe
1952*	New York	(1)	7	Stengel	Berra	Reynolds, Lopat, Raschi, Sain
	Chicago	(3)	7	Richards	Lollar	Dobson, Pierce, Grissom, Rogovin
1953	Chicago	(3)	14	Richards	Lollar	*Pierce,* Trucks, Dorish, Fornieles
1954	Chicago	(3)	16	*Richards/* Marion	Lollar	*Consuegra,* Trucks, Harshman, Keegan
1955	Boston	(4)	17	Higgins	White	Sullivan, Susce, Delock, Nixon
1956	Cleveland	(2)	13	Lopez	Hegan	*Score,* Wynn, Lemon, Garcia
1957	New York	(1)	8	Stengel	Berra	*Shantz,* Sturdivant, Turley, Kucks
1958	New York	(1)	14	Stengel	Berra	*Ford,* Turley, Shantz, Ditmar
1959	Chicago	(1)	6	Lopez	Lollar	Shaw, Wynn, Pierce, Donovan
1960	Baltimore	(2)	8	Richards	Triandos	H. Brown, Barber, Wilhelm, Pappas
1961	Baltimore	(3)	13	*Richards/* Harris	Triandos	Pappas, Barber, Estrada, Fisher
1962	Los Angeles	(3)	8	Rigney	Rogers	Chance, Lee, McBride, Belinksy
1963	Chicago	(2)	12	Lopez	Martin	*Peters,* Pizarro, Wilhelm, Herbert
1964	Baltimore	(3)	12	Bauer	Brown	Bunker, Roberts, Pappas, McNally
1965	Baltimore	(3)	10	Bauer	Brown	Pappas, Barber, McNally, Bunker
1966	Minnesota	(2)	10	Mele	Battey	J. Perry, Kaat, Boswell, Grant
1967	Chicago	(4)	11	Stanky	Martin	*Horlen,* Locker, Peters, John
1968	Cleveland	(4)	9	Dark	Azcue	*Tiant,* McDowell, S. Williams, Siebert
1969	Baltimore	(1)	13	Weaver	Hendricks	Palmer, Cuellar, McNally, Phoebus

Year	Team	Rank	Pitchers' WAL	Manager	Catcher	Staff
	Minnesota	(1)	5	Martin	Roseboro	J. Perry, Boswell, Kaat, Hall
1970	Minnesota	(1)	6	Rigney	Mitterwald	Hall, J. Perry, Blyleven, Zepp
	Baltimore	(1)	5	Weaver	Hendricks	Palmer, McNally, Cuellar, Hardin
1971	Oakland	(1)	11	Williams	Duncan	*Blue,* Hunter, Segui, Dobson
	Baltimore	(1)	6	Weaver	Hendricks	Palmer, McNally, Dobson, Cuellar
1972	Baltimore	(3)	12	Weaver	Oates	Palmer, Cuellar, Dobson, McNally
	Oakland	(1)	8	Williams	Duncan	Hunter, Holtzman, Odom, Blue
1973	Baltimore	(1)	14	Weaver	Williams	*Palmer,* McNally, Cuellar, Alexander
	Minnesota	(3)	9	Quilici	Mitterwald	Blyleven, Decker, Kaat, Corbin
1974	Oakland	(1)	10	Dark	Fosse	*Hunter,* Holtzman, Blue, Fingers
	Baltimore	(1)	4	Weaver	Williams	Grimsley, Cuellar, Palmer, McNally
1975	New York	(3)	6	Virdon/ Martin	Munson	Hunter, May, Medich, Dobson
	Kansas City	(2)	2	*McKeon/* Herzog	Martinez	Busby, Splittorf, Pattin, Fitzmorris
1976	New York	(1)	7	Martin	Munson	Figueroa, Ellis, Hunter, Holtzman
	Kansas City	(1)	2	Herzog	Martinez	Fitzmorris, Bird, Leonard, Splittorf
	Texas	(4)	2	Lucchesi	Sundberg	Blyleven, Umbarger, G. Perry, Briles
1977	Texas	(2)	18	Lucchesi/ *Hunter*	Sundberg	*Blyleven,* Ellis, G. Perry, Alexander
	Boston	(2)	9	Zimmer	Fisk	Jenkins, Stanley, Cleveland, Tiant
1978	New York	(1)	11	*Martin/* Lemon	Munson	*Guidry,* Figueroa, Tidrow, Gossage
	Oakland	(6)	5	*McKeon/* Winkles	Essian	Keough, Johnson, Langford, Broberg
1979	Baltimore	(1)	11	Weaver	Dempsey	Flanagan, McGregor, Palmer, D. Martinez
	Chicago	(5)	9	*Kessinger/* LaRussa	May	Baumgarten, Kravec, Trout, Wortham
1980	Baltimore	(2)	7	Weaver	Dempsey	Stone, McGregor, Palmer, Flanagan
	Oakland	(2)	2	Martin	Essian	Norris, Keough, Langford, Kingman

Year	Team	Rank	Pitchers' WAL	Manager	Catcher	Staff
	Minnesota	(3)	3	*Mauch/* Goryl	Wynegar	Erickson, D. Jackson, Koosman, Zahn
1981	New York	(3)	7*	*Michael/* Lemon	Cerone	Righetti, John, Guidry, May
	Kansas City	(4)	4	*Frey/* Howser	Wathan	Gura, Leonard, Splittorf, Gale
1982	Seattle	(4)	12	Lachemann	Sweet	Beattie, Bannister, G. Perry, M. Moore
	Toronto	(4)	10	Cox	Witt	Stieb, Clancy, Leal, Gott
1983	Texas	(3)	13	Rader	Sundberg	*Honeycutt,* Hough, Darwin, Smithson
	Baltimore	(1)	9	Altobelli	Dempsey	Boddicker, McGregor, Davis, D. Martinez
1984	California	(2)	5	McNamara	Boone	John, Witt, Romanick, Slaton
	Detroit	(1)	4	Anderson	Parrish	Petry, Morris, Berenguer, Wilcox
1985	Kansas City	(1)	12	Howser	Sundberg	Leibrandt, Saberhagen, Jackson, Gubieza
	Detroit	(3)	13	Anderson	Parrish	Morris, Petry, Terrell, Tanana
1986	California	(1)	4	Mauch	Boone	Witt, McCaskill, Sutton, Romanick
	New York	(2)	8	Piniella	Pagliarulo	Tewksbury, Guidry, Drabek, J. Niekro

Note: Managers in *italics* managed the most games of the two listed.
Pitchers in *italics* are the individual NERA winners.
AL East and West leaders are listed from 1969 to 1986.
*Tie for best park-adjusted pitching staff.

The 1911–14 A's are not listed. With Chief Bender, Jack Coombs, Eddie Plank, and the rest, they were a legendary staff, winning three pennants in four years. Unfortunately, the Thorn–Palmer study reveals them as frauds. The A's *hitters* won the pennants; the pitchers were actually anchors dragging the team down. In 1913 the hurlers cost the team ten games, in 1914 four, and in 1911 one. Luckily the hitters—Eddie Collins, Home Run Baker, Stuffy McInnis, and the like—were strong enough to overcome the pitching and win with ease.

The 1982 Milwaukee Brewers eked out a

BEST NERA STAFFS (AL)

Year	AL Team	(Rank)	Games Saved	Manager	Catcher
1926	Philadelphia A's	(3)	24	Connie Mack	Mickey Cochrane
1977	Texas Rangers	(2)	18	Frank Lucchesi/Hunter	Jim Sundberg
1955	Boston Red Sox	(4)	17	Mike Higgins	Sammy White
1954	Chicago White Sox	(3)	16	Paul Richards/Marion	Sherm Lollar

BEST NERA STAFFS (NL)

Year	NL Team	(Rank)	Games Saved	Manager	Catcher
1957	Brooklyn Dodgers	(3)	19	Walter Alston	Roy Campanella
1906	Chicago Cubs	(1)	18	Frank Chance	Johnny Kling
1970	Chicago Cubs	(2)	17	Leo Durocher	Randy Hundley
1907	Chicago Cubs	(1)	16	Frank Chance	Johnny Kling

MOST TIMES A REGULAR STARTER ON BEST NL STAFF

NL Pitcher	No. of times
Don Sutton	7
Tommy John	7*
Mordecai Brown	5
Ed Reulbach	5

*Includes both leagues.

MOST TIMES A REGULAR STARTER ON BEST AL STAFF

AL Pitcher	No. of times
Jim Palmer	8
Lefty Grove	6
Rube Walberg	6
Mike Cuellar	6
Dave McNally	6
Bert Blyleven	6*
Wes Ferrell	5
Catfish Hunter	5

*Includes both leagues.

pennant on the last day of the season over Baltimore, thanks to their sluggers, nicknamed "Harvey's Wall Bangers." They would have won comfortably if the pitchers had not cost them four games over the season.

The Worst Staffs

The 1927 Phillies were the most futile flingers of all times; they cost their club twenty-three games.

The 1911 Boston Braves' pitchers lost twenty-two games more than they should have. Ironically, Johnny Kling—who shepherded the 1906–7 Chicago Cubs' pitchers—was their catcher.

The 1915 Philadelphia A's lost twenty-one on pitching alone (that was the year Connie Mack broke up his 1914 champions).

In recent years the worst staffs were the 1974 Padres, nineteen losses; the 1967 Astros, eighteen; the Padres of 1977, fourteen; and the 1979 Oakland A's, fourteen.

How much does a manager help or hurt the staff? John McNamara suffered with the two Padres' staffs. In 1986 he was in Boston, guiding the finest staff in the league and laughing at Fenway Park's jinx on pitchers.

13

The Top of the Hill

Who were the 100 best pitchers of all time? Walter Johnson? Grover Alexander? Cy Young? Sandy Koufax? Tom Seaver? Sure—but who were the other ninety-five?

What yardstick do you use? Wins? ERA? Strikeouts? Linear Weights? No-hitters?

To start with, we have divided the pitchers into decades—actually two twenty-year spans and eight decades. The war-torn 1940s ripped a big three or four years out of the careers of the best pitchers of their era, so we have given the 1940s only six men, and allotted the extra four to the 1970s. Likewise, we have selected only seven men for the period 1860 to 1879, and thirteen for 1880 to 1899.

We believe these divisions make sense for another reason. Every year the human animal gets stronger, jumps higher, runs faster; the Olympic records are proof of that. While batting skills may not have accelerated at the same pace as running or shot-putting, inasmuch as batting involves reflex more than power, pitching skills have certainly leapt

forward. While it might be an overstatement to say that Cy Young could not make a big-league team in the 1980s, he would certainly not dominate the game the way he did in the opening years of the century.

HIGHER, FARTHER, FASTER

Every year the human animal becomes bigger, stronger, faster, better. Every year the caliber of athlete is hiked up another notch. If Cy Young, Ty Cobb, Babe Ruth, and other oldtimers were magically reincarnated today in their former primes, the Nolan Ryans and Cal Ripkens might play them right off the Astroturf—and if not, for a hero is by definition an exception, certainly the average player of days gone by would be left in the dust.

The proof is in the sensational improvement in track-and-field records. Back in great-grandfather's day, in the summer of 1924, Rogers Hornsby whacked National League pitchers at a .424 clip. Across the

271

THEY ALSO HIT—SOMETIMES

*The fact that I am such a great pitcher overshadows my wonderful
work with the willow when I step up to the plate.*

—Dizzy Dean

Dizzy Dean was still in his street clothes in the Cardinals' dugout as the Tigers took their batting practice before the final game of the 1934 World Series. Dashing to the batting cage, he grabbed a bat out of the hands of a startled Hank Greenberg stepped to the plate, and whaled two pitches into the left-field stands. "There you go," he said, flipping the bat back to its owner. "That's the way you do it."

In uniform an hour later, Diz drilled two hits in one inning to tie the World Series record. He also shut the Tigers out 11–0. Like most pitchers before 1973, the year of the d.h., Dean preferred talking about his pitching. And, also like most pitchers, his hitting was not that good (his lifetime average was .225).

Most pitchers were more like Lefty Gomez, who got only one hit in All Star play. A left-handed swinger, he said, "It was a hell of a line drive; I pulled it over shortstop." His only World Series hit "handcuffed Burgess Whitehead at second base. That winter he had a nervous breakdown."

So folks were surprised when Lefty boasted that he had once broken a bat. "I ran over it backing the car out of the garage."

Once, picked off second, he trotted back to the dugout, where manager Joe McCarthy shook his head and asked, "What happened?"

"I don't know," Gomez shrugged, "I've never been on second before."

There are some pitchers who have never been on first. Bob Buhl of the 1962 Braves had a perfect record at bat: seventy times up, seventy outs. Dean Chance went to bat 662 times in his career and struck out 420 times. Lefty Grove whiffed 593 times.

Joe Niekro hit only one home run in his life, in 1976. It came off his brother, Phil, and won the game 4–3.

Gaylord Perry was such a weak hitter that his manager, Al Dark, predicted, "A man'll land on the moon before Gaylord

sea, in Paris, the world was following the *Chariots of Fire* Olympics; Finland's Albin Stenroos won the marathon with a time of 2:41:22.

Sixty summers later, Alberto Salazar was whipping that time by more than thirty minutes. Poor Stenroos would limp in some twenty minutes behind Joan Benoit, the 1984 women's Olympic champ.

In that same interval, the Olympic shot-put record went from forty-nine feet to almost seventy-three feet, an improvement of 47 percent. The 1500-meter swim record went from over twenty minutes to under fifteen minutes, or 33 percent faster.

Even the women are beating their fathers' and grandfathers' records. In 1984 Ulrike Meyfarth's winning Olympic high jump (6 feet, 7 inches) would have won the men's event in 1948.

Or take the 400-meter swim. Johnny "Tarzan" Weissmuller could not win a bronze medal today—in the women's events. He would not even qualify for the hits a home run." He was right. On July 20, 1969, forty minutes after Neil Armstrong stepped onto the moon, Perry's first and only home run fell to earth in Candlestick Park.

In the white major leagues of this century, by common consent, the best hitting pitcher was Wes Ferrell, one of the greatest all-round athletes ever to play the game. As a pitcher, he won twenty games each of the first four years he pitched in the American League. Wes could have starred in the outfield as well. In 1931 he slugged nine home runs in 116 at-bats, while hitting .319. That equals about forty for a full season. It is also a record for home runs by pitchers in one year. Wes swatted seven in 1933 and seven more in 1935 and ended his career with thirty-eight. No pitcher has ever topped that. Ferrell batted .280 for a career, with a fine .451 slugging average. In 1931 he pitched a no-hit game *and* hit a home run and a double and knocked in four runs.

Red Ruffing was so good with the bat that he often pinch-hit for Tommy Henrich and Bill Dickey. (Of course, big Red was right-handed, and they were lefties.) Ruffing hit .364 in 1930, .330 in 1931, and .306 in 1932. No pitcher has ever hit as many doubles (97) or knocked in as many runs (273).

In 1937 Big Jim Tobin hit .441, and in 1942 he almost hit six home runs in six consecutive times at bat. He pinch-hit one over the fence, came back the next day to pinch-hit another, went in the third day to pitch, and his first time up hit a long drive to the base of the center-field fence, then hit three straight home runs over it. He won the game 6–5—it was hard to win for the Braves back in those days.

Tobin is one of four men to pitch a no-hitter and hit a home run in the same game. The others are Cy Young, Catfish Hunter, and Rick Wise, who hit *two* in his 1971 classic.

In 1966 Tony Cloninger of the Braves hit two homers in a game twice within a two-week period. The second two were grand slams.

Ken Brett, George's pitching brother, hit home runs in four straight games in 1973. It was actually five, but in the fifth game the ump made him stop at second, thinking the ball had bounced over the wall. Only the relievers in the San Francisco bull pen (Brett was playing for the Phils at the time) saw it clear the fence on the fly, but they were not saying anything.

U.S. women's trials. If his old movie mate, Jane, were calling for help from ravenous crocodiles, Johnny could splash to her aid in five minutes, four seconds, only to find that young Tiffany Cohen had gotten there almost a full minute ahead of him, rescued Jane, and was already swinging away through the jungle, triumphantly ululating.

No doubt about it, the human athlete is far, far better today than he or she was sixty, or even twenty, years ago.

If Jim Thorpe, the 1912 Olympic champ, could not make the 1988 Olympic team, there is great doubt that Ty Cobb could make the 1988 Detroit Tigers' outfield either. Could Cobb hit Nolan Ryan with his hands spread apart on the bat? Could Walter Johnson win with nothing but a fastball? Could the overweight Ruth compete with today's superbly conditioned athletes? If the best women of the 1980s are superior to the best men of 1912–50, and if the best women today are not good enough to play in the majors, the conclusion seems inescapable:

the best men of the 1920s could not play today either.

WHY DO BASEBALL RECORDS GO DOWN?

Then why don't baseball records reflect the improvement? Why hasn't the home-run record improved 50 percent as the shot-put record has? Why isn't Mike Schmidt hitting ninety homers a year, why isn't Roger Clemens striking out 550 men a year?

One reason is that track-and-field pits man against an unchanging measure—the marathon is always 26 miles, 365 yards; the tape measure for the high jump is the same now as it always was. But baseball pits man, not against changeless units of measure, but against other men, who are improving as fast as he is.

It is true that batting averages today are an anemic version of the 1920–30 era. But this is a result of changing rules and playing conditions, most of which have aided the defense over the offense—for example, night ball, bigger gloves, and deeper fences.

For a batter who comes to bat 500 times, each hit represents two points on his yearly average. The season lasts twenty-six weeks. Thus only one less hit a week will cut a man's batting average by fifty-two points a year, making .250 hitters out of .300 hitters and .350 hitters out of .400 hitters. How many hits a year do today's batters lose to bigger gloves alone?

If Mike Schmidt today swung against a pitching machine—the same one that Babe Ruth had faced in 1927—instead of against a human pitcher, Smittie could very well be hitting eighty or ninety home runs now.

The Population Squeeze

The second factor is population. In great-grandfather's day a baby boy had three times as great a chance of growing up to play with the Yankees as a baby boy born in the 1960s did. Where once baseball took only the cream, it now takes the cream of the cream.

In 1901, when Cy Young won thirty-three games, the population of the United States was 84 million. Each major leaguer represented 95,000 white U.S. and Canadian males. By 1950 the population was 166 million and the ratio was 1:170,000. Today, with the influx of blacks and Latins, plus the gigantic population boom in general, each player is the best of 290,000 western-hemisphere males, from the equator to the North Pole.

"The game is diluted," oldtimers cry. Nonsense. It was diluted in Christy Mathewson's and Lefty Grove's days. It was Babe Ruth, not Roger Maris, who deserved the asterisk in the record books: hit when the player/population ratio was only 1:125,000. We close our eyes and visualize Matty challenging Honus Wagner, Walter Johnson blazing them in to Ty Cobb. Alas, it was not exactly that way. Matty faced Honus Wagner only about eight games a year. Just from population increase alone, Roger Clemens faces a Wagner-caliber hitter three times as often. Baseball saw no less than eleven .400 hitters in the first thirty years of this decade, but we have not seen one in the last forty-five years. Four-fifths of the fans in the country have never watched a .400 hitter.

And every year the population squeeze gets tighter. In 1960 it had reached 1:360,000, as the gates were finally opened to blacks and Latins. After expansion in 1961, the ratio went down for the first time since 1900, and Maris immediately broke Ruth's mark, which had been protected for a quarter of a century. In 1962 the National League added two more teams, bringing the ratio down to 1:290,000; Sandy Koufax broke Rube Waddell's strikeout mark that had stood since 1904, and Maury Wills erased Cobb's stolen-base mark. Other expansions followed in 1969 and 1971, and for the first time, baseball growth slightly exceeded population increase. Nolan Ryan promptly broke Koufax's mark, and Lou Brock surpassed Wills'.

However, with no expansion in the last fifteen years, the ratio has climbed back to 1:300,000. And, as SABR's Bill Deane points out, the baby boom of the 1950s is a demographic bubble that is further tightening the noose. The player pool is growing by two million every year. At that rate, baseball would have to add one new team every three years just to stay even. To get back to the ratio in Grover Alexander's day, it would have to double the number of teams.

Nor is it just numbers. Each generation is taller and stronger than its father's generation. In 1927 the average weight of the New York Yankees' starting pitchers was 170. In 1984 the Detroit Tigers' starters ranged from 200 pounds (Jack Morris and Dan Petry) to 215 (Milt Wilcox). And in 1985 Detroit added the beefy Walt Terrell.

Taking a different statistical path, Dick Cramer, who developed the Yankees' and White Sox' computer programs, calculates that if Ty Cobb had played in 1911 under the same conditions as 1976, one would have to subtract ninety-four points from his batting average to equate it to a modern average. Thus Cobb's .420 that year would have been about .326 in 1976.

The same logic applies to Johnson's strikeouts, Alexander's victories, Mathewson's ERA, and the rest. Today's players face better hitters or pitchers far more often.

So .400 hitters—or sixty-two-homer hitters and 400-strikeout pitchers—are not cre-

ated on the playing field. They are created high in the glass-enclosed suites of Park Avenue, where baseball's decision makers create whatever level of hitting or pitching competition they wish. Do you want .400 hitters every other year, as we had in the 1920s? Just return the game to the conditions of the 1920s by changing the rules to raise the league batting average to the .280–.290 level again and add more teams until the player-to-population ratio is 1:100,000 again. Do you want pitcher dominance similar to that in Walter Johnson's day? Just recreate the playing and population conditions of 1910.

While returning the game to the "Golden Age" of the 1920s would produce more individual record breakers, it would dilute the competition. Great-grandpa rarely saw a seven-game World Series and only in 1908 saw a pennant playoff to break a tie finish. Now almost every other World Series goes the full seven games, and we have seen five pennant playoffs (not championship series) since 1946. Baseball is better now than it ever has been, and it will only get better.

HOW TO CHOOSE THE "BEST"?

While Christy Mathewson and Cy Young might not compete in today's game—and certainly would not dominate, any more than Paavo Nurmi could breeze away with today's Olympic marathon—they were the greatest of their time. And who can ask for more? Thus we are dividing the game into decades for judgment.

The decades are approximations, and each man's lifetime total record is considered, not just his record within the decade. Because World War II destroyed almost half of one decade, and along with it, the careers of most of the potential stars of that generation, we have cut its quota somewhat and allotted the unused slots to the 1970s, where population increase has clustered more stars than in any previous decade. We decided to stop with the 1970s and leave it to later writers to add the names of those who came to the fore in the 1980s—Dwight Gooden, Fernando Valenzuela, Roger Clemens, and the rest.

We decided on a few guidelines. Should we consider excellence over a span of years or brilliance in a short term? We selected the former. We decided to deemphasize strikeouts, just a glamorous way to make outs, and pyrotechnics in single games, such as no-hitters. We also decided, reluctantly, to ignore World Series performances, because it seemed unfair to those men who did not get into World Series.

That left us with two main criteria: We have included ten stars of the Negro leagues, since we take literally the words "100 best" of all time. The Negro leaguers we have selected were giants of their times—white newspapers compared Rube Foster to Addie Joss, John McGraw compared Jose Mendez to Mordecai Brown and Christy Mathewson, and Monte Irvin called Leon Day better

than Bob Gibson. They played the best of the whites—Johnson, Alexander, Feller, and more—and beat them often enough to have earned their place alongside the Juan Marichals, Ferguson Jenkins, and Luis Tiants who climbed on their shoulders into the white majors.

We were tempted to add Masaichi Kaneda and Kazuhisa Inao of Japan. If there were some reliable cross-league criteria to use, we might have done so. Instead, Japanese achievements must remain tantalizing question marks.

Relief pitchers present a statistical problem. Comparing a starter and a reliever is somewhat like comparing a third baseman and a shortstop. You can do it, but the numbers just do not match up. Relievers almost always have lower ERAs than starters. There are two reasons. One, in perhaps one-half or one-third of their innings, they start with one or two outs. Two, they throw hard for two innings and do not have to pace themselves for nine.

So then, here are our choices of the 100 best starting pitchers, presented by decades, in alphabetical order:

1860–79

Pitcher	W–L	WAL	WAL W–L	Pct.	NERA
Tommy Bond	193–115*	7	161–147	.523	3.16
Jim Creighton	(Active before league play)				
Jim Galvin†	361–310*	14	350–321	.522	3.30
Bobby Mathews	166–138*	NA	NA	NA	NA
Dick McBride	0–4*	0	0–4	.000	4.31
Al Spalding†	48–13*	3	34–27	.557	2.78
Will White	299–166	18	216–179	.547	2.84

Best: Al Spalding

*Does not include National Association (1871–75) records: for Bond, 41–48; for Galvin, 4–2; for Mathews, 132–111; for McBride, 152–76; and for Spalding, 207–56. Spalding's combined won–lost record of 255–69 makes for a percentage of .787.

†Hall of Fame.

1880–99

Pitcher	W–L	WAL	WAL W–L	Pct.	NERA
Bob Caruthers	218–97	19	167–138	.530	2.84
John Clarkson*	326–177	33	285–218	.567	2.84
Clark Griffith*	240–141	22	213–168	.559	2.93
Guy Hecker	177–150	14	179–149	.544	2.82
Bill Hutchinson	182–158	NA	NA	NA	NA
Tim Keefe*	344–225	37	322–247	.566	2.71
Silver King	205–152	18	197–161	.550	2.84
Jim McCormick	264–214	20	259–219	.542	2.98
Kid Nichols*	360–202	47	328–234	.584	2.69
Hoss Radbourn*	308–191	27	277–222	.555	2.73
Amos Rusie*	243–160	35	237–166	.588	2.67
Jesse Tannehill	197–116	13	170–143	.543	3.16
Mickey Welch	311–207	20	279–239	.539	3.08

Best: Amos Rusie

*Hall of Fame.

1900–09

Pitcher	Actual W–L	WAL	Expected W–L	Pct.	NERA
Mordecai Brown*	239–130	34	219–150	.593	2.56
Rube Foster*	Negro League				
Addie Joss*	160–97	22	150–107	.584	2.60
Christy Mathewson*	373–189	42	323–238	.576	2.69
Joe McGinnity*	247–144	21	216–175	.552	3.02
Eddie Plank*	326–193	26	284–234	.548	3.02
Rube Waddell*	194–141	25	192–143	.573	2.75
Ed Walsh*	195–126	28	189–132	.589	2.54
Vic Willis	244–204	19	243–205	.542	3.16
Cy Young	510–313	72	484–339	.588	2.69
Others					
Jack Chesbro*	197–132	11	175–154	.532	3.27
George Mullin	228–196	2	213–211	.502	3.59
Jack Powell	246–255	8	259–242	.512	3.49
Ed Reulbach	181–105	19	162–124	.566	2.90

Best: Cy Young

*Hall of Fame.

1910–19

Pitcher	Actual W–L	WAL	Expected W–L	Pct.	NERA
Babe Adams	194–140	15	182–152	.545	3.18
Grover Alexander*	373–208	56	346–235	.596	2.69
Eddie Cicotte	208–149	20	199–158	.557	3.00
Walter Johnson*	417–279	67	415–281	.596	2.52
Carl Mays*	308–126	18	185–149	.533	3.10
Jose Mendez	Negro League				
Jack Quinn	242–217	18	247–212	.538	3.27
Dick Redding	Negro League				
Hippo Vaughn	178–136	19	176–138	.560	3.00
Joe Williams	Negro League				
Others					
Red Ames	183–167	8	183–167	.523	3.39
Chief Bender*	212–128	9	179–161	.527	3.33
Slim Sallee	173–143	12	170–146	.538	.321

Best: Walter Johnson

*Hall of Fame.

1920–29

Pitcher	Actual W–L	WAL	Expected W–L	Pct.	NERA
Wilbur Cooper	216–178	17	214–180	.543	3.18
Stanley Coveleski*	215–142	27	205–152	.577	2.86
Red Faber*	254–113	26	210–157	.572	3.10
Bill Foster	Negro League				
Burleigh Grimes	270–212	12	253–229	.525	3.42
Waite Hoyt*	237–182	17	227–192	.542	3.30
Eppa Rixey	266–251	21	280–237	.542	3.21
Joe Rogan	Negro League				
Dazzy Vance*	197–140	25	193–144	.588	2.93
Nip Winters	Negro League				
Others					
Pop Haines*	210–158	10	194–174	.527	3.39
Sam Jones	229–217	5	228–218	.511	3.55
Dolph Luque	194–179	17	204–169	.547	3.16
Herb Pennock*	240–162	7	208–194	.517	3.49
Reliever: Fred Marberry	148–101	12	130–101	.522	3.24

Best: Stanley Coveleski

*Hall of Fame.

1930–39

Pitcher	Actual W–L	WAL	Expected W–L	Pct.	NERA
Tommy Bridges	194–138	26	192–140	.578	2.93
Dizzy Dean*	150–83	20	137–96	.588	2.78
Martin Dihigo*	Negro League				
Lefty Gomez*	189–102	19	165–126	.567	2.98
Lefty Grove*	300–141	57	278–163	.630	2.51
Carl Hubbell*	253–154	35	239–168	.587	2.79
Ted Lyons*	260–230	31	276–236	.539	3.08
Satchel Paige*	Negro League				
Red Ruffing*	273–225	13	262–236	.526	3.39
Lon Warneke	193–121	18	175–139	.557	3.10
Others					
Paul Derringer	223–212	12	230–205	.529	3.36
Larry French	197–171	16	200–168	.543	3.21
Mel Harder	223–186	15	220–189	.538	3.30
Bobo Newsom	211–222	9	225–208	.520	3.49

Best: Lefty Grove

*Hall of Fame.

1940–49

Pitcher	Actual W–L	WAL	Expected W–L	Pct.	NERA
Leon Day	Negro League				
Bob Feller*	266–162	28	242–186	.565	3.02
Emil Leonard	191–181	21	207–165	.556	3.08
Hal Newhouser	207–150	33	212–145	.594	2.77
Hilton Smith	Negro League				
Dizzy Trout	170–161	25	190–141	.574	2.93
Others					
Harry Brecheen	133–92	21	133–92	.591	2.75
Claude Passeau	162–150	15	171–141	.548	3.18
Virgil Trucks	177–135	20	176–136	.564	3.08
Bucky Walters	198–160	19	198–160	.553	3.16

Best: Bob Feller

*Hall of Fame.

1950–59

Pitcher	Actual W–L	WAL	Expected W–L	Pct.	NERA
Murry Dickson	172–181	13	190–163	.538	3.33
Whitey Ford*	236–106	32	203–139	.594	2.77
Bob Lemon*	207–128	19	186–149	.555	3.10
Ed Lopat	166–112	14	153–125	.550	3.16
Billy Pierce	211–169	23	213–167	.561	3.08
Allie Reynolds	182–107	8	153–136	.529	3.36
Robin Roberts*	286–245	24	289–242	.544	3.21
Curt Simmons	193–183	13	201–175	.535	3.33
Warren Spahn*	363–245	33	337–271	.564	3.08
Early Wynn*	300–244	11	283–261	.520	3.45

Reliever

Hoyt Wilhelm*	143–122	30	162–103	.611	2.52

Best: Warren Spahn

*Hall of Fame.

1960–69

Pitcher	Actual W–L	WAL	Expected W–L	Pct.	NERA
Jim Bunning	224–184	19	223–185	.547	3.21
Don Drysdale*	209–166	25	212–163	.551	3.02
Bob Friend	197–230	11	224–203	.525	3.39
Bob Gibson*	251–174	39	252–173	.593	2.84
Larry Jackson	194–183	17	206–171	.546	3.24
Sandy Koufax*	165–87	24	150–102	.595	2.77
Mickey Lolich	217–191	6	210–198	.515	3.52
Juan Marichal*	243–142	25	218–167	.566	3.02
Jim Perry	215–174	8	203–186	.522	3.45
Milt Pappas	209–164	13	199–174	.534	3.33

Relievers

Stu Miller	105–103	9	112–96	.538	3.24
Ron Perranoski	79–74	8	85–68	.555	3.02

Best: Bob Gibson

*Hall of Fame.

1970–79

	Actual W–L	WAL	Expected W–L	Pct.	NERA
Gaylord Perry	314–265	36	326–253	.563	3.08
Phil Niekro	319–261	34	320–252	.559	3.11
Steve Carlton	323–229	32	308–246	.556	3.13
Tom Seaver	311–205	46	304–212	.578	2.84
Don Sutton	310–239	16	291–258	.530	3.39
Ferguson Jenkins	284–226	26	281–229	.551	3.18
Jim Kaat	283–237	13	273–247	.525	3.42
Tommy John	264–210	22	259–215	.546	3.21
Nolan Ryan	253–226	15	254–225	.530	3.33
Jim Palmer	268–153	33	244–177	.580	2.88
Bert Blyleven	229–197	38	251–175	.573	2.88
Jerry Koosman	216–205	19	229–192	.544	3.24
Luis Tiant	229–172	19	219–182	.546	3.24
Vida Blue	209–161	9	194–176	.530	3.42
Relief					
Rollie Fingers	114–118	11	127–105	.547	3.05
Rich Gossage	101–89	12	107–83	.563	2.84
Sparky Lyle	99–79	12	100–75	.571	2.88
Best					
Tom Seaver					

Well, there you have either the 100 best pitchers who ever lived, or 100 of the best pitchers who ever lived, whichever way you wish to look at it.

Which one was *the* best? You could say that the best would have to be the best of the 1970s, since every decade has been better than the one before it. Our own subjective choice as the greatest athlete pitching in the 1970s is a man who has done things with a baseball that no man before him ever did—and he did it against the greatest hitters and pitchers of all time. We refer to Nolan Ryan.

But our objective choice for pitcher of the 1970s is dictated by the numbers—Tom Seaver.

And if you want to measure earlier generations against their own contemporaries and not against some future superman who will be better fed, better trained, better educated, and better equipped, then we would single out for special consideration the following pitchers:

Walter Johnson worked harder than any man ever worked for victories, with that record number of 1–0 games—he won thirty-eight and lost twenty-seven.

Grover Alexander played in the tiniest park any pitcher has had to contend with and still pitched ninety shutouts, sixteen of them in one season. And he has one of the best wins-above-league records of anyone.

Lefty Grove got a late start and played entirely in the lively ball era but dominated most pitching categories, with more annual titles in most departments than any other man in any other era.

Bob Feller's four missing wartime years will tantalize us forever. Satchel Paige and

Lefty Grove

Smokey Joe Williams also fall into this category.

Sandy Koufax, in four brief years, accomplished feats that most other pitchers could not duplicate in twenty years.

If we must pick one, and surely we must, then we will choose the man who has both the highest lifetime WAL percentage and the lowest NERA of all time. That man, of course, is Lefty Grove.

THE JIM CREIGHTON AWARDS

From 1956 through 1986 the baseball writers chose fifty-two Cy Young winners. One wonders why they bother. They almost automatically—thirty-three times—rubber-stamped the biggest winner in the league or—fourteen times—the biggest winner on the league or division champion.

There have been only five exceptions; four of those were relief aces on a division winner. That leaves only one man out of forty-eight who won on excellence alone, in spite of not playing for a winner: Bruce Sutter, relief specialist on the fifth-place Cubs in 1979.

It's hardly worth going through the empty ritual of balloting. The Most Valuable Player award is not quite so predictable, but nearly.

The Rookie-of-the-Year award is different. Here the writers actually strive to reward excellence wherever it may be found, once even dipping into a ninth-place team to honor Tom Seaver of the Mets.

In 1973 Seaver became the first man to win the Cy Young without winning twenty games. Since then, other than relievers, only Mike Scott has matched this feat (excepting Fernando Valenzuela's Cy Young award for thirteen victories in the strike-shortened 1981 campaign).

How many Cy Young awards would Cy Young have won? We think he would have won four: in 1892, 1901, 1902, and 1903.

In the first year he led the league in all the usual categories—wins (thirty-three), ERA, and strikeouts. But these traditional litmus tests are more symbolic than indicative. Before we vote, we would want to know how each man did in other meaningful categories:

> Opponents' On Base Average—how many men did he put on base?
> Pitching Average—how hard was he to hit?
> NERA—how effective was he in preventing runs?
> WAL—how many extra wins did he give his team?

Young led in three of these four key categories; Earl Moore beat him in park-ad-

Jim Creighton

justed pitching average. When you list the league leaders in these critical headings, the decision is virtually made for you: Cy Young was the best.

In the National League, if there had been a vote that year, the writers would presumably have selected Wild Bill Donovan, the league's top winner (25–15 for third-place Brooklyn) or possibly Deacon Phillippe

(22–12) or Jack Chesbro (21–10) of the champion Pirates. But we are more interested in the other, more fundamental indicators. We admire Noodles Hahn (22–19 for last-place Cincinnati). But staying with our own criteria, we would want to consider Vic Willis (20–17 with fifth-place Boston). Willis was the toughest man to get on base against, the toughest man to hit, the toughest man to score on, and, naturally, the toughest to beat. He led in all four of our key categories—OOBA, PA, NERA, and WAL. We vote for Willis, gloves down.

Unfortunately, we were not voting in 1901, and neither was anybody else. So, to rectify that, we thought it would be fun if we, and you, selected the best men for all seasons, starting with 1876. (For the years before 1901, however, we will not compute PA or OOBA.)

We cannot very well give a Cy Young award to the best pitcher of 1876 (Cy was only a lad of nine at the time), so we decided to call our award the Jim Creighton award, in honor of the game's first great pitcher.

We decided to bestow the Creighton awards through 1986, even though the baseball writers began giving Cy Young awards in 1956. After all, the writers did not have the advantage of our WALs, NERAs, PAs, and OOBAs, so naturally they can be forgiven for making so many egregious errors in their selections. In the following charts, we indicate the leaders in each category each year, followed by our choice for the Creighton and the writers' pick for the Cy Young. The reader is at liberty to cross off both our choices and the writers' and write in his own.

In 1902 we have a hard decision between Cy and his young rival, Rube Waddell. Again Young (32–11 with third-place Boston) was the biggest winner, both actual and relative, but Waddell, the strikeout king

(24–7 with the champion A's), was most effective in getting hitters out. It is a classic dilemma between the most valuable pitcher—the big winner—and the most excellent.

We opted for value over excellence and chose Young over Waddell.

The next year, however, there was no contest. Young swept every category.

As the writers have weighted the Cy Young award in favor of the big winner, we have weighted our Jim Creighton awards

heavily toward the WAL leader. WAL and NERA are value indicators, measuring in essence wins and earned runs. PA and OOBA are excellence indicators, measuring hits and walks, which are, after all, means to the end, which is high WALs and low NERAs. Where there was no clear-cut dominating pitcher, we confess that we reverted to the writers' sin and went for the big winner in conventional wins, particularly on the pennant winner. Hey, we're human too.

AMERICAN LEAGUE AWARDS

Year	WAL	NERA	PA	OOBA	Jim Creighton Award	Cy Young Award
1901	Young	Young	Moore	Young	Young	
1902	Young	Siever	Waddell	Bernhard	Young	
1903	Young	Young	Young	Young	Young	
1904	Chesbro	Chesbro	Chesbro	Young	Chesbro	
1905	Waddell	Waddell	Waddell	Young	Waddell	
1906	Hess	Rhoades Pelty Hess	Pelty	Joss	Pelty	
1907	Walsh	Walsh	Winter	Young	Walsh	
1908	Joss	Joss	Joss	Joss	Joss	
1909	Plank Bender Krause	Krause	Morgan	Joss	Krause	
1910	Johnson	Coombs	Ford	Walsh	Coombs	
1911	Johnson Ford	Gregg	Gregg	Walsh	Gregg	
1912	Johnson	Johnson	Johnson	Johnson	Johnson	
1913	Johnson	Johnson	Johnson	Johnson	Johnson	
1914	Johnson Leonard	Leonard	Leonard	Leonard	Leonard	
1915	Johnson	Johnson	Morton	Morton	Johnson	
1916	S. Coveleski	Cicotte	Shawkey	H. Coveleski	H. Coveleski	
1917	Bagby S. Coveleski	S. Coveleski	S. Coveleski	S. Coveleski	S. Coveleski	
1918	Johnson	Johnson	Sothoron	Johnson	Johnson	
1919	Cicotte Johnson	Johnson	Johnson	Cicotte	Johnson	
1920	S. Coveleski	S. Coveleski	Ehmke	S. Coveleski	S. Coveleski	
1921	Faber	Faber	Faber	Faber	Faber	
1922	Faber	Faber	Faber	Faber	Faber	
1923	S. Coveleski Vangilder Hoyt	S. Coveleski	S. Coveleski	Shawkey	S. Coveleski	

Year	WAL	NERA	PA	OOBA	Jim Creighton Award	Cy Young Award
1924	Johnson Pennock	Baumgartner	Johnson	Johnson	Johnson	
1925	Lyons Blankenship Pennock	Blankenship	Blankenship	Blankenship	Blankenship	
1926	Grove	Grove	Grove	Rommel	Grove	
1927	Lyons	Moore	Thomas	Lyons	Lyons	
1928	Grove Braxton	Braxton	Braxton	Braxton	Braxton	
1929	Grove	Grove	Earnshaw	Marberry	Grove	
1930	Ferrell Grove	Grove	Grove Hadley	Stewart	Grove	
1931	Grove	Grove	Hadley	Grove	Grove	
1932	Grove	Grove	Bridges	Grove	Grove	
1933	Harder Hadley	Harder	Bridges	Marberry	Harder	
1934	Harder Gomez	Gomez	Gomez	Gomez	Gomez	
1935	Grove	Grove	Whitehead	Grove	Grove	
1936	Grove	Grove	Grove Pearson	Grove	Grove	
1937	Gomez	Stratton	Stratton	Stratton	Stratton	
1938	T. Lee	Grove	Feller	Stratton	Stratton	
1939	Grove Feller	Grove	Feller	Lyons	Feller	
1940	Newsom Rigney	Newsom	E. Smith	Lyons	Newsom	
1941	T. Lee	T. Lee	Benton	Benton	T. Lee	
1942	Hughson Newhouser Lyons	Lyons	Newhouser	Bonham	Lyons	
1943	Chandler	Chandler	Haefner	Chandler	Chandler	
1944	Trout	Trout	Newhouser	Trout	Trout	
1945	Newhouser	Newhouser	Newhouser	Wolff	Newhouser	
1946	Newhouser	Newhouser	Newhouser	Newhouser	Newhouser	
1947	Feller Haynes Newhouser	Haynes	Shea	Hutchinson	Feller	
1948	Bearden Lemon Newhouser	Bearden	Shea	Scarborough	Bearden	
1949	Trucks	Garcia	Byrne	Hutchinson	Page	
1950	Garver	Garver	Wynn	Wynn	Garver Wynn	
1951	Pierce	Pierce	McDermott	Hutchinson	Pierce	
1952	Shantz	Reynolds	Shantz	Shantz	Shantz	
1953	Pierce	Pierce	Pierce	Pierce	Pierce	

Year	WAL	NERA	PA	OOBA	Jim Creighton Award	Cy Young Award
1954	Trucks	Consuegra	Turley	Consuegra	Trucks	
1955	Sullivan	Pierce	Score	Pierce	Pierce	
1956	Wynn Ford Score	Score	Score	Score	Score	
1957	Bunning Sullivan	Sullivan	Turley	Sullivan	Sullivan	
1958	Ford	Ford	Turley	Ford	Ford	Turley
1959	Pascual Wilhelm	Wilhelm	Score	Mossi	Wilhelm	Wynn
1960	Bunning	Bunning	Estrada	Brown	Bunning	
1961	Pascual Hoeft Donovan	Donovan	Pascual	Donovan	Donovan	Ford
1962	Aguirre	Aguirre	Aguirre	Aguirre	Aguirre	
1963	Pascual Peters	Peters	Downing	Ramos	Peters	
1964	Ford Chance	Chance	Horlen	Horlen	Chance	Chance
1965	Stottlemyre McLain McDowell	McDowell	McDowell	McLain	McDowell	
1966	Peters J. Perry Kaat	Peters	McDowell	Wilson	Kaat	
1967	Horlen	Horlen	Siebert	Merritt	Horlen	Lonborg
1968	McLain McDowell Tiant	Tiant	Tiant	Tiant	Tiant	McLain
1969	McLain Cuellar	Bosman	Messersmith	Cuellar	Cuellar McLain	Cuellar McLain
1970	McDowell	McDowell	McDowell	McDowell	McDowell	J. Perry
1971	Wood Blue	Blue	Blue	Blue	Blue	Blue
1972	G. Perry	G. Perry	Ryan	Nelson	G. Perry	G. Perry
1973	Blyleven	Blyleven	Bibby	Blyleven	Blyleven	Palmer
1974	Hunter G. Perry	G. Perry	Ryan	Hunter	G. Perry	Hunter
1975	Palmer	Palmer	Blyleven	Hunter	Palmer	Palmer
1976	Palmer Fidrych	Fidrych	Ryan	Fidrych	Fidrych	Palmer
1977	Blyleven	Blyleven	Ryan	Blyleven	Blyleven	Lyle
1978	Guidry	Guidry	Guidry	Guidry	Guidry	Guidry
1979	Eckersley Koosman	Eckersley	Kravec	McGregor	Eckersley	Flanagan

Year	WAL	NERA	PA	OOBA	Jim Creighton Award	Cy Young Award
1980	Burns Gura Norris	May	Norris	May	Norris	Stone
1981	Stieb	Lamp	Stieb	Gura	Stieb	Fingers
1982	Stieb	Sutcliffe	Beattie	Stieb	Stieb	Vuckovich
1983	Stieb	Honeycutt	Stieb	Hoyt	Stieb	Hoyt
1984	Blyleven	Blyleven	Blyleven	Blyleven	Blyleven	Hernandez
1985	Stieb	Stieb	Stieb	Saberhagen	Stieb	Saberhagen
1986	Clemens	Clemens	Clemens	Clemens	Clemens	Clemens
Most Titles						
	Johnson (9) Grove (9) Coveleski (4) Newhouser (4)	Grove (9) Johnson (5) Coveleski (3) Pierce (3)	Johnson (4) Ryan (4) Newhouser (3) Turley (3) Score (3) McDowell (3)	Young (5) Johnson (4) Grove (4) Joss (3)	Grove (7) Johnson (6) Stieb (4) Young (4) Coveleski (3) Pierce (3)	Palmer (3)

Note: From 1956 to 1966, only one Cy Young award was presented in the major leagues; in these years, NL pitchers won seven.

NATIONAL LEAGUE AWARDS

Year	WAL	NERA	Wins	Jim Creighton Award	Cy Young Award
1876	Bradley	Bradley	Spalding	Bradley	
1877	Bond	Bond	Bond	Bond	
1878	Ward	Ward	Bond	Bond	
1879	White	Bond	Ward	Bond	
1880	Ward	Keefe	McCormick	Ward	
1881	Derby	Weidman	Corcoran/ Whitney	Derby	
1882	Radbourn	Corcoran	McCormick	Radbourn	
1883	Radbourn	McCormick	Radbourn	Radbourn	
1884	Radbourn	Radbourn	Radbourn	Radbourn	
1885	Clarkson	Keefe	Clarkson	Clarkson	
1886	Ferguson	Ferguson	Keefe/Baldwin	Ferguson	
1887	Clarkson	Casey	Clarkson	Clarkson	
1888	Keefe	Keefe	Keefe	Keefe	
1889	Clarkson	Clarkson	Clarkson	Clarkson	
1890	Rhines	Rhines	Hutchison	Hutchison	
1891	Nichols	Ewing	Hutchison	Hutchison	
1892	Young	Young	Hutchison	Young	
1893	Rusie	Breitenstein	Killen	Rusie	
1894	Rusie	Rusie	Rusie/Meekin	Rusie	
1895	Hawley	Maul	Young	Hawley	
1896	Nichols	Rhines	Nichols	Nichols	
1897	Nichols	Rusie	Nichols	Nichols	

Year	WAL	NERA	Wins	Jim Creighton Award	Cy Young Award
1898	Nichols	Griffith	Nichols	Nichols	
1899	Young	Willis	Hughes/ McGinnity	Willis	
1900	Garvin	Waddell	McGinnity	McGinnity	

Year	WAL	NERA	PA	OOBA	Jim Creighton Award	Cy Young Award
1901	Willis	Willis	Willis	Willis	Willis	
1902	Taylor	Taylor	McGinnity	Taylor	Taylor	
1903	McGinnity Mathewson	Leaver	Mathewson	Phillippe	Mathewson	
1904	McGinnity	McGinnity	McGinnity Brown	McGinnity	McGinnity	
1905	Mathewson	Mathewson	Reulbach	Mathewson	Mathewson	
1906	Brown	Brown	Reulbach	Brown	Brown	
1907	Brown Pfiester Lundgren	Pfiester	Lundgren	Brown	Brown	
1908	Brown	Brown	Brown	Brown	Brown	
1909	Mathewson Brown	Mathewson	Fromme	Mathewson	Mathewson	
1910	Brown	Cole	Cole	Adams	Cole	
1911	Alexander Mathewson	Mathewson	Alexander	Mathewson	Mathewson	
1912	Cheney Marquard	Tesreau	Tesreau	Mathewson	Tesreau	
1913	Seaton	Brennan	Seaton	Mathewson	Seaton	
1914	James Doak	Doak	Doak	Rudolph	Doak	
1915	Alexander	Alexander	Alexander	Alexander	Alexander	
1916	Alexander	Marquard	Cheney	Rudolph	Alexander	
1917	Alexander	Anderson	Anderson	Alexander	Alexander	
1918	Vaughn	Vaughn	Vaughn	Vaughn	Vaughn	
1919	Vaughn	Alexander	Alexander	Adams	Alexander	
1920	Alexander	Alexander	Grimes	Adams	Alexander	
1921	Grimes	Adams	Glazner	Adams	Adams	
1922	Cooper	Douglas	Ryan	Adams	Adams	
1923	Luque	Luque	Luque	Alexander	Luque	
1924	Vance	Vance	Vance	Vance	Vance	
1925	Luque	Luque	Luque	Luque	Luque	
1926	Kremer	Kremer	Petty	Kremer	Kremer	
1927	Alexander Haines	Kremer	Vance	Alexander	Haines	
1928	Vance	Vance	Vance	Vance	Vance	
1929	Grimes	Grimes	Hubbell	Lucas	Grimes	
1930	Vance	Vance	Vance	Vance	Vance	

Year	WAL	NERA	PA	OOBA	Jim Creighton Award	Cy Young Award
1931	Brandt Meine Walker	Walker	Hubbell	S. Johnson	Walker	
1932	Hubbell	Warneke	Swetonic	Hubbell	Warneke	
1933	Hubbell	Hubbell	Schumacher	Hubbell	Hubbell	
1934	J. Dean	J. Dean	J. Dean	Hubbell	J. Dean	
1935	Blanton	Blanton	Blanton	Blanton	Blanton	
1936	Hubbell	Hubbell	Mungo	Hubbell	Hubbell	
1937	Melton Dean Turner	Melton	Mungo	Turner	Turner	
1938	B. Lee	B. Lee	Vander Meer	Root	B. Lee	
1939	Walters	Walters	Walters	Hamlin	Walters	
1940	Walters Passeau	Passeau	Higbe	Tamulis	Passeau	
1941	Wyatt White	White	White	Wyatt	White	
1942	Cooper	Cooper	Vander Meer	Cooper	Cooper	
1943	Andrews Lanier Cooper	Lanier	Wyatt	Wyatt	Cooper	
1944	Walters	Heusser	Walters	Raffensberger	Walters	
1945	Passeau Roe Wyse	Prim	Prim	Prim	Wyse	
1946	Pollet	Pollet	Blackwell	Beggs	Pollet	
1947	Branca Spahn	Spahn	H. Taylor	Spahn	Spahn	
1948	Sain	Brecheen	Barney	Roe	Sain	
1949	Pollet	Staley	Staley	Staley	Staley	
1950	Blackwell	Blackwell	Blackwell	Jansen	Blackwell	
1951	Roberts Spahn Maglie	Maglie	Queen	Roberts	Maglie	
1952	Roberts	Hacker	Hacker	Hacker	Hacker	
1953	Spahn	Spahn	Gomez	Spahn	Spahn	
1954	Roberts Antonelli	Antonelli	Antonelli	Roberts	Antonelli	
1955	Friend Roberts	Friend	S. Jones	Newcombe	Friend	
1956	Spahn Burdette Antonelli	Burdette	Newcombe	Newcombe	Newcombe	Newcombe
1957	Drysdale	Podres	Podres	Podres	Podres	Spahn

Year	WAL	NERA	PA	OOBA	Jim Creighton Award	Cy Young Award
1958	S. Jones	S. Miller	Koufax	S. Miller	Spahn	
1959	Craig Law S. Jones	Law	Haddix	Haddix	Law	
1960	Drysdale	Drysdale	Koufax	Drysdale	Drysdale	Law
1961	O'Toole	O'Toole	Koufax	Spahn	O'Toole	*
1962	Broglio Gibson	Gibson	Gibson	Koufax	Gibson	Drysdale
1963	Koufax Ellsworth	Ellsworth	Koufax	Koufax	Koufax	Koufax
1964	Koufax Drysdale	Koufax	Koufax	Koufax	Koufax	*
1965	Marichal	Marichal	Koufax	Marichal	Marichal	Koufax
1966	Koufax	Koufax	Marichal	Marichal	Koufax	Koufax
1967	Bunning P. Niekro	P. Niekro	Hughes	Hughes	Hughes	McCormick
1968	Gibson	Gibson	Gibson	Gibson	Gibson	Gibson
1969	Gibson	Carlton	Seaver	Dierker P. Niekro	Seaver	Seaver
1970	Jenkins Gibson Holtzman	Gibson	Simpson	Jenkins	Gibson	Gibson
1971	Seaver	Seaver	D. Wilson	Seaver	Seaver	Jenkins
1972	Carlton	Carlton	Sutton	Sutton	Carlton	Carlton
1973	Seaver	Seaver	Seaver	Seaver	Seaver	Seaver
1974	P. Niekro	Capra	Capra	Barr	P. Niekro	Marshall
1975	R. Jones	R. Jones	Warthen	R. Jones	R. Jones	Seaver
1976	Denny	Denny	Richard	Messersmith	Denny	R. Jones
1977	Reuschel	Candelaria	Seaver	Seaver	Seaver	Carlton
1978	P. Niekro	Swan	Richard	Swan	P. Niekro	Perry
1979	P. Niekro	P. Niekro Kison Schatzeder	Carlton	Candelaria	P. Niekro	Sutter
1980	Carlton	Carlton	Soto	Sutton	Carlton	Carlton
1981	Carlton	Ryan	Seaver	Valenzuela	Seaver	Valenzuela
1982	Rogers	Rogers	Lea	Lea	Rogers	Carlton
1983	Denny Soto Hammaker	Hammaker	Gooden	Hammaker	Hammaker	Denny
1984	Peña	Peña	Gooden	Hershiser	Sutter	Sutcliffe
1985	Gooden	Gooden	Fernandez	Tudor	Gooden	Gooden
1986	Scott	Scott	Scott	Scott	Scott	Scott

*From 1956 to 1966, only one Cy Young award was presented in the major leagues; in these years, AL pitchers won four.

MOST TITLES

WAL	NERA	PA	OOBA	Creighton Award	Cy Young Award
Alexander (6)	Mathewson (3)	Koufax (6)	Mathewson (5)	Alexander (5)	Carlton (4)
Brown (5)	Alexander (3)	Vance (4)	Adams (4)	Seaver (5)	Koufax (3)
Mathewson (4)	Vance (3)	Seaver (4)	Alexander (4)	Mathewson (4)	Seaver (3)
Spahn (4)	Gibson (3)	Alexander (3)	Hubbell (4)		
Roberts (4)	Carlton (3)				
Gibson (4)					
P. Niekro (4)					
Nichols (4)					

JIM CREIGHTON AWARDS
AA (American Association)

Year	WAL	NERA	Wins	Jim Creighton Award
1882	White	Driscoll	White	White
1883	White	White	White	White
1884	Hecker	Hecker	Hecker	Hecker
1885	Caruthers	Caruthers	Caruthers	Caruthers
1886	Foutz	Foutz	Foutz/Morris	Foutz
1887	Kilroy	Smith	Kilroy	Kilroy
1888	King	King	King	King
1889	Duryea	Stivetts	Caruthers	Caruthers
1890	Stratton	Stratton	McMahon	Stratton
1891	Haddock	Crane	Haddock/McMahon	Haddock

Union Association

Year	WAL	NERA	Wins	Jim Creighton Award
1884	Daily	McCormick	B. Sweeney	Daily

Players League

Year	WAL	NERA	Wins	Jim Creighton Award
1890	King	King	King/Baldwin	King

Federal League

Year	WAL	NERA	Wins	Jim Creighton Award
1914	Falkenberg	Ford	Hendrix	Hendrix
1915	Davenport	Moseley	McConnell	Davenport

Lefty Grove emerges as the all-time Creighton champ, with seven trophies to put on his crowded mantelpiece. Walter Johnson took home six of the coveted awards, and Grover Alexander and Tom Seaver five each.

We agreed with the writers only thirteen times.

The top choice of the writers was Steve Carlton, with four Cy Youngs. We gave him only two Creightons.

The writers voted Tom Seaver tops three times, but we liked him best five times.

The writers chose Jim Palmer best three times; we agreed with them only once.

We gave Dave Stieb four Creightons and

Actually two Creightons and two Cy Youngs should be given each year beginning in 1969, when the two leagues split into four divisions.

First, there are two races in each league, not just one, and two champions. Thus, there should be two MVPs and two Cy Youngs.

Second, the present six- and seven-team divisions are analogous to the old eight-team leagues, more so than the unwieldy twelve- and fourteen-team leagues are.

Since the intention of the divisions is to double the competition, then there should be competition within the divisions for everything—batting champs, home-run kings, ERA champs—just as there is competition for the division title. So an MVP and a Jim Creighton (or a Cy Young) should be given to the best player and best pitcher in each division.

We have followed the tradition of giving only one award for each league. If we had given one for each division, Tom Seaver would probably have picked up another, for a total of ten. Bob Gibson would have added two, and Phil Niekro, Steve Carlton, Bert Blyleven, and Jim Palmer one each.

BEWARE

The practice of linking contract bonuses to the Cy Young award (and the MVP) is fraught with danger. Winning the Cy Young, or even coming in third, can trigger tens of thousands of dollars worth of bonus payment in a player's contract.

The danger of collusion and favoritism is obvious. A writer who likes one candidate and dislikes another can easily bestow his vote on the one and withhold it from the other. Sometimes the third-place finisher in the Cy Young balloting gets only a single vote, which could be worth thousands.

There is precedent for such fears. Ted Williams, the 1947 Triple Crown winner, lost the MVP award by a single vote when one Boston writer, for personal reasons, refused to name Williams even tenth best on his ballot. There was no bonus clause in Williams' contract then, as there would be today.

The threat of scandal is not an idle one. If a player should be accused of splitting his bonus with a writer who voted for him, one can imagine the bombshell this would be. We wonder why commissioner Peter Ueberroth has not moved to outlaw such bonus clauses.

An objective trigger, such as winning the league WAL or NERA title, would be far safer than the present subjective trigger of the Cy Young voting. Those are awards that a pitcher wins for himself; they are not bestowed or withheld by someone else who could be suspected of having a personal motive in casting his vote.

THE CY YOUNG CURSE

The Cy Young award carries a heavy price. Half the winners have fallen victim to the Cy Young curse: the year after they win, their careers take a nose dive. They are like the man Abraham Lincoln described who was tarred and feathered and run out of town on a rail: "If it wasn't for the honor of the thing, I'd rather walk."

The winners and their records, both before and after winning, are:

CY YOUNG

Year	AL	W–L	Next Year	NL	W–L	Next Year
1956	—	—	—	Newcombe	27–7*	11–12
1957	—	—	—	Spahn	21–11*	22–11*
1958	Turley	21–7*	8–11	—	—	—
1959	Wynn	22–10*	13–12	—	—	—
1960	—	—	—	Law	20–9	3–4
1961	Ford	25–4*	17–8	—	—	—
1962	—	—	—	Drysdale	25–9*	19–17
1963	—	—	—	Koufax	25–5*	19–5
1964	Chance	20–9*	15–10	—	—	—
1965	—	—	—	Koufax	26–6*	27–9*
1966	—	—	—	Koufax	27–9*	rct.
1967	Lonborg	22–9*	6–10	McCormick	22–10*	12–14
1968	McLain	31–6*	24–9*	Gibson	22–9*	20–13
1969	McLain	24–9*	3–5	Seaver	25–7*	18–12
	Cuellar	23–11	24–8*			
1970	J. Perry	24–12*	17–17	Gibson	23–7*	16–13
1971	Blue	24–8	6–10	Jenkins	24–13*	20–12
1972	G. Perry	24–10*	19–19	Carlton	27–10*	13–20
1973	Palmer	22–9	7–12	Seaver	19–10	11–11
1974	Hunter	25–12*	23–14*	Marshall	15–12–21*	9–14–13
1975	Palmer	23–11*	22–13*	Seaver	22–9*	14–11
1976	Palmer	22–13	20–11*	R. Jones	22–14	6–12*
1977	Lyle	13–5–26	9–3–9	Carlton	23–10*	16–13
1978	Guidry	25–13*	18–8	G. Perry	21–6*	12–11
1979	Flanagan	23–9*	16–13	Sutter	6–6–37*	5–8–28*
1980	Stone	25–7*	4–7†	Carlton	24–9*	13–4†
1981	Fingers	6–3–28*†	5–6–29	Valenzuela	13–7†	19–13
1982	Vuckovich	18–6	0–2	Carlton	23–11*	15–16
1983	Hoyt	24–10*	13–18	Denny	19–6*	7–7
1984	Hernandez	9–3–32*	8–10–31	Sutcliffe	16–1	8–8
1985	Saberhagen	20–6	7–12	Gooden	24–4*	17–6

*Led league in wins or saves.

†Strike-shortened season.

Phil Niekro three. There is plenty of room in their trophy cases for them, since the writers disdained to give either of them even one Cy Young. Sudden Sam McDowell and Bert Blyleven each took home two Creightons but no Cy Youngs.

THE WORST

"Success is counted sweetest by those who ne'er succeed," said Emily Dickinson.

Everyone loves a winner. But for every winner there has to be a loser. Every Bobby Thomson faces a Ralph Branca.

The easiest way not to lose is not to compete, to sit on the sidelines and hoot at the other guy who is out there taking risks. We, from the safety of our grandstand seat, pay tribute to those who had the courage to get into the arena and give their best. It is no disgrace to fight and lose. After all, as Charlie Brown points out, even Babe Ruth struck out 1,330 times (although, as Lucy replies, not consecutively).

The Worst Careers

The biggest loser in history was Cy Young. He won 510 games, but he lost 313. Nobody else is even close; Walter Johnson is next with 279 losses. Behind them come five more Hall of Famers and a probable Hall of Famer:

Pitcher	Losses
Cy Young	313
Walter Johnson	279
Eppa Rixey	279
Phil Niekro	2
Robin Roberts	251
Warren Spahn	245
Early Wynn	244

Some other record failures:

Pitcher	Hits Against
Cy Young	7,078
Walter Johnson	4,925
Grover Alexander	4,868

Pitcher	Runs Against
Red Ruffing	2,117
Burleigh Grimes	2,037

Pitcher	HR Against
Robin Roberts	502

The Worst Years

George Washington "Grin" Bradley had his ups and downs. He was the first man to pitch an official major-league no-hitter, in 1876, when he won forty-five games, sixteen of them shutouts. Three years later he became the first man to lose forty games, with a mark of 13–40.

In 1883 twenty-year-old rookie John R. Coleman gave up the amazing total of 809 hits and lost 48 games, both records that, like Cy Young's wins and losses, will probably never be broken. He won only twelve. Coleman can be excused a bit; he slaved for the last-place Philadelphias, who won seventeen and lost eighty-one.

Will White lost a total of seventy-three games in two years—thirty-one in 1879 and forty-two in 1880. But two years later Cincinnati turned around and finished in first place, and White turned his forty-two losses into forty wins.

In the modern era, pitchers are not kept in to take that much punishment. The most anyone has lost since 1901 are the twenty-nine defeats suffered by Vic Willis of the seventh-place Braves in 1905, another mark that may never be tied. Traded to the third-place Pirates in 1906, Willis came back and won twenty-two.

The most losses over the past twenty-five years is the twenty-four hung on poor Jack Fisher of the Mets in 1965.

Actually, when one thinks about it, it is no disgrace to lose. It means the manager had confidence enough to send a pitcher in again and again.

In 1906 rookie Joe Harris of the last-place Red Sox was 3–21, but he was the victim of some bad luck. He pitched a twenty-four-inning game and lost it. It was the last good game he ever pitched, and he left the major leagues with a lifetime record of 4–29.

Forty-eight years later, Don Larsen was also 3–21, but you never know how things will turn out. He was traded to the Yanks, played in the World Series and pitched a perfect game, and no one remembers his twenty-one losses.

A couple of rookies, Russ Miller of the 1928 Phils and Steve Gerkin of the 1945 A's, both lost all twelve of their decisions. Terry Felton lost all thirteen decisions he had in 1982, and washed out of the big leagues with a lifetime mark of 0–16.

Pedro Ramos and Phil Niekro both suffered through four seasons with the most losses in their leagues. Ramos' came consecutively, 1958–61, as his team, the Washington Senators, finished eighth, eighth, fifth, and seventh.

The height (or depth) of failure must be to lead the league in losses while pitching with a second-place team. Believe it or not, seven men have done it:

Year	Pitcher	W–L	Team	ERA
1915	Dick Rudolph	27–19	Braves	2.37
1917	Eppa Rixey	16–21	Phils	2.27
1923	Herman Pillette	21–19	Tigers	3.85
1947	Hal Newhouser	17–17	Tigers	2.87
1958	Ron Kline	13–16	Pirates	3.53
1968	Ray Sadecki	12–18	Giants	2.91
1980	Brian Kingman	8–20	A's	3.84

Two men did it with third-place teams: in 1902 Vic Willis was 27–20 with the Braves (2.20 ERA), and in 1923 Wilbur Cooper was 17–19 with the Pirates (3.57 ERA).

In Willis' losing year, he led the league in strikeouts and complete games and was second in victories. Newhouser was second in strikeouts, and first in complete games. Most of these men compiled excellent records in other years. How, then, could they lose so many games while pitching on winning ball clubs?

Brian Kingman's story is a case study. In 1980, the year of "Billy Ball" in Oakland, Martin took the last-place A's and made them contenders within a year; the pitching staff turned in a modern record of ninety-four complete games. Everyone had a great year—except Kingman. Writing in *Sport* magazine, Brian said he was shut out five times and lost six other games by one run.

The A's scored only 2.9 runs per game for Kingman but smothered Steve McCatty with 5.1 runs per nine innings. The two pitchers' ERAs were almost identical, but McCatty had a 14–14 record, and Kingman was 8–20. As Kingman also pointed out, Dennis Leonard of Kansas City had vir-

POLITICS AND PITCHING

From that indefatigable researcher, Bill James, comes the information that hitting suffers—and therefore pitching improves—in presidential election years.

There have been twenty-five presidential elections between 1880 and 1984 (we threw out 1912 and 1920 because of changes in the ball in those years). We checked NL and AL league batting averages for each of the twenty years, plus the old American Association—forty-six league averages in all. Batting averages went down thirty-four times, up nine times, and stayed steady three times. Furthermore they usually bounced back up the next year.

Hitting reached its all-time nadir, and thus pitching its all-time peak, in 1968—a presidential year.

The Republicans are definitely a pitchers' party; the Democrats are not quite so overwhelmingly so. Here's the party breakdown:

	Down	Up	Flat
Rep.	23	2	1
Dem.	11	7	2
Total	34	9	3 = 46

You can almost bet on it. When batting averages go down, the odds are 2:1 that the Republicans will win the election. When they go up, the odds are more than 3:1 that the Democrats will win. Only twice did batting go up in Republican years—AL hitters improved in 1924 (Calvin Coolidge) and 1956 (Dwight Eisenhower).

There must be some reason why hitters weaken in Republican years and pitchers become strong. James theorizes that the country cannot stand too much excitement—a double dose of oratory and base hits—all in the same summer.

We await other discoveries. Do sunspots affect batting or pitching? (We checked that—apparently not.) How about the stock market? Women's hemlines? The mating habits of Canadian hares? We await the results of further research with eagerness.

tually the same ERA as well, yet his club scored 5.3 runs per game for him and he won twenty, while Kingman lost twenty.

Meanwhile, Martin, "the great motivator," was "a screaming maniac" at every error. Kingman said Martin called two ninth-inning pitches in one game, and both of them were smacked for home runs that lost the game 5-4.

In another game, Kingman was pitching a one-hitter and leading 1-0 when Martin came out and told him to throw high fastballs to Cleveland's Mike Hargrove (.304). The first two were head high; the third was over Mike's head, but he hit it somehow for a two-run single.

Kingman lost another game 1-0, obeying Martin's iron-clad rule to throw a fastball on the 2-0 count. Toronto's Al Woods (.300) whacked it for a homer.

Brian's final loss came after five innings of relief. He was pulled with two runners on base, and both scored to drive him down to defeat number 20.

The longest losing streaks in this century were:

Year	Pitcher	Team	Lost	W–L
1915–16	John Nabors	A's	24	1–25
1910–11	Cliff Curtis	Braves	23	10–35
1963	Roger Craig	Mets	18	5–22
1978–79	Matt Keough	A's	18	10–32

Not every victory is deserved, nor is every defeat. In 1972 Steve Arlin of the Padres put together a string of seventy-one innings in which he gave up only thirty-three hits. Yet he lost twenty-one games that year after losing nineteen the year before. No wonder he went into dentistry.

Appendix:
The Evolution of Pitching—
A Timeline

What follows is a complete historical timetable of rule changes and strategic innovations that affected the balance between pitching and batting. The effects of these changes can be seen very clearly for the period for which statistics are available, that is, from 1876 to the present. The summaries below highlight significant changes and developments that occurred prior to 1876.

1830s: In the English game of rounders, which is the forerunner of town ball and in turn baseball, the bases were separated by 36 to 60 feet, and the "tosser" stood some 15 to 20 feet from the striker.

1845: In the original rules of the Knickerbocker Base Ball Club of New York, the distance between pitcher and batter was unspecified. The ball had to be pitched (straight arm, straight wrist, underhand), not tossed overhand, and "for the

bat"—meaning that the pitcher was at the service of the batter, who could say where he wanted the pitch. In the rival "Massachusetts Game" that flourished in New England until the mid-1850s, the ball was tossed overhead to the "striker" from a distance of 35 feet. Three swinging strikes and the batter is out, but there are no provisions for called strikes or balls.

1854: The pitching distance of the "New York Game" is established as "not less than 15 paces" or yards.

1858: Strikes are called by the umpire after he has warned the batter that he is failing to swing at good pitches.

1860: The pitcher must deliver his pitch from 45 feet from the striker's point, or home base, but he can deliver from as much as six feet to one side or the other of the pitcher's point. He can run up if he pleases. Also, the ball is reduced in size to a maximum circumference of 10 inches, more nearly the size of the modern ball. An umpire can now call strikes against a batter who is deliberately taking good pitches to delay the game.

1862: The pitcher is virtually immobilized within a box 12 feet wide and 3 feet in length. He may not even take a step in delivering the ball.

1864: The box is now 6 feet long and 6 feet wide. Fair balls caught on the bound are no longer outs, but one-bounce fouls continue as outs. An umpire who suspects a pitcher is intentionally delivering wide ones to delay the game—and thus create a tie—might call balls against him; three balls give a batter his base.

1866: The box is still 6 feet wide, but now only 4 feet long. The umpire can now call balls against a pitcher, after a warning, without consideration of his intent. However, in practice an umpire will never call a ball or a strike on the first pitch delivered, nor until a warning has been offered to the pitcher or to the batter as appropriate. The net effect of this practice is that the pitcher can throw as many as four unfair balls (balls that bounced before reaching the striker, or are over his head, or behind him) before a fifth gives the batter his base, and the batter can take four fair pitches before a fifth strikes him out.

1868: The pitcher can take a full step before pitching.

1871: The batter may call for a pitch at the height he prefers, requesting a high ball, a low ball, or a fair ball (the last being a pitch between the shoulder and the knee).

1872: The prohibition against the underhand throw (snapping the wrist), which had been honored principally in the breach, is formally rescinded. This rule change makes the curve ball legal.

1875: A pitcher will have a "ball" called against him for every three pitches not delivered at the correct height—that is, nine unfair pitches produces a base on balls. The batter receives a warning if he takes a fair pitch with two strikes on him; the next pitch he takes that is in the location he requested will be strike three.

LEAGUE AVERAGES AND RULE CHANGES

Year	National League					Other (AA, U, P, AL, F)					Rule Changes/Comment
	BA	ERA	HR (Post 1900)	BB*	K	BA	ERA	HR	BB	K	
1876	.265	2.31	-	336	589						Box 6 ft. by 6 ft. Distance 45 ft. Bats only 2 in. diameter. Walk on 9 balls, as outlined under 1875. Bond of Hartford popularizing a more nearly sidearm delivery.
1877	.271	2.81	-	346	726						Base on balls not charged as an at bat, as was the case in 1876. Livelier ball experimented with, as was 50 ft. pitching distance.
1878	.259	2.30	-	364	1081						Return to dead ball, as fans preferred low-scoring games.
1879	.255	2.50	-	508	1843						Base on balls on 8 balls, not 9; every pitch had to count as a ball, a strike, or a batted ball—no more warnings except with two strikes.
1880	.245	2.37	-	740	1993						Catcher must catch strike-three pitch on the fly to record putout. Note batting decline from 1877 on.
1881	.260	2.77	-	1034	1784						Pitching distance 50 ft. Two-strike warning eliminated—now a strikeout. Base on balls on 7 balls. Scoring increases.
1882	.251	2.89	-	960	2161	AA.244	2.72	-	629	1185	Foul caught on one bounce no longer an out. Shoulder-high delivery permitted in National League and American Association.
1883	.262	3.13	-	1121	2877	.252	3.30	-	1198	2417	
1884	.247	2.98	-	1821	4335	AA.240 / U.245	3.24 / 2.99	- / -	1996 / 1134	5655 / 4830	Base on balls on 6 balls. All restrictions on pitching motion removed in AA. NL permits from-the-shoulder delivery only. Dilution of talent with Union Assn. Note Ks.

Year											
1885	.241	2.82	-	1845	3338	.246	3.24	-	1685	3369	Base on balls on 7 balls. Box 4 ft. by 6 ft. Raised-leg windup banned. Flat bat introduced; unsuccessful.
1886	.251	3.31	-	2389	4315	.243	3.45	-	3182	4730	Flat bat banned. Box 4 ft. by 7 ft.
1887	.269	4.05	-	2732	2837	.273	4.29	-	3320	3075	HBP goes to first base in NL; AA had adopted rule in 1884. No high-low strike-one zone for all batters. Walk on 5 balls; K on 4 strikes. Note Ks, BBs. Box is 4 ft. by 5½ ft. K-zone: top of shoulder, bottom of knee.
1888	.239	2.83	-	2093	3998	.238	3.06	-	2634	4234	Foul tip is not an out except with two strikes. K on three strikes.
1889	.264	4.12	-	3612	3492	.262	3.84	-	3704	4177	BB on four balls. Radical rise in BBs, not in Ks, also in batting.
1890	.254	3.60	-	3771	3707	AA .253 / P .274	3.86 / 4.23	- / -	3747 / 4182	4233 / 2986	Pitching distance in Players League 51 ft., 1½ in. also used more lively ball; note PL batting. Talent diluted, with AA especially weak.
1891	.252	3.34	-	3802	3642	.255	3.72	-	4249	4027	Free substitution allowed, leading to pinch hitters, relief pitchers in years to follow.
1892	.245	3.28	-	6178	5955			-			AA folds; NL becomes 12-team league. Batting and attendance decline.
1893	.280	4.66	-	6142	3339			-			Pitching distance 60 ft., 6 in. Pitcher's box eliminated, replaced by slab 12 in. by 4 in. Note boost to batting, decline in Ks.
1894	.309	5.32	-	5807	3304			-			Foul bunt a strike; to this time, foul balls on any pitch counted as neither a strike nor a ball. All-time worst year for pitchers, best for batters.
1895	.296	4.78	-	5101	3602			-			Foul tip a strike. Bat diameter increased to 2¾ in. Slab lengthened to 24 in.; widened to 6 in.
1896	.290	4.36	-	4854	3522			-			
1897	.292	4.31	-	4716	3727			-			

	National League					Other (AA, U, P, AL, F)					
Year	BA	ERA	HR (Post 1900)	BB*	K	BA	ERA	HR	BB	K	Rule Changes/Comment
1898	.271	3.60	-	5092	4247						
1899	.282	3.85	-	4972	3856						Balk rule modernized. Last year of NL at twelve teams.
1900	.279	3.69	253	3034	2697						AL not yet a major.
1901	.267	3.32	224	2685	4241	AL .277	3.66	229	2780	2736	Foul ball now a strike in NL. Note radical shift of K/BB ratio from previous year. AL adopts foul strike rule for 1903. Catcher required to stay close behind batter.
1902	.259	2.78	97	2620	3895	.275	3.57	259	2815	2744	
1903	.269	3.27	150	3179	3767	.255	2.95	184	2266	4199	Foul strike rule in AL. Mound limited to 15 in. high.
1904	.249	2.73	175	3131	4277	.244	2.60	155	2611	5026	Note batting decline since foul-strike rule in NL since 1900, in AL since 1901.
1905	.255	2.99	182	3264	4462	.241	2.65	155	3008	5107	
1906	.244	2.63	126	3423	4537	.249	2.69	134	2835	4560	
1907	.243	2.46	141	3425	4210	.247	2.54	103	2883	4476	
1908	.239	2.35	151	3222	4180	.239	2.39	116	2897	4928	Year of Pitcher, not matched until 1968. NL shutouts, 164, a record till 1968, (pro rata). Note ERAs. Spitball is prevalent.
1909	.244	2.59	151	3614	4435	.244	2.47	110	3048	4921	AL shutouts, 146, a record till 1968. (pro rata).
1910	.256	3.02	214	4023	4511	.243	2.53	145	3462	5276	Cork-centered ball introduced in NL, second half of season; also for World Series. Note home-run rise to follow, also BA.
1911	.260	3.39	314	4282	4792	.273	3.34	195	3635	5093	
1912	.273	3.40	284	3876	4629	.265	3.34	153	3772	5143	

Year											
1913	.262	3.06	310	3529	4595	.256	2.93	160	3791	4861	Brooklyn Dodgers bat .213.
1914	.251	2.78	266	3593	4699	F.263 A.248	3.20 2.73	295 148	3623 3933	5115 5140	Federal League provides dilution of talent 1914–15.
1915	.248	2.75	225	3269	4729	F.255 A.248	3.03 2.94	249 160	3637 4214	4529 4857	Phillies of NL—team ERA of 2.15.
1916	.247	2.61	239	3013	4827	.248	2.83	142	4122	4698	
1917	.249	2.70	202	3061	4500	.248	2.66	136	3830	4146	White Sox of Al—team ERA of 2.16.
1918	.254	2.76	138	2522	2898	.254	2.77	98	3199	2978	
1919	.258	2.91	206	2612	3294	.268	3.21	240	3363	3576	Ruth hit 29 homers.
1920	.270	3.13	261	3017	3636	.283	3.79	369	3807	3635	Trick pitches banned; new balls used more frequently in wake of Chapman death; lively ball in AL. Ruth hits 54 homers. Bill Doak glove (with pocket) introduced. Hitter's decade to come.
1921	.289	3.78	460	2882	3356	.292	4.28	477	3943	3607	All-time high BA for AL; Detroit bats .316. BBs now begin to outpace Ks, pattern for years to come. Lively ball comes to NL.
1922	.292	4.10	530	3438	3355	.284	4.03	525	3782	3580	
1923	.286	3.99	538	3496	3408	.282	3.99	441	4107	3601	
1924	.283	3.87	498	3206	3383	.290	4.23	397	4136	3239	54,030 balls used in NL; only used 22,095 five years earlier.
1925	.292	4.27	634	3453	3372	.292	4.39	533	4315	3318	Resin bag allowed.
1926	.280	3.84	439	3470	3359	.281	4.02	424	4206	3456	
1927	.282	3.91	483	3412	3496	.285	4.12	439	4029	3399	Yankees have .489 slugging average.
1928	.281	3.98	610	3831	3389	.281	4.04	483	3827	3704	
1929	.294	4.71	754	3945	3472	.284	4.24	595	4065	3566	
1930	.303	4.97	892	3688	3852	.288	4.65	673	3958	4080	Year of Hitter in this century. Phillies (NL) team ERA 6.70, NY (NL) BA .319. NL ERA highest in century except for AL in 1936.

	National League					Other (AA, U, P, AL, F)					
Year	BA	ERA	HR (Post 1900)	BB*	K	BA	ERA	HR	BB	K	Rule Changes/Comment
1931	.277	3.86	492	3503	3864	.278	4.38	576	4165	4044	Ball deflated in NL—note decline in HR, ERA. From this year to 1942, AL becomes hitters league; for period, compare AL-NL walks.
1932	.276	3.88	649	3138	3848	.277	4.48	708	4402	4002	
1933	.266	3.34	460	2974	3528	.273	4.28	608	4375	3915	Note NL batting decline since 1930; pitchers not so fearful, walks decline, too.
1934	.279	4.06	656	3240	4146	.279	4.50	688	4611	4285	
1935	.277	4.02	662	3288	4066	.280	4.45	663	4546	3542	
1936	.278	4.02	607	3603	4205	.289	5.04	758	4855	4033	St Louis Browns' ERA 6.24. AL slugging "only" .421, less than NL slugging of .448 in 1930, but walks 32% higher.
1937	.272	3.91	624	3644	4554	.281	4.62	806	4775	4454	
1938	.267	3.78	611	3705	4087	.281	4.79	864	4924	4255	
1939	.272	3.92	649	3819	4258	.279	4.62	796	4660	4320	Last NL BA over .270 up to present day.
1940	.264	3.85	688	3769	4322	.271	4.38	883	4496	4729	Pitcher must place only one foot on rubber at start of delivery.
1941	.258	3.63	597	4147	4411	.266	4.15	734	4744	4425	
1942	.249	3.31	538	4068	4195	.257	3.66	533	4317	4139	Only sub-4.00 ERA in AL since 1920 except for 3.99 in 1923. Note HR decline in AL, continues through 1946; NL homers also decline. Wartime "balata" ball (deadened).
1943	.258	3.37	432	3980	4062	.249	3.30	473	4324	4503	
1944	.261	3.67	575	3972	3919	.260	3.43	459	3951	4244	
1945	.265	3.80	577	4151	3865	.255	3.36	430	4145	4186	
1946	.256	3.42	562	4379	4429	.256	3.50	401	4405	5228	

Year	BA	ERA	BB			BA	ERA	BB			Notes
1947	.265	4.07	886	4464	4492	.256	3.71	679	4745	4633	First plus-4.00 ERA in NL since 1936. Note HR boost, both leagues.
1948	.261	3.95	845	4396	4717	.266	4.28	710	5232	4306	BB in AL highest in century; to be exceeded in 1949-50.
1949	.262	4.04	935	4393	4577	.263	4.20	769	5627	4369	NL HR tops, exceeding 1930.
1950	.261	4.14	1100	4537	5007	.271	4.58	973	5418	4558	Strike zone narrowed; first change since 1887. Last .270 BA in AL till 1979.
1951	.260	3.96	1024	4379	4748	.262	4.12	839	4889	4595	K totals highest since AL in 1910—but scoring is high! Everyone is swinging for the fences.
1952	.253	3.73	907	4147	5240	.253	3.67	794	4630	5154	Brooklyn has slugging average of .474.
1953	.266	4.29	1197	4220	5309	.262	4.00	879	4469	4911	NL HR total highest ever, pro rata.
1954	.267	4.07	1114	4414	5086	.257	3.72	832	4619	5129	
1955	.259	4.04	1263	4240	5419	.258	3.96	961	4814	5405	NL-AL BB totals were similar only three years earlier—now look!
1956	.256	3.77	1219	3982	5694	.260	4.16	1075	5019	5813	
1957	.260	3.88	1178	3866	6150	.255	3.79	1024	4309	5814	AL BBs less than NL for only time in 1945-1975!
1958	.262	3.95	1183	4065	6192	.254	3.77	1057	4062	6051	In NL, BBs are 60.9% of K—lowest in majors since 1908—decade of pitcher is presaged.
1959	.260	3.95	1159	3974	6525	.253	3.86	1091	4210	6081	NL BB-K ratio is 57.7%, best since introduction of 3-strike, 4-ball count in 1889.
1960	.255	3.76	1042	3937	6824	.255	3.87	1086	4447	5993	AL expansion has surprisingly little impact except in Ks.
1961	.262	4.03	1196	3995	6622	.256	4.02	1534	5902	8330	NL expansion likewise. Dodger Stadium replaces Coliseum; the hitters' parks are disappearing.
1962	.261	3.94	1449	5265	9032	.255	3.97	1552	5671	8535	Strike zone expanded as Frick panics—zone that prevailed 1887-1949 returns. Mets bat .219.
1963	.245	3.29	1215	4560	9545	.247	3.63	1489	5031	9228	BAs in decline—the rout is on. Shea Stadium replaces Polo Grounds.
1964	.254	3.54	1211	4394	9256	.247	3.63	1551	5227	9956	

| | National League | | | | | Other (AA, U, P, AL, F) | | | | | |
Year	BA	ERA	HR (Post 1900)	BB*	K	BA	ERA	HR	BB	K	Rule Changes/Comment
1965	.249	3.54	1318	4730	9649	.242	3.46	1370	5306	9634	Astrodome replaces Colt Stadium.
1966	.256	3.61	1378	4404	9312	.240	3.44	1365	4927	9493	
1967	.249	3.38	1102	4672	9468	.236	3.23	1197	4993	9945	AL BA lowest ever—when it was .239 in 1908, the ERA was also 2.39 as walks were half 1967 totals and homers ⁷⁄₁₀. Chicago White Sox ERA of 2.45.
1968	.243	2.99	891	4275	9502	.230	2.98	1104	4881	9641	NL BA lowest since 1908; homers since 1946; ERA since 1919. Yankees bat .214. Walks are 44.5% of strikeouts in NL, all-time low. Cardinals ERA 2.79.
1969	.250	3.58	1470	6397	11628	.246	3.62	1649	7032	10845	Expansion of NL to 12 teams; also AL. Strike zone narrowed, mound lowered to 10 in.—still, most strikeouts ever, pro rata in NL.
1970	.258	4.05	1683	6919	11417	.250	3.72	1746	6808	10957	First 4.00 ERA since 1961. AL has first .250 BA since 1962.
1971	.252	3.47	1379	6059	10542	.277	3.47	1484	6447	10414	AL backsliding—HR figure is like that of 1966, pro rata.
1972	.248	3.46	1359	5985	10544	.239	3.07	1175	5742	10174	AL BA below .240 again—danger; AL HR lowest since 1949, pro rata.
1973	.254	3.71	1550	6453	10507	.259	3.82	1552	6647	9855	BB-K ratios higher—in NL, highest since 1958; in AL, highest since 1961. Designated hitter in AL.
1974	.255	3.62	1280	6828	9971	.258	3.62	1369	6135	9524	
1975	.257	3.63	1233	6730	9793	.258	3.79	1465	6674	9490	
1976	.255	3.50	1113	6263	9602	.256	3.56	1122	6128	9143	

Year										Notes
1977	.263	3.91	1631	6487	10488	.266	4.06	2013	7270	11234	Atlanta ERA 4.85. AL goes to 14 teams. HR explosion—lively ball? AL ERA over 4.00, first time since 1961.
1978	.254	3.58	1276	6279	9905	.261	3.76	1680	7287	10153	
1979	.261	3.73	1427	6188	9920	.270	4.22	2006	7413	10115	AL has first .270 BA since 1950, highest BB/K ratio since 1960. Highest ERA since NL 1953. Haitian ball implicated.
1980	.259	3.60	1243	5469	9849	.269	4.03	1844	7221	10363	
1981	.255	3.49	719	4107	6332	.256	3.66	1062	4761	6905	Year of strike: hitters affected more than pitchers.
1982	.258	3.60	1299	5964	10300	.264	4.07	2080	7338	10921	
1983	.255	3.63	1398	6424	10749	.266	4.06	1903	7094	10967	
1984	.255	3.59	1278	6149	10929	.264	3.99	1980	7171	11571	
1985	.252	3.59	1424	6373	10674	.261	4.15	2178	7465	11777	
1986	.253	3.72	1523	6560	11648	.262	4.18	2290	7667	13058	Look at those HR, BB, and K totals!

*Because nearly all pre-1900 homeruns were inside the park, the figure is not relevant for purposes of comparison.

Index